In Memory of Akram Midani,
Dean, College of Fine Arts,
Carnegie Mellon University

D1220721

PITTSBURGH FILMMAKERS
477 MELWOOD AVENUE
PITTSBURGH, PA 15213

4/14/12

PN 1998 A3 B89
WORLD OF LUIS BUNUEL: ESSAYS
IN CRITICISM, THE
Mellen, Joan (Ed.)
Film: Directors/Filmmakers

DATE	ISSUED TO
4/16/12	Alexis Kunsak

PN 1998 A3 B89
**WORLD OF LUIS BUNUEL: ESSAYS
IN CRITICISM, THE**
Mellen, Joan (Ed.)
Film: Directors/Filmmakers

DA

THE WORLD OF *LUIS BUÑUEL*

The World of
LUIS BUÑUEL

Essays in Criticism

Edited by
JOAN MELLEN

New York
OXFORD UNIVERSITY PRESS
1978

Copyright © 1978 by Joan Mellen

Printed in the United States of America

Library of Congress Cataloging in Publication Data
Main entry under title:

The World of Luis Buñuel.

  Filmography: p.
  Includes index.
  1. Buñuel, Luis, 1900–   —Addresses, essays,
lectures. I. Mellen, Joan.
PN1998.A3B89   791.43′0233′0924   77-26743
ISBN 0-19-502398-6
ISBN 0-19-502399-4 pbk.

For AMOS VOGEL,
Ally, with Buñuel, in the subversive

Preface

. . . .

Luis Buñuel stands with Eisenstein, Chaplin, Renoir, Dovzhenko, Mizoguchi and Fellini as one of the greatest directors ever to work in cinema. European critics have long recognized Buñuel's importance, but only recently has his reputation in America begun to match his magnificent achievement—having created films of rare artistic quality for nearly fifty years.

The World of Luis Buñuel offers a sample of critical assessments of his remarkable films, from *Un Chien Andalou,* his first work, made in 1928, to *That Obscure Object of Desire* (1977). It draws in particular upon articles in French and Spanish not before translated into English. French journals like *Positif* and *Jeune Cinema* have published debates on Buñuel's work. They are represented here together with a selection from the special double Buñuel issue of *Études Cinématographiques* which appeared in 1963.

Translated into English for the first time are such Spaniards as José Luis Egea, writing during the Franco years in *Cine Cubano* as a young filmmaker for whom Buñuel provided inspiration as a legend and teacher before Egea had the opportunity to see a single Buñuel film. Other selections from the number of *Cine Cubano* devoted exclusively to Buñuel testify to how deeply Buñuel's films have touched viewers in the Spanish-speaking world. If the French have responded most to the surrealist in Buñuel, Hispanic writers have welcomed him as a satirist and critic of the angst-ridden decadence of Spanish culture, with its anachronistic hidalgos (played most convincingly by Fernando Rey) living in genteel poverty in remembrance of glories past.

The British, as well, quickly applauded Buñuel's contribution to the art of film, as evidenced by director Tony Richardson's introduction to Buñuel's films and by the critical essays of David Robinson and Tom Milne reprinted in this volume.

Buñuel demands a critic equal to his own vision; he has inspired distinguished men of culture such as Mexican novelist Carlos Fuentes, who offers a critical overview enlivened by his personal friendship with Buñuel. Noted French critic André Bazin, who has written brilliantly on *Los Olvidados,* and Henry Miller, who recognized presciently the significance of *L'Age D'Or,* are also represented.

There are several pieces by Buñuel himself, a letter by his son Juan, and an article by his scriptwriter, Jean-Claude Carrière, allowing us a glimpse into the thinking which produced *Un Chien Andalou, Viridiana,* and *The Exterminating Angel.* There are articles by Raymond Durgnat, Irving Louis Horowitz, Charles Thomas Samuels, and John Simon which form a debate on the merit and meaning of *The Discreet Charm of the Bourgeoisie,* that dazzling reaffirmation in the mid-1970's of the themes which have haunted Buñuel throughout his career.

This book reveals the many moods of Buñuel: realist and surrealist, Marxist and anarchist, anti-cleric and mystic, Freudian and post-Freudian. For Luis Buñuel, whose vast intellect ranges over the conflicts which have engulfed our century, has unceasingly exposed to us with grace, wit, and ironic distance the roots of our social and personal malaise, even as he slyly hints at our prospects for a more liberated future.

Joan Mellen

Contents

. . . .

On *Nazarin*

On *Viridiana*

5 A Debate on *The Discreet Charm of the Bourgeoisie* 361

6 A Buñuel Filmography 405

I

Introduction

. . . .

An Overview of Buñuel's Career

Joan Mellen

. . . .

Before he directed those masterpieces of his career which began arriving almost annually in 1961 with *Viridiana*, Luis Buñuel, citing Friedrich Engels, set out the artistic aims which would continue to govern his work into his seventies. Through the surreal, visualizing the impulses of the unconscious, he would, he said, "shatter the optimism of the bourgeois world, and force the reader (or spectator) to question the permanency of the prevailing order." The artist, Buñuel stated, is obliged neither to offer solutions nor to "take sides." It is enough, as he has since asserted, that his films make certain "the powerful can never affirm that everyone agrees with their acts."

Of all the directors working today, Buñuel possesses the most iconoclastic and radical view of the world. He finds the society of his time decadent and antithetical to human liberation. Deploying the imagery of surrealism and sardonic humor, Buñuel has set out to undermine those values and institutions we take for granted and which have so alienated us from our feelings and desires that we have become paralyzed and frustrated without realizing how. He has sustained a fiery, dissident sensibility throughout a long career, beginning with *Un Chien Andalou*, made when he was twenty-nine, and highlighted by a brilliant artistic outpouring in his sixties and seventies reminiscent of the creative life of William Butler Yeats. Church, state, and bourgeois culture itself have been targets of Buñuel's satire; and every one of his films may indeed be seen as a parody of our entrapment by that bourgeoisie, defined always by Buñuel as those in power today, the masters and beneficiaries of this planet's wealth.

I   BUÑUEL AND THE "BOURGEOISIE"

This bourgeoisie—the ruling class of our time—is treated by Buñuel as would an entomologist (a profession for which he once studied), scrutinizing the insects beneath his microscope—a not unfitting simile since, to Buñuel, this class is insect-like in its amorality. The surreal *L'Age d'Or* (1930) is an examination of its decadence, as are *The Exterminating Angel* (1962), *Diary of a Chambermaid* (1964), *Tristana* (1970), *The Discreet Charm of the Bourgeoisie* (1972), *The Phantom of Liberty* (1974) and *That Obscure Object of Desire* (1977). His delineation of the psychopathology of the everyday life of the middle class and those who serve it reveals the bourgeoisie as complacent, in a state of spiritual paralysis, and so self-destructive that its demise as a viable class and cultural force may even occur without a revolution on the part of its victims. For how durable, morally coherent, or culturally stable can a ruling class be which must contend with cows in its beds (*L'Age d'Or*) or donkeys in its pianos (*Un Chien Andalou* [1928]), mocking its pretenses of propriety, sobriety, and calm control? Buñuel's surrealism is ever in the service of exposing the limitless savagery of the bourgeoisie, its brutality the surest index of an awareness on its own part that, power notwithstanding, only savage repression can prolong its day.

Sexual repression and cruelty continually characterize this bourgeoisie. In *L'Age d'Or* a father, servant of the wealthy, kills his child for distracting him and causing a cigarette he is rolling to be spoiled. The mode of the film is the surreal, the style expressionistic. But the cruelty belongs not to Buñuel, but to the world he depicts. Religion is already in the service of the ruling class; at one point, a statue of Jesus dissolves to a man in a top hat, a smiling, typical bourgeois. At the center of *L'Age d'Or*, the bourgeoisie cavorts at a grand party during which the kitchen catches fire. The wealthy guests remain blithely indifferent, ignoring the screams of servants struggling for their lives. Such, Buñuel observes, is the morality of the privileged few.

But Buñuel's bourgeoisie finds little joy in its supremacy. More than those classes which enjoy none of its privileges, it is tortured by doubt, sexual repression, and guilt. The hero of *L'Age d'Or* loses the heroine to her Oedipal attachment to her father, an orchestra conductor. At the moment his concert begins, the embrace of the lovers is broken. And to the chagrin of her lover, this woman later openly embraces and kisses her father, moaning in an ecstasy reserved for this particular attachment. That her lover slapped the face of her *mother* when she spilled her drink on him by accident delighted this woman, for her affection is directed solely to her male parent.

Buñuel's method is to depict unconscious longings as real, as indeed for the surrealists they are. He is fond of quoting André Breton's paradox: "the most admirable thing about the fantastic is that the fantastic does not exist; everything is real." This statement points accurately to Buñuel's style as a filmmaker. Not content to play about the surfaces of reality, Buñuel would bring the unconscious into view by so integrating it with everyday life that the film itself renders it empirically real.

Freudian psychology, not unexpectedly, plays an important role in Buñuel's work. Dreams, which Freud described as the "royal road" to the turmoils of the unconscious, pervade his films. In *Los Olvidados* the boy, Pedro, dreams of battling his delinquent friend, Jaibo, for the sexual favors of Pedro's mother (an act feared by Pedro and which will actually occur). The mother awakens and in slow motion offers a hunk of raw meat to Jaibo. Pedro and Jaibo wrestle over this bloody piece of flesh, which represents all Pedro's hunger—for physical survival no less than for Oedipal gratification. The social fate of injured and perpetrator alike is determined from infancy by the culture, nowhere better expressed than in this battle for possession of the woman, symbolized by ripe, red meat, by raw flesh, a grotesque object connoting sexual and sadistic distortion, expressing both the debased role of men and the sad fate of women. The Oedipal in Buñuel is at once perverse and associated with terror, a nameless repressed dread induced by the nature of parental authority, possessive and authoritarian—no less true for Pedro, whose mother neither wanted nor loves him.

In *Robinson Crusoe* (1952), a brilliant adaptation of the Defoe novel, Crusoe dreams of his diabolical father wasting water while refusing to offer any to his sick, thirsty son. This father intones,

"God will not forgive you . . . you will die," the reprisal for
Crusoe's rebellion, his having refused to settle down into his
father's middle-class style of life. Intercut in this dream is a shot of
the skull of Crusoe senior floating in the water, a wish fulfillment
for a son anxious to liberate himself at last from a stern, oppressive patriarch who has associated his own self-righteous domi-
nance with that of God himself.

Buñuel exposes how in the depths of the unconscious we
struggle with bourgeois norms dictating to us how to live; these
values, not our own, are strictures which prevent us from living
free and satisfying lives. This is the theme of *Belle de Jour* (1966),
which concerns a woman who cannot reconcile sex and love and
within whose unconscious, revealed to us through her fantasies,
are buried both the guilt of having rebelled against the Church
and its notions of female purity, and the self-hatred engendered
by this rebellion.

II   BUÑUEL AND RELIGION:
"THANK GOD—I AM STILL AN ATHEIST"

The complicity of religion with bourgeois rule has haunted this
director who was educated among the Jesuits. The close of *L'Age
d'Or* finds Christ returning with a young woman to his castle
from which will soon issue screams and gunshots. We hear the
martial drums which punctuate so many Buñuel soundtracks. In
this episode, borrowed from the Marquis de Sade, Buñuel's Christ
appears ready to participate in the very perversities of those he is
presumed to have "saved." Whether religious or political, repression breeds the acts it presumes to prevent—an ongoing Buñuelian theme.

Religion and the clergy are forever cropping up in Buñuel's
films. "I am an atheist still, thank God," Buñuel has quipped,
indicating how all of us, even in our rebellion, are shaped by the
culture and upbringing we resist—a facet of the irrationality of so
much of bourgeois life, his primary concern in *The Phantom of
Liberty*. At the end of *The Milky Way* (1969), a film simultane-

ously irreverent and redolent of the mysteries of religion, the camera dollies in on a strange character who seems to have materialized out of nowhere. The movement of the camera is relatively rare for this director, so ascetic in his style that he renounces cinematic devices as "tricks." The camera movement itself tells us that this man's words will bear a close relationship to Buñuel's own perceptions. "My hatred of science and technology will surely drive me back one day to the absurd belief in God," he proclaims. And then he is gone, one more Buñuelesque voice longing for a redeemer who, should he come, would no doubt be subject to the director's uncompromising irony.

For lest we misguidedly bring Buñuel too quickly back into the fold, organized religion is also represented in his work by the ridiculous figure of *Simon of the Desert* (1965), eating and defecating for thirty-seven years atop his ridiculous stone pillar. Institutionalized religion is represented as an instrument of unspeakable misery in the documentary *Land Without Bread* (1932). A church is filled with ornate statuary while famished parents steal the morsels of bread given their children at school in this isolated Spanish community. The narrator remarks matter-of-factly: "The only things of luxury are the churches," as ironic "Ave Marias" are heard on the soundtrack.

The only cleric who gains Buñuel's unqualified support is his Nazarin, a priest, excommunicated by the Princes of the Church for attempting to put Christ's teachings into practice. What counts for Buñuel is that Nazarin applies to his own life the perceptions enunciated by Jesus, and like Jesus he is a man willing to stand up to the repressive ruling order. "I'm fond of the character in *Nazarin*," Buñuel has remarked, "he's a priest. So what? He could just as well be a hairdresser or a waiter. What interests me is that he sticks to his ideas, that they are unacceptable to society and that, after his adventures with prostitutes, thieves, etc. they lead him to irrevocable condemnation by the forces of order." Paraphrasing Dostoevsky's "The Grand Inquisitor," the work which inspired this film, Buñuel has said, "If Christ were to return, they'd crucify Him again. It is possible to be *relatively* Christian, but the *absolutely* pure, the absolutely

"I'm fond of the character in *Nazarin*," Buñuel has remarked, "he's a priest. So what? He could just as well be a hairdresser or a waiter. What interests me is that he sticks to his ideas, that they are unacceptable to society and that, after his adventures with prostitutes, thieves, etc. they lead him to irrevocable condemnation by the forces of order."

innocent man—he's bound to fail . . . I am sure that if Christ came back, the Church, the powerful churchmen, would condemn Him again."

Nazarin's credo is revolutionary and socialist. "Everything," he insists, "belongs to those who need it." He is no match for the prelate who dismisses his behavior as out of keeping with the "dignity" appropriate to a priest. The scene between the two ends as the camera dollies in on the milk and chocolate on this Church father's table for a symbolic close shot expressing Buñuel's sense that the Church has always been cynical and greedy, placing its own material splendor and comfort before all else. A parallel scene at the end of *Tristana* (1970), in which gluttonous priests down hot chocolate and cake at the table of the dying Don Lope in the hope of being remembered in his will, reiterates the same motif.

Nazarin is too honest to believe in such banalities as miracles. "Blasphemous fools," he admonishes his followers, "Miracles from *me?*" In contrast, we have the depiction of a ridiculous Christ at the end of *The Milky Way* who pretends to have effected a miraculous cure of a blind man. Buñuel has Christ *spit* into the man's eyes to restore his sight. But the camera, focusing on the man's feet, testifies that, spitting miracles notwithstanding, the man remains as blind as before. His feet hesitate before a ditch which he obviously cannot see. Buñuel once remarked, "I believe one must search for God in man." It is the mockery of true dedication which fuels Buñuel's desire to unmask the role of organized religion and the ways in which it has been antithetical to the teachings it invokes.

But if religion helps little to alleviate suffering in this world, Buñuel's films find that small measures and nominal reforms accomplish less, providing only a moral cover for the established order. One kindly prison director cannot save the vulnerable Pedro from the jungle environment of *Los Olvidados.* The reformer, Vasquez, cannot even remove the chains from mistreated political prisoners in the underrated *Fever Mounts in El Pao* (1959), if only because he chooses solely to loosen their shackles in lieu of a challenge to the basic injustice of their imprisonment. All, therefore, that changes when Vasquez himself assumes power is that a different group of political prisoners find their way into the jails of El Pao. Through the telephone, Vasquez hears once again, in a marvelous use of asynchronous sound, the clinking of chains around the legs of these new prisoners.

The hypocrisy of "change," religious or secular, either as charity or as political reform, which leaves power intact, is a subject of abiding importance to Buñuel. In *La Mort en Ce Jardin* (1956) the priest, Father Lizzardi, wears a wristwatch which is the gift of an oil company and a symbol of the alliance between the Church and capitalism, at once establishing that little challenge to the status quo will issue from the Lizzardis of this world. This same cleric enjoins a dying prisoner, brutalized by the police, to "remember your soul." Buñuel, seemingly absent, is bitter and enraged.

The Reverend in *The Young One* (1960) insists that his mattress be turned when he discovers that a black man had slept on it the preceding night. He objects not to the lynching of Travers, the innocent black fugitive unjustly accused of raping a white woman, but to his being tied to a post in a manner which prevents him from sitting down. Justice is perceived by this representative clergyman in terms of how the victim is trussed; he is concerned with the form of injustice as opposed to its roots. Buñuel urges examination of the very structure of our laws and an exposure of those on whose behalf they have been enacted and implemented. Short of this, we will remain mired in the arbitrary, in ration- alization, self-deception, and deceit. In *The Discreet Charm of the Bourgeoisie* the "worker-bishop" turned gardener first absolves of his sins the penitent murderer of the bishop's parents, who is now old and frail. Then he executes him, blood lust and the desire for revenge rendering a sham the religious pretense of absolution. Despite his long years with the Church, its teachings have entered only the surface of this "worker-bishop's" consciousness, sug- gesting that its precepts have been formal only since the Church as an institution has always endorsed the violence of the strong.

Liberation comes to those in Buñuel's films, like the young couple in *Mexican Bus Ride* (1951), who can escape and transcend the damaging oppressiveness of the Church. We know their joy is assured when we hear that because no church exists in the rural area where they live, their marriage ceremony must consist of an ancient primitive ritual. The beginning of the film finds them setting off, as custom decrees, to spend their wedding night alone on an uninhabited offshore island.

Charity in Buñuel reeks of hypocrisy, if only because it is so obviously ineffectual, the donor aware of this no less than the recipient. In *Viridiana* the heroine's cousin, Jorge, buys a little dog as an act of kindness to free it from a pathetic fate, tied as it is to a peasant's cart and forced to run behind. But no sooner has Jorge rescued the little creature than another identical cart with another little dog tied behind enters the shot. As long as the structure of bourgeois life remains unaltered, neither isolated random acts of beneficence nor, for that matter, new technology will alleviate the suffering of the many, a central preoccupation of Buñuel. The horse-drawn carts are replaced in the next cut by a large truck lumbering down the road, conveying not progress but the greater menace of a bourgeoisie armed anew with modern technology. The dead weight of this present—in which, as Buñuel stresses, religion features as a primary hindrance to human liberation—is symbolized by the surreal image of those two recalcitrant Jesuits tied to a piano in *Un Chien Andalou,* his first film.

III BUÑUEL THE PATIENT REVOLUTIONARY

Hope is kept alive in these dark films of Buñuel, where the rule of the bourgeoisie seems interminable, by the director's faith in his enemy's historical demise. The frenzy and anxiety of bourgeois power reveal the futility of its war against humanity's deepest yearnings. Both *The Exterminating Angel* and *The Discreet Charm of the Bourgeoisie*—and, to a lesser extent, *The Phantom of Liberty*—are parables of bourgeois paralysis and destruction from within, through the loss of that energy and self-confidence essential for the maintenance of power. In *The Exterminating Angel,* bourgeois guests at a dinner party find themselves incapable, for what seems like months, of leaving the drawing room of their hosts. The household servants, those yet healthy and spiritually whole who have not made themselves inwardly subservient to their employers, feel irresistible impulses to flee and leave the party before it has even begun. Only the major-domo, who perceives his identity solely in terms of serving the rich, a prototypic "Uncle Tom," remains to suffer with them. Buñuel reveals his bourgeoisie in paralytic decline and as indiscriminately rapacious. The guests slaughter and devour the pet sheep of the family, an act symbolic of their political behavior during the tenure of their rule.

The deteriorating situation strips this ruling class of the veneer of convention. Without their social and psychological defenses, their worst impulses emerge. It is not that they were above ruthless behavior before, but that such cruelty was previously confined to class-approved targets. Before the paralysis sets in, a guest throws a glass through the window at a man described as "just a passing Jew." Their hastening incapacity causes them now to treat each other in ways once reserved for their victims. Buñuel uses the narrative device of their entrapment in one room to reveal the character and qualities they ordinarily take great pains to conceal.

"I trust to their discretion," says the host, commenting in vain hope that decorum might yet conceal cruelty, certain as he is that his guests will depart the morning after the dinner, in a foreshadowing of the title of Buñuel's later film on the same theme. But this bourgeoisie, grown too weak and corrupt even to preserve itself, can no longer afford to be "discreet." The parable carries an implicit call to combat, as will the march of the fascists at the end of *Diary of a Chambermaid.* For although this decadent bourgeoisie seems on the verge of collapse, it would take us all down with it, as it does the subservient major-domo, if the "sheep" do not take up arms against it. By resort to a magical incantation not unlike the ritual of prayer, the guests manage to emerge. They repair to a church for the *Te Deum* they promised in thanksgiving should they escape from their nightmare alive.

But in the last scene of the film they are paralyzed anew, this time unable to leave the church. The priests themselves, having been not merely the servants of the bourgeoisie but *willing* servants, are trapped in the church with them. Buñuel cuts to a group of demonstrators being slaughtered by the police, followed by a flock of sheep that runs into the cathedral where the bourgeois figures remain trapped. As the rioters are gunned down, the scene discloses that those servants who first escaped from the house at the beginning of the film will have the following choices: returning like sheep to the side of their masters; being shot in cold blood if they protest ineffectively; or preparing a fight to the finish. Those who reject the last of these alternatives will share the doom reserved for their "betters." This dramatic moment was foreshadowed in the earlier parable of the animals. The household bear rediscovered his natural tenacity and boldness, remaining free in the house and never entering the drawing room of starving and mad guests. The workers, who now, like sheep, rush into the church, will be slaughtered as well. Buñuel's is a cold and dispassionate view devoid of sentimentality toward the victims who have waited so long to rebel no less than toward their oppressors.

Animals figure often in Buñuel's films and are sometimes portrayed as the moral betters of human beings, functioning as an admonition to their cruel "superiors." The finest instance of this theme occurs at the end of *Robinson Crusoe* when, looking back for one last glimpse of the island, Crusoe hears, in an exquisite use of asynchronous sound, the barking as if from an echo chamber of his dog, Rex. Dan O'Herlihy, as Crusoe, in a fine moment of understated feeling, wipes away an invisible tear of homage to his one companion of so many years whose loyalty and love made his days on the uninhabited island emotionally surmountable. That the companion happened to be an animal is incidental, and the moment is shot as if we were indeed at a religious ceremony. Buñuel's animals, without ulterior motives, or greed or cruelty beyond the need to survive, are manifestations of our own better and potential selves.

The Discreet Charm of the Bourgeoisie, made ten years after *The Exterminating Angel,* continues the theme of bourgeois demise, as its six main characters, powerful figures in government and narcotics traffickers on the side, find themselves incapable of sitting down together to finish a meal. Dreams abound in this film—fantasies in which these bourgeois friends are insulted, jailed, and destroyed by dissident revolutionaries. They dream, moreover, each other's nightmares. Buñuel in his seventies has not become a mystic; it is simply that their fates are interchangeable. What they fear for their friends is what they themselves most dread; as members of the same privileged class, there are more similarities than differences among them. Their equilibrium has been shattered at last, and Buñuel now finds his bourgeoisie confused and disoriented by the challenge to its hegemony by revolutionaries stalking the Ambassador from Miranda, the most prominent of the six.

Buñuel, seventy-two years old in 1972, perceives the enemy dreaming of its own destruction, beset by nightmares, and filled with an anxiety it has lost the power to assuage. Its usual methods for calming itself and dispersing challengers, ranging from sexual indulgence *(L'Age d'Or)* to the unrestrained violence of fascism *(Diary of a Chambermaid)*, no longer work. Buñuel's characters in *The Exterminating Angel, The Discreet Charm, The Phantom of Liberty* and *That Obscure Object of Desire* are in fact his enemies. He maintains considerable aesthetic distance from them all because they are decadent and unreliable, selfish and unpredictable in their callousness. Rarely in any Buñuel film are we offered heroes with whom to identify or heroines whose fate we may follow sympathetically. Buñuel departs from a nineteenth-century style of linear narrative particularly in the episodic *Discreet Charm* and *Phantom of Liberty*. He is motivated not only by the sense that daring ideas demand new forms, but by his awareness that the thoroughly unwholesome people at the forefront of his stage permit him to look forward to a social era in which they will no longer be the arbiters of taste and will cease to rule empires at their whim, an epoch anticipated by Buñuel with no less conviction because it has not yet come into existence.

IV THE IMAGE OF WOMAN

In *Viridiana, Belle de Jour,* and *Tristana,* Buñuel condemns the victimization of women by the bourgeois patriarchy centered in Spain and France. Lacking self-confidence and any sense of their value as human beings, Buñuel's women become simultaneously frigid and callous. Meanwhile, the films themselves, placing the sexual perversions of their female characters in perspective, reveal the manner in which women have been psychologically deformed by the Church and expose the values of bourgeois culture in general which have conspired to keep them in a condition of subservience and servitude. Viridiana, abandoning her novitiate, becomes a "sinner," one who would partake of life's sensual joys. Her escape into felt existence is shown by Buñuel to be infinitely more pure than was her narrow, confined life as a nun, and he has remarked about *Viridiana:* "My heroine is more virginal at the end than she was at the beginning."

Buñuel's camera itself is complicit in Viridiana's awakening, focusing on her legs as she sensuously draws off her stockings in the manner of a seasoned prostitute. It focuses on the udders of the cow she is too timid to milk, their paradoxically female and phallic quality a compelling temptation to the young nun. Even when at the end she offers herself to her cousin Jorge, a cynical libertine, her capitulation is seen by Buñuel as an expression of a hitherto repressed physical self, initiating a life preferable to her strangled, unfelt existence at the convent; such is the measure of Buñuel's disdain for the distortions of human need inherent in the deadening of sensual life by the Church.

Viridiana, reincarnated, becomes Belle de Jour, a modern French woman whose frigidity with her gentle, handsome husband is related directly to a repressive religious upbringing not unlike that of her predecessor. She re-emerges in the Buñuel canon as Tristana, a young Spanish woman whose fate it is to be deflowered by an analogue to Viridiana's uncle, Don Jaime, here called Don Lope, their continuity expressed by the fact that both are played by Fernando Rey.

Viridiana, Severine of *Belle de Jour,* and Tristana, out of the psychic distortion caused by guilt and repression of their basic needs, have come to associate sexual release with masochism. The destructiveness and unhappiness of all three women, but especially that of Severine and Tristana, belie Buñuel's ironic quip that "sex without religion is like an egg without salt." It may be true, as Buñuel has said, that "sin multiplies the possibilities of desire," but he also demonstrates, through Severine in particular, that sex divorced from the whole of human needs and used as a surrogate for feeling valued can be debilitating and perverse in proportion to the degree of repression inflicted upon the young. Severine is caught in a double bind because she desires but does not love the hoodlum Marcel, and loves but never desires her husband, Pierre. Her fantasies are introduced by straight cuts, as we hear the ringing of the harness bells of horses bearing a coach down the avenues of the Bois de Boulogne, the vehicle a symbol of Severine's desires. In one such reverie she is splattered with mud, in another molested by crude men while her husband looks on. In real life she can be awakened only by sex in which she is treated as dirty, defiled, and worthy only of punishment.

But Buñuel is not arguing that women are masochistic either

by genetic or emotional predisposition. He focuses on images reflective of the very social institutions which formed Severine from her earliest childhood and which have made her what she is. In one flashback, a priest tries to force the wafer of communion down her reluctant throat.

When her husband, having been shot by her lover, becomes paralyzed and helpless, Severine's masochistic daydreams cease. In the final sequence the harness bells sound once more, indicating that we are entering one of Severine's fantasies. Pierre, asking her what she is thinking, as he had done earlier in the film, rises from his wheelchair. Only when he is paralyzed in life can he become gentle in Severine's fantasies and not the agent of her degradation he had earlier been. We hear the sound of a cat, another emblem of Severine's stealthy sexuality, as she, perverse as ever, uncured, can be satisfied only with her husband a cripple and maimed, incapable of sex. Her guilt is now assuaged, her sense of deserving only pain fulfilled at the expense of life itself. And the coach, which always appeared occupied in her reveries, now passes empty down the long avenue of the Bois. Reality is miserable enough to suffice.

The ending of *Belle de Jour*, which has mystified many critics, is chilling in its evocation of the hopelessness of Severine's struggle to find release. The relationships finally open to her involve either whoredom or numbness. Her conditioning closes in, and Buñuel, as unsentimental as ever, resists the easy assertion that all problems have solutions.

Tristana is Belle de Jour transported to autocratic Spain. Her lecherous guardian, Don Lope, a pretentious liberal full of rhetoric of free love and anti-clericalism, which serve him primarily as a means of striking poses and seducing vulnerable women, tells her that her mother lacked brains, the better to intensify her feelings of inadequacy and to ensure her need of his authority. Tristana dreams of Don Lope's head in the shape of a phallic bell clapper swinging portentously from a church tower, a nightmare to haunt her even after his death. And at the end, she indirectly kills him by refusing to notify his doctor as he lies dying. Instead, a destroyed Tristana, rendered perverse and cruel by the repressive environment in which she has struggled for survival with vanishingly small success, opens the window to allow the falling snow and chill to envelop the still-warm corpse.

V BUÑUEL'S AESTHETIC DISTANCE: NEITHER VICTIM NOR EXECUTIONER

It is his seeming distance from his subject matter which has led many to view Buñuel as amoral—an artist so mired in his own satire that he is even unable to sympathize with the weak, a director who could himself shoot a goat and stand by and watch bees devour a donkey in *Land Without Bread* to gain an image of the precarious lives of the Hurdanos. Buñuel looks beyond useless empathy which finally will assuage no one. His focus, even in *Los Olvidados,* is not on Pedro, the devastated child in quest of love, but on the social order which has destroyed him. The last shot of Pedro—as an abandoned corpse on a rubbish heap—serves to ignite an anger undiluted by sentimental catharsis.

Buñuel, in fact, warned us of his artistic demeanor from the moment that impassive man, acted by Buñuel himself, slit a woman's eyeball with a razor in *Un Chien Andalou.* Since then, he has indeed violated our comfortable view of reality through our very organ of perception, even as his camera eye is violated by what it must reveal. The sliced eyeball, viscous fluid running, as a cloud indifferently bisects the moon, is followed by other unspeakable acts in *Un Chien Andalou,* a title bearing no relation to the images of the film. An automobile runs over a girl on an empty street while an indifferent crowd suddenly and mysteriously disappears.

Buñuel's films are replete with the cruel. This cruelty is both accidental and motivated, and before it all are helpless. Buñuel's is indeed that world of the bourgeoisie in which the most unscrupulous have been rewarded with complete power. The director's outrageous images throughout a long career point to this unmitigated reality as he penetrates in film after film the attractive façade of the powerful.

His characters cannot be heroes in the old-fashioned sense. But this does not prevent Buñuel from portraying them with subtlety.

The Ambassador in *The Discreet Charm* arranges his dope pushing aided by the secrecy of the diplomatic pouch in a reference to crimes sanctioned by authority and fostered by the diplomatic mailbag. To thwart a terrorist bent on finishing him off, he first attempts seduction, and then a wily hypocrisy. "I'd even be a socialist if they believed in God," he cajoles. Like so many of his class, he will say and do anything in a spot. He will even, if need be, embrace the revolution—if only for the necessary duration. In fact, he believes in nothing, only in the violence required to preserve his power, and before long a gun emerges from his soup tureen.

Eating is another bourgeois preoccupation. Extending the idea of the dinner party of *The Exterminating Angel*, Buñuel locates in the devouring of food a powerful symbol of both bourgeois power and bourgeois self-indulgence. Nothing so dramatically intimates its defeat to come as the inability of the six protagonists to finish a meal. As the selections in this volume by Simon, Samuels, Durgnat, and Horowitz reveal, *The Discreet Charm* has occasioned considerable debate, starting with Buñuel's designation of the bourgeoisie as the ruling class of our time, the determinants of refinement, and, as such, an accurate barometer of our psychic, social, and moral health.

But all are victims in Buñuel, the despoiling and the despoiled, Don Lope and Tristana alike; all are manipulated by a hostile social order. If some of Buñuel's people, like Jaibo in *Los Olvidados* and Don Lope in *Tristana*, seem unattractive, it is because the social milieu from which they take their identity is so decadent and inhuman. The perverse in Buñuel often becomes the only response compatible with remaining alive. It is because Buñuel blames for our depravity the institutions of religion, the patriarchal family, and a society structured according to class and privilege that he can sympathize even with characters as damaged and destructive as the murderous Jaibo. He forces us to feel compassion for the hypocritical seducer, Don Lope, as an aging man in one memorable shot; Don Lope clutches in futility the perfume atomizer with which he has made one last effort in vain to win Tristana by simulating the youth he has long since left behind. Purged of his obsession to kill women, Archibaldo de la

The perverse in Buñuel often becomes the only response compatible with remaining alive. (*Los Olvidados*)

Cruz is redeemed as a human being once again, symbolized by his rescue of an insect in *Ensayo de un Crimen* (1955), an act of compassion performed as well by Don Jaime in *Viridiana*. The latter, however, harbors simultaneous thoughts of raping his niece and reasserts emphatically his refusal to see his illegitimate son Jorge, whom he has gratuitously rejected. The effort to live differently contends with compulsive behavior which is the result of a debased culture's effect on victimizers no less than on victims.

For even the vicious are victims of forces of which they are as much the shaped as the shapers. Buñuel thus enables us to empathize with the distress and pain even of the vicious like Jaibo, a sadist who has kicked the cart of a legless man down a long street and out of the cripple's reach. At the moment of Jaibo's death, we are led to pity him. Shot by the police, he lies dying, as Buñuel superimposes a shot of a mangy black dog, an emblem of the character himself. "I'm alone, alone," Jaibo cries out in his last moment in that despair which fueled his cruelty and rage. He wins our empathy as we perceive the magnitude of his loneliness as a social outcast, his having been utterly abandoned and thus driven to punish and lash out at others indiscriminately. It is not that understanding the causes of cruel behavior can exonerate it or lessen our need to resist it. But, equally for Buñuel, we need to understand its cause if we are to surmount cruelty and gain the essential insight that the tormentors are themselves afflicted by the society they reflect.

Buñuel never permits an attribution to the victim of the sins of those who have made him what he is. In this spirit, he peoples his films with grotesquely injured and deformed characters—dwarves, lepers, the blind, the abandoned, and the sexually perverse. Their very presence charges the director's anger. "In a world as badly made as ours is," Buñuel has said, "there is only one road—rebellion."

VI   BUÑUELIAN STYLE

Buñuel's use of the language of film is so spare as to seem to the eye to be almost non-existent. "Once the camera starts dancing and becomes the star of the picture," Buñuel has declared, "I lose interest and leave the theatre." Music unaccounted for in the shot by, for example, a character playing an instrument or placing a record on the phonograph is also rare in Buñuel's films. *Diary of a Chambermaid, Belle de Jour,* and *Tristana,* to cite three instances, contain no music at all. Close-ups are rarely used in Buñuel's films and are awarded only to the deserving. Or they occur at great moments of epiphany on the part of previously deluded characters. At the close of *Nazarin,* the enchained Nazario and his guard pass a woman selling fruit from a cart. As, suddenly, out of pity, she offers Nazarin a pineapple, the drums of Calanda, sounded during Semana Santa in Buñuel's home town in Aragon, beat thunderously on the soundtrack. At first, Nazarin cannot look at the woman; by now, life has taught him no longer to believe. But in a burst of hope liberated by her gratuitous act, he recovers faith in life and in people, exclaiming, "May God repay you, lady." Buñuel now grants him a close-up, symbolic of his renewed belief in the value of living and in the potential of human beings for simple kindness. The close-up is awarded by Buñuel when it accompanies spiritual recovery.

A tracking shot is equally rare in a Buñuel film. Indeed, the *smaller* the space with which he has to work, the more likely it is that Buñuel will move his camera, as in the dolly shots in the bedroom of Viridiana on the morning Don Jaime asserts that he raped her the night before, and then, out of conscience (and truth) denies it. There are also diagonal tracking shots in the crowded drawing room of *The Exterminating Angel,* the camera squeezing by the disheveled guests, trapped and struggling to find a way out of what one of the characters calls the "sinking ship" of the bourgeoisie. In both instances, Buñuel parodies the tracking shot by not allowing himself sufficient space in which to continue it. He refuses to admit a superfluous camera presence into his art, as if it would undermine the film's autonomy as a living world co-existent with our own, analagous to the co-presence of our conscious and unconscious lives. In *Los Olvidados,* Pedro, angry at being made an object of Buñuel's scrutiny while working at the reformatory chicken farm, even throws an egg against the camera lens.

The long tracking shot, therefore, is intruded by Buñuel only when he wishes to add a rare judgment of his own. In the last shot of *Viridiana,* there is a long traveling shot out of the room in which Viridiana, Jorge, and the maid, Ramona, sit playing cards—a *menage-á-trois* to be. Viridiana's final hand has already been dealt, her fate charted, and the tracking shot away from the room conveys this truth. Her inexorable descent into sensuality was clear the moment two of her charity cases attempted to rape her and she gripped in simultaneous terror and release the pair of phallic jumprope handles used as a belt by one of her attackers, the very rope which had earlier served as the suicide implement of her uncle, Don Jaime. As the camera retreats down the corridor, Viridiana will proceed along the path that separates her more and more from her early ideals of chastity and charity. The slow movement of the camera away from the image of Viridiana, her hair now permanently down, awaiting her turn with Jorge, fixes the scene in our minds as the unvarying emblem of her future.

Like all satire which would challenge the structure of things as they are, Buñuel's films are replete with irony. His aim is to demolish the bourgeois façade of liberal pretense concealing naked ruthlessness, as in *Land Without Bread*. His narrator and alter ego says of the starving, pathetic children of the Hurdanos, "they are given the same education as children all over the world." The run-down tenement in the Mexican slum of *Nazarin* is called the "Meson de Heroes," house of heroes, a Buñuelesque irony which plays back upon itself because Buñuel does indeed find in its bedraggled inhabitants a richness of feeling which for him carries the resilience to survive horror and as such the presence of human dignity. A marvelously ironic *double entendre* occurs in *Nazarin* as his clerical superior discusses the charge that Nazarin is guilty of sexual misconduct because he is sheltering a woman in his room. "I know you're incapable," says the ironically named Don Angel. And through the pun, Buñuel implies that when all the pontificating is said and done, sexuality lies very close to the consciousness of us all, including that of seemingly pure and celibate Church fathers like Nazarin's superior.

Buñuel has told François Truffaut, "I may introduce some irrational elements—under cover of a dream—but never anything symbolic." For Buñuel believes the grotesque to be more than metaphor, clarifying and revealing our feelings. Yet the vast hydroelectric dam overseen by Francisco in *El* is brilliantly symbolic of the herculean effort required by this character to contain his violent and destructive feelings. And that the lovers in the throes of orgasm in *The Exterminating Angel* use the terminology of death ("my death, oh, my refuge!") to describe their ecstasy portends perhaps the death throes of their class even as in this particular film, with its two categories of people—the powerful and those who serve them—it signals the menace to the society they continue to rule. "What's the value of the German mark?" demands the Ambassador from Miranda in *The Discreet Charm of the Bourgeoisie* when the international situation is mentioned. He is careful to invest his money anywhere but in his own country, his question both symbolic of the behavior of the entire bourgeoisie and revealing of this particular character. Symbols do heighten the reality of the Buñuel films as the action repeatedly moves from the particular to the general, and as the fate of one always intimates the fate of many.

Assiduously avoiding the didactic and refusing to preach about the vagaries of the bourgeoisie, Buñuel comments through style. Rarely does he allow his themes to emerge through an uncinematic and static use of dialogue, characteristic of lesser directors. A pristine example is his revolutionary appeal through the use of jump cuts at the close of *Diary of a Chambermaid,* one of Buñuel's finest and least appreciated films.

The fascist gamekeeper, Joseph, who for twenty years has served the bourgeois landowners at the center of the film, murders and rapes a little girl. An upright, respectable figure, he is soon freed, for the bourgeoisie has little quarrel with the fascists, the most zealous of its advocates, and then only when they act prematurely. Joseph even fulfills his lifelong ambition after the crime, opening a little cafe in Cherbourg, emblematic of the petit bourgeois aspirations of those who serve the powerful. There he will tend to the needs of the army he hopes will engineer a fascist uprising and install a military regime.

The final sequence locates Joseph at the door of his cafe, chanting in rhythm with the marchers in a fascist parade. He leads them in the cry, "Vive Chiappe," the name of the very prefect of police who in 1928 closed Studio 28 for showing Buñuel's *L'Age d'Or.* The fascist marchers pass Joseph and turn the corner. By means of three jump cuts, they become dramatically smaller until by the third shot they appear to have been wiped off the face of the earth. The jump cuts leap ahead to the moment of an anti-fascist revolution, a point echoed by the juxtaposition of the last of the three shots with that of a stormy sky. A clap of thunder signals the director's outrage as he orchestrates the revolution from the skies. And the film ends.

Such overt intrusions of style announce the real hero of the Buñuel films, his the only consciousness we can respect. It is the director himself, impatiently revealing the hidden malevolence of the bourgeois world, breaking down the barriers between art and life, and challenging our complacency by preventing us from assimilating his vision to our leisured amusement or discounting his satire as irrelevant to our own experience.

Sometimes Buñuel achieves this with a sound overlap, as when the voice of Pierre enters Severine's first fantasy in *Belle de Jour* to ask her about her thoughts. And often the sound overlap serves as unexpected counterpoint, deflating a character just when we have been prepared to admire. His servant, Saturna, calls *Tristana's* Don Lope a "fine man," as we observe Don Lope's insolent attempt to seduce a young woman on the street. Buñuel always grants his audience more information than that afforded his characters. Later Don Lope will argue in his defense that he exempts from his sexual advances the wife of a friend and "the innocent flower," words overlapped by a shot of Lope's young charge, an as yet unspoiled, childlike Tristana, soon to be the helpless object of his lust and a victim of his male and class superiority.

Much of Buñuel's style illuminates his belief in the interchangeability of the conscious and the unconscious life. He has spoken of his "love for the instinctive and the irrational," contending that "the cinema seems to have been invented to express the life of the subconscious." A typical example of Buñuel's mature use of the surreal comes near the close of *The Milky Way*. A priest sits lecturing at an inn outside a young man's bedroom door because, compulsively, he had "forgotten some important points" in his earlier dining room tirade. The prelate rants on while inside the room a young man and woman lie separated in twin beds, driven apart, Buñuel implies, by dogmas fostered by religion and the repression of natural, unencumbered sexual feeling. Without warning, Buñuel cuts to a shot of the priest, now seated in the middle of the room, continuing his speech uninterrupted. Such, Buñuel smiles, is the power of religion and orthodoxy to enter our heads, to inhibit us unawares, and to invade our very being with its unflagging and persistent efforts to prevent us from living as we choose.

Only in Buñuel do we find so brilliantly interwoven the psychopathology of our time and the values of the age which nurture that damaged psychology. Buñuel, as a Swiftian satirist, never hesitates to exaggerate, offering images just barely beyond the pale of credibility.

But in no way are the sexual obsessions of Buñuelian characters warmed-over Krafft-Ebing. The jealous, obsessive husband of *El* who decides to sew up his wife's vagina with scissors and sutures differs only in degree from the possessive, materially compulsive bourgeoisie of reality. And the vagaries of Francisco of *El* are treated by Buñuel as symptomatic of an entire world order in disintegration, a chaos from which escape is impossible, even as Francisco, seeking refuge from his driven behavior during his last years in an isolated monastery, has learned nothing from his obsession and continues to be as jealous as ever of his now remarried wife. The last shot of *El* takes place in this Colombian monastery, his final retreat, as a wavering Francisco disappears into a long, unlit cavern. It is the tunnel of his obsessions and the darkness of his ignorance about the thwarted passions which have been distorted in his psyche and which, as a consequence, it is his destiny to re-enact forever. This chilling image at the end of *El* offers a fearful warning of the sickness the bourgeoisie would unleash on us all if it is not displaced, along with its Church, from the society it afflicts.

Similarly, throughout *The Discreet Charm of the Bourgeoisie,* Buñuel intercuts shots of his six central characters walking aimlessly down an interminable highway; one of these shots in fact ends the film. In this last scene, there is no sound at all. Buñuel then intercuts on the soundtrack the cries of a crowd as if at a sporting event, foreshadowing perhaps a day of popular condemnation of the six at some future judgment, as in the fantasy of the pope's execution in *The Milky Way.*

In this earlier film, Jean, one of the pilgrims to Santiago de Compostela, daydreams about a group of revolutionaries, armed and led by a woman, marching up a hill to their goal—the execution of the pope. In one of Buñuel's wittiest sound overlaps, the man sitting next to Jean is disturbed by the sound of gunfire issuing from—Jean's dream, foreshadowing the motif of the *The Discreet Charm,* in which the bourgeois characters dream each other's nightmares, completing them interchangeably. In this surreal use of the relation of sound to image, Buñuel reveals that only in our unconscious lives can we as yet dream each other's dreams. In a repressive world, we are still unable to share them consciously and to experience a common purpose. And here

Buñuel expresses one of the central ideas of his later work. The inhumanity of their rule has so come to torment the bourgeoisie that the aspirations of their victims begin to inhabit their own inner lives—which have, by now, after the long period of their predominance, grown empty and devoid of life-enriching images of their own.

In the final scene of *The Discreet Charm*, the shouts accompanying the six seemingly carefree bourgeois characters give way to silence, and their aimless walk continues. At the final moment they have their backs to us, as if we were soon to be shed of them permanently, along with their hold on us—one of the most economical of the dramatic revolutionary gestures with which Buñuel has concluded a film.

Buñuel thus compels us to confront a future which, while it has not yet emerged in the external world, is nevertheless already formed and present within our unconscious lives. The nihilistic emptiness of bourgeois life is reiterated in the final sequence of *The Phantom of Liberty*, in which animals peer into the camera, preferable surrogates for the human beings whose irrationality and arbitrary violence Buñuel finds in this moment of social decline symptomatic not of freedom, as he had in such earlier surrealist work as *L'Age d'Or*, but of the death throes of a superfluous, utterly venal, and unproductive social group.

But just as the captured revolutionaries of *The Phantom of Liberty* cry, "long live the chains," Buñuel refuses us any facile glorification of the oppressed. However maimed Joseph of *Diary of a Chambermaid* may be, damaged representative of the oppressed classes that he is, he remains a sadist who has chosen to ally himself with the powerful, and he fills us with the fear and loathing appropriate to the closet fascist.

Buñuel remains the observer from above, enveloping the hypocritical clergy in his sardonic smiles, as he watches the priest of *Diary of a Chambermaid* grant the bourgeoise Mme. Monteil permission to engage in unorthodox sexual practices, if not to enjoy them, with the understanding that she will provide for the falling church roof and other less immediate necessities. Laden with cakes, he departs, not merely a compromised individual, but a representative of his class, a co-conspirator with the wealthy and, as such, a co-defendant in Buñuel's court of justice. So are the priests, at the end of *The Exterminating Angel*, paralyzed and trapped within the cathedral with the wealthy dinner guests whose interests they have so diligently served. In *Diary of a Chambermaid* there is even a sexton who writes fascist pamphlets with Joseph under the cover of night.

Buñuel's hatred of the bourgeois order is unrelenting, but he is romantic neither about its easy demise nor in underestimating the price exacted from its victims. His fidelity to harsh truth is joined, nonetheless, to an unalterable conviction that transcendence is both possible and in process. It is this dialogue between hope and pain which makes Luis Buñuel one of the most humane and revolutionary artists working in film. Such is Buñuel's art, replete with irony and wit, lucid, ever focused, and providing through more than thirty films a veritable cultural heritage.

II

Biographical Glimpses

. . . .

Out of Innocence

J. Francisco Aranda

. . . .

Calanda is a village of 3,000 inhabitants, 115 kilometers from Zaragoza, on the foothills of the Teruel range. It would be a nondescript place but for two phenomena which give it a claim to fame. First, it is the birthplace of one of the most delightful of Spanish dances, the Calanda *jota*—a slow bolero, of aristocratic solemnity and great choreographic invention. It is arguable that ballet owed its birth to the boleros of Calanda and Alcañiz, a few kilometers away. In the sixteenth century, when the bolero reached its apogee, the kingdom of Aragón extended to include among its other Mediterranean territories, Naples; and it may be that Aragonese dances, brought there by the Spanish governors, imported steps which, having been systematized in Italy, provided the origins of the first known academic ballet. (It might also be mentioned that Gaspar Saenz, one of the best contrapuntalists of Spanish Renascence music, was born in Calanda.)

The other reason for the village's celebrity is the Miracle of Calanda. A man very devoted to the Virgin of the Pilar, having had a leg amputated, dreamed that Our Lady disinterred the member and stuck it back on his stump. The flesh, even though it was already putrefying and worm-eaten, resumed its vital functions. No other miracle can compare with this. To revive a dead man or return sight to one who is blind, can be faked; to see a man who has been without a leg walking with it once more is a proof too absolute to allow a possibility of doubt.

This country—once ruler of European destinies, now eking a living out of arid lands—oscillates between these two poles. The

From *Luis Buñuel: A Critical Biography* by J. Francisco Aranda, translated by David Robinson (New York: DaCapo Press), 1976. Reprinted by permission of Da Capo Press and Martin Secker & Warburg Limited.

31

landscape itself affords contrasts: on three sides are the dry, ploughed fields; on the fourth the Sierra, with rocks and richly colored flora, with trees and little streams of transparent water. Unlike Alcañiz the village presents no remnants of former glories. The people go about in their dark working clothes, with felt hats over their eyes. They are savage, and were until recently mostly illiterate. Yet sometimes, talking to them, there is still a sense of ancient tradition and underlying elegance. Their pleasures are violent and aristocratic. On feast days they organize hunts with packs of dogs, and bring back quantities of game. Afterward they gorge themselves with an enormous banquet of meat, liberally washed down with the sharp, sweet wine of Cariñena, and accompanied by *jotas* sung in voices that resemble the rasp of files. Best of all is Semana Santa (Holy Week). Then four hundred men go into the streets with great drums. From the evening of Good Friday, the day of Our Lord's Crucifixion, until the morning of His Resurrection, two days later, the percussion echoes for many kilometers around. The strongest keep up the drumming with all their might, and stop only for swigs from their leather wine bottles. Others take the place of those who succumb to exhaustion.

In the middle of the village is the church—an ugly one—which forms the end of a triangular plaza. In the center of this is a crude monument. This was first dedicated to the victors of the Civil War, and "Die for God and the Fatherland." Later, as the slogan became less fashionable, a bust of Goya, who was born in a village not far away, was substituted. Perhaps one day a monument to Luis Buñuel will replace Goya on the same pedestal.

The Buñuel family comes from Calanda. Its genealogy can be traced back to Spain's glorious sixteenth century. Some Buñuels emigrated to Aragón; a less distinguished branch established itself in the north, and it is supposed that they were the founders of Buñuel, a Navarrese village fronting the south of Huesca. Luis Buñuel's grandfather was born at the beginning of the nineteenth century and died at the end of it. He had two sons, Joaquín, who died of cholera at the end of the century, and Leonardo, the father of Luis. Leonardo was a restless boy. At fourteen he left home to join the army as a bugler. He took part in the Cuban War against the United States and rose to the rank of Captain. After the war he stayed in Cuba and opened a fancy-goods store in partnership with two associates, Vizoso and Lasteleiro, who subsequently between them made one of the largest fortunes in Spanish America. Leonardo had no such ambitions. In 1899 he visited his birthplace and announced that he would choose the healthiest and prettiest woman in the village. This he did.* Leonardo fell in love, and married, at forty-three years of age, a girl more than twenty years younger than himself, María Portolés. She was the daughter of the landlord of the *posada* (inn) facing the church. Although educated as a *señorita*, she was accustomed to lend a hand at the bar. Once married, he settled in Calanda for good, buying an estate there.

Don Leonardo had fine features and large clear eyes. Although he had no formal education, he acquired a culture. Friends who still remember him talk of his lively intelligence and the wide range of his knowledge. When he moved to Zaragoza he mixed with the intelligentsia of the Aragonese capital, where rich land-owners made up a considerable part of the bourgeoisie. He died in 1923.

Luis's mother was born in 1883 and died on 29 June 1969. She was a model wife, and made the marriage very happy. A woman of remarkable beauty, she was tall, broad-boned, with such an aristocratic bearing that even when she was past sixty, heads still turned when she went to mass along the Paseo de la Independencia. She brought up her children in the most devout and strict conventions of those days. There were seven of them: Luis, the first-born and strongest, born in 1900; María (1901), Alicia (1902), Conchita (1904), Leonardo (1910), who became a radiologist, Margarita (1912) and Alfonso (1915–61), an architect and adherent of the Spanish Surrealist group. To know the Buñuel family is a considerable help in understanding the work of Luis, which can be so disconcerting at times. Their character is a mixture of energy and honesty. They are violent and gentle at the same time. Their taste for paradox and bizarre expressions is inborn; the constant slips on the treacherous ground of blasphemy, inevitable. Anec-dotes on this subject are numerous and delightful. When Señora Buñuel's daughters were imprisoned, she protested to the police,

*Even today, when a girl of the village repeatedly refuses offers of marriage, risking remaining an old maid, the villagers say: "She'll marry when Buñuel comes back from Cuba."

asking "How dare you imprison people who are all descendants
of canons?" For her, Luis was a saint. To prove it she showed me
his portraits on an improvised altar in a wardrobe where they
were surrounded by photographs of the late Popes. Knowing the
Buñuels, it was impossible to question her sincerity. Looking
into her great limpid eyes, one felt submerged in a deep, trans-
lucent lake. Surrealism is not the creation of Luis, or of his
family: the world is surreal. But above all, Spain.

At the end of the last century the Buñuels had a fine house in
Calanda. Just before Luis was born they pulled down their
cottage on the outskirts of the town in order to build a new one,
where they intended to live. They rented a stately mansion from a
noble Lower Aragonese family, the Ram de Viu, who had palaces
in Alcañiz and Cataluña. There Luis was born. In his autobiography, written for the Museum of Modern Art in 1938* and
never till now published, he recalled:

> I was born February 22, 1900, in Calanda, a town in the province of Teruel,
> Spain.
>
> My father had spent almost all his life in America, where, as a wholesale
> merchant, he succeeded in amassing something of a fortune. When well in his
> forties he decided to return to his native town, Calanda, where he married my
> mother who was then barely seventeen. I was the first of the seven children of
> this marriage who are now living in Spain.
>
> My infancy slipped by in an almost mediaeval atmosphere (like that of
> nearly all the Spanish provinces) between my native town and Zaragoza. I feel
> it necessary to say here (since it explains in part the trend of the modest work
> which I later accomplished) that the two basic sentiments of my childhood,
> which stayed with me well into adolescence, are those of a profound eroti-
> cism, at first sublimated in a great religious faith, and a permanent conscious-
> ness of death. It would take too long here to analyze the reasons. It suffices
> that I was not an exception among my compatriots, since this is a very
> Spanish characteristic, and our art, exponent of the Spanish spirit, was
> impregnated with these two sentiments. The last civil war, peculiar and fero-
> cious as no other, exposed them clearly.

Luis was baptized in Calanda. Then his parents moved to
Zaragoza, the capital of Aragón, to live in a flat at number 29,
Paseo de la Independencia. From then on Luis spent four months
every summer, as well as Holy Week and other holidays, at

*It was written in English and is printed here without editorial revision or
correction.

Calanda. From 1915 to 1931 he spent his holidays at San Sebastian, but always returned home for Easter, to take part in the Procession of the Drums, in which he was one of the most dogged performers. In the country the Buñuels lived in the rebuilt house, surrounded by a beautiful garden full of cypresses and running down to the edge of the river. He played with his brothers and sisters and the village children, and was a quiet little boy. Like all the sons of good provincial families, he learned to serve at mass, and sang in the choir with a very good voice. Sometimes he played games with the girls, pretending to be the priest saying mass—a very common first sexual manifestation among Spanish children. All the Buñuel children liked dressing up. Sometimes they organized theatrical entertainments with texts of their own invention. Conchita recalls one in which they all wore kerchiefs on their heads (like the bandits in *L'Age d'Or* and characters from so many Buñuel films) and Luis recited:

> With this pair of scissors
>> And will to fight, it's plain
> We'll have a revolution
>> And capture all of Spain.

At other times they had shadow shows. Luis was kind to his sisters, but also very attracted to the other girls, whom he sometimes gave dolls which he had taken from the house. There were elements of sadism, natural enough in little boys, in his games. One of them, typically Calandan, consisted of poking a match inch by inch toward the eyes of a little girl, very slowly, to see how long she could resist closing them. When she gave up, she had to shout "Coñe!" ("Cunt!") and run away. "We tried doing the same thing to bats," Buñuel recalls. "They never said 'Coñe!' of course, though we always hoped they would." Other times they dared one another to swallow cigarette butts picked up in the street and washed down with water, or to eat sandwiches spread with ants*—an activity which has given rise to tortuous interpretations of Buñuel's gastronomic habits. In fact, his only peculiarities were to be a vegetarian between the ages of eighteen and twenty, and always to eat day-old bread.

*Buñuel denies this.

"At six he was sent to the College of the Brothers of the Sacred Heart, an order which, having been expelled from France, had finally settled in Zaragoza. There he encountered the idiom which was later to become an important part of his culture. At seven he moved to the Jesuit College, where he worked for his *baccalaureat* until he was sixteen. He always had top marks, receiving the 'Laurel Crown' and the titles of 'Emperor,' 'Carthaginian Consul' and so on, which embarrassed him immoderately and more than once led him to misbehave deliberately so that they would not award him such honors."

This extract from a letter from Alfonso Buñuel (26 January 1955) brought a protest from Luis, who wrote in another letter:

"My marks at the Jesuit College were sometimes good and other times bad; and I *never* was Emperor or Prince, although I had one or two minor prizes." The records of the college itself show that Buñuel is, as usual, exact. His worst marks were generally for mathematics. There is a record of a second prize for good conduct, honorable mention in French and Latin, and good marks for piety, politeness and neatness, and other Jesuitical virtues. An exquisite photograph shows the infant Buñuel invested with the Image of the Immaculate Conception at the Congregación Mariana. The present Rector also reveals that he was a school-friend of Buñuel in the last baccalaureat year. It is strange, he told me, that he should have left the college in this last and most difficult year; "but it could not have been a case of being expelled, because that would have been established in the school records." The Rector remembers him as a serious boy, bigger, better dressed and much more responsible than the majority of the others in his class. "We very much envied him, because he was like a man, which is what we all wanted to be."

Such details are not irrelevant. Everyone's childhood is decisive in his subsequent development. For the artist, the atmosphere and the landscape in which his early years are passed form the character of his work. Buñuel is one of the most outstanding illustrations. It is impossible to understand his cinema without taking into account his character as a Spaniard and an Aragonese, and all that goes with these things. Most of the errors and the elaborate and difficult interpretations put upon Buñuel's work come from this ignorance: indeed, for many years most critics thought that they were dealing with a Frenchman. If he had been French, the anti-clerical content and the insistence on religious problems would have had a different character. It might have been an intellectual and rational game, perhaps with a degree of wishing to *épater le bourgeois*. As it is, there is no question but that Buñuel's is far from an *Encyclopédiste* mentality; and that, as his autobiography suggests, religion was an anxious preoccupation from which he liberated himself by reacting violently against it. The same may be said of his social vision. Buñuel is the product of a bourgeoisie which entered the new century with the "Generación del '98,"* defeated, disillusioned, with few supports to prop their pride of caste. His family shared in an urban culture, liberal and semi-intellectual, at the same time as they were landowners. They remained in contact with the land. Above all, they were the children of that generation which achieved its revolution. During the first quarter of the century they were deeply conscious of national and personal crisis. And there were many among them who reacted as he did.

Throughout his work, Buñuel attacks—sometimes bitterly and angrily—those things which constituted his own youthful patrimony. In *L'Age d'Or* and *El* there are gardens recalling the family garden in Calanda, complete with the horrid, scaled-down reproductions of classical statuary, the creation of the society which built its neo-Gothic or *art nouveau* villas. The brilliantly conceived, idiotic decorations of the house in *El* are, according to Buñuel's sister Conchita, like those of their home in Calanda. The house in *Viridiana* must be a recollection of the home of his respected canon uncle. Buñuel's work is a pitiless analysis of the atmosphere which surrounded him. It is full of aesthetic reminiscences (literary, musical and plastic) of the nineteenth century, as, it may be mentioned in passing, is all Surrealist art. Some enemy of the Surrealists has said that "to be a Surrealist you have only to come from a 'good family.'"

Living in the country acquainted him with agricultural life: in his films he often alludes to the way men treat beasts of burden. In almost all of them, too, he returns to the landscape of Calanda.

*1898 was the year in which Spain lost her last colonies.

Buñuel uses a large proportion of exteriors, stressing landscapes of dust and soil. At most he frames only a narrow strip of sky. But this sky tells you nothing. In the midst of the land, among the dry tree-trunks, the rocks and the stones—there he places the center of his interest, the human being, geometrically composed and dwarfed in a very particular kind of long shot. A frame from Buñuel is unmistakable, distinguishable among thousands, linked with the great tradition of Griffith, Ince, Pudovkin, Dovzhenko, Ivens, but carried to an extreme of exasperation. In all his work there emerges a plastic style which has its own grandeur. We are far from the narcissism of Welles: yet despite himself Buñuel has an aesthetic personality, a way of going directly to what he has seen and felt, without aiming to beautify it. And the content, the absolute presence of the matter and its space, illuminates the unique message of his "being." The physical type of the Aragonese peasant appears in very many of his films: short-legged, bearded, wearing the old, dirty clothes of a laborer, with skins and a crumpled hat. (Cf. *L'Age d'Or, Nazarin,* etc.) The Jesuits taught him to be conscious of his duties and obligations, even the disagreeable ones, and this has enabled him to express all he wants to express in the cinema, with regal discretion. All his life Buñuel has borne this formation with an elegance that Voltaire, James Joyce and Jean-Paul Sartre—good students who emerged from just such a school as his, as equally vehement anti-Catholics—might themselves have envied.

Other constant themes in his cinema also appear to be tastes from his youth: Alfonso Buñuel recalled in a letter:

"Entomology and the study of animals in general attracted him. He always had some live animal in his room: snakes, rats, giant lizards, owls and so on. He was a favorite pupil of the entomologist Cándido Bolívar, whom he helped in classifying insects in the Museum of Natural History in Madrid, near to the Student Residence in which he lived.

"Extremely fond of music, he played the piano and violin from childhood; and I remember him playing the ocarina in the morning, before he had breakfast. His favorite composer was Richard Wagner, whom he greatly venerated, especially *Tristan and Isolde"* (the music of *Un Chien Andalou*, *L'Age d'Or* and *Cumbres Borrascosas*).

Conchita writes:

"When he was about thirteen he started to study the violin, at his own very strong desire; and he seemed to show an aptitude for it. He used to wait till we had gone to bed, then, with his violin all ready, would come to the room where we, his three sisters, slept. He would begin by telling us the 'plot,' which as I recall it was a very Wagnerian tale, although he was not aware of it at the time. I don't think his music was so Wagnerian, but it was a gift which enriched the adventures of my childish imagination.

"In those days we spent the summers at our house in Calanda. There he managed to form an orchestra, and at the great religious ceremonies, from the choir of the church, he would launch the strains of Perosi's *Mass* and Schubert's *Ave Maria* over the admiring populace. My parents often went to Paris, showering us with new toys on their return. From one of these trips came a theatre which, looking back, I reckon must have been about one meter square. It had a back-cloth and scenery. I remember two sets: a throne-room and a wood. The cardboard characters represented a King, a Queen, a Jester, Courtiers. They were only ten centimeters high, and always faced the front, even when they were moving sideways, pushed by a wire. To augment the cast my brother brought in a ferocious lion, which normally stood on an alabaster base and served as a paperweight. Also he used a gilt Eiffel Tower which until then had passed its time between the kitchen, the drawing room and the barn. I can't remember whether the Eiffel Tower represented a fortress, or some sinister personage in the play, but I do recall that I saw it enter the throne-room, leaping and bounding, harnessed to the tail of the lion. A week before the shows, Luis started preparations. He rehearsed with his chosen ones who, as in the Bible, were few; though many were called. He arranged chairs in one of the barns. Invitations were prepared and distributed among those boys and girls of the village who had achieved the age of twelve. At the last moment he prepared a small collation of sweets made of egg-white and, as a drink, water flavored with vinegar and sugar. As we were persuaded that this drink came from an exotic land, we drank it with pleasure and devotion. To make him admit us, his sisters, my father had to threaten him with prohibition of the event.

"He ate like a squirrel, and even when the temperature was below zero and there was snow on the ground, he wore as little clothing as possible, and monkish sandals on his feet. My father was opposed to all this, but underneath, very proud of having a son capable of these things. He hid his pride, and was particularly angry with Luis when he saw him lift up his feet one after the other and wash them in the wash basin—in cold water—every time he washed his hands. At that time, or perhaps a little earlier (I find dates very confusing) we had in the house a rat as big as a hare, which was perfectly repulsive with its vixen tail, but which we treated as one of the family. Whenever we went anywhere we took it in a parrot's cage, and for quite a time it made our lives very complicated. The poor creature died like a saint, and with definite symptoms of poisoning. As we had five servants, it was not easy to discover the murderer. At all events we had forgotten it even before its smell had completely vanished from the house. We always kept some animal. Monkeys, parrots, falcons, toads and frogs, some sort of snake, a large African lizard which the cook, in a moment of fright, killed outright with the kitchen poker and an iron. I still remember the ram, Gregorio, who practically crushed my femur and pelvis when I was ten years old. I believe that they had brought him from Italy when he was little. He was always untrustworthy, and only liked Nene the horse. We were already older when we had a big hatful of grey mice. They belonged to Luis, but he allowed us to look at them once a day. He had selected several couples which, well fed and housed, procreated without cease. Before leaving home, he took them to the barn and let them go, so that they might increase and multiply.

"We all loved and respected everything that lived, even vegetable life. I believe that they also respect and love us. We could walk through a forest of wild animals, like those Salgari describes, without fear of molestation. There is one exception. THE SPIDERS. Horrid and fearful monsters which at any moment can deprive us of all the joy of living. Thanks to a strange, 'Buñuel-esque' morbidity, they are a principal theme of our family conversation. Our discussions on spiders are legendary. One story alleges that my brother Luis, seeing a monster with eight eyes and a twisted mouth emerge when he was eating in an inn in Toledo, fell into a swoon and did not recover until he arrived back in Madrid.

"Nearly all the animals which we bought belonged to my brother Luis and I never saw beings better cared for, each one according to its biological needs. Even today he still loves animals and I think that he even tries not to hate spiders. In *Viridiana* we are shown a long, long cart-track, and a poor dog tied beneath a cart. Looking for locations for the film, he had been very upset to see this actual scene, but played for real. He tried to put a stop to it once or twice, but the habit is rooted among Spanish peasants, and it was like fighting windmills. While they were shooting these scenes, he ordered a kilo of meat to be bought every day for the dogs, and for any others that might come into the neighborhood.

"We had many delightful adventures. In one of those summers that we spent at Calanda, we experienced the greatest adventure of our childhood. At that time Luis was thirteen or fourteen. We decided to go to a nearby village without the permission of our parents. We were joined by some cousins of our own age, and left the house, I don't know why, all dressed up as if for a holiday. The town, five kilometers away, was called Foz. We had estates and smallholdings there. We visited everyone, and everyone gave us sweet wine and little cakes. The wine produced such euphoria and Dutch courage in us that we did not hesitate to go to the cemetery. For the first time I walked there without fear. I recall Luis stretching out on a grave as if on the autopsy table and asking to be cut open. I also remember our efforts to help one of our sisters to release her head from a hole which the weather had worn in a tomb. She was so firmly stuck that Luis had to tear away the plaster with his nails in order to free her. After the war I went back to the cemetery to remember. It seemed much smaller, and older. Thrown into a corner was a crumbling little white coffin, with the mummified remains of a child, which made a strong impression on me. A big cluster of red poppies was growing where its stomach once was.

"After our heedless and sacrilegious visit to the cemetery, we undertook to walk across the bare and burning hills in search of the—to us—fabled 'Brown Cave.' The sweet wine continued to sustain us and enabled us to do what older people had not dared to do: to jump into a deep, narrow hole, to drag ourselves along a horizontal fissure, and arrive at the first cavern. Our only speleological equipment consisted of a stub of wax candle, left over from some burial, which we had picked up in the cemetery. We walked as long as its light held out. Suddenly everything went— lights, courage, joy. Luis insisted that the fluttering bats were prehistoric beings; but that he would protect us. Later, when someone said that he was hungry, Luis chivalrously offered himself to be eaten. Because my brother was my idol, I whimpered that *I* wanted to be the one to be eaten, since I was the littlest and silliest of the senior group of Buñuel children. I have forgotten the anguish of all those hours, just as one forgets physical pain. I remember however the joy of being found, and the fear of punishment. There was no punishment, on account of our pathetic state. We made the return journey to home, sweet home in a cart drawn by Nene. My sister was unconscious, though I am uncertain whether from drunkenness, weakness or discretion. Our parents only addressed us in the most formal terms for the next few days. When he thought we were not listening, my father recounted the adventure to visitors, exaggerating the dangers, and praising Luis's offer to be eaten. Nobody mentioned my offer, though it was just as heroic."

Luis's autobiography takes up the story:

> My eight years as a student with the Jesuit fathers only increased these sentiments instead of diminishing them. Until my baccalaureat at sixteen years of age one can say that I had not been a part of modern society. I went to Madrid to study. The change from the province to the capital was as amazing to me as it would have been to a crusader who had suddenly found himself on Fifth Avenue, New York City.
>
> When I graduated with my bachelor degree my father asked me what I wanted to study. I had two chief interests: one, music (I had taken several violin courses) and the other, natural sciences. I asked my father to allow me

to go to Paris and enroll in the Schola Cantorum and continue the study of composition. He refused, arguing that with the career of an artist one was more apt to die of hunger than to prosper. This was the attitude of any Spanish father (and perhaps of a father of any nationality). Flattering my other interest, he urged me to go to Madrid to study for the career of Agricultural Engineer.

In 1917 I therefore found myself settled in Madrid in the Students' Residence, which in Spain is the only really modern institution of pedagogy, inspired and created in imitation of the English universities, by the Institución Libre de Enseñanza.

A curious thing is that in Spain the career of engineer is the most difficult and honorable which a young man can pursue. The aristocratic thing to do in Spain is to study to be an engineer or a diplomat. The only young men who had access to these careers were those who, besides having the necessary intelligence and application, had sufficient funds, as the cost was excessive for the modest Spanish way of living.

In agricultural engineering there was the absurd situation in which, although it was essentially a career of natural sciences, it was necessary for one to study mathematics for several years. And, if my inclinations led me to the study of nature, I in no way felt inclined to solve equations with the grade of "n." Nevertheless I studied mathematics for three years. With this they succeeded in making me hate my studies.

Determined to try on my own and without my father's permission, I enrolled in 1920 as a pupil of the learned Spanish entomologist, Dr. Bolívar, director of the Museum of Natural History of Madrid. This and the following year I dedicated to the study of insects which, as far as my material future was concerned, was less lucrative than if I had studied music at the Schola Cantorum.

I worked with interest for over a year, although I soon arrived at the conclusion that I was more interested in the life or literature of insects than in his [*sic*] anatomy, physiology and classification.

During that time I formed a close friendship, in Students' Residence, with a group of young artists who were to influence me strongly in finding my bent. Some of them have become famous, such as the poet, Federico García Lorca, the painter, Salvador Dalí, Moreno Villa, poet and critic, etc. I began to collaborate in the vanguard of literary publications, publishing some poems and preferring to chat with my friends in the café rather than to sit at the table with the microscope at the Museum of Natural History.

My new literary leanings made me realize that my goal was art and letters rather than natural sciences. Thus I changed my career and began the study of Philosophy and Letters in the University of Madrid, and graduated with a degree in 1924.

I cannot say that I was a good student. I alternated between interminable gatherings of our group of friends and the writing of poems, and sports. In 1921 I became amateur boxing champion of Spain, because, as the saying goes, "In the land of the blind, the one-eyed man is king."

Alfonso Buñuel, in the letter already quoted, relates this episode:

"In his adolescence, apart from natural sciences and intellectual pursuits, he was a great athlete: very muscular in build, unbeatable at elbow-wrestling. As an amateur boxer he made public appearances in Madrid, losing the amateur heavyweight championship on points at nineteen.

"His father having finally forbidden him boxing, especially in public, he went to the ring rather nervously. In the previous bout, it happened that one of the boxers was killed. With great trepidation Luis was on the defensive in every round. The judges, seeing his superiority over his opponent, asked him to adjourn the fight. The opponent accepted another round, and Luis said: 'Twenty more or none at all'; so his opponent was declared winner on points."

Of Luis's friendships, Alfonso adds:

"In the Residencia he formed warm friendships with various other inmates: Federico García Lorca, Pepín Bello, Salvador Dalí,* José María Hinojosa, José Moreno Villa. His group was in general that whole generation of writers and their circle: Alberti, Guillén, Dámaso Alonso, Ramón Gómez de la Serna, Altolaguirre, Pedro Garfias, Barradas, Palencia, Vázquez Díaz, José Ortega y Gasset, Adolfo Salazar, etc." He might also have included two very great friends, Vicens and Sanchez Ventura.

Buñuel's period in the Residencia de Estudiantes is important. The Residencia was a formative place, an exceptional catalyst of talents in the story of modern Spanish art. Its history has still to be written, and will be a significant one. To understand it, it is necessary to link it with two sister institutions: the Institución Libre de Enseñanza and the Instituto Escuela. Since 1920 almost all Spain's outstanding names in the sciences, arts and sociology—internationally celebrated figures—have come from these three centers.

The contact between young intellectuals, their shared existence, the interminable talks in the common rooms, dormitories and cafés to which Buñuel refers, describing them as idling away the time (and the description is correct if we apply the Aristotelian

---

*Dalí was never a formal member of the Residencia, though he was a constant visitor there.

definition of idling as the germinating period of creation), resulted in the work of the Generation of '27. Buñuel, Val y Gay and García Lorca would organize lectures, shows and excursions. Federico was later to found, with Eduardo Ugarte as secretary, "La Baracca" ("The Barn"), a touring theatrical company; with this company Buñuel was to visit Las Hurdes where he would subsequently make the film of the same title; and he was to develop the literary and cinematographic activity described in Chapter 3.

In the Residencia there were concerts, poetry recitals, entertainments, literary discussions, scientific lectures, a Sociedad de Cursos y Conferencias. The cinema had begun to interest intellectuals in France after 1918, and consequently in the Spanish center—always in the forefront—there was a favorable atmosphere for what they were beginning to call "The Seventh Art."

Buñuel interested himself in the theatre, especially the puppet theatre, thanks to his friends Juan Chabas and Federico García Lorca, who wrote some excellent farces for puppets. The three of them met a little man called Mayeu who was presenting children's shows in the Retiro Park, passing the hat around to make a little money. Chabas and Buñuel organized shows of a superior kind, helping Mayeu to prepare the plays and performances. They ended up taking the show to the Residencia where they presented performances with this delightful theatre which Lorca had already conscientiously rehearsed with Manuel de Falla, during his adolescence in Granada.

Buñuel was also an amateur actor. His troupe were much admired for their interpretation of Zorrilla's *Don Juan Tenorio* which they played every 1 November. The performance was faithful, but the students let themselves and their fantasy loose on the production and the decors. Each year the director and designer changed. Sometimes it was Lorca, sometimes Buñuel. As actor, Buñuel always played Don Juan: exuberant, exaggerated, nervously moving from one side to the other, and carrying a portable typewriter for writing love-letters. The students of the Residencia saw in the ultra-romanticism of *Don Juan Tenorio* a fount of Freudian significances and other precursors of Surrealism, which practically all the members of the group were to assimilate.

(Buñuel notes: "My first contact with Freud was reading in 1921 *Psychoanalysis of Daily Life,* translated and with an introduction by Ortega y Gasset. This introduction earned the Spanish philosopher a letter of harsh censure from Freud.") The custom of presenting this annual performance still continues as a sort of ritual among the survivors who remain in Madrid. Something resembling the Residencia production was seen in 1951 when Salvador Dalí mounted *Don Juan Tenorio* for the National Theatre, with settings which he had designed and used in America. Buñuel's stage experience in the Residencia was later to prove useful when he began his professional career with the direction of *El Retablo de Maese Pedro,* and afterward came to direct film actors.

Generally the activities of this period influenced the whole artistic formation of Buñuel. His passion for insects is reflected in all his films. Insects played a great part in Spanish literature at that period, in the work of Lorca, Dámaso Alonso and others, providing our writers with an authentic poetic image—of anxiety, fear, desire, terror. Buñuel's use of big close-ups of insects interpolated in the action of his films, has been attacked as affected and pretentious; but those who make this criticism fail to recognize the expressive origins of such images. Although they come from entirely personal sources, their use is never simply gratuitous: they always have an additional purpose, as shock images, as methods of transition between sequences, as a reminder to the spectator of the other dramas that are played out on the sidelines of the main theme. As well as symbols of unbalanced states of mind, too, there is an element of objective vision, a gesture of curiosity and affection toward these other living creatures.

His Surrealist formation can also be traced to his years in the Residencia. Although his orthodox initiation into the movement dates from his stay in Paris, his first literary works, published in Madrid, already clearly show his inclinations. The beginnings of Surrealism in Spain were contemporary with the French movement.* We can trace the germs from 1916 and the appearance in

---

*Buñuel in fact corrects this statement. He says that it was only four months after the première of *Un Chien Andalou* that he introduced Dalí to the Surrealist group in Paris.

Barcelona of Francis Picabia's* Dada magazine *391*. In 1919 a
Dada group formed in Barcelona around a fashionable milliner,
Joan Prats, and some of his dilettante friends. Almost at the same
time Dada made its appearance in Madrid. If the rapid assimilation of Surrealism in Barcelona was due to the city's thirst for
cosmopolitanism, in Madrid it had an indigenous origin which
made it quite different from French Surrealism. Although integrated in the international Paris group, Buñuel's Surrealism
always retained its essentially Spanish character.

Madrid in 1920 was a hubbub of "isms," which were later noted
and classified by Ramón Gómez de la Serna, who was very
roughly Spain's equivalent to Apollinaire. Encouraging all his
contemporaries, inciting them to discover new forms, accustom-
ing them to his extravagant literary techniques, he was the
catalyst if not the master of the new styles. The Spanish Surrealist
group was undoubtedly on the march before 1925. There is a
study of this movement,† which represented an important, though
not exclusive activity of the Generation of '27; and the present
writer has made a *Chronology of Spanish Surrealism*. The Surrealist influence and the style of the new "belief" were marked in
Buñuel's Spanish friends—Dalí, Hinojosa, Prados, Lorca, Alberti,
Bello, Duran, Garfias, Gerardo Diego and later Ceruda Alexandre
and many others. It is important to recognize that these owed not
everything to French Surrealism; only Juan Larrea was indebted
to Paris. Spanish Surrealism did not drink at the same fountains
as the French—Swift, De Sade, De Quincey, Hegel, Lautréamont,
Jarry—but from *La Celestina* and the Spanish picaresque novel,
and the nineteenth century indigenous theatre.

For Buñuel, as a good Aragonese, fantasy is impossible: paradoxical though it may seem, his Surrealism is without fantasy, a
purified form of Surrealism. Surrealism was a movement of revolt
against the last century's strict and stultifying naturalism. Buñuel
is a materialist, but no longer admits *only* what he can see and
touch. He accepts as real, things which we do not *know* but
which can be sensed, although they may continue to remain

---

*Picabia, whose baptismal name was Francisco Martinez de Picabia, was of
Spanish-Cuban origin.
†H. B. Morris, "Surrealism and Spain," Cambridge University Press, 1972.

undemonstrable by experiment. (It is strange, however, to observe that since Surrealism many of these things have become capable of scientific demonstration.) Generally, even despite Maurice Nadeau's classic *Histoire du Surréalisme* (1945), there is still misconception about what the movement really was. For many it was simply an aesthetic movement. And in effect it was so from the time of the defection to an artistic formalism of some of its members, who were for other reasons expelled from "the party." Fundamentally, however, it was a philosophical and active position applied to the contemporary world as an embattled intellectual movement, and deeply involved in the social and political currents of the time. To an extent elevating reality through a process of poeticizing it, its practitioners fought against and despised the idea of "art for art's sake" and the idealist aesthetic still dominant in many areas of the old European capitalist culture. If Surrealism in Spain never had a defined program as it had in France, it nevertheless possessed the advantage of alliance with the temperament and art of a people traditionally devoted less to logic, and more to reality than the French. With the Spanish, Surrealism does not imply an intellectual distortion of reality, but a rupture: "The ship on the sea and the horse on the mountain," pleaded Lorca. To put the boat on the mountain and the horse on the water would be worse, for the Spanish Surrealists, than simply a fantastic paradox: it would be an injustice and an offense against nature and the natural order. Hence the Spanish are able to understand Buñuel, and not find in his work any of the betrayal and renunciation of which some French critics accuse him.

It is quite true that Buñuel's work can be divided into distinctive periods according to its language: the first and the latest by orthodox Surrealist vocabulary; and the middle period by images and situations apparently belonging to the commercial cinema, although in reality we can discover within them the same processes as in the other films. It is also true that Buñuel has changed in the course of thirty years, as all men must; and as he has himself said: "At seventy you see things with a different passion and from a different viewpoint. In thirty years the world has changed, and you have to attack with different weapons." Yet his feelings and convictions have continued unchanged. Buñuel's processes of intellectual connection do not observe traditional logic. He affirms the absurd, but only in that part of cinematic structure which is not concrete: in the development of the sequence and its articulation with the rest. But his material is, in a wholly Spanish style, always objective, undistorted. I cannot bring to mind a single shot or a single frame in Buñuel which does not contain some real, familiar, everyday object, directly shown. Here lies the difference between him and Jean Vigo, the son of a Catalan, and the cinema's other great Surrealist. Vigo also employs objective reality, but records it with the illuminations, the unexpected angles of an eccentric vision which gives new significances to the object, through aesthetic addition. For Buñuel the element of surprise and contradiction in things resides in those things just as they are. He shows pig-killing quite faithfully in *Cumbres Borrascosas,* just as it might be seen in any village; but when he presents it to us it seems incredible, inadmissible. When he presents the actual world as harsh and cruel, it is no sadistic deformation. On the contrary, Buñuel shows violence with discretion, in brief shots, which never linger over details, but bring us a genuine sense of shame. Vigo, as artist and poet, was the prophet of a new social class. Buñuel is the chronicler of a dying class; and without wanting to make anything more beautiful or optimistic than it is, simply and laconically offers us his document.

This Spanish essence of Buñuel clearly links him quite as much with his contemporaries of the Generation of '27 as with the artists with whom he was associated in his French period. His intellectual origins in the Residencia de Estudiantes are fundamental to a knowledge of him. His contact with it continued after his years as a student of philosophy and literature. After going to Paris in 1925, Buñuel continued regularly to visit the Residencia, and kept up his contact with his friends—even after his marriage, when he was living in an apartment in Calle Menendez y Palayo, between 1934 and his departure for France in 1937.

Returning to 1924:

> Upon completing my career, I found myself at loose ends. My only out was to try for a professorship in an institute or university, a profession for which I felt I had no calling. As I was twenty-four years old I realized that I must think seriously about getting established, but nevertheless I felt more undecided and perplexed than ever. This is a fault prevailing among the Spanish. Instead of a youth's developing according to his likes and aptitudes, he must follow the course marked out by his parents. The student, upon leaving the bosom of his family and feeling himself independent, is more drawn to life itself than to study. The Spanish University did very little, one must realize, to attract the students or inspire their affection.
>
> My nervousness and uncertainty was dissipated immediately when my mother gave me permission to go to Paris. My father had died the year before.

This was the time of Primo de Rivera's dictatorship. Buñuel lived in a time in which politico-social problems were becoming progressively graver. The bourgeoisie tried to ignore them. The Residencia with its educated bourgeois élite and its English-style education of exclusive minorities had felt an ill-defined anxiety, which manifested itself in the pre-Surrealist rebellion. The liberal and progressive tone of the Residencia would not succeed in shaking the young artists out of their heritage and their "symbolist" education.

Buñuel, like Larrea and Hinojosa, will breathe the cosmopolitan air of Paris. He will perhaps be the first of the Institute's ex-students to react, the first of the Generation of '25 (or the Generation of the Dictatorship, or the Generation of '27, to use alternative titles for it) to adopt a radically new position. It is a fact of considerable importance, which can explain the late acceptance and understanding of his work as much as his present-day recognition, now that a new generation has taken a fresh step forward, and the Buñuel period can be regarded as "classic." Despite this Buñuel remains firmly linked to his Generation of the Residencia. He overcomes a crisis, but it will be expressed in terms of conflict. It is the path which leads from "Modernism" to realism, from idealism to Marxism. His whole work reflects the path of a nation from the "Golden 1900s" through the Dictatorship and the Civil War up to our own times.

The Discreet Charm of Luis Buñuel

Carlos Fuentes

. . . .

COMING: From the moment Christ dies on Good Friday right up to the celebration of his rising on Holy Saturday the town of Calanda resounds to the ceaseless beating of drums. All afternoon, all through the night to the flare of torchlights, all through the following morning everyone, man, woman or child, beats until the tense goatskins burst or become ragged and bloodied. For the hands of the townspeople are now raw; the knuckles are bare bone; the fingers are open sores and the ancient, severe, monotonous, rising sound of the drums, the heartbeat of Calanda, can be heard for miles around the bleak Aragonian countryside.

It is the birthplace of Luis Buñuel, the seat of a family that built its fortunes in colonial Cuba and then abandoned the billiard-green rum and sugar tropics for this grey, stormy and stony Greco landscape that is Aragón: The birthplace of Luis Buñuel is also the birthplace of his film characters Tristana and Viridiana, and the place where his four sisters have chosen to die. They have already ordered a funeral repast of black olives, black sausage and caviar, and all four of them, shrouded in black, beat the drums for 24 hours during Holy Week until their knuckles glow red and white, and then one of the Buñuel sisters, an obsessive poker player, goes into the church, starts collecting religious prints from the faithful, forgets where she is, shuffles the holy cards and is about to deal them back, remembers where she is, crosses herself and dips her wounded fingers, along with the beggars and hags and incestuous dwarfs, in the sacred fount of Spain.

GROWING: In the provincial capital of Saragossa stands the Jesuit school Buñuel went to as a boy. It has a stone courtyard

From *The New York Times Magazine* (March 11, 1973). © 1973 by The New York Times Company. Reprinted by permission.

with vaulted archways and stealthy brothers eying each other and the world with keenness and suspicion. You must understand Spain in terms of survival, and even the upholders of the status quo have been persecuted in this land of paradoxes. Like the Moors and Jews before them, the Jesuits were expelled from Spain and her colonies in the 18th century; they were too meddlesome, too astute, too rationalistic. And they did not teach Christian resignation, but pragmatic politics, the uses of flattery and veiled menace, wile and implacable logic. They survived and came back to polarize generations of conservatives and radicals. Voltaire, Luis Buñuel and Fidel Castro can be counted among their disciples.

There exist two tinted photographs of Buñuel as a child. In one of them, dressed in white and holding a beribboned white candle, he prepares for First Communion. In the other, clad in a velvet Lord Fauntleroy suit, he is a charming and discreet little bourgeois gazing with bulging eyes at the surviving ruins of Spain. Buñuel was born in 1900, two years after a most traumatic national experience: the loss of the remnants of empire in the war with the United States, the final collapse of the rigid design of the Counter Reformation. The "critical generation" of 1898 had set about dissecting the national corpse. Ortega y Gasset spoke of an "unvertebrated Spain" and tried to revive her brain with the thick blood of modern German philosophy. Santiago Ramón y Cajal introduced modern scientific methods. And while Europe fought the war that ended the illusion of unlimited peace and progress under liberal bourgeois rule, all these renovating trends met at the students' residence in the University of Madrid.

Frederico Garcia Lorca and Rafael Alberti, Salvador Dali and Luis Buñuel: Spain would speak again, Spain would see again. The campus revolutionaries read Marx and Engels, Dostoevski and Freud. And they had a sense of humor: Buñuel and Lorca would shave closely, powder their faces, dress in nun's garb and board tramways, winking at the male passengers, nudging them with hips and elbows as panic crept. Some, like Lorca, had to stay on in Spain and dig into the roots, later to surface with the poetic images buried under the necrophilic tons of granite at the Escorial. Others, like Buñuel, felt that they could only understand the

Spanish crisis from the viewpoint of the European crisis. Buñuel packed his Aragonian burro and trotted over the Pyrenees to join the surrealist revolution in Paris.

See anew, think anew, mock and scandalize your way through the trembling cardboard facades of the old, positivist, capitalist, academic order; proclaim on Anatole France's death that a corpse has just died; insult the likes of the poet Paul Claudel and the St. Cyr Military Academy; remember your friends stupidly butchered on the Marne and Verdun battlefields; vilify and destroy a society of hypocritical exploiters. All power to dreams, all power to love, all power to the subconscious; spring from false, everyday "reality" to the super-reality where the impossible opposites—dream and vigil, art and life, politics and morality, good and evil, saint and demon, man and woman—are once more, as in the origins of being, united, one.

The roster was immense: André Breton and Louis Aragon, Tristan Tzara and Max Ernst, Giorgio de Chirico and Benjaim Péret, Pablo Picasso and Francis Picabia, Marcel Duchamp and Joan Miró, Paul Eluard and Man Ray, Hans Arp and Yves Tanguy. The space was limited: From the Place Blanche in Montmartre to the cafes on the Boulevard Montparnasse. The achievements were extraordinary. The elements of vision and speech were dissembled and associated anew, and poems, paintings, sculptures, plays, magazines, manifestos and mischievous happenings came crashing through the rusty cracks of the *Belle Epoque.*

For a time Buñuel neither painted, wrote nor composed. Apart from being a competent boxer and entomologist, he could dabble in stage direction with Falla's "Puppet Show of Maese Pedro" at the Amsterdam Opera; he could scribble a few movie reviews for the surrealist magazines (but his thematic choices would be significant: Stroheim and Keaton); he could even become Jean Epstein's assistant in the filming of "Mauprat" and "The Fall of the House of Usher." But in 1928, he obtained a loan from his mother, called in his boyhood friend Dali and made *Un Chien Andalou.* Cyril Connolly was at one of the first showings and said that the effect of excitement and liberation was indescribable. He added that the spectators had been offered the first vision of the fires of disenchantment and madness that smoldered under the complacent postwar world. Nurses were on hand to assist people in the audience who might faint when the eyeball of that impudent flapper gets slashed by a razor as the moon is crossed by a drifting cloud. Pianos are stuffed with dead donkeys and with a ballast of struggling Jesuits strangled by horse's reins; pale hermaphrodites are run down by speeding cars on indifferent boulevards; a man erases his lips, and a woman's pubic hair sprouts on his face, and this in turn liberates the following image, which is a black sea urchin; striped boxes contain mutilated hands; hands are full of swarming ants; fourth floor apartment doors open on wintry beaches where the dummies of lovers will rot this coming spring, buried chest-high in the sand. . . . Free association, said Buñuel and Dali; no preconceived ideas, pure poetic freedom. But the images *were* inspired by psychoanalysis, and most of them drifted off in the direction of Dali's future paintings.

The first break with Dali came on the first day of shooting *L'Age d'Or*, their second joint venture. They got the money from a Parisian angel called the Comtesse de Noailles, who at the same time was financing Cocteau's *Le Sang d'un Poète*. The Castor-and-Pollux relationship between the two Spaniards seems to have been severely damaged when Dali fell in love with Gala, Paul Eluard's wife, and Buñuel tried to strangle the lady on a rock at Cadaqués because he saw in her a diabolical influence. In any case Dali stayed on the set of *L'Age d'Or* for exactly one day. From then on, it was Buñuel on his own, and this, the greatest of the surrealist films and one of the most personal and original works in the history of the cinema, is also a primer of Buñuelian obsessions, procedures, manias and illuminations.

A scientific prologue on the ways of the scorpion gives way to the arrival by launch of a party of bankers, officials and philanthropic dowagers who disembark on a barren beach where the littered skeletons of popes and bishops have become gigantic rock formations, and there they proceed to lay the cornerstone of Western civilization on a pile of excrement—and to murder the original inhabitants, a group of guerrilla-fighters. Which leads us to modern-day Rome and what is certainly the first critique of the consumer society ever. The hero (Gaston Modot), who has been dreaming the previous scene, is now actually being led by two policemen; he is accused of making love in a dream, and his eyes wander over advertisements that further entice his erotic appetites: cosmetics, women's stockings and underwear. Excited by the lustful call of the economy, he decides to have his pleasure at once; but the object of his desire, a dreamy-eyed nymph of the upper classes (Lya Lys) is safely ensconced in her father's house, and that worthy gentleman is hosting a concert of Wagnerian music to a packed garden of attentive society leaders.

To get to her, the hero must kick animals, humiliate the maimed, batter down doors and destroy property with the anarchical fury of James Finlayson doing battle against Laurel and Hardy. He is as indifferent as the concert guests to the brutal murder of a child by her gamekeeper father; he slaps a dignified matron on the face; pulls the orchestra leader's white beard and finally rapes the girl (who all this time has been sucking the toe of a marble statue) on the garden gravel as the *Liebestod* surges to its climax and, desire achieved, disillusion sets in. The silken nymph becomes a big cow seated on the connubial bed; old age arrives; the temple of the body is in ruins; the garden of sex withers; snow falls and the scene shifts violently to the snowbound castle of the Marquis de Sade's "One Hundred Twenty Days of Sodom"; the sexual revelers depart, led by a Christ figure, and the wind slashes the tufts of a woman's hair on a cross to the strains of a bullring *pasodoble.*

L'Age d'Or opened in 1930 at the Studio 28 in Paris to an uproar worthy of Hugo's "Hernani" or Stravinsky's "Rite of Spring." The *camelots du roi* and other Catholic and Fascist gangs threw brimming inkpots at the screen and slashed the paintings by Dali, Ernst and Tanguy exhibited in the lobby. The right-wing press egged the gangs on and howled against Buñuel. Finally, Police Commissioner Chiape had the film banned. But one of its first spectators, Henry Miller, had now written that *L'Age d'Or* was a unique and incomparable film, the only one he had seen that revealed the true possibilities of the cinema.

Buñuel's career was launched with an explosion; yet, with the exception of the stark and cruel documentary about Spain's most miserable region, *Land Without Bread* (1936), commissioned and then withdrawn by the authorities of the Spanish Republic, he was not to direct another film during the following 19 years. Why? Again, the politics of survival.

First, the survival of the Republic after the Franco uprising and Fascist intervention: Buñuel worked as a courier and press agent for the Loyalist government. Then, the survival of Luis Buñuel himself. He had been called to Hollywood by Irving Thalberg after the *Age d'Or* sensation; he was told to stay put, get into the mood watching Lili Damita potboilers and wait for something to come up. Buñuel resigned in a huff from M.G.M., produced a few B-movies in Spain and, after the fall of the Republic, found himself an exile in New York, working with Iris Barry in the Museum of Modern Art documentary film section and for Nelson Rockefeller's wartime Office of Inter-American Affairs. The arrival of Dali in the United States and the publication of the Catalonian painter's autobiography put an end to that. Buñuel was described in it as an incendiary atheist, wholly responsible for the subversive content of *L'Age d'Or;* Dali's highly respectable scenario had been treasoned by Buñuel.

The illusion was reproduced by the New York press and, to avoid embarrassing MOMA, Buñuel resigned and, with $40 in his pocket, a wife and two young sons, traveled to Mexico, where other Spanish Republican exiles had found a home and work. There he vegetated, until the producer Oscar Dancigers offered him a full-length film in 1947. Its horrors can scarcely be conceived. It was to be (and became) a triangular alternation of Mexican *rancheras* sung by Jorge Negrete, the personification of sombreroed *machismo*, tangos sung by an Argentine weeping willow called Libertad Lamarque and rumbas danced by a curvaceous tropicality known as Meche Barba. The film did not survive.

But Buñuel did; he made three more situation comedies before he could stage his own comeback with the fiercely beautiful *Los Olvidados*, a brutally unsentimental view of a teenage gang in a Mexico City slum. It won him the director's award at Cannes in 1951, but it did not win him much greater freedom, and it is a measure of the man's stubbornness that he was able to translate all those low budgets, hammy actors, despicable sets and 13-day

schedules into personal statements, unified, mysterious and replete with implicit meanings. His films during this time dealt
with jealousy (*El,* where the middle-class Othello decides to sew
up his wife's vagina before retiring to a monastery), solitude and
survival (*The Adventures of Robinson Crusoe,* where Defoe's
hero screams at the sea to hear his own voice and finds solace in
the feminine clothes he can salvage from the wreck) and fetishist
murders (*The Criminal Life of Archibald de la Cruz,* where the
would-be killer's perfectly planned crimes all fail miserably and
only accidental deaths occur. A nun falls down an elevator shaft).

But even the most awful films of Buñuel's Mexican period have
at least one unforgettable scene. A case in point is his flawed
version of *Wuthering Heights,* a nightmare of miscasting in
which Cathy speaks with an Italo-Polish accent, Heathcliff with
Andalusian pronunciation and the Mexican actors sound like
Cantinflas. Yet all is redeemed by the final scene at Cathy's tomb,
where *l'amour fou,* necrophilia, homosexuality, murder and incest blend in a fantastic visual statement: Desire encompasses and
surpasses good and evil, for the alternative to desire is solitude,
and solitude is death. That scene alone is worth 20 William Wyler
versions. With Manuel Barbachano's production of *Nazarin,*
Buñuel was back in Cannes, and won the first prize for his gospel
according to a wandering priest, a religious Quixote whose will
for good results in disaster, loss of faith in God and rebirth of
faith in man—by means of a pineapple.

Finally, with Gustavo Alatriste's backing, he returned to a
forgiving Spain with an innocent script about a gentle novice
called Viridiana. The script was read by the Government censors,
but it was literally "read." Fortunately, censors are incapable of
reading between the lines or imagining what cold print can
become when translated into images—especially Buñuel images.
Denounced as a traitor for working in Franco Spain, Buñuel
quietly shot his script, improvising all the way, sending each
day's work by air to Paris, where he edited the film, and presenting the finished product at Cannes in 1961, with the Spanish
censors' approval. The censors had proved unable to really read;
now they proved equally incapable of seeing. Along with the
Golden Palm at the festival *Viridiana* got a lambasting from the

Vatican's *L'Osservatore Romano.* Were the Spanish censors napping? For the "innocent script" now included sexual perversion, rape, suicide and a debauched parody of Christ's last supper. The Spanish censors were summarily dismissed from their jobs; the film was banned in Spain. And Buñuel had won an international audience.

Two twin parables open and close the most recent period of his work, and both are intimately linked to the theme of survival. The first was *The Exterminating Angel,* or how to escape from an endless supper party: After a night at the opera, a group of upper-class Mexicans meet for dinner and then find that, for some unexplained reason, they cannot leave their host's house or communicate with the outside world—as isolated as shipwrecks, they unlock their true nature, their moral cannibalism, while the social code breaks down. The last was *The Discreet Charm of the Bourgeoisie,* or how to get together for an impossible meal: The six elegant characters constantly plan to get together for a series of gastronomical feasts, but the very act of eating is constantly interrupted by myriad invasions of the rational and irrational facts of their lives—illicit love affairs, drug smuggling, army maneuvers, menaces from Latin American guerrillas, dreams told by total strangers in coffee shops that have run out of coffee, dreams they dream themselves, dreams they dream another one has dreamed.

In between them, he made *Simon of the Desert,* depicting the useless gesture of a man perched on top of his column like a theological Jonathan Seagull, masochistically invoking his own temptations and ending, in the Devil's company, in a New York discothèque. Jeanne Moreau wryly battled her way up from the kitchen and employed her employer's lusts and fantasies in *Diary of a Chambermaid* and Catherine Deneuve dreamily battled her way down to the whorehouse in that marvelous blending of reality and imagination, fate and desire in the mirror of a woman's erotic fantasies that is *Belle de Jour. The Milky Way* portrayed an ambiguous pilgrimage, cutting through times and spaces, in search of lost heresy. Buñuel's most intimate, autobiographical, Spanish, provincial movie was *Tristana,* with its immediate, tangible symbols of fear, deception, mutual damnation and ridiculous social convention.

SEEING: In his sixties, Buñuel finally achieved the choice of subject matter, the means, the creative freedom so long denied him. But Buñuel has always proved hardier than the minimal or optimal conditions of production offered him; he constantly remarks that, given a $5-million budget, he would still film a $500,000 movie. An obsessive artist, Buñuel cares about what he wants to say; or rather, what he wants to see. A really important director makes only one film; his work is a sum, a totality of perfectly related parts that illuminate each other. In Buñuel's films, from *Un Chien Andalou* to *The Discreet Charm of the Bourgeoisie*, the essential unifying factor is sight. His first image is that of a woman's eye slit by a razor and throughout the body of his work there is this pervading sense of sight menaced, sight lost as virginity is lost; sight as a wound that will not heal, wounded sight as an interstice through which dreams and desires can flow. Catherine Deneuve's absent regard in *Belle de Jour* is calculated. She is constantly looking outside the confines of the screen, enlarging the space of the screen, looking at something beyond that isn't there, that probably connects the two halves of her life.

But Buñuel's violent aggressions against sight actually force us back to his particular way of seeing. His world is seen first as a grey, hazy, distant jumble of undetermined things; no other director shoots a scene from quite that neutral, passive distance. Then the eye of the camera suddenly picks out an object that has been there all the time, or a revealing gesture, zooms into them, makes them come violently alive before again retiring to the indifferent point of view.

This particular way of seeing, of making the opaque backdrop shine instantly by selecting an object or gesture, assures the freedom and fluid elegance of a Buñuel film. Sight determines montage; what is seen flows into what is unseen. The camera fixes on a woman's ankle or the buzzing box a Korean takes to a brothel; the woman's shoes lead to desire or the Korean's stare to mystery, mystery and desire to dream, dream to a dream within it and the following cut back to everyday normality has already compounded reality with the fabulous; the meanest, most violent or weakest character has achieved a plurality of dimensions that straight realism would never reveal. The brutal gang leader in *Los Olvidados* is redeemed by his dream of fright and solitude: A black dog silently races down a rainy street at night. And you cannot altogether hate the stupid, avaricious people in *The Discreet Charm;* their dreams are too funny; they are endowed with a reluctantly charming dimension; they are doomed, yet they survive.

Cruel and destructive: Such were the adjectives reserved for his early films; now they are elegant and comical. Has the dynamite-flinging miner of Asturias, as Henry Miller called him, mellowed so much? On the contrary: I believe his technique has simply become more finely honed, his sense of inclusiveness through sight wider. More things are seen, understood, laughed at and perhaps forgiven. Besides, the author is debating himself. Is that a Buñuel stand-in who drones in *The Milky Way:* "My hatred towards science and technology will surely drive me back to the despicable belief in God"?

Sight connects. Buñuel has filmed the story of the first capitalist hero, Robinson Crusoe, and Crusoe is saved from loneliness by his slave, but the price he must pay is fraternity, *seeing* Friday as a human being. He has also filmed the story of Robinson's descendants in *The Discreet Charm,* and these greedy, deceptive people can only flee their overpopulated, polluted, promiscuous island into the comic loneliness of their dreams. Sight and survival, desires and dreams, seeing others in order to see oneself. This parabola of sight is essential to Buñuel's art. Nazarin will not see God unless he sees his fellow men; Viridiana will not see herself unless she sees outside herself and accepts the world. The characters in *The Discreet Charm* can never see themselves or others. They may be funny, but they are already in hell. Elegant humor only cloaks despair.

So in Buñuel sight determines content or, rather, content is a way of looking, content is sight at all possible levels. And this multitude of levels—social, political, psychological, historical, esthetic, philosophic—is not predetermined, but flows from vision. His constant tension is between obsessive opposites: pilgrimage and confinement, solitude and fraternity, sight and blindness, social rules and personal cravings, rational conduct and oneiric behavior. His intimate legacies, often conflicting, are always there: Spain, Catholicism, surrealism, left anarchism. But, above all, what is always present is the liberating thrust that could only come from such a blend of heritages. Certainly no other filmmaker could have so gracefully and violently humanized and brought into the fold of freedom, rebellion and understanding so many figures, so many passions, so many desires that the conventional code judges as monstrous, criminal and worthy of persecution and, even, extermination. The poor are not forcibly good and the rich are not forcibly evil; Buñuel incriminates all social orders while liberating our awareness of the outcast, the deformed, the maimed, the necrophiles, the lesbians, the homosexuals, the fetishists, the incestuous, the whorish, the cruel children, the madmen, the poets, the forbidden dreamers. He never exploits this marginality, because he makes it central to his vision. He has set the highest standards for true cinematic freedom.

And finally, this respect for freedom of his characters is translated into respect for the freedom of his audience. As they end, his films remain open, the spectator remains free. A flock of sheep enter the church of *The Exterminating Angel* as civil strife explodes in the streets. An empty carriage rolls down a wooded lane while the horses' bells jingle in *Belle de Jour*. Nazarin accepts a gift of a pineapple from a humble woman as the drums of Calanda start pounding and the whole structure of the priest's mind turns and opens toward the future. Viridiana sits down and plays cards with her cousin and the cook as they listen to rock recordings. A bell with the face of her victim and victimizer telescopes Tristana back to the very beginning of her story. The mad husband in *El* zigzags his way down a monastery garden where he thinks he has achieved peace of mind. The six listless characters in *The Discreet Charm*, driven by an irrational urge, trudge down an unending highway.

If the end in a Buñuel film can mean exactly the contrary, the beginnings of his films can be terrifying. *L'Age d'Or* starts with a scorpion and that scorpion, encircled by fire, is committing

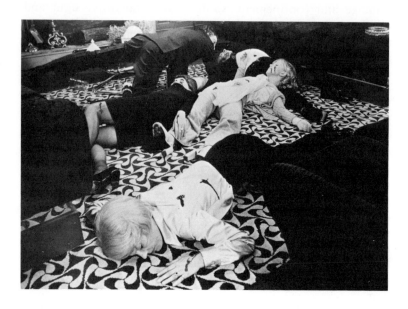

Buñuel has written: "The camera is the eye of the marvelous. When the eye of the cinema really sees, the whole world goes up in flames." (*The Discreet Charm of the Bourgeoisie*)

suicide with its own poisonous tail. It is the center of a flaming eye. Buñuel has written: "The camera is the eye of the marvelous. When the eye of the cinema really sees, the whole world goes up in flames."

BEING: He lives in a Mexico City suburb behind a high brick wall crowned with bits of broken glass. A dusky maid opens the white metal gate; a nameless shaggy dog, huge as a rug, leaps; a tiny bitch called Tristana barks. The interior is as impersonal as a dentist's office. The only decorative element that strikes the eye is a portrait of the youthful Buñuel by Dali, hardly visible under the staircase. On the second floor is Buñuel's monkish bedroom, a bed without springs or mattress; he sleeps on hard wooden boards, covered only by a rough blanket. Then comes the office, deceptively camouflaged by encyclopedias and autographed photos of Dominguín executing *verónicas*. The really interesting books are hidden behind the neutral volumes; and secrets— personal photographs, clippings, reviews, letters—remain secret.

On the third floor there are vast naked terraces and a sort of gymnasium where Buñuel practices his favorite sport: exercising on crutches; he says it's great for the spine. Once, there was a magnificent collection of firearms here, and a workshop where Buñuel made his own gunpowder and bullets and then practiced shooting at spiders in the garden below. That hobby ended when Buñuel thought he had calculated such a perfect trajectory that the bullet, on hitting a man's chest, would simply bounce off. He asked one of his sons to become a living target so as to prove the point. Cautiously declining to participate in this William Tell charade, the son asked Buñuel to experiment by firing at the phone book first. Buñuel fired and the bullet went right through the directory.

Activity in the house shuttles between an open air roasting pit, the Provençal dining room where Jeanne, Buñuel's statuesque wife (they have been happily married for the past 45 years) serves enormous dishes smothered in garlic, spices and Burgundy, and Buñuel's very private domain: the bar where he mixes the Buñueloni (gin, vermouth and Carpano) and, on demand, the Yves Tanguy (Fernet-Branca, grenadine, stout and plenty of ice).

Think of Picasso, Ortega y Gasset, Manuel de Falla: Most famous Spaniards age to look like retired picadors (matadors tend to die young). Buñuel looks like the picador plus the bull. A massive, bald, olive-colored head that seems about to charge as Buñuel takes his hand to his deaf ear and the whole square, husky body bends forward with rough, aggressive movements that suddenly take on a chivalrous grace: There's a fight going on between gravity and jest, between reserve and spontaneity. The ski-jump nose, not unlike the Hope-Nixon model, twitches inquiringly; the nostrils flare and determine the furious grimace of the mouth, the clenched teeth, the fires of disapproval in the enormous, beautiful, protruding green eyes. Then a mischievous twinkle, a liquid laughter, rushes from the eyes to the thin, crooked, smiling lips.

Short-sleeved sports shirts, gray cardigans, formless gaberdine slacks, Mexican sandals, a blue package of Gauloises near the sinewy, freckled hands. At 73, he walks two hours every day and claims to have all the conceivable ailments, but in such a dispersed fashion that they never come to a head. He goes to bed at 9 P.M. and gets up at 5 A.M., starts drinking his daily liter of alcohol at 11 each morning, receives friends at the bar in the afternoon. The simplicity of his life-style has not changed since, with *Belle de Jour,* his income rose steeply. ("Please, Buñuel," I asked him the other day at lunch at La Coupoule in Paris, "how much do you earn? American readers like to know precisely how much a man earns." Buñuel laughed and answered, "Say I make $20,000 on a film; that will enrage Serge Silberman, my producer.")

Perhaps his one luxury is a yearly trip to Madrid in winter, where he takes the topmost apartment in the Torre de Madrid and, wearing a muffler and beret, he walks around the old, nostalgic places. He remains very close to his four sisters and is quite proud of his four nephews, all of them scientists specializing in pharmacology, neurology, medicine and psychiatry. The psychiatrist has revolutionized clinical treatment in Oklahoma by permitting patients with diverse mental ailments to mingle freely among themselves and with "normal" people. Two of the nephews are candidates for Nobel prizes.

His two tall, athletic sons, Juan Luis and Rafael, envy their father's upbringing. Their complaint is that they had nothing to rebel against in a household where the ideas of surrealism, anarchism and atheism were common currency. Juan Luis does wire sculpture and has just won the Georges Sadoul prize in Paris for his first long film, a humorous tale of modern-day witchery called *A Meeting with the Happy Death.* Rafael, who looks like Gary Cooper in *The Virginian,* writes plays and rides a motorcycle. He is married to Joyce, a handsome New York-born girl, and they have a child, Buñuel's sole grand-daughter, Juliette, age 5.

Jeanne Moreau declares that she would like to board as a pupil in the Buñuel home, get up at dawn, have a cold shower and be scolded by the master if she came back after sunset.

SAYING: We started sipping two potent Buñuelonis and talking movies, books and politics. Whose work in the cinema influenced him most at the beginning? "The comedians, certainly. And Stroheim. Especially that scene in *The Merry Widow* where Mae Murray is dancing on a stage and John Gilbert looks at her face, Roy D'Arcy at her sex and the old man, Tully Marshall, at her feet. Of course, it's the old fetishist millionaire who finally gets her. But the one film which really inspired me and made me see the cinema for the first time as a valid medium of artistic expression was Fritz Lang's *The Three Lights*." What about the current cinema? He doesn't go much to the movies, does he? "I usually leave after the first couple of reels. Besides, I'm deaf and my remarks are too loud. I was hissed out of a theater showing Ray's *King of Kings*. When the Devil tempts Christ, he offers him a dazzling, golden city in the desert, full of minarets and cupolas. My loud-voiced commentary was: 'He's offered Christ Disneyland!' I'm a Kubrick fan, ever since *Paths of Glory*. Fabulous movie; that's what it's all about: codes of conduct, the way people behave when the codes break down. *A Clockwork Orange* is my current favorite. I was very predisposed against the film. After seeing it, I realized it's the only movie about what the modern world really means. Also Fellini's *Roma;* the sense of pure spectacle, the freedom to do without cumbersome plots. I sent him a wire with congratulations . . ."

What about extra-cinematographical influences? A critical cliché always compares him with Goya. "That's very superficial. The critics talk about Goya because they ignore all the rest, Quevedo, St. Theresa of Avila, the Spanish heterodoxes, the Spanish picaresque novel, Galdós, Valle Inclán. Unfortunately, culture has become inseparable from economic and military power. A powerful country can impose its culture and universalize second-rate artists, like Hemingway, whose fame can only be a result of American power. But Spain's weakness has meant a worldwide ignorance of her marvelous literature."

Apart from Spanish culture, what were his really formative readings? "Freud, the Marquis de Sade, Marx and Engels, Jean Henri Fabre the entomologist. You know, my literary tastes change like the weather. I can love an author in the morning and hate him that same night. I was crazy about Thomas Hardy 30 years ago. The irrational climate, the obscure passions. I reread him recently and fell asleep. Lots of rhetoric, zero mystery. George Meredith used to amuse me enormously. The unbearably exquisite elegance of the social life he describes, the parties. That taught me a lot. And then, of course, all the surrealists were great fans of Miss Emily Brontë's. *Wuthering Heights* was *the* great love story for us. I wanted to do it back in 1930 with lots of Wagner on the sound track. When I finally shot it in Mexico, it came out as an anachronism, a sentimental homage to my own youth.''

What is his attitude toward "cultural values?" He has been quoted as saying that he'd like to blow up the Louvre. "Yes, when somebody says that a man's life is as insignificant as a worm's compared to the treasures in a museum. But I'd knock down a man who says *his* life is worth more than the Louvre. In any case, I've always felt an instinctive antipathy toward dead culture. I'm completely lacking in conceptual memory. Things only come alive for me thanks to visual memory. When I was preparing *Simon of the Desert,* I closeted myself for months at the Bibliothèque Nationale in Paris, read everything about the early Christian stylites, how they dressed, what they ate, how they survived for years on top of those pillars. All useless. The film is nothing but a series of visual gags.''

That would be, of course, one way of defining all his films, starting with, *Un Chien Andalou.* How was that particular film born? "It all began with two twin dreams Dali and I had. He dreamed obsessively of a hand crawling with ants. I dreamed of a slit eyeball. We wrote the script by associating images and eliminating anything that had a political, historical, esthetic or moral connotation. Critics have invented a thousand interpretations. In fact, *Un Chien Andalou* is a desperate appeal to violence and crime." It is true that critics have a field day digging out symbols whenever a Buñuel film is presented. How does he feel about this? "I've never introduced a symbol on purpose in any of my films. I make pictures about things that amuse and interest me. Take *Viridiana,* for example. As a child, I dreamed of making love to the Queen of Spain, who was very blonde, very white, like a sublime nun. I imagined I stole into the palace, drugged Her

Majesty and then raped her. *Viridiana* is the crystallization of this masturbator's dream. A picture is not an algebraic equation. It can't prove anything. They've said my films are violent and destructive, and therefore immoral. The truth is that I've never chosen a subject first—charity, for example, or virginity, or cruelty—and then straitjacketed my characters with the problem. I have no previous answers. I look, and looking is a way of asking." Many people agree that *L'Age d'Or* is the greatest and most significant work of the entire surrealist movement. What, actually, did the surrealist experience mean to Buñuel? "Well, for one thing, group solidarity was a tremendous thing among the surrealists. Breton would call us in to sit in judgment if we deviated from the group morality. I learned then that being free is not doing whatever you want, but acting in solidarity with friends you love and respect. But then, by choosing a certain morality, you are not really free at all. Only crypto-Fascists pretend they are ideologically free. Surrealism taught me that man is never free yet fights for what he can never be. That is tragic."

I'd like him to talk about his experiences in the United States. What did he do at the Museum of Modern Art in New York? "I was asked to edit Leni Riefenstahl's documentaries on the Nazi rallies at Nuremberg. The purpose was to use them as anti-Nazi propaganda. I showed the final result to René Clair and Charlie Chaplin in New York. Chaplin rolled with laughter, pointed at Hitler and said the Führer was a bad imitation of Charlot. But Clair had misgivings: Riefenstahl's images were so damned good and impressive, no matter how you edited them, that the effect would be the contrary of what we were aiming at, a real boomerang. Audiences would be overpowered and come out feeling that German might was irresistible. The matter was taken to the White House. President Roosevelt saw the film and agreed with Clair. So it was quietly sent to the archives."

What about his fight with Dali at the time? "The morning Dali's opinions were published in New York, I walked into my office at MOMA and found the typists and phone girls reading The Motion Picture Herald and wringing their hands and crying: 'Oh, Mr. Buñuel, what an awful thing!' I resigned so as to avoid embarrassing my good friends there. Then I called Dali and gave him an appointment at the Pierre Hotel. I had decided to give him a good beating. But when I saw him walk down the lobby, I felt a surge of sympathy for the man, too many fond memories came back, our youth. . . . So I just called him a son of a bitch and told him our friendship was over. He looked nonplused and said, 'Luis, you understand that my remarks were not intended to hurt you, but to publicize myself.' I've never seen him since. But I do hope I can invite him to drink a glass of champagne before we both die." And the United States in the thirties and forties? "It was very different. People were kind, honest and incredibly punctual. And the comfort, the bathrooms! But then something went wrong. Innocence became too powerful. And innocence in power means ignorant danger. The United States became a country of suspicious bureaucrats, aggressive and chauvinistic. I still enjoy having a martini at the Plaza, though. The Plaza makes the best martinis in the world."

Does he also enjoy filming? "Not at all. I hate it, hate the confusion on the set, the noise, can't stand having more than one person talk to me at a time, hate giving orders. . . ." Yet he is said to be, with Alfred Hitchcock, the fastest, surest, most precise of all filmmakers. "I do my homework. Before arriving the first day on the set, I know exactly how each scene will be shot and what the final montage will be. Believe me, I learned all the tricks filming on two-week schedules in Mexico. I can cut a film in two days. That leaves my mind free while shooting to improvise, to keep an eye both on the general feeling and the minute details hovering above and beneath the actual process of filming."

To what extent does he improvise? "Well, I can only give you examples. In *Viridiana* this novice arrives with a suitcase. So what does she carry inside it? I hadn't foreseen that detail. So I thought, if a mechanic carries wrenches and oilers and screwdrivers, then a novice will carry a cross, nails and a hammer and a crown of thorns. Likewise, that crucifix that becomes a penknife in the same film. It wasn't premeditated. I found it was sold as a tourist trinket in Albacete where I was shooting and decided it would be funny." Buñuel, the superb movie technician, is said to hate technique. "No, what I detest is gimmickry, exhibitionist technique. The camera's presence mustn't be felt. Once the camera starts dancing and becomes the star of the picture, I lose interest and leave the theater. No esthetics whatsoever, none. I used to have great fun with my Mexican cameraman, Gabriel Figueroa. I would let him prepare these beautiful shots of clouds and volcanoes, then tell him to swing the camera around and shoot a couple of old goats on a rocky hill."

What about actors? "Possibly the best actress I've ever directed is Jeanne Moreau. Incredibly subtle and professional. And Fernando Rey; great actor. I get along very well with actors. But maybe they don't get along too well with me." He rarely concedes them a close-up; that seems to be reserved for insects. Is that what he means? "No, no, I mean too many of my actors have had untimely deaths soon after working for me. The girl in *Un Chien Andalou*, Simone Mareuil, took a bath in gasoline, went to a park, set herself on fire and danced ablaze for a while. The actor in the same movie, Pierre Baltcheff, committed suicide. Gérard Philipe died a few months after making his last film with me. And there's a scene in *The Criminal Life of Archibald de la Cruz* where the star, Miroslava, has her wax image cremated. Well, the day the film opened, she was actually cremated. She had killed herself the day before. And many, many more died too. . . ." What about nonprofessionals? "I used many at the beginning. We were short on cash, so friends participated: Max Ernst, Prévert, Dali, myself. I prefer professional actors; I've had a tough time with dwarfs, particularly. The dwarf in *Nazarín* spoke badly, forgot his lines, made everyone feel nervous. I found him in a slum and liked him because he didn't look like a dwarf but like a gargoyle. He was a cobbler and a bigamist. After acting in my films, he started living with four women. The film became his sexual fetish. So tiny and so vicious."

Sex is very powerful in his films because it is felt rather than seen. What is his attitude toward sex? "Personally, I'm monogamous and discreet. An old man can easily make a fool of himself, like Don Lope in *Tristana*. I believe in a chaste eroticism. You can attribute that to my Jesuit education. Sexual pleasure for me is directly linked with the idea of sin and only exists in a religious context. The sexual act cannot be reduced to a chapter on hygienics; it is an exciting, dark, sinful, diabolical experience. Sex is a black tarantula and sex without religion is like an egg without salt. In the *Summa Theologica,* Saint Thomas says that fornication between man and woman, even if they be married, is nevertheless a venial sin. Now, I think that's a very sexy idea. Sin multiplies the possibilities of desire."

He always declares that his last film will really be the last one he'll ever make. Thankfully, he always does one more, so that it's become a joke to talk about Buñuel's next last film. "I'm a professional loafer. I like sitting around looking at the flies. Then I suddenly get bored, call in my writer Jean-Claude Carrière and get rolling once more." He lives a hermit's existence while keeping up a highly creative output. "I suppose I'm like everybody else. You accumulate experience during your childhood and youth and then go off to a silent corner and try to remember. There comes a time when it's foolish to believe that you must live in order to create. No; just a hole and a spider spinning its web and remembering what the world outside was like."

Politics? "Forty years ago, everything was very clear-cut. We thought we knew the issues. There was a defined line, moral, artistic, political; it all went together, a new art that would enlarge the conscience and sensibility of man, along with a revolutionary politics, without leaders, without supermen, not these masses of Chinamen screeching '*maomaomao,*' like cats. The enemies were capitalism, the bourgeoisie, private property, chauvinism, religion, the police, institutional violence coated with middle-class sentimentality. We could then attack the bourgeoisie, surprise it, because it was so sure of itself and its institutions. Now that's all changed. Publicity, the media, absorb everything, make everything innocuous, fashionable. Just before he died, Breton told me: 'Dear friend, it is no longer possible to scandalize anybody.' Maybe he was right. But the thing is, the world of 1973 is not better than the world of 1923. It's even worse, because of the confusion and the deceit. There is no longer an international revolutionary politics. There are only the imperialistic policies of superpowers who can blow us all to bits."

Does he then think that the revolutionary artist, lacking the self-confidence of the twenties and thirties, is no longer a decisive social factor? "I'm pessimistic; but I hope to be a good pessimist. In any society, the artist has a responsibility. His effectiveness is certainly limited and a writer or painter cannot change the world. But they can keep an essential margin of nonconformity alive. Thanks to them, the powerful can never affirm that everyone agrees with their acts. That small difference is very important. When power feels itself totally justified and approved, it immediately destroys whatever freedoms we have left, and that is fascism. My ideas have not changed since I was 20. Basically, I agree with Engels: An artist describes real social relationships with the purpose of destroying the conventional ideas about those relationships, undermining bourgeois optimism and forcing the public to doubt the tenets of the established order. The final sense of my films is this: to repeat, over and over again, in case anyone forgets it or believes the contrary, that we do not live in the best of all possible worlds. I guess that's all it amounts to. In any case, I believe that the class struggle is no longer the central social problem. The real issues are birth control and ecology. The real issue is survival."

DYING: We walk in silence down a wintry Parisian boulevard. Buñuel is a friend, a warm, humorous, magnificent friend, and one can be with him without having to say anything.

We reach his hotel and go up to his room. He always reserves the same one; the windows open on the black and grey tombstones, the naked trees of the Montparnasse cemetery. It has rained all day, but at this hour of the afternoon a very pure, diaphanous light seems to drip from the fast moving clouds. Buñuel starts packing for the flight back to Mexico City.

Every now and then, he gazes at the trees and murmurs: "I'm not afraid of death. I'm afraid of dying alone in a hotel room, with my bags open and a shooting script on the night table. I must know whose fingers will close my eyes."

Buñuel Is Written with a Tilde and Is Seventy Years Old

José Luis Egea

· ·

When I was sixteen or seventeen years old, I used to steal copies of *Cinema Universitario* from a bookstore. At other times, I managed to read it at a friend's house, occasionally accompanied by *Objetivo*, which had been banned only a year or two before.

These publications contained two categorical statements. One, an obvious one, namely that Spanish cinema was in a bad state, that it was a barren desert due to lack of freedom. Another, hypothetical, unverifiable, based on faith, suggested that there was a certain Luis Buñuel, exiled in Mexico, who gave the true measure of what Spanish cinema could be. Our cinema director was far away, and worshipped like a Virgin of Sorrows, or an Antonio Machado, then still alive. Each of us, thanks to these publications, books acquired outside of Spain, or to meager information from friends who had managed to see some of his films abroad, each of us, I repeat, was an eager young cinophile, restless and curious, who knew everything about Buñuel but actually knew nothing. Our relationship with him did not extend beyond Revelation. We were like initiates to a Mystery. We knew indeed that he existed. And this kind of lay faith was our weapon, our final argument, the card we unexpectedly threw on the table when the fascist of the moment, some censor or official of cultural oppression, if not a "theoretician" or "critic," affirmed with total audacity that "Spaniards are not cinematically gifted." We might have writers . . . Ah, the Golden Age! . . . sculptors. . . . Ah, the image makers! . . . painters. . . . Ah, Velazquez! . . . but cineastes. . . . We would make a face, and, like someone enumerating the seven Virtues in opposition to the Seven Sins, we'd reply: Ah, Cervantes! ah, the Generation of 98,

From *Cine Cubano* 71/72. Translated by Toby Talbot.

ah, Alberti, Lorca, Hernández, Machado! ah, Sánchez! ah, Goya! ah, Picasso! and ah, ah, ah, BUÑUEL! So there! Now, let's see what they have to say. AND BUÑUEL, eh? And BUÑUEL? And the echo, perhaps the echo was repeated in the void: Buñuel, ñuel, el, l. . . .

From the age of eighteen to twenty I was living in Paris. I didn't see any of Buñuel's films, because I had no money to go to the movies. The few times I went, my preferences ran toward more current directors, including the most recent. For example, I remember the extraordinary impression I experienced one day when I saw a first film; it was *A bout de souffle* [*Breathless*], and its director was a certain Jean-Luc Godard, a critic on *Cahiers*. I used to discuss cinema with my French friends. When they learned that I wanted to study directing, they would invariably ask: "Oh, but are films made in Spain, and what are they like?" I talked to them, enraged by their ignorance, of our cinematographic wasteland. They would sagely shake their heads—"Spain, that exception to democratic Europe"—and nostalgically "showed solidarity" with our plight. Whereupon, once again, I would pull from my sleeve the card printed Unknown Spanish Author: lots of folklore, chastity, wimples, cassocks, uniforms, many model families, but in our cinema there was one Universal Creator, none other than (attention!) none other than BUÑUEL! I can recall perfectly my exasperation when one of my listeners, a leader of *Positif*, asked in utter seriousness: *"Mais, ce Buñuel, il est mexicain, ou français, n'est-ce-pas?"* And I, though I was Basque, became enraged: *"merde, il n'est pas français, il est espagnol, aragonnais,* a simple Aragonese, for your information, BUÑUEL is an ARAGONESE!"

Another thing that annoyed me was the conversion into an N of the Ñ, a common error in all the European texts which discussed Buñuel.

I returned to Spain without straightening out this graphic detail.

If, in the catacombs of San Sebastian, Buñuel was a universal artist, in the cenacles of Madrid, in the bars near the official school of cinema, and within its classrooms and corridors, there was a full-fledged practicing cult. Students would comment on certain scenes: "That's very Buñuelesque, you'll see how they pass on it." I remember that in my classes there were two favorite adjectives for categorizing a film, a situation, the nation, a girl, a meal, or whatever: "Kafkaesque" or "Buñuelesque." Kafkaesque and Buñuelesque was in all likelihood our configuration and reality. Until one day . . .

It was the year of our Lord 1961, when a star announced that He would be coming to Spain, to Madrid, to shoot a film! There were those who thought that Buñuel—like Jesus Christ, like José Antonio Primo de Rivera, the founder of the Falange—had lived his thirty years in privacy, and was now ready to reside in public before expiring. Be that as it may, the fact is that there was an Incarnation, and to that I can testify. All heaven broke loose. Overnight, there began circulating through leftist cinema channels, among the critics, and at the School, scores of authentic anecdotes ("I swear it's true!"), anecdotes about the Redeemer. Carlos Saura, our first year teacher at the School; Aranda, the future evangelist official of the Master; Emilio Sanz de Soto, the cosmopolitan man from Tangiers; Ricardo Muñoz Suay, one of the "alma mater" of the inevitably historic Conversations on Cinema held in Salamanca, the officiator of secret ceremonies and a specialist in initiating neophytes to the Cabala; Juan Antonio Bardem, whose name also began with B; Domingo Dominguín, who in addition to fighting bulls knew how to read, and prior to his conversion had left a section of rump as tribute to the gunshot of the "Marxist hordes"; Paco Rabal, who became the priest in *Nazarin,* all of them and others too, who joined later, were bearers of the Glad Tidings, proselytizing apostles of the Faith, direct, physical witnesses of the Incarnation, because—how much suffering and hope was at last realized! It turned out that Buñuel *really existed.* The *sacrarium* was in the skyscraping—streets, in the Tower of Madrid.

Luis Buñuel in person! To get to see him, to speak to him, became the yearning of many and the privilege of few. The Apostles, from time to time, allowed an anecdote to escape, a phrase, an expression, an opinion expressed by the Master. One even managed to assist in the shooting. For them, the initiates, Buñuel became Luis. "And Luis said . . . ," "Luis believes

that . . . ," "Yesterday, while having breakfast with Luis . . ."
I must confess that this tendency to spiritual proprietorship
became very widespread. From the day he began shooting *Viridiana*, we "in" students smiled ironically at those who were not
"in."

I guess we were all very good, very proper, and behaved
ourselves very well, because one day, unexpectedly, we students
were invited to tea with Buñuel! There was wine and sausages, a
historic photograph of—Bardem, Saura, Buñuel, Picasso, Fer-
reri!—and numerous others—"move closer to Luis, boys"—in
which most of the students at the school appeared. A few of us
were bashful, and did not pose. We confined ourselves to some
wine and playing football in the CEA field[1] now demolished and
the nostalgic site of a famous, prolonged workers' strike, which
was illegal, as all are in our country. A friend chided me because
I—"the elitist, petty bourgeois, narcissistic little gentleman"—
had not posed for the photograph. And my inner reply was: it's
dialectically immoral. I HAVEN'T SEEN ONE BUÑUEL FILM!
Sponsoring homages struck me as a ceremony of the establishment, of institutionalized assimilated bohemia. Today I believe
that, objectively speaking, things are not that schematic.

We had an actress friend at the school. She was blonde, good-
looking, tall, and had performed in Argentina and Poland. Her
name was Victoria Zinny Pilutzky, and she claimed to have been a
councilwoman in the municipal government of Buenos Aires.
She was known for her conceit, but we friends forgave her
completely because, as I mentioned, she was extremely attractive.
One day she appeared at the school saying that she and Paco
Rabal were going to be in *Viridiana*. Nobody believed her, since
we were accustomed to her fantasies, and because we knew that
people more experienced and qualified than she had not met the
requirements necessary for appearing in the film. For example,
Juan Julio Baena, who before serving as the policy-director-
repressor of the School of Cinema had worked as a cameraman,

[1]CEA were film studios built in the 30's, with the original intention of shooting
exclusively Spanish films. Several businessmen and intellectuals—I think Luis
Buñuel was among them—contributed money to help. The tea was given on the
occasion of Buñuel's sixty-first birthday.

was not successful in "getting placed" with Buñuel. But Victoria, this time, was telling the truth. Years later, on page one of *France Soir*, a photograph announced her wedding with an Italian magnate.

The position of cameraman was filled by Pepito Aguayo (Senior), a short man who had been a bullfighter, and who knew so much about photography that people claimed he did not use a camera meter, but measured the light by squinting his eyes and using the palm of his hand. In circles close to Baena, it was said that Aguayo had been chosen out of irony, because Buñuel was not interested in modern technique, but in the efficacy of a "pompous" photography which only a "true" bourgeois could provide. In short, the film was made, it went to Cannes, won the Grand Prize, and became the *Viridiana* scandal: the "V" bomb, or "B" bomb, which authorities on culture have still not agreed upon. Correct graphics aside, the fact is that the bomb unquestionably exploded and that its profound repercussions are still being felt. The man who was General Director of Cinematography at the time collapsed, the Minister of Information died of a heart attack, the UNINCI Production Company disappeared, its members and affiliates dispersed, and the film *Viridiana,* as colophon, was officially declared "non-existent." Since non-existent things do not exist, it has not been shown in Spain to this day.

Thereafter, logically, a new factor entered the worship ritual among the cult devoted to the Master. "Hunting" for a private screening of *Viridiana* became a sport practiced by people of all persuasions. A costly 16mm print existed, whose projection was catalogued and controlled by "accredited" individuals. The comments at such projections were of this nature: "It's strong, but not terribly." Gradually, very gradually, some young people, initiated in the B. Ritual, began making headway toward a few cinema passes. On such occasions, the comments were not merely laudatory but outrightly panegeric. And remarks like "Buñuel's hot," or references to how "macho" he was at least had some relationship with reality, since the film was precisely one made by L.B.

I say and write L.B., not Luis Buñuel, because a "Ukasse" of the Administration—a new and recent name in Spain to label the government—decreed, provisionally, not only the "inexistence" of the film-ceremony, but also that of the priest-director. And in the pages of *Nuestro Cine* we would write L.B. in the same manner as C.M. for Carlos Marx (Karl Marx), or "conflicts among groups" for struggle between the classes, etc., etc., etc.

Several months later, I received a telephone call from Ricardo Muñoz Suay (ay!). It had to do with the presentation of a group of youthful offerings to the Master. (Let the children approach me. . . ."). I seem to recall that this Lodge meeting was attended by Santiago San Miguel, Victor Erice, Pedrito Olea, Antonio Artero and myself. Santiago, Victor, Pedro and I are Basques, that is, timid, and we speak little. We were rather anxious, because Ricardo had explained to us that Buñuel's deafness was only a ruse which he used to avoid replying to an interlocutor whom he disliked. We measured each of our opinions, fearful that the Master might raise his hand to his ear in his characteristic gesture. Pedro had brought along a French book on Buñuel's cinema. At a particular moment in the conversation, Pedro turned very red, and overcoming all sorts of inhibitions, dared to approach the Messiah to autograph the book. A few moments of tension followed. Nobody knew how it would end. Buñuel laughed slyly, asked for a ballpoint pen and wrote a few words. I don't know if it was due to coincidence, bad luck or irony, but I believe I can affirm that Pedro's name was half crossed out when Buñuel wrote his own autograph over it. Antonio Artero, founder, general secretary, member of the executive committee of the central committee, the director, cornerstone and single militant of the P.P.B.—Partido Popular Batturo (Popular Party of Aragon)—held a brilliant dissertation with Buñuel on the greater number of vowels that rustic Aragonese has in comparison with Spanish. Buñuel set forth a contrary example: the Spanish which Valencians speak is the most sibillant, whispered, and sinuous, and is filled with all sorts of imaginable consonants. A language made more for "conspiring" or insinuating than for communication. When Buñuel departed, Ricardo affirmed that: a) what Buñuel had said about Valencians—like himself—was obviously a joke; b) Buñuel was, despite everything, one of *our* men. This was the year 1962, if I recall correctly.

1962 represents a highly significant date for all Spaniards because, in the words of a Swedish record, "there's a light in Asturias/which warms all of Spain/for that is where/there's an uprising in all the mines. Fraga Iribarne emerged as Commissar and Great Master of culture . . . and of tourism. There was talk of Europeanization, liberalization, tion, tion, tion, tion. . . . In sum, the great colonial-hostel boom began. In that year—I don't know if it was due to my inveterate habit of being contrary—I returned to Paris. This time I went with some money. I bought a newspaper and read: "Study of the Ursulines: *Land Without Bread, Un Chien Andalou, Nazarin, Viridiana, Los Olvidados.*" I didn't think about it twice, and buried myself in the monastic art cinemas, ready to savor to the hilt the vibrant experience of that cathartic communion, of that definitive confirmation of the miracles so long hidden. And?

Do you know that if one places a succulent, abundant dish before a dog that has not eaten in days, he will, instead of lunging upon the food, devour it bit by bit, knowing instinctively the perils of indigestion? Do you know that the opposite happens in human beings, and hence children so often fall ill? (Note: At least that is what the priests at school used to say.) Too many dishes, too many films at one time for a dog conveniently uninformed and deformed!

My first sensation was one of bewilderment. I liked *Land Without Bread* and *Nazarin* enormously. *Un Chien Andalou* left me bewildered. I was enthusiastic about *Los Olvidados.* And I didn't care for *Viridiana* at all. In order to understand these impressions, it is necessary to explain the ultimate basis for my pre-judgments (my prejudice).

Of all the needs fascism had engendered in us, perhaps that of SEEING reality reflected in images was the one we felt most urgently. Without further shadings. The System had imposed a radical break with the cultural movement prior to the civil war. Information on contemporary culture was scarce. We were unaware, for example, of the importance and virulence of the surrealist movement of the 30's, and of the significance of the Spanish contribution to the latter. Italian neorealism in the cinema struck us then as inadequate and sentimental. The bad taste, vulgarity, reactionism and hypocrisy of the official Spanish cinema made us long for a "realist" cinema of the here and now, and one that was "well made." To make a film well was, for us, another weapon against the System. And the possibility of making a movie struck us as a radical event, like a vow taken before the gods, a definitive irrevocable act, confirming that we "were right."

It is not surprising, therefore, that a propos of a Bergman film I wrote at that time as follows: ". . . surrealism and expressionism were the two ultimate efforts at survival of bourgeois art. . . ." Yes, ignorance, dogmatism and frustration. And the Buñuel legend, that everyone fed upon, was compensation for all those frustrations. Finally, realities have little to do with the sublimations one makes out of obligation and necessity.

Hence my stupor, my incomprehension of *Un Chien Andalou*. Hence my taste for *Nazarin, Los Olvidados,* and *Land Without Bread.* Hence, also my rejection of *Viridiana*. It wasn't the film *I wanted it to be.* It wasn't the film that one "of us" *ought* to make in Franco Spain of 1961. Where was the everyday reality of our nights, of that "time of silence" of ours? But . . .

There was a "but" which disturbed me, which broke the certainty of my opinions. This "but" was that, throughout *all* the films, including *Un Chien Andalou,* one could hear amid the shadows of the movie house several muffled and simultaneous guffaws. When I laughed, I did so involuntarily, and in unison with other people scattered throughout the hall. It was at the end when I realized that those of us who reacted similarly were all Spaniards. What was there in those films, in that director, that provoked such ludic unanimity? What voice, what echo, what resonance was there, which beckoned us, summoned us unconsciously, powerfully? Why had Buñuel, contrary to my schemes, been so collectively "ours"? Why, on leaving the hall, did I feel such delight in pronouncing Buñuel with an ñ, before my French friends? Why did I take pleasure in explaining the phrases, the gestures, the winks, the sly twists, the oaths and ironies which their Cartesian minds did not manage to grasp fully?

I returned to Madrid without answering these questions for myself.

In the summer of 1963, I attended for several weeks the shooting of *Tears for a Bandit*. At that time, the Censors had prohibited several versions of the *Tristana* script. It seemed unlikely that Buñuel would again shoot amongst us. In the Saura film there was a scene—later destroyed by censorship—in which an executioner performed *garrote vil*[2] upon several Andalusian bandits. The scenes were shot in the square in Colmenar de Oreja, a little village near Aranjuez. Several cinephiles, critics, "friends" and intellectuals of the small Madrid world, attended the shooting. Cameras took many pictures, because the executioner was Luis Buñuel, no less, and the garroted men were several famous intellectuals, while the town crier for the event was the dramatist Antonio Buero Vallejo. At the last minute, for some reason, the afore-mentioned intellectuals did not appear, and the executed men were played by common men in costume. Antonio Buero Vallejo did, however, fill his role, and very well indeed. Wrapped in his black inquisitorial robes, his pale head covered with a feathered hat, he looked like a figure out of a picture of the period, some bird or vulture of ill omen.

Angelino Fons and I, who wandered around among the horses and costumed figures all day, exchanged glances and complicit remarks from time to time. More than one critic, more than one decorator, more than one cinephile and, even, a stray homosexual, hovered around Buñuel-Executioner in order to be photographed. Angelino donned the purple habit of a penitent priest, to form part of a scene in which he carried a big black wooden cross. At the end of the afternoon, when the work was finished, we took a picture together, holding the two ends of a cross. An enormous white "Cadillac," the production car, brought us back to Madrid. That was the last initiate Ceremony of the Buñuel

[2]The *garrote vil* is a monstrous instrument for imposing the death sentence in Spain. It consists of a thick piece of wood pounded into the ground, at the foot of which a small seat is set for the guilty man. From a metal collar at neck height, a long screw protrudes which crosses the wood and ends in a wheel crank. As the executioner turns this crank, the screw squeezes the collar against the guilty man's Adam's apple and neck, producing death by cervical dislocation and asphyxiation. There are several engravings by Goya which describe this simple, sadistic mechanical apparatus. Upon occasion, death apparently delays about twenty minutes in occurring. Around the 60's, I believe, the collar began to be constructed of steel, instead of nineteenth century iron.

Cult that I attended. In April, Julian Grimau was shot. Months later, two anarchists were executed by *garrote vil*. Buñuel was not the executioner, and the protagonists truly died. There were no photographs. We were in the midst of liberalization. The reign of Ambiguity was beginning.

From 1964 to 1970, several socio-cultural phenomena altered our personal and collective situation. The birth and death of the so called misnomered "Spanish New cinema" the proliferation of Special Auditoriums and Art Cinemas[3], the increase of bookshops, the growth and crisis of publishing houses, the hard, spasmodic installation of a babbling industrialized culture, of an unflinching commercialization of cultural products assimilated by the horde in compulsive consumership. And simultaneous to all this, the slogan "Opening to Europe" as a new expansionist, oligarchical device. An "opening" dictated from above, *controlled* from above, maintaining the same means in the same hands: censorship, absence of political freedom, declaring strikes and workers' unions to be illegal, etc., etc. The reign of Ambiguity: the reign of television, of the utilitarian automobile and of armed force—the Triumverate of rising values. A coincidence implicit in itinerary to the Scotch shower[4]. Censorship plus Art and Experimentation, Europeanization plus dictatorship, tourist hotels plus emigration of manpower, economic development plus popular repression, the Education Law plus student massacre with the University occupied in perpetuity by the Armed Police, the Press Law plus closing of publications, a monopoly of foreign information plus dependency on UPI, Reuters and the CIA. "Law and Order." "Law and Order," etc., etc. During those five years, there were several bullet wounds during

[3]In Spain, there are two types of elitist movie houses: the "Special Halls" and "Art Cinema" houses. Contrary to what happens in other countries, the price is *more* expensive in the commercial movie houses. These cannot exceed a limited number of seats—about 500—nor be established in cities of less than 50,000 inhabitants. Since they enjoy a more "open" censorship criterion, and other economic advantages, they turn out to be an excellent business, generally far removed from art or any experimentation. The confused legislation that controls them enables the impresarios to move from one category to another according to the expediencies of each season, and, even, of each program.

[4]The "Scotch shower" consists of projecting over the body alternating, sudden streams of very hot and very cold water, to activate blood circulation.

demonstrations. Enrique Ruano, Xavier Echevarrieta and two workers from Erandio were killed. It was precisely during those five years that a "special" public, particularly in Madrid and Barcelona, gained access to a substantial part of Buñuel's work. A "Scotch shower" type of access—disordered, opportunistic, elitist, scarce. But access, in the end.

Amid this confusing atmosphere I was able to acquire a fuller knowledge of Buñuel's films, seeing some of them for the first time, re-seeing others, gradually advancing my understanding and comprehension, evaluating them in their proper light, that is demystifying them. We were able to see or re-see in sporadic, semi-private screenings held at the Film school, and then on a circuit of art cinemas: *Viridiana* (only privately, since it "doesn't exist"), *Los Olvidados, Nazarin, Ensayo para un crimen* or *The Life of Archibaldo de la Cruz, The Exterminating Angel, Diary of a Chambermaid, The Young One, El*, and *Land Without Bread*.

For me, personally, one of the most important results was the ability to gain specific knowledge of Buñuel as a concrete film director. Seeing these films not only impelled me to try to understand them, to "read them," but enriched me by raising new questions, creating new spaces in my entire esthetic and cultural framework.

To my mind, one of the clearest and most positive constants in Buñuel's work is his highly personal sense of humor, his capacity for irony. A capacity directed not only toward the reactionary customs, practices and individuals in his films but toward the profession of film directing itself, and of course, toward the spectator. I think that it is due to this capacity for sarcasm that Buñuel paradoxically converts terrible actors, amid a dreadful, badly lit set, into a distanced, ironic, element which is not at all "realistic," but is extremely effective.

The mechanism of demolition, of revulsion, in Buñuel's films rests definitively upon two fundamental pillars: evident truths, and a break from the prevailing "mental order."

Gross elemental truths appear as the generally *populist* response to the magical-repressive values of a society and of characters who engender only misfortune and unhappiness. The violence and *spontaneity* of these "great truths" merely serve to denounce the *artifice* and fragility of superstructures such as the State, Religion, Order, Official Culture, etc., with their repressive common denominator. The "exaggerations," the "coarseness" of the repulsive elements in Buñuel are, unquestionably, tinged by a profound belief in man's right to happiness; they are filled with a democratic and humanistic sense of existence. It is noteworthy that this deeply humanistic position is extended to the *human condition in its totality,* including the world of the repressers. Furthermore, in certain instances, the latter are presented as victims of the same repression which they exercise upon a third party and presented as unhappy, thwarted beings, limited, alienated by their own police function. They are seemingly trying to tell us that the garbage permeating our society likewise taints those who throw it.

The break in the prevailing "mental order" is, as I stated, the other key aspect of Buñuel's work. This break, this revulsion, must be understood in its total dimension, that is, directed toward every class of conservative values, whoever they may be. Bourgeois materialism, the downright practicality of "mental stability," of "that's how things are," receive as much of a flogging as the mythical-religious framework of the same bourgeoisie. Meanness, servility, and the dirty tricks of the oppressed as well. The mental peace of pat formulae, the *one-dimensional* view of life, are continually subject to question. The world of dreams, of the imagination, is used by Buñuel a) to reveal the concealed side of people and things, their total reality, their true condition; b) as a *negating* force of the "normal" abnormal everyday order. Sustained by imaginative freedom and lapidary expression of truthful truths, Buñuel continually provides an unveiling of the human condition, an authentic humanization of existence. He struggles, aspires to, and explores what Marx designated as the means and end of Revolution: the conscious construction of human existence, man definitively human, definitively NEW, the beginning of true History. In this sense, and to the degree that we are so, does the subjective aesthetic dimension of Buñuel's cinema remain "ours," revolutionary. I believe that it is quite clear that my intention is not to claim that Buñuel is a "Marxist" or that all of his films can be measured and classified in the same manner. I merely wish to indicate that those general aspects in the Buñuel films that I know, both on an expressive and ideological level, form part of the contradictory combination of liberating tendencies developed in that great dialectical synthesis that constitutes a Social and Cultural Revolution of Civilization.

Interest in biology and the study of animal and plant life, curiosity about the world of Nature as a potential source and mirror of human life, belief in the right to happiness, contempt for the social and ideological order of the bourgeoisie, profound humanist faith, a deep-rooted individualism in the struggle for "moral regeneration" of a humanity that has deteriorated because of the Repressive Order, denunciation of the magical-religious opium, a more immediate pessimism toward the chaos of common ignorance and superstition, a realistic view and assumption of all of man's defects and virtues, in the past and present, an imaginative poetic exaltation, an ingrained belief in love, exposure of cynicism and hypocrisy, all these ideological components, all of these *often self-contradictory* values, what do they recall? What do they resemble? What do they evoke? Have they not historically been the *essential* elements of our peoples' democratic and revolutionary thinking? Have they not in all likelihood constituted the traditional common property of the libertarian movement for at least a century? Have they not permeated the very *values*, all the desperate popular revolutionary uprisings against Kings, Governments, Inquisitions, Obscurantisms? Have they not existed from the time of the 1873 revolts of the cantons up until the youthful revolt against "established society" that was prompted by Opus Dei fascism of 1970[5]? Did they not largely

[5]The Opus Dei is a religious-political sect which, at the present time, dominates the government's political and administrative organization. Its members are, therefore, placed in key positions of the fundamental sectors of the economy. The dominating ideology of this sect is a clever mixture of traditional clerical-authoritarian-fascist thought with "modern" pretensions, based on the technocratic implantations imported from reactionary Yankee sociology. In sum, the Opus is the sectarian mythical-religious-elitist organization whereby the class in Power defends and imposes its political and economic dictatorship, in other words, the ultimate expression of Spanish fascism.

affect the Institución Libre de Enseñanza, Ferrer's Modern School,[6] the Popular Atheneums, the October Revolution of 1924 in Asturias, the anarchist-syndicalist movements, the great popular republican blossoming, the very marrow of the highly complex, tragic civil war of 1936–39, the cultural movement of 1927–39? In my opinion that is a fact. If not, why to this day would they remain so relevant?

In 1970, the film *Tristana* acquired, within the *inner dialectic* of the cultural market as manipulated by *Power*, a specific dimension.

As previously stated, the script for *Tristana* had been rejected upon several occasions over the years. It was in 1969, I believe, that Buñuel—following the rule that applied to all—presented once again the script of *Tristana* to Initial Censorship. The censors, once more, failed to authorize it. The Spanish producers decided to shoot the film in Portugal. Immediately, a conflict involving prestige arose for the Ministry of Information and Tourism. Overnight, in the eyes of European "clientele," the image of a culturally repressive State began to take shape. *The best-Spanish-director-has-to-make-his-film-abroad.* The international reverberations of Buñuel's name, the co-production with French participation, aroused fear of a "scandal" which would destroy the liberalization and Europeanization slogans of Opus-fascism. In these circumstances, the Ministry held a private conversation with Buñuel. During this interview, according to rumor, Power indicated to Author the permissible limits. In a word: through a "gentlemen's agreement" it authorized the shooting. I wish to point out that the foregoing is rumor. Lack of freedom necessitates, among other things, that such matters, which ought to be open to all, be revealed at this undeveloped whispered level.

---

[6]Francisco Ferrer was a teacher of more or less acrasian ideology, shot at the beginning of the century in Barcelona, by order of Alfonso XIII. He was accused of directing the disturbances in which the Catalonian people tried to prevent the embarcation of colonial troops to Morocco. In reality, the feudal-colonial oligarchy accused him of other "charges": sexual education of boys and girls, etc. The press at the time labeled the events as the "Tragic Week." The monarchist newspaper *ABC*, in an article by Luca de Tena in December, 1970, established a parallel ("again an anti-Spanish campaign") between protests on behalf of the Ferrer case and the protests against the War Council of Burgos.

What is objectively certain, however, is that the shooting of the film was authorized, and that, by the mere acceptance of this situation, Buñuel was in an obvious *privileged* position over other Spanish scriptwriters and directors, for whom the censors' decisions are *indisputable,* and for whom conversations or private arrangements with the Administration do not normally exist.[7] In short, *Tristana* was able to be made without obstacles, and furthermore, it passed Final Censorship, which is exercised after a film is completed.

In the spring of that year, a question began to take shape, which is now of paramount importance: in cinema, fascist forms of power not only stifle the possibilities of existence for a culturally competitive "quality" cinema, but also jeopardize a national industry of production. The inner logic of the present filmmaking structure in our country leads, among other things, to *the disappearance of film as a genuine cultural expression,* and to the conversion of the labor and industrial infrastructure into an excellent and cheap "background" for foreign, particularly North American, companies. Hence, we are headed for a typical *colonial* situation. We are in fact *in it.*

At the same time, as the Ministry is searching for films of Spanish directors which can compete in the Festivals, one finds that a large number of them are banned, prohibited, cut or under "consideration." Furthermore, the industrial crisis reduces to almost zero the number of products from which to choose. At which point the publicity for *Tristana* and *Cabezas Cortadas,* or if you prefer, the Buñuel "brand" and the Glauber Rocha "brand," are launched. It is hoped that these "opening" exceptions will conceal the repressive rule. And that these two films and those two names will become—*against the individual will of both directors, to be sure, and unrelated to the esthetic significance of the two films*—the black guignol of *Spanish* cinema, both outside and inside of Spain. Patches to conceal our cultural and human impoverishment, silk garments to cover the ugliness of our brutal repressiveness, the wretchedness of our condition and of our alienation.

[7]This "irregularity" likewise indicates the artificiality of the actual legal norms regarding our cinema.

Buñuel's latest film as of 1970 has been hailed as one of the greatest box-office successes. Money has suddenly opened the eyes of distributors and exhibitors, who have "discovered" Buñuel and his films as potential commercial gold mines, and who have "ventured" to show several of his works which until now have been regarded as "odd." How contradictory is our reality, and how difficult to deal with it: A problem: the System presents the trick card: "Prestige-Privilege"; how to find the unknown quantity which will convert prestige into a *weapon*, and not into privilege. *A problem to be resolved now and by all.*

With such positive marketing indices for the Buñuel "brand," Juan Julio Baena—one of the most "liberal" policy-directors or one of the most police-like "liberal" directors to have passed through the Official School of Cinema—was invited to give a talk and colloquium to students. Why is it that the same individual who prohibited any kind of free assembly or student society, that the same person who banned and confiscated rehearsals and films, the same one who continually called for armed police intervention, the same one who imposed his personal and dictatorial criterion upon all the students and subordinate personnel, the same one who thrust the School into a theretofore unknown chaos and confusion, the same one who committed all sorts of irregularities and arbitrary actions, for which he did not hesitate even when it came to violating his own "legality," why is it that this same individual decided in 1970 to set the Buñuel record straight? Well, simply, in order to behave, on a reduced scale, in accordance with the mechanisms of the Paternal System. To "isolate" the "long-haired, red, dirty, toxic, immoral rebels." To stand up as a "defender of Culture" in order to purchase the good will of a few through the lure of a name, in order to insinuate that if the "reds" left him alone, he would support a School without "changes," without "problems," and with "Buñuel," in other words, with "quality." An "efficient, European" school, with "room for everyone if they fulfill their duty," a duty which consisted merely in "studying and working," "Law and Order," "Evolution and not Revolution." "Coca-cola refreshes best." "Put a tiger in your tank."

A group of students sent a letter to Buñuel protesting his

presence at the School. Others went to ask his pardon for the contents of what they considered an inopportune letter. In conclusion, Buñuel did not attend the School. He played "hooky."

That summer, three construction workers were shot to death in Granada, during a demonstration. That summer, the government militarized the Madrid metro[8], which had been paralyzed by a strike. That autumn, a metallurgical worker was shot in Eibaz during a demonstration against the War Council of Burgos. That summer and that fall, those of us film directors who worked in Spain found ourselves at a standstill amid a crisis of unknown proportions. María del Carmen Andújar—how Spanish the name!—the young president of the "Raphael Club," declared in the news weekly *Triunfo* that her idol is "not leftist," but "a normal fellow," and that "to be leftist is abnormal." The justification of euthanasia? No: simply the codification of rules of behavior.

A few days ago a film club in Barcelona organized a cinema weekend in Andorra, a small independent principality in the Catalonian Pyrenees, between the French and Spanish borders. The program, announced in a specialized Spanish magazine, offered films, some in complete versions, others in partial sequences, which, in all likelihood, would not be seen in the normal Spanish circuits. One of the films was Luis Buñuel's *Simon of the Desert.* On that weekend, the 18th-19th-20th of March in 1971, the centennial of the Paris Commune, a street demonstration took place in several Spanish cities. In Valencia, the monument of the founder of the Falange was blown up. Friends of mine, a couple, drove about eight hundred kilometers to see Buñuel's film, the cause of numerous complications when it was shown in the International Week of Films of Human and Religious Values in Valladolid.

We saw a documentary by Chris Marker on Cuba. The film was in French, and a great protest was made because the majority of the audience wanted to hear Fidel's voice in our own language, which the dubbing prevented. To be sure, the program announced "The Battle of the Ten Million, with Fidel Castro," in the same

---

[8]In Spain the underground railroad which circulates under the streets of the city is called the "Metro."

manner as one might say, "with Marlon Brando." And, naturally, it is always annoying to be prevented from hearing the "star" in the original version.

When the projection of *Simon of the Desert* began, the hall was jammed with five hundred people. We had come from all parts of the peninsula. And when the lights went on again, after the predictable "outpouring" of laughter, imprecations, and bravos, a huge ovation sounded for the young seventy-year-old Buñuel. For a man capable, still, of making a film that was so up-to-date, so revulsive, so humanist, so ironic, so provocative, so much *ours*, so "underground," so "Spanish."

It was after seeing *Simon of the Desert* that I realized *Tristana's* full range, the enormous sadness of that classic, the mature and melancholy self-criticism, its stature as a great film, the pathos of its individual and generational "testament." It is that—the combination of blatant libertarian outrage and the powerful impotence of ingrained individualism—which is at the core of the work of Buñuel that I've been able to see and love.

In a final scene in *Tristana*, one of the characters, Don Lope, (who can simultaneously represent the real or literary image of Baroja, Don Guido, Unamuno, Bradomín and many others), winds up, senile, drinking hot chocolate and buttered toast in the company of some priests. From the depths of my being, and in commemoration of his birthday, I wish that Luis Buñuel never, ever peacefully drink chocolate with any Represser, even if the latter invites him on his birthday. Salud!

The Buñuel Mystery

Jean-Claude Carrière

∙ ∙ ∙ ∙ ∙ ∙ ∙ ∙ ∙ ∙ ∙ ∙ ∙ ∙ ∙ ∙ ∙ ∙ ∙ ∙

Luis Buñuel is shooting a new movie in Spain. He is filming the narrow, winding streets and the cloisters of Toledo, a city he knows quite well since he lived there once, not far from the cathedral. The weather is raw. Some days he wears a black beret, which he pulls down tightly on his head. Other days, he wears a peaked cap, and there's always a viewer hanging around his neck. "For no particular reason," he notes. "It's only to prove that I'm a movie director."

Since *Viridiana,* in 1961, he has been back twice to shoot in Spain. This film is called *Tristana.* It is a strange story of love and honor, which is based on a novel by the great Spanish writer, Benito Pérez Galdós, who died in 1920. Galdós is not all that well-known outside Spain, but his world is very similar to Buñuel's, and the director has already taken the subject for his film *Nazarin* from him. In point of fact, Buñuel says that *"Tristana* is one of Galdós' worst novels."

Buñuel sets the action in Toledo among the provincial middle class in the years 1928 to 1935, before and during the Civil War. The project was forbidden in 1963 by the Spanish government when Buñuel first proposed it. And when it came up again in 1969, it was again forbidden, but eventually it was authorized.

Though he is Spanish by birth, Buñuel became a Mexican citizen six years ago. That's why he can make films in Spain even though most of them cannot be shown there. In spite of that, he is very famous in Spain.

In *Tristana,* he again uses Catherine Deneuve, the star of *Belle de Jour,* and his friend Fernando Rey, whom he directed in *Viridiana.* The Italian actor, Franco Nero, is also in the film.

From *Show* (April 1970). Translated by Alice Mayhew.

When he's not working on the set, Nero's busy with his own Super-8 camera shooting Buñuel from every angle.

Buñuel was seventy in February, but his energy is undiminished. He is quite deaf, but he seems to have come to terms with that. On the set he paces around, explaining things, gesticulating, leaning close to hear. And then all of a sudden he will roar with laughter until tears come to his eyes. Passersby in the Toledo streets ask for his autograph. He grumbles, but signs, murmuring, "Dali would be jealous."

I know something of Buñuel. I met him for the first time in 1963 and have collaborated on four scripts with him: *The Diary of a Chambermaid*, *The Monk* (not yet filmed), *Belle de Jour*, and *The Milky Way*. Altogether, I have spent more than a year working closely with him and I have watched him shoot often. I have even occasionally taken small roles under his direction, my favorite being in *The Milky Way*, the role of a bishop who speaks in Latin. "Simply because," Buñuel remarked, "it is more and more difficult to find an actor who speaks correct Latin."

I spent a week with him during the filming of *Tristana*. This was the first time I had seen him film in Spanish, and the first time that I had watched him shoot a script that I was familiar with but hadn't worked on. I watched him with a fresh eye. I thought of the unbelievable pile of nonsense and the hack articles that have been written about him, and I told myself that the time had come for me to add my stone to the edifice.

A great deal has been written about him—much too much. In an attempt to seize upon all the facets of a highly complicated man, he has been made out to be a tissue of contradictions. He is described simultaneously as an atheist and theist, revolutionary and bourgeois, an intellectual and a peasant, a recluse and an extrovert, fierce and sentimental, irrational and reasonable, a poet and a rationalist, as both very French and very Spanish. He is all these things and more. He is indifferent and resigned to all the junk that is written about him, my own included. His sense of humor protects him.

His unwillingness to talk about himself is matched by the genuine humility with which he talks about his films. He wishes above all to be simple, absolutely simple, and it is not the least of Buñuel's contradictions that he is both profoundly simple and deeply complicated. He makes an effort to be clear and direct. His manner is like his cinematic style—straightforward and without the least affectation. It is impossible to fault him on this. He never talks self-importantly about his "work," about which he shows a marvelous detachment. He never looks at his films a second time, nor reads what's written about him. He is angered when he is accused of being warped or a sadist, a profaner of things sacred, a blasphemer or a cruel director, attracted only by the horrible and the morbid. And he makes fun of people who try to set him on a pedestal. He works patiently away at destroying his legend. Yet, whether or not he wishes it, there is a tenacious and subtle Buñuel mystery.

Mystery is *his* word. He believes that works of art begin in mystery, in the inexplicable. He cannot heap enough sarcasm on those who claim to explain and understand everything, and on the famous "French mentality," the legacy of Descartes and Voltaire, which thinks it can reduce the world to something that is completely intelligible. He likes, whether he is working or dreaming, to give himself over to the images which simply come to him and take him by surprise. "When we were working on the script of *Un Chien Andalou* with Dali, we had only one rule: Keep only the pictures that we cannot explain rationally."

But if Luis Buñuel has evolved since *Un Chien Andalou*, and if the films he makes today do not attempt to reflect the surrealist style faithfully, this same passionate taste for the irrational is still very much a part of him. His "images" loom constantly in his work. Dream and daydream play a tremendous role, mixing with the real until, as in *Belle de Jour*, they are inextricably joined. I have never understood—and hopefully I shall be lucky enough never to understand—why the last five minutes of *The Milky Way* moved me so.

Buñuel loves to repeat what André Breton once said about somebody: "He's a jackass. He never dreams." He claims that the irrational governs the world—and, even more so, the cinema.

The Buñuel mystery.

On the surface, he makes films as everybody else does, out of the same materials. His technique is commonplace. He is completely free of artiness. He avoids pretty picture-making and sneers at critics who speak of his artist's palette or his painter's eye. "Sometimes I just let my cameraman photograph clouds. That gives him pleasure. He enjoys it." He does not attach particular importance to acting. He steers clear of unusual angles or sophisticated camera work. He shoots very fast, commenting that he gets bored after the seventh week. He made *The Exterminating Angel* in eighteen days, *Viridiana* in twenty-three. It is frequently said that he neglects details, that he could do better. In the bad days, in Mexico, he put his name to a number of films that he now doesn't want his friends to see.

I watch him shoot. As usual, he arrives on location not knowing exactly where he's going to place his camera. He never prepares a shooting script. He looks around briefly and makes a quick decision. The solution is usually the simplest, or sometimes just the easiest. He may even say, "No, not that way. It's too difficult." He arranges the actors and the extras very carefully, but he doesn't trouble much about the details of the background. He looks through the camera sight frequently. Someone gives him a headset so that he can hear the dialogue, because he's so deaf. He doesn't give the actors any direction before the run-throughs, merely places them and corrects as they go along.

When an actor pleases him—as, for example, Jeanne Moreau in *The Diary of a Chambermaid*—he doesn't add a thing, allowing the interpreter his own sensibility and his own reactions. But, other times, he might take the actor aside for an hour if necessary, if he hasn't gotten it, and give him directions down to the minutest detail, even a frown. His directions are sometimes astonishing. He told Georges Marchal to disappear behind a coffin in *Belle de Jour,* "as the sun sets on the horizon." In the same film, Francisco Rabal is supposed to come out of an elevator after committing a holdup, and look around nervously. Buñuel thought he overdid it. Rabal asked, "Okay, what shall I think about?" "Think about your aunt," Buñuel told him. The remark has become part of the legend.

His camera is constantly on the move. He believes a moving camera, even if the movement is minute, creates a sort of hypnotic effect. He gives his cameraman very simple, but very precise directions.

On the set, the atmosphere around him is animated. He sees

and senses everything. Buñuel has practiced hypnotism and is very telepathic. This may explain the immediate contact he has with people, the extras, the technicians, the newspapermen. There is a sense of profound harmony, great intimacy, deep mutual respect. And always a great feeling of fun.

As soon as he is ready, he starts to shoot. He leans slightly forward, his legs bent, and sways gently back and forth. Great concentration. Once he's satisfied with a take, he goes on to the next. He uses only from about 55,000 to 65,000 feet of film, which is very little. He has the reputation of being well-organized and very economical, never behind schedule. He takes what he needs, knowing in advance exactly how it will come out. The actual cutting takes only eight to ten days.

He shoots with serenity and sureness and never displays the kind of anguish which sometimes paralyzes other directors. "I place my actors in the camera and follow them in the setting as long as I can. When I don't know what to do anymore, I stop and change the angle."

This sense of calm does not prevail during the period when the script is being worked out. He has often remarked that for him the film is made at the writing stage. It is then that the problems arise and must be solved.

He trusts to chance for his choices of subject. Sometimes he uses original stories (*The Exterminating Angel, The Milky Way, Viridiana*), or he adapts novels he likes (*Nazarin, Tristana,* and *The Monk,* which no doubt he will film one day), or he accepts suggestions from producers but so completely transforms them that they ultimately appear original (*Diary of a Chambermaid, Belle de Jour*). Nobody can guess what will attract Buñuel. Many people have proposed stories thinking they had found "the perfect story for him." He almost always rejects them.

I remember how surprised I was when I learned he had agreed to make *Belle de Jour,* because, naively, I thought the novel uninteresting. He wrote me immediately: "Just between us, a ridiculous theme, but intriguing. A multitude of whores with terrible conflicts between the super-ego and the id. Just the opposite of what today's cinema holds up before us. A very, very well-laid-out plot, and to boot a very alluring fictitious world."

"Just between us, a ridiculous theme, but intriguing. A multitude of whores with terrible conflicts between the super-ego and the id. Just the opposite of what today's cinema holds up before us." (*Belle de Jour*)

His whole vision of the film is these few sentences. Afterward, he was astonished at the commercial success of the film, which he thought too complex for popular taste.

The Milky Way was the fulfillment of an old desire to make a film about heresy. He had long been fascinated by the history of heresies, with which he is well-acquainted—particularly by the mentality of the heretic, which involves the kind of fanaticism that can accept dogma whole hog, except for a single detail which the heretic adds or subtracts. This detail is what the man feels he, personally, adds to the understanding of the "truth." And for this detail, the man is ready to kill or to die. This phenomenon interested Buñuel first from a strictly religious point of view, but then, also, because it has universal implications.

But Buñuel could not decide how to adapt this idea for the movies. In 1967, we were together in Venice for the presentation of *Belle de Jour*. He asked me to spend some weeks with him in Spain to see if we could find a story and style that would dramatize it. We packed some theology textbooks in valises and set off.

In Spain, in the hills of Granada in a peaceful hotel, we were completely isolated, fifteen miles from the nearest village. It was autumn and the weather was magnificent. There was nobody in the hotel except some hunters who left each day at dawn and returned very late. We spent several weeks there, far from the world, walking in the forests, and talking about divine grace and original sin. It was a time of great contentment. The scenario worked itself out slowly. After a month, we had about fifty pages. Serge Silberman, who had produced *Diary of a Chambermaid*, came to see us. He read the fifty pages in a half hour and agreed to make the film. "We're going to take you to a nice house in the country," Buñuel told him, taking him gently by the arm, "a very comfortable house. The people will be dressed in white and won't do you any harm." He was telling him he was crazy to produce a film like *The Milky Way*. Silberman didn't agree.

Buñuel exhibited all the doubts and concerns of the creative artist during the writing of the script. He is much more author than director. And yet, paradoxically, he writes only rarely and with difficulty. When he is faced with it, he needs someone else who will actually take pen and paper after they have talked it out together. I have played that role four times. I am well aware that Buñuel's universe is so particular and so personal that it's useless to offer him ideas that are supposed to arouse his enthusiasm. When a difficulty arises, he thinks up a half dozen possible solutions, and, if he asks for advice, it is only to help choose from among them. His imagination is both brilliant and boundless. I often have the impression when I'm working with him that I am his first audience. He will be silent for a long time, gazing out the window; he lights a cigarette and puts it out (he smokes and drinks a bit too much, which worries him but doesn't seem to do him any harm), then he bursts out laughing, tells a story, gets lost in some digression, and finally finds what he's looking for. Sometimes his critical sense, which is very acute, overwhelms his imaginative side and he suffers periods of depression when everything seems stupid and childish to him. Sometimes he needs help to sweep these doubts away, find his direction again, and give his imaginative side pre-eminence again.

He likes to work regularly, five or six hours a day, roughly. That gives me time to sketch out what we've talked over, write dialogue and type up a draft. In the evening, when we go out to the Madrid cafes, there is not a word about work. He is just delighted to be with friends in his favorite spots.

He has an instinctive sense of how a film script should be constructed. From this point of view, the scripts of *El, Belle de Jour,* and *Tristana* could pass as models. He places great importance on the last image of one sequence and the first image of the following one, to the relationship of the parts to each other. For him, dialogue poses no problems. Ideally, it is as simple as possible, no cleverness, no play on words. The details, which, as far as he is concerned, "make the film," he finds as he goes along. Sometimes he is conscious of "playing Buñuel" and he fights against it. He will make a joke. He'll say, "If this is too short, we'll put in a dream." He tries to disconcert, to surprise, to do something one would not expect of him. He has said: "I do not make films for the 'public,' I put the word 'public' in quotes. If this 'public' is conventional, hidebound, perverted, that's not its fault but society's. It's very, very difficult and happens rarely that one can make a film that pleases the 'public,' as well as one's friends and the people whose judgment counts for one." He is one of the rare filmmakers—perhaps the only one—who makes films to please himself.

He includes in the script all the directions, as for costume or decor, that may help him when he comes to shoot, but never the technical directions. He prefers to leave something to discover for the actual filming so that it will not become a mere formality. "If everything is in the scenario, why bother making the film?"

In the movie world, which he detests, he lives like a hermit. When he's not working, he reads and rests in his house in Mexico, where he lives with his French wife, two dogs and his parrot. In his bar there is a framed map of the Paris *métro*. In the living room, there is his portrait by Salvador Dali, a friend from other days whom he doesn't see anymore.

He has three children. Raphael lives in New York where he runs an off-Broadway theater. Jean-Louis, a sculptor and film-maker, lives in Paris. Juliette is his youngest and is named in honor of Sade and his *Prosperités du Vice*.

Luis Buñuel is seldom seen at the film festivals. And even less frequently at the receptions and cocktail parties. He maintains that he manages his time so well that he is able to spend months doing nothing. That's what he says. He'd have to prove it.

He goes to the movies very rarely and, because of his deafness, sees only pictures with subtitles, but he's very impatient and usually leaves after twenty minutes. Nevertheless, he has seen Bergman's *Persona* twice and *The Saragossa Manuscript*, a Polish film made by Has, two or three times. He has a weakness for this film and for Potocki's book which inspired it. Several years ago he was very struck by a film by the Brazilian Glauber Rocha, *Black God, White Devil*, and *The Hunt*, a film by a young Spanish filmmaker, Carlos Saura. He still admires Fritz Lang and he likes Fellini up to *La Dolce Vita*.

His true masters, as he acknowledges, are writers, not film-makers. Buñuel has been nourished by many cultural traditions, first the Spanish, particularly the picaresque novels up to the time of Galdós. And yet many Spaniards find him more French than Spanish. It was in France, particularly during the surrealist movement, that he really found his style. He made his first film, *Un Chien Andalou*, in 1928 with some money his mother gave him. In 1930, he made *L'Age d'Or*, which André Breton called the only authentically surrealist film ever made.

These two films, his intimacy with members of the surrealist group, his discovery of the works of Sade and Freud all marked him indelibly, as he is the first to point out. He can talk all night and with great emotion about this time of his life. He tells the story of how he was once denounced by the surrealists because he had sold the script of *Un Chien Andalou* to a bourgeois literary review. He was subjected to a trial complete with public defender and prosecutor. "I was despondent," he recalls, "and such was the strength of our convictions at that time that I felt I should have to commit suicide." In the end his sentence was to smash the review's printing press with a hammer.

Today Buñuel likes to repeat Breton's words that, "It is now impossible to scandalize anybody." Nevertheless, he asserts that the struggle goes on, because the adversary is still the same, even if he has changed faces. Buñuel is still on the alert, still concerned about being true to himself. A long time ago he understood that to try to be original just for its own sake was not interesting, and once such originality became an end in itself it led to mere pyrotechnics. He is fond of repeating, with the hint of a smile, the words of a Spanish scholar: "Everything that does not come out of tradition is plagiarism."

He doesn't try to be original; he simply is, quite naturally and without any apparent effort. Even more, he doesn't try to scandalize. It simply happens. There's an enormous difference.

That is not to say that Buñuel is not conscious of his power. He has said that, "The cinema is a tremendous weapon and can be dangerous if wielded by a free spirit." But, above all, beyond all the success and all the scandals, he stands aloof from the fashions of the day, especially those he has made himself, and insists on just being himself—the final mark of originality.

Even so, aside from the struggle, it seems to me that much of Buñuel's work recalls the words of André Breton in the *Second Manifesto of Surrealism:* "Everything leads me to believe that there is a certain point in the life of the spirit at which life and death, the real and the imagined, the past and the future, the communicable and the incommunicable, the exalted and the lowly, cease to be seen as contradictory. One would search in vain in the whole spectrum of surrealist insight for anything except the exact point where one could hope to determine where these contradictions fall away." It is this "exact point" that I have seen in a flash at certain moments in Buñuel's work. For those who know how to watch him, Buñuel no longer seems merely a dealer in contradictions. There is a great deal of discussion about his obsessions and manias as a film creator, but I have never been struck by this side of him. I believe him to be the exact opposite of the author who simply goes on repeating himself. Clearly, there is a distinguishable Buñuelian universe, filled with brilliant and unique images; but this universe is a boundless kingdom. One cannot catalogue it. I asked Buñuel one day if he was aware that he habitually used certain themes and certain favorite images. He smiled, "Yes, there are these elements that recur in my films. But I spot them too late. When I do, I never use them again."

There are a lot of pealing bells, wood fires, animals, drum rolls, and priests in his work. A great many priests. In this regard, a few words about Buñuel's relationship with the Catholic religion are in order. Many people have commented on it, often quite mistakenly and away from the point. They say he is fascinated by Catholicism, that he has a love-hate attitude towards it, and numerous well-meaning souls have suggested that he will end by being "saved," and wind up in the bosom of the Church.

I fear they deceive themselves. The relationship between Buñuel and his religion is, like everything else about him, marvelously simple. Buñuel is deeply and sincerely an atheist. The famous witticism, "I am an atheist, thank God," does not apply to him. It's an old Spanish joke that people have stuck on him. Raised in the Catholic religion and educated by Spanish Jesuits, he long ago rebelled against his religion, which he considers to be one of the major forces responsible for social injustice.

It is nevertheless true that he is uninterested in anything outside the Christian universe, which has been the only one he has ever known. Although he lives in Mexico, he displays a complete indifference toward the art and civilization of the Indians. He is equally bored by Africa and the Orient. He is at ease only with the Christian myths, traditions and legends that he knows intimately. He knows the Gospels well, even if he doesn't admire them. He has read the Church Fathers, the lives of the saints, the history of the great heresies. This reading, this familiarity with the Christian spirit has stamped most of his films. Both *Viridiana* and *Nazarin* could be taken as apocryphal parables, and are therefore considered to be dangerous, which explains the embarrassed though divided attitude of the Church toward his films. *Simon of the Desert* and *The Milky Way*, aside from their satirical and comic aspects, concern the relation between man and the sacred, or perhaps even more they are about man's efforts to speak to the empty heavens.

In Toledo it is winter. A cold wind blows in the narrow streets.

Luis Buñuel is making a picture once again. He often insists, so they say, that this one will be the last: He said it about *Diary of a Chambermaid*, about *Belle de Jour*, about *The Milky Way*. But he goes on, because of some interior and private need that he doesn't try to explain. He will go on making films for a long time.

Some Spanish friends come to see him, and also his sister Conchita, who lives in Saragossa. He includes them in some back-ground shots. In the evening, after he has finished shooting, he retires early.

He says the best time of his life was when he was in his fifties, but he doesn't complain too much at being old. He has arrived at a certain serenity. He likes solitude—at least part of the time. He can sit watching an ant on a twig or the clouds in the sky for long periods. If he were to retire to a desert island, the book he would take would be the *Souvenirs d'un Entomologiste*, by J.-H. Fabre, a nineteenth-century French scholar. He has a passion for this work, in which he sees a love of nature and of all living things equal to his own.

He is, literally, incapable of killing a fly.

He is not preoccupied by death. He would like to have time to prepare himself and to leave his affairs in order because he likes to maintain order in his house and his documents. When a journalist asked him why he did not come back to live in Europe, he responded, "Because of fear of death. I don't mind dying, but not while I'm moving."

On his deathbed, to scandalize his friends one last time, he would like to summon a priest. And afterward he would like his tombstone removed from time to time so that the newspapers could be brought to him. "It's nothing to die," he says. "What's hard is to be not with it."

He's up in the morning at six. He's first on the set and welcomes the technicians. He asks how they are. He marks the first position for the camera precisely.

He doesn't like it when his generosity, his modesty, his talent for friendship are discussed. But many of his friends say that the great masterpiece of Buñuel is Buñuel himself. He is the man that everyone who is around him would dream of being.

His square face is carved out of beautiful brown stone. Sometimes he grows a mustache, "but never a beard, because I would
look like Hemingway."

Square shoulders, strong muscles, a hearing aid in the left ear,
clear and wide eyes.

He was born with the twentieth century. I hope he lives as long
as it does.

III

Buñuel the Filmmaker

. . . .

Poetry and Cinema

(Text of an address delivered at the University of Mexico in 1953)

Luis Buñuel

· ·

Octavio Paz said once that "A chained man need only shut his eyes to make the world explode." Paraphrasing him, I would say that the white eye of the screen need only reflect the light that is properly its own to blow up the universe. But, for the time being, we can sleep easily, for the cinemagraphic light that reaches us is carefully filtered and metered. In none of the traditional arts is there so great a disproportion between potential and achievement as in the cinema. A film acts directly upon the spectator, presenting him with concrete people and things; in the silence and darkness of the theater, it isolates him from what we might call his normal psychic habitat. For these reasons, it can stimulate him more effectively than any other form of human expression. It can also more effectively stultify him. The bulk of current film production seems, unfortunately, to have this as its mission, and the screens of our film houses daily parade evidence of the moral and intellectual void in which the cinema is wallowing. The fact is that the cinema limits itself to imitating the novel or the stage—but with this difference: that as a medium it is less richly endowed with the means of psychological expression. It is repeating *ad nauseam* the same old stories that the nineteenth century had already wearied of telling but that nonetheless drone on in the modern novel.

A moderately cultivated man would toss aside a book based on any one of the subjects that make up the plots of our biggest films. Yet that same man, comfortably seated in a dark theater, is

From *Buñuel: An Introduction* by Ado Kyrou (New York: Simon & Schuster), 1963. Reprinted by permission of Georges Borchardt, Inc.

dazzled by a light and movement that exert an almost hypnotic power over him; he is fascinated by the faces of people and by the rapid shifts of scene, so that he placidly accepts the film bromides, no matter how stale.

The filmgoer is robbed of an important share of his critical faculties by this lulling influence. I will give one concrete example—*Detective Story*. The structure of the story is perfect; the director is excellent, the actors exceptional, the production original. But all this talent, all this know-how, all the complicated steps involved in producing a film have been devoted to a story that in content is both stupid and remarkably low in moral caliber. It makes me think of that extraordinary machine in *Opus 11*; it is a gigantic apparatus made of the finest grade of steel; it has a thousand complex gears, tubes, manometers, levers; it is engineered as precisely as a watch, but on the scale of an ocean liner; its sole function is to postmark the mail.

The essential element in any work of art is mystery, and generally this is lacking in films. Authors, directors, and producers take great pains not to disturb our peace of mind, and they keep the marvelous window of the screen closed to the liberating world of poetry. They would rather have that screen reflect subjects that could perfectly well be sequels to our everyday life; they prefer that it repeat over and over the same hackneyed drama to make us forget the tedium of our daily work. Their approach is, of course, sanctioned by conventional morality, official censorship, and religion; it is ruled by good taste, and seasoned with an innocuous humor together with all the other prosaic imperatives of reality.

Anyone who is eager to see good films will rarely be satisfied by the big expensive productions or by those that have won critical praise or wide popular acceptance. The personal story, the private individual drama, cannot, in my opinion, interest anyone who is truly alive to the contemporary world. If the spectator shares in the joys, sorrows, and anguish of a character on the screen, it can only be because he sees in that character the reflection of the joys, sorrows, and anguish of society as a whole and, by extension, his own. Unemployment, the instability of society, the fear of war, and so on—these are the things that affect all men today and, accordingly, they affect the spectator. But that Mr. So-and-So is not happy at home and casts about for a girl friend to provide him some fun, and that he then abandons her to return to his self-sacrificing spouse—all this is unquestionably moral and edifying but it leaves us completely indifferent.

Sometimes that which is the essence of cinema springs unexpectedly from an otherwise insipid movie—a slapstick comedy, or a banal romantic film. Man Ray once said something very significant: "The worst movies I've ever seen in my life, the kind that put me sound asleep, always have five minutes that are marvelous. But the best, the most highly praised films, have barely five minutes that are even worthwhile." What this means is that in all films, good or bad—and beyond and despite the intentions of directors—cinematic poetry struggles to come to the surface and reveal itself.

In the hands of a free spirit the cinema is a magnificent and dangerous weapon. It is the superlative medium through which to express the world of thought, feeling, and instinct. The creative handling of film images is such that, among all means of human expression, its way of functioning is most reminiscent of the work of the mind during sleep. A film is like an involuntary imitation of a dream. Brunius* points out how the darkness that slowly settles over a movie theater is equivalent to the act of closing the eyes. Then, on the screen, as within the human being, the nocturnal voyage into the unconscious begins. The device of fading allows images to appear and disappear as in a dream; time and space become flexible, shrinking and expanding at will; chronological order and the relative values of time duration no longer correspond to reality, cyclical action can last a few minutes or several centuries; shifts from slow motion to accelerated motion heighten the impact of each.

The cinema seems to have been invented to express the life of the subconscious, the roots of which penetrate poetry so deeply. Yet it is almost never used to do this. Among modern film trends,† the best known is the so-called neorealism. The neorealistic film offers the spectator what seem to be moments from real life, involving real people caught as they move about the street, and having even authentic scenery and interiors. With

---

*Jacques B. Brunius, a French writer.
†This was said in 1953.—A.K.

The cinema seems to have been invented to express the life of the subconscious, the roots of which penetrate poetry so deeply. (*Belle de Jour*)

some exceptions, among which I would single out *Bicycle Thief*, neorealism has done nothing to spark what is properly and characteristically cinematic—I mean the mysterious and the fantastic. What is the point of all the visual dressing up if the situations, the motives that animate the characters, their reactions, and even the plots themselves are drawn or copied from the most sentimental, conformist literature? The most worthwhile contribution—and it comes not from neorealism generally but from Zavattini* specifically—is the raising of a humdrum act to the level of dramatic action. In *Umberto D*, one of the most interesting of the neorealistic films, an entire ten-minute reel is devoted to showing a maid go through a series of actions that only a short while ago no one would have considered worthy of being filmed. We see the maid go into the kitchen, light the fire,

---

*The great Italian screenwriter, whose credits include *Bicycle Thief*.

put on a casserole, throw water several times on some ants that are advancing Indian file across the wall, take the temperature of an elderly man who feels feverish. Despite the trivial side of the situation, we follow her movements with interest and even with a certain suspense.

Neorealism has introduced a few elements to enrich the language of cinematic expression, but nothing more. Neorealistic reality is incomplete, conventional, and above all, rational. The poetry, the mystery, all that completes and enlarges tangible reality, is utterly lacking. Neorealism confuses ironic fantasy with the fantastic and the grotesque.

"The most admirable thing about the fantastic," André Breton has said, "is that the fantastic does not exist; everything is real." I was talking with Zavattini some months ago, and I said to him that I was not in sympathy with neorealism. Since we were lunching together, the first illustration that came to mind was a glass of wine. For a neorealist, I said, a glass is a glass and nothing more. We see it being taken from the sideboard, being filled with wine, carried presently to the kitchen where the maid will wash it, or maybe she will break it, which will result in her being fired or in her not being fired, and so on. But this same glass, seen by different human beings, can be a thousand different things, because each person pours a certain dose of subjective feeling into what he is looking at, because no one sees things as they are but as his desires and his state of mind make him see them. I am fighting for the kind of film that will make me see this kind of glass, for it is this kind of cinema that will give me a total vision of reality, enlarge my knowledge of things and of people, and open to me the marvelous world of the unknown, of everything that I do not find in any newspaper or on any street.

Do not think from what I have just said that I am for a cinema exclusively dedicated to the expression of the fantastic and mysterious, for a cinema that flees from or despises daily reality and aspires only to plunge us into the unconscious world of dreams. A few moments ago I indicated all too briefly the capital importance I attach to the film that deals with the fundamental problems of modern man, and so I must emphasize here that I do not consider man in isolation, not as a single case, but in the context of his relationships with other men. I will let Friedrich Engels speak for me. He defines the function of the novelist (and here read film maker) thus: "The novelist will have acquitted himself honorably of his task when, by means of an accurate portrait of authentic social relations, he will have destroyed the conventional view of the nature of those relations, shattered the optimism of the bourgeois world, and forced the reader to question the permanency of the prevailing order, and this even if the author does not offer us any solutions, even if he does not clearly take sides."

The Moral Code of Luis Buñuel

Donald Richie

. . . .

Several years ago a critic, talking with Buñuel, mentioned that the director had made a number of purely commercial films. "Yes," answered Buñuel: "I have made several frankly bad pictures, but not once did I compromise my moral code. . . . My bad films were always decent. I am against conventional morality." Upon being asked what this meant, he answered: "Morality—middle-class morality, that is—is for me immoral. One must fight it. It is a morality founded on our most unjust social institutions—religion, fatherland, family culture—everything that people call the pillars of society."

In all of Buñuel's films this energetic battle against the "morality" of the world has been the director's major theme. In his first picture, the celebrated slitting of the eyeball with the razor indicates his intention: the old way of looking at the world, the way of traditional morality, the traditional squeamishness of middle-class culture—all of this must go. And the attack has continued, unabated, all during the director's career.

Yet, if one saw the aim of such attacks as simple destruction, one would misunderstand the aims of the director. His is, after all, a code in itself and Buñuel has his own morality. The greater theme running through his best films is that institutions such as church, state, and family are corrupting only because they give man an entirely false idea of himself. Specifically, they imply that men are, somehow, more than human. Buñuel's moral code rests on an assumption that men are only, or merely, human.

His films are filled with illustrations of this. In *L'Age d'Or* the great civic ceremony is interrupted by the cries of the mud-covered

Reprinted by permission of the author. This article was written in 1963 for the Japanese magazine, *Eiga Hyron*. Since the original English version of the piece is lost, this is a translation by Donald Richie from the Japanese.

couple making love nearby. In *Viridiana,* the young heroine comes to realize that she is not a saint, but only a limited human girl. She sits down to the card game at the end, admitting that she too is part animal and that she must learn to take comfort in that. In *Nazarin,* the priest has also learned that he cannot work miracles, that he is only human, and that he must live with this fact.

The institutions that Buñuel hates are always attempting to suggest that a man is more than he is because only in this way can a civilization be built. A civilization is intended to take care of its members. But church and state can do nothing for conditions shown in *Land Without Bread* and *Los Olvidados.* Thus these institutions are blind to human realities. Civilization is itself a hypocritical pretense.

There are many illustrations of this in the films of Buñuel. One of the most explicit occurs in *L'Age d'Or.* At the party there is a fire and a maid falls dead. The guests literally do not notice this extraordinary incident because society is traditionally blind to anything which might disturb its own idea of itself. Later a father shoots his little boy. The explanation is that the child tore up a cigarette he was rolling and therefore deserved to die. This is at once accepted with relief and belief by the other guests. These incidents do not disturb them, but when the hero dares to slap one of their members, the girl's mother, then society turns against him because one of its own members has been threatened.

This is acutely observed. Buñuel sees man-made society as both self-seeking and self-perpetuating, something like the anthill or the beehive, something, in short, inhuman. And it is interesting how very often Buñuel uses insect images to suggest this.

His heroes hate and destroy them (*L'Age d'Or, Wuthering Heights*), or, hating them, endure them (*Un Chien Andalou, Land Without Bread*), or make them kill each other (*Robinson Crusoe*), or—paradoxically—attempt to save them (*The Criminal Life of Archibaldo de la Cruz, Viridiana*). A recurring metaphor for man-made civilization is that which opens *L'Age d'Or*—mating scorpions doing battle.

Buñuel sees men as only human, and one of his favorite ways is to focus his attention not upon the aspiring head nor the expressive hands but upon the much more typical and human-like feet. It is upon these, he says, that man finally rests. The ignoble foot is at least as typical of the human and probably far more important than the head. In *El, Archibaldo, Susanna, Viridiana, The Diary of a Chambermaid,* and many more films, feet are typically emphasized.

The image of feet as basic is enriched in that feet are also, iconographically, a sexual symbol—a fact made explicit in a scene in *L'Age d'Or.* Buñuel uses such symbols in a fairly straightforward fashion. He was, after all, originally a surrealist, and a naked presentation of symbols is a part of that pictorial style. The director is also, and to that extent, Freudian, since it is upon Freudian assumptions that the surrealist school built its assumptions. But it might also be argued that, in Buñuel's instance, the appeal of such symbols is that all point toward a kind of natural man which society itself must deny.

The Freudian connection between feathers, on the one hand, and sex in general, masturbation in particular, is interesting mainly in Buñuel's use of this symbol. It is used explicitly in *L'Age d'Or* when the hero tears feathers out of the pillow and when later a cloud of feathers falls on the heroine's face. Later use of the symbol is richer and more evocative. There are feathers in *Viridiana,* in *Los Olvidados,* and particularly in *Robinson Crusoe.* Here the implications are particularly interesting. The implication is that Robinson is hard, inhuman, a puritan and, consequently, a hypocrite since he denies his own body. Robinson, alone, refuses to ease his body; with Friday, he refuses to ease his heart and mind. Away from the human society he still apes, he remains its dupe. He will not be natural.

Another way that Buñuel states this theme of necessary naturalness is through his use of animals. In his films the animals are blood brothers of man. A lovely icon occurs in *Los Olvidados* when the donkey sticks his head through the window and into the room where the children are asleep. He too is one of the family; he is not less human than they are animal. Buñuel has an entire bestiary—the giraffe in the uncut *L'Age d'Or,* the dogs in *Los Olvidados, Ascent to Heaven,* and *Viridiana,* the roosters in *The Brute* and *Los Olvidados,* the pigeons in *Los Olvidados* and

Viridiana, the turtle in *Cela S'Appelle L'Aurore,* and all the other animals in *Land Without Bread, Nazarin,* and *La Mort En Ce Jardin.* For Buñuel, these beasts are reminders of the true human estate.

Not, however, that Buñuel is suggesting that humans and animals are identical. What he wants is to remind us of our animal beginnings; he still wants, he has said, to make a kind of insect-comedy in which the girl acts just like a bee, the man acts just like a beetle, etc. He also wants to point out that aspiration cannot lie through church, society, family, since it is precisely humanity that they deny. Rather, fulfillment can come only from a choice—and this is often the choice of another person. This is a romantic solution—and indeed, one expects romanticism from a moralist so firmly set against those institutions which so powerfully control such a majority of lives.

This is perhaps why all of Buñuel's films share the same subject: love. Along with one of his favorite authors, Sade, Buñuel sees love as so very important that nothing else matters. Love is seen realistically; its feet are firmly planted in lust, and various fixations and compulsions are those branches from which it grows. Love is difficult and it may be only partially achieved, but it is all that matters. This is why the lovers in *L'Age d'Or* have such difficulties, and why Buñuel has for so long been fond of *Wuthering Heights,* that story of an unfulfilled and powerful love. What he shows us in his films is that the love of the old man for shoes in *The Diary of a Chambermaid,* and the living and murderous jealousy of the hero in *El,* must be equated with the more conventional romance of *Wuthering Heights*—that love is love, no matter what form it takes.

It is precisely this ability to love which, finally, separates us from the animal—which is why Robinson Crusoe, refusing even self-love, almost turns into an animal. We must retain the innocence and assurance of the beasts and then, disregarding all inhuman constructions and delusions—church and state—must realize ourselves through a love which may take almost any form.

People who call Buñuel a sadist miss the point. The point is that, for Buñuel, even sadism is a form of love. Once Truffaut, speaking about this with the director, suggested that, like Gide, Buñuel sought to disturb, to disquiet. Buñuel answered: "One must not make people think that all is for the best in this best of all possible worlds; I do not try to make anything which is either unworthy or reassuring." Buñuel, indeed, does not want to reassure—that is the task of church and state—but he might have added that he seeks to make one wonder, to doubt, that he seeks to shock because through this shock will come further self-knowledge, and perhaps even an awakening to the falseness of this man-made world.

Many of Buñuel's moral means are disturbing precisely because they are so personal to him. His mistreatment of the blind—in *L'Age d'Or, Los Olvidados, Viridiana,* and other pictures—is an opaque icon in that one is not sure how it should be read. It shocks through its undirected lack of all conventionality. One may read it as a symbol—those who do not see the world as it is deserve to be punished—but the shock remains. The films of Buñuel are filled with these concrete but inexplicit images, drawn, one would suspect, from the director's own life, which disturb precisely because they remain mysterious.

Buñuel is a teacher, he is didactic, and he is a moralist. His is a tough but compassionate code, an honest appraisal of man, a completely unsentimental but moving assessment of life. He teaches a new and better morality. He assumes a metaphysical importance but is at the same time aware of his own limitations.

There is in *Saint Simon* [*Simon Of The Desert*] a superb image which reminds me of Buñuel himself. The saint, devoted to his god, sits high on a pillar for all of life; self-imprisoned on his column, he spends his days in prayer. He is, to that extent, inhuman. But down the pillar, discolored over the years, winding and twisting its way to the ground, is the excrement of the saint. Saint though he is, his bowels must still move. So there he sits, near God indeed, but supported on a pillar of excrement. The image is ambivalent and may be read several ways. One is that the church, God, man's inhuman aspirations, are really built upon unacknowledged human attributes. Another is that it is because we are standing upon our excrement that we are raised the higher. Another is that this true God, which is love, may be reached only by our acknowledging our own true nature as men.

"I am still an atheist, thank God," says Buñuel, bringing all the interpretations together.

Style and Anti-Style

Raymond Durgnat

· · · · · · · · · · · · · · · · · · · ·

When Buñuel was offered a selection of subjects, he usually chose
the least unpromising and adapted it to be, as completely as
possible, a Buñuel film. In no circumstances would he betray his
moral positions. Now that he is relatively free, he begins from a
mental image which fascinates him: "It may be a picture I've
seen: for example, an image of St. Viridiana, an image capable of
triggering off other images, which in turn lead to a complete idea.
There's also reality, as transmitted by everyday news items; and
direct observation, as in *Los Olvidados*." Once shooting has
begun, he works very rapidly, rarely needing more than two or
three takes ("otherwise I get bored"). However, he leaves considerable scope for improvisation, especially in letting the actor take
over and fill out a characterization. He has described how he and
his cameraman occasionally come to line up a virtuoso effect,
then roar with laughter and do it again, simply and flatly.

His style is self-effacing. In his cheaply-budgeted Mexican
features, he relies extensively on that rather old-fashioned heads-
to-knees group-shot which the French call *le plan Américain* and
which the Americans favored because, graceless as it is, it permits
the fastest possible flow of actions and reactions within a scene,
while keeping that scene a unity in the spectator's mind. He uses
relatively long takes, reserving quick cutting for certain climaxes.
His pans, tracks and angle-shots are as spare, curt and functional
as Hawks's. Even when his images are strikingly composed, they
often give an effect of clutter, because the objects or backgrounds
of everyday life are left to lie around, instead of being "edited
out." The lighting is often flat and matter-of-fact, although in

From *Luis Buñuel* by Raymond Durgnat. Copyright © 1967 by Movie Magazine
Ltd. Reprinted by permission of the University of California Press.

dream-sequences, and particularly throughout *Los Olvidados* and *Viridiana*, it becomes low-key and starkly mysterious. Buñuel's later films are less impecunious in effect than the earlier Mexican films, but still his meanings generally lie in the scene which is created, and in its straightforward intensification through the camera's eye, rather than in subtle relationships between the scene and the style. In this sense his most beautiful films are *L'Age d'Or* and *Los Olvidados*.

In 1927 he wrote appreciatively of the American tempo in films, for its way of disclosing only the kernel of a scene before driving on. In sheer unsentimental speed Buñuel compares with certain American directors. The American vice that goes with the American virtue is the slick manipulation of timid conventionalities and rigid formulae. Buñuel gets the speed up in a world which is real, unpredictable, and bristling with radical confusions and tragic paradoxes. Nor is the pace maintained mechanically. It slows during the guerrilla sequence of *L'Age d'Or* to suggest a weary exhaustion, or throughout *Cela S'Appelle L'Aurore* to allow the moral implications of each stage in the plot to develop in the spectator's mind, so that he can observe the hero's solutions lucidly.

If his films conspicuously lack the formal elegance which often masquerades as beauty, they also lack the languid loitering among trivial finesses which often mimics emotional sensitivity. The conventional association of beauty with nostalgia and yearning, with a static admiration, is at best a perversion of true romanticism, and more often a sterile acquiescence in its defeat. Hence, perhaps, André Breton's: "Beauty will be convulsive, or it will not be. . . ." For Buñuel too, the notion of beauty as yearning is superseded by a feeling for beauty as desire. Desire either drives on towards satisfaction, and therefore quiescence, then maintaining itself as a quiet resolution which is matter-of-fact rather than lyrical (or rather, lyrical *only* because matter-of-fact), or else it is frustrated, smothered by apathy or other degradations, including complacency. In his films, aestheticism is always related to a sterile fastidiousness. George Steiner commented how exactly Buñuel catches the kinds of self-conscious elegance that go with Fascism. Even when establishing beauty as nostalgia, his films move with a rapidity which makes of beauty a convulsion, a moment in a process, perhaps a climax, but no more important than the process as a whole. His films surprise by the speed with which beauty blossoms out of the ordinary, and disconcert by the speed with which they move from the beautiful to the anticlimax of the continuing process. Buñuel's interest in processes and connections drives his films with a rapidity that is at once surgical, stoic and dynamic.

Because the unconscious knows nothing of conventional ideas of beauty, these convulsive moments are often ugly or grotesque or scandalous. One might speak of convulsive or visionary moments, rather than of beauty. The shocks are in no sense an assault on the spectator's detachment and lucidity, though they may be an assault on his complacency or his sentimentality. If the inexplicable abounds in Buñuel's work, it is so that his moral arguments are constantly related to the inner world of desires and feelings, related in a way which asserts their irrational existence as categorical imperatives of man's nature. Buñuel is a moralist, but also protests against the rationalist, as well as puritan, attempt to apply moral standards to every impulse and feeling of man.

In his detachment from his own lyricism, Buñuel is more Brechtian than Brecht. He has no need of alienation effects, which in practice delight us aesthetically, thus de-alienating themselves. In his theories, Brecht was a rhetorician, and he pays the price for it. Buñuel needs no alienation effects, because the complexity of his characters and of their predicaments, and the sardonic restraint of his style, force the spectator to careful moral judgments at every turn.

Conversely, it might be said that Buñuel's detachment debars him from the deeply tragic. Often, he seems to slide into the derisive, the grotesque, or the ironic, to indicate tragedy without indulging it fully, except perhaps in *L'Age d'Or* and *Los Olvidados*. There is some truth in this comment, though it is obviously no longer possible to make the tragic a touchstone of an artist's significance. Far more than the erotic shocks, it was the derisive quality of Buñuel's films which made English audiences, in their turn, so derisive towards them. It's that derisiveness which is so honest, so much more tragic than noble tragedy; and, with the Theatre of the Absurd, it has asserted itself as a major twentieth-century mode.

The lack of sympathy for Buñuel's characters, in their absurdity, is often the spectator's response, not the director's. For example many critics thought of Don Jaime (Viridiana's uncle) simply as a morbid fetishist. Buñuel pointed out that whatever his faults might be, there was a great deal of kindness and nobility in his attitudes. Once one refrains from, in effect, destroying Don Jaime by ridicule, his story takes on a more deeply tragic tone without so immersing the spectator in the tragic that he can't see the tragically derisive too.

Indeed, psychoanalysis, suggesting that a man's conscious experience is only part of his subjective experience, suggests also that an "entomologist's" eye might reveal the unconscious self-image. Buñuel's rather sceptical attitude towards the merely conscious is expressed by the way in which connections and conflicts become *series* of moods. Often, lighting produces a swift, sudden dilatation of atmosphere, which flares up like a match, and dies.

On another level, Buñuel takes lyricism with a pinch of salt, because for him nothing is more astonishing than anything else. His shock moments may shock the spectator, but cause no slackening in Buñuel's fast, hard style. The pace and emphasis of his films confirm his declaration that he is absolutely fascinated by such ordinary remarks as "Give me a match." Vis-à-vis life's possibilities for indifference, this remark is pregnant with the rich mystery of a groping for fraternity, of a human initiative in an arbitrary world, which is all the more beautiful for being quite unself-conscious. Buñuel's shock moments are bearable because of the terseness in his handling of them. This terseness doesn't arise from a tactful timidity, since a timid director would never entertain such extraordinary ideas. It arises from Buñuel's acceptance of the atrocities as an integral, unsurprising part of existence. Something of this comes over even to the most conventional-minded spectator, who is all the more shocked to find he can bear such shocks. Buñuel's films are extremely insidious.

If everything is holy, nothing is sacred. And if everything is fascinating, it's because everything is ambivalent. Indeed, Buñuel's films are profoundly dialectical in that every character, every event, is not an assertion of any one point, but is a synthesis between opposing polarities. The use of drama as a model for human experience implies an extensively dialectical approach to life. Many an artist's intuitive feeling for these dialectics, whether Hegelian, Freudian, Marxist or moral, has been obscured by the academic devotion to Aristotelian logic. Every character, every plot-point is then an affirmation of either A-and-not-B or B-and-not-A, instead of charting the changing interrelationships of both A and B. One need only cite the debates as to whether Shakespeare means Henry V to be the hero or the villain of his history cycle. But either conclusion is interesting only since Shakespeare has radically criticized both sides, and the sophistication of his viewpoint lies in its uneasiness and ambivalence. Excessive simple-mindedness prevails if the spectator feels that because Don Jaime is ridiculous, he isn't tragic, or that, conversely, because the hero of *El* finishes in a tragic predicament, he isn't also funny. The play of contradictions in Buñuel's work is extremely sharp.

Aristotelian logic also underlies the common distortion of works of art by the attribution of excessively cut-and-dried symbolic meanings, although artists work by conglomerates of associations. Nowhere is this associative quality more apparent than in the Buñuelian motif of insects.

To kill or not to kill an insect is a decision which faces several characters. It is morally all the more indicative as the act involves no retaliatory consequence, because it is a matter of impulse rather than reflection, while from conventional viewpoints it has no moral significance. Thus the insect motif sometimes suggests a reverence for life. But this reverence is amused and sardonic, and has its markedly un-Schweitzerian aspects. The sudden death of an insect can also imply that a man can die as abruptly, and as unimportantly. Further, the cut-ins of insects, with the omnipresence of animals generally throughout Buñuel's films, jolts us by its reassertions of the ubiquity, the viability of alien modes of instinct on a planet which we ludicrously tend to think of as ours. Our planet is, also, a reticulation of other worlds. Meeting aliens from outer space is bagatelle, since the tortoise on the lawn is just as alien down here.

Conversely, the interaction between the human and insectoid levels make the latter a metaphor for the former, for the undercurrents of blind, impersonal, weird life-force in man. Buñuel's own remarks on his "entomological" interest in people strengthens one's impression that Buñuel characters who have lost their biological integrity as a result of tabus, repressions, and so on, to become mere units in the social ant-heap, often take on insect-like movements. The insect world is a metaphor for all that is tragically derisory in alienated man. A Kafka hero similarly finds himself slowly turning into a beetle. In contrast to Shakespeare's imagery, Buñuel's motifs are, as we shall see later, occasions for dissonances, contradictions, ambivalences, for a radically non-hierarchical view of the universe.

This sense of life's disorder explains, too, why Buñuel's films are often visually messy. His characters' rooms or surroundings are often littered with objects: tools, stores, objects of every kind. Formal pleasure is degraded by the impurity of things. The world around is non-symbolic; it is just what it is, a disorder from which man selects what he needs to live with, and whose selected objects also lie around in something of a mess. In *The Young One* and *Robinson Crusoe*, objects breathe an intense practicality, every room has an intense, lived-in quality: everything is fully itself, not a symbol for something nebulous, introverted or idealistic. Buñuel's is a very concrete world. At the same time, the lack of clear-cut formal organization gives the films something of a dream atmosphere. (Organic living is anyway none too neat.) Buñuel's preference for group-shots and long-shots (rather than intercutting close-ups) also helps to relate characters constantly to their background and to one another. In this context, a simple move into close-up has a lyrical effect (which helps explain why Buñuel's "moments" can blossom so rapidly). Throughout *Robinson Crusoe*, Buñuel maintains just the balance between order and disorder which gives full beauty to Crusoe's civilizing of his island, for his life is organic and creative as opposed to an extraneous routine.

The sensuous or sensual shocks in which Buñuel's films abound usually lie in the *idea* rather than in the photographic texture. His films dwell on the physical in a key-signature that's conspicuously absent from the bourgeois experience. Egg-yolks or milk are poured over thighs, a woman's back is stroked with a pigeon. The world is, physically, unprocessed, unhygienic, has a farmyard smell, is *obscene*.

Buñuel's untidiness compares interestingly with the work of another untidy director, Jean Renoir. Renoir's Heraclitean world, in which all passes, flows and is all the more precious, is also subversive and at times leads into Buñuel's. One thinks of Boudu with his goat, of the torture of the goose in Renoir's version of *Diary of a Chambermaid*, of the Walter Brennan character in *Swamp Water*. But Buñuel's harsher sense of the affinities and disjunctions between the human and the inhuman, between instinct and repression, is more grinding, and more conscious of the perverse. Renoir's generous sense of the flow of impulse, instinct and life is spontaneously lyrical, in contrast with Buñuel's wry, stoical affirmation that most of the time man hardly manages to be man at all.

So marked is Buñuel's lyrical reticence, and so often does his lyricism run at cross-purposes to conventional expectation, that Buñuel's films often disappoint the sophisticated spectator when he sees them for the first time. If he likes them it is because, as Jean-Luc Godard observed, a film doesn't have to be consistently exciting to please audiences. All it needs is a few bold ideas or moments which will hold up the duller parts. But even when initially they disappoint, Buñuel's films prove barbed. As one thinks about them afterwards, they haunt one uneasily until one returns to re-examine, to re-experience and then to grope for the answers to their perplexing questions, to seek clues in every line of dialogue. Then one realizes that every detail counts; the "shocking" moments fall into their context, flat moments reveal unsuspected tensions.

His films abound also in *argument*. But we may be misled by this word unless we remember that the logic of Buñuel's films is, of course, a dramatic logic. Its content may be moral and philosophical, but its form is dramatic. Fiction is so much a matter of particular people, particular circumstances, particular cases, that the relationship between the particular story and reality in general can never be logically established. Dramatic logic is suggestive rather than exclusive, divergent rather than convergent. It's not "this *must* follow from that" but "had you realized that these apparently distinct factors could be related?" The value of dramatic logic lies not in its irrefutability, but in the insights which it offers, and the lived experience of those insights. By sharing certain experiences with the screen characters, the spectator explores himself and others simultaneously. What he had cursorily dismissed now becomes not only a theoretical possibility but, in the fullest sense, comprehensible.

Like most artists, Buñuel uses not the "typical case" beloved of critical assumption but the significant case, which is often extreme or otherwise atypical. He does so for much the same reason that psychology has worked from the insane and the neurotic to the normal. His films move convincingly from the exceptional back to the ordinary, from the bizarre to the everyday, from the realistic to the climactic, in such a way as to illuminate the inextricability of each.

Our interest in Buñuel as a moralist could be understood as implying that his films are *films à thèse,* Euclidean theorems concocted to prove some moral generalization. But, in Buñuel's words: "It is absurd to pose a problem *a priori* and try to prove something in a film. It's not at all like a geometrical theorem or an algebraic equation. It's often said that my films are violent or destructive, and therefore immoral. Without wanting to defend my works on this particular point, I can tell you what my position is about morals in the cinema. I never place myself before a problem—say, charity, or virginity, or cruelty—and then organize my characters around it, while knowing all the answers in advance. To do so would seem like cheating." There is, of course, no contradiction between a refusal to preach and the fact that his characters face various issues, through the evolution of which Buñuel is able to express himself. The appearance of several issues in the course of one film, or even of one situation, prevents it from being a study *in vitro* of any one issue. Buñuel is expressing himself, not in the sense of issuing manifestos, but in the sense of sharing experiences with us. For him the cinema is never a pulpit, not even for erotic blasphemies: "If a work of art is clear, then my interest in it ends . . . Mystery is the essential element of every work of art. . . ."

The Films of Luis Buñuel

Tony Richardson

. . . .

The cinema's prophets are few and lonely; none more formidable than the Spaniard, Buñuel.

Luis Buñuel was born in 1900 at Calanda in Aragon, of well-to-do parents. He was educated at the University of Madrid as a scientist and became, for a time, assistant to the great neurologist Ramon y Cajal. Later he was sent by the Spanish Government to Paris as scientific attaché to the League of Nations. Apocryphally, his school-friend Garcia Lorca, the poet, was the first to turn Buñuel's interest away from the football field to the arts, but it was not until he became absorbed in the life of mid-'twenties Paris that this interest was to be fulfilled.

Artistically, Paris was then in the lively and muddy spate of surrealism. "La Revolution Surréaliste" was on the bookstalls; Ernst, Breton, Arp, Man Ray, Miró, Tanguy, di Chirico, Picasso and Salvador Dali were writing and exhibiting. Buñuel became friends with Dali, and by him was persuaded to collaborate in the making of a film, *Un Chien Andalou*. Surrealists such as Man Ray had already experimented with the possibilities of film, and the general artistic licence had enabled other artists, like Clair, to use surrealism for their own ends. But, in general, most of the avant-garde films of the time now seem tame and set, with the clichés of art tailored to theory. To see *Un Chien Andalou* in their context is to see first the conventionality of the theoretical approach that produced it, then, sharply, the force and passion of its makers.

Opening with a sensational sequence of a razor slicing a young girl's eye, "to shock the audience into free association," the film

From *Sight and Sound* (January–March 1954). Reprinted by permission of the author.

explores the relationship between violence and sexuality, and the consequences of the moral constraints of society. In their creation of an autonomous world, the makers claimed to reject any elements that could be fitted into any recognizable conscious pattern: inevitably, they did not succeed. Narrative lines tentatively emerge; symbolism (textbooks changing into pistols) is sometimes overt; the labored desire to outrage constantly obtrudes. The images of protest and revolt—a man trying to rape a girl is yoked to two *frères des écoles chrétiennes* and to two grand pianos on which are dead asses—now seem brashly naïve. Only in one scene, as a couple watch an accident in the street below, is there an indication of the later Buñuel, who was to use the freedom of surrealism to expose and penetrate reality.

Buñuel himself says that the collaboration with Dali was complete in this film: it is impossible to speculate on which elements are whose. The differences are to be found rather in the attitude to the various images than in particular contributions. M. Ado Kyrou, in his lively, militant *Le Surréalisme au Cinéma* comments on the piano sequence:

> Dali voit une image-scandale, une composition bien agencée, tandis que Buñuel voit une image-choc, une composition révendatrice. Pour Dali, qui a toujours prétendu n'accorder aucun intérêt à touté question sociale le scandale est un moyen de publicité; pour Buñuel, le scandale est un acte révolutionnaire.

Despite the credits, their collaboration was to end after only a few days' work on the script of their next project, *L'Age d'Or*. In this film Buñuel came of age.

II

By its first sequence, a brusque documentary account of scorpions, the film asks to be accepted as fact rather than as fiction. In style and subject this sequence symbolizes the theme of the film. Among the rocks where the scorpions are found are a band of cutthroat beggars, hideous, blind and maimed, planning to attack the descent of civilization on their territory in the form of robed and mitered bishops, consecrating the bitter crags. But, weak and exhausted, they die before they can reach the priests; and civilization, complete in top hats and frock coats, in cassocks and nuns' habits, has arrived to lay the foundation stone of a new city—imperial Rome. The mayor's official speech is interrupted by cries of violent lovemaking. Buñuel now introduces his main theme, the conflict of love with the moral and conventional pressures of society. The lovers are separated by force, but later meet at a fashionable music party where, after delay and subterfuge, they again begin to make love, only to be interrupted when an imperturbable butler calls Modot, the hero, to the telephone. The girl is left alone to satisfy her desire on the big toe of a statue in the garden. On the telephone, the president of Modot's country (he is a diplomat) accuses him, by neglect of his duties, of starting a revolution. Clouded by guilt, he returns to the girl; but he attracts her no longer and she leaves him for the old, flabby, bearded conductor of the orchestra. At the same time, the survivors of the debauch at de Sade's Château de Selliny leave the castle. Symbol both of what love has become and by whom it has become what it is, the old, poxed, gouty roués are led by Christ.

Surrealism is born out of despair; its only power is to hasten the general cataclysm by its own prophetic chaos. Max Ernst said of it, *"In turning topsy-turvy the appearances and relationships of reality, surrealism has been able, with a smile on its lips, to hasten the general crisis of consciousness which must perforce take place in our time."* No other work of the period expressed this so completely as *L'Age d'Or*. All civilization is oppression, suffering, frustration; above, the cynical emptiness and callous show of the rich; below, the misery, hunger and incipient revolution of the poor; individuals are ridden with inhibition, anxiety and guilt; beauty is, like Hans Schwitters' haphazard, delicate collages of tram tickets and paper money, the momentary chance of an afternoon's boredom—clouds pass in the mirror as the girl, restless and lonely, waits for Modot's arrival. Buñuel has taken a traditional romantic theme, love thwarted by circumstance, and seen it with "un œil à l'état sauvage," stripped of any sentimental associations; love is a fierce lust with clumsy embraces and frustrated satisfaction. The honesty of his attitude is explosive and cauterizing.

Yet it is not despair that finally pervades the film but a savage glee, almost optimistic in destruction. In a world where Marcel Schwob predicted "Le rire est probablement destiné à disparaître," surrealism answered disintegration with its own laughter. When Modot is deserted by the girl, he bundles out of a window, in fury, a burning plough, an enormous pine, a bishop, a toy giraffe. This same lusty and joyous iconoclasm gives unity to the film and binds the coda (which at first seems superfluous) to the main theme. It springs partly from a young man's desire to shock and outrage, partly from the ironic tradition of the picaresque; violence turned to joke. After a subtitle, "Parfois le dimanche," buildings explode and collapse; a tumbril is driven through a fashionable party; and a maid rushes in, faints, as flames leap out of a doorway behind her, while the guests unconcernedly chatter on. Surrealism gave Buñuel power to denounce but also, like Clair, freedom to romp.

But, though the props are still surrealist—the man with "patches" of living flies, the cow on the bed—and the general form loose and episodic, there are indications that Buñuel had exhausted the surrealist approach and had already begun to shape events into drama. Surrealism had become a technique for exposing and analyzing reality rather than a means of creating an independent world of fantasy. Its freedom had, too, as M. Kyrou points out, given him the means to introduce technical innovations, such as his use of the "monologue intérieure" and the brilliant sound montage, that were startling for his time. But he was to abandon surrealism completely in his next film, *Land Without Bread* (1932).

III

Land Without Bread is a documentary of the mountain district, Las Hurdes, in Northern Spain. Reality here surpasses the bitterest nightmares of surrealism. The land is barren and infertile; for two months the whole population live on nothing but unripe cherries; their bodies and necks are swollen with monstrous goiters; their crowded homes are bare, squalid, crumbling; children lie dead and abandoned in the gutters; there are idiots and morons everywhere; at night the crier tolls for those who have died of plague and typhus. Whatever slight alleviation there might be is destroyed by the peasants' ignorance and superstition. They are often bitten by vipers, whose bite is not mortal, but is made so by an herb they rub into the wound. Their miserable agriculture lacks tools and method, and effort is crippled by disease and apathy.

All this Buñuel records with a flatness and lack of comment that make it the more alarming. No moral is drawn, no response instructed, no easy attitude given. Buñuel is content, as was Goya in Los Desastres de la Guerra, to let the naked record speak for itself. In one sequence only, where bees attack a dying ass, is there any element of his old sensationalism. Though the material is organized with masterly skill, the very conception of "art" here seems irrelevant. It is the most profoundly disturbing film I have ever seen.

After *Land Without Bread*, Buñuel was brought to Hollywood at Chaplin's instigation, but none of the projects he worked on proved acceptable. He returned to Spain and produced a number of commercial films, and during the Civil War he was sent to the Republican Embassy in Paris. Afterwards, he went to America again, where he worked for some time at the Museum of Modern Art: he was asked to leave when it was discovered that he had made *L'Age d'Or*. Then he worked in Hollywood on the dubbing of Spanish films, until in 1947 he went to Mexico with a vague plan concerning a film version of Lorca's *La Casa de Bernarda Alba*. This fell through, but he made one commercial film before, in 1950, he directed what is perhaps his greatest work, *Los Olvidados*.

IV

In *L'Age d'Or*, Buñuel had begun to create dramatic action; in *Land Without Bread* he had approached reality directly; *Los Olvidados* was the fulfillment of both these developments. This intense dramatic vision sees the story of a group of delinquent boys living on the outskirts of Mexico City in the terms of Blake's "Innocence and Experience." Everyone in the film, so concentrated in its logic, is set at some place in that scale. At the one end is the pathetic Indian boy, Ochitos; at the other, the brutal, lecherous blind beggar and the cruel, embittered Jaibo, leader of the gang; between them is Pedro, the Innocent twisted and brutalized by Experience.

As in all Buñuel's films, the treatment is conceptual. The characters are simplified to whatever aspect or passion Buñuel is creating, and all irrelevant traits are suppressed. The unique force of the film comes from the combination of austerity and strictness in conception with a startling, often ironic, poetry of expression, with its images of donkeys, black hens, doves that can cure fever, cripples, torn meat, pariah dogs, in an almost timeless setting of arid squalor. The images underscore the logic. Pedro at first guards tenderly his pet hen with its brood of chickens; later, he savagely beats a pullet to death. The prophecies and thunderings of *L'Age d'Or* have become fact, the horrors actual, the vision immensely darkened.

All the characters have to struggle to scrape a living from the misery and poverty of their surroundings; Jaibo's gang batter a boy to death, drag a legless man from his cart, bait and stone the blind musician, who, in turn, bullies the patient Ochitos and tries to rape the young girl, Meche. They live in hate and fear of each other, their only contact savage, brutish matings, out of which the unwanted Pedros are born, and the city has new dangers and vices. Perhaps only Goya has created horror so acute. Buñuel's vision is too uncompromising to permit any softening of its bestiality; but—and one cannot say this emphatically enough, in view of what many critics have written—he never uses horror inartistically. There is no sensationalism in the handling of violence in this film; terror is balanced by pity, hopelessness by humanity. And throughout there is a strong, warm delight in any momentary respite from suffering—the little girl entranced on the carousel, Meche pathetically bathing her face in milk to soften her skin—and a pity that can encompass not only the helpless Ochitos but Pedro's selfish, callous mother. Toughened and dulled by the appalling savagery of her existence, she neglects

Pedro, is easily seduced by Jaibo, but, alone of Buñuel's characters, she is allowed a moment of consciousness. Compelled by the authorities, she goes to see Pedro in jail. He has become a vicious, desperate animal, love turned to resentment and hate. As she begins to reproach him, she understands suddenly her own responsibility for what he has become; impulsively she wants to comfort him, to ask forgiveness. Pedro shrinks from her. There is nothing to be done, nothing to be said. She turns and walks out of the room. If one defines tragedy as "the balance and reconciliation of discordant and opposite qualities," it is the word for *Los Olvidados*.

V

Those who can find only harshness and violence in Buñuel's work should see *Subida al Cielo* (1952), with which he followed two commercial films, *Susana* and *La Hija del Engaño*. Written by the Spanish poet Manuel Altolaguirre, and set in an Indian village in the Mexican jungle, this is a feckless poetic comedy, whose mixture of folklore and fantasy is similar to Lorca's *Don Perlimperlin*. The plot is simple: Oliverio, about to be married, has to break off the ceremony as his mother is dying; to respect her wishes, he must get her will ratified by a lawyer, and it is the two-day bus journey that this entails, with its adventures and delays, that forms the substance of the film. The bus is stranded in a storm; it gets stuck in a river; a woman has a premature delivery; the party stop at the driver's home to celebrate his birthday; and, besides these distractions, Oliverio is pursued by the local tart (splendidly incarnated by Lilia Prado). His mental conflicts are deliciously portrayed in a jaunty dream sequence in which, while his mother mounted on a pedestal unconcernedly knits, Oliverio dumps his wife in a river and is drawn along an immense umbilical cord to the tart, in a bus transformed to a lusciously romantic patch of jungle. Eventually, goaded as much by irritation as by desire, he sleeps with the girl, during a torrential storm, on the top of the mountain, Subida al Cielo. He returns to find his mother dead, but by pressing her thumbs onto the document he is able to secure the distribution of property she had wished.

In itself the idea for the film is contrived, and the characters— the chirpy cripple, the respectable, prim Spaniard, the opinionated politician—are stock types. But Buñuel has given it a wonderfully poetic cast. From the first moment when the lovers, in a flower-wreathed canoe, embark for their honeymoon island, the film is impregnated with a rich sensuousness. The births, the loves, the deaths of the people underlie the farcical comedy, the journey mirroring the rhythm of life. Towards the end of the film, there is an exquisite change of key from the noisy gaiety of the beginning. When the bus half sinks in the river, all efforts to extricate it with oxen and tractor fail, and the tractor itself flounders. While the passengers try to rescue it, the farmer's daughter, a wise, wide-eyed tot, casually leads the oxen and the bus out of the water. By the time the bus returns, she has died from a snakebite, and the whole party attend her funeral; this mood is sustained by the death of the mother; and Oliverio and his wife, matured by their grief, stand hand in hand gazing out over the dark sea.

Yet, if these deeper complexities inform the film, the prevailing mood is one of happiness. Buñuel parodies himself in the dream sequence; the cripple jokes about his peg-leg; and the descent of the American Tourists, the Shriners' Convention, self-consciously speaking bad Spanish to each other and doggedly trying to buy an *old* sombrero, is satirized gently and without malice. Buñuel himself has praised *The Treasure of Sierra Madre* for putting Mexico so truly on the screen. This may be true of the deserts and the bitter traditions of the hacienda, but the other Mexico of the tropics, with its rich fruitfulness and lazy Indians, has never been so spontaneously and so poetically caught as in this enchanting film.

Two more commercial films, which I have not seen, followed: *Una Mujer Sin Amor* and *El Bruto*. Buñuel describes them as uninteresting, though the stills of the latter, with black cockerels and seduction among the carcasses hanging in a butcher's shop, look characteristic, and a poster has the intriguing description "fascinatingly bestial."

VI

Buñuel's next film, *El* (1953), is a complete contrast in mood; uneasy, wintry, keen. The story of a paranoiac, it seems, in tone and in its upper-middle-class setting, a return to *L'Age d'Or*. El (Arturo de Cordova) falls in love with his friend's fiancée (Delia Garces) and violently pursues her. Half-fascinated, half-repelled, she agrees to marry him; after the wedding, he becomes jealous to the point of insanity over every trifle. She confides in her mother, her priest, her ex-fiancé, but they discount her stories; these confidences enrage him even more, and he attempts to kill her. She leaves him and he, after complete breakdown, enters a monastery.

Relentlessly Buñuel watches, as if it were a snake, the paranoia unwind its fascinating coils; he gloats in the incidental comedy of its writhings (as when Cordova jabs a knitting-needle into a key-hole through which he imagines someone to be spying). Sometimes, though, one feels that Buñuel himself twists the tail of the snake to produce fascinating wriggles for their own sake. This is accentuated by the inadequacy of the players, neither of whose personalities are interesting enough to encompass the range and subtlety of characterization demanded. But the failure lies deeper. The conventional, commonplace script has only been partly assimilated by Buñuel. The ruthlessness of his study of the paranoiac sits uneasily with the elements of comedy-of-situation in the script; it called, perhaps, for the hand of a Sturges. There are signs, too, of production difficulties and confusions in narration.

Buñuel's personality is most evident in the blasting anti-Catholicism of the film—a subject to which he always reacts in his grandest, most authoritative manner. The paranoiac is portrayed as deeply religious, and it is at a ceremony for the initiation of young priests, at which he is a lay official, that he first sees the girl. This magnificent sequence presents the heavy, oppressively ornamented setting, the strain on the blanched faces of the boys, the weary ritual of the bishop, and Cordova's desperate attempt to keep his attention on the solemnity of the occasion while, despite himself, it wanders on to the legs of the spectators. The climax of the film provides a further opportunity. Cordova, desperate and exhausted, has gone into a church; in a rapidly mounting cross-cutting sequence all the congregation, the altar boy, the priest himself, seem to him to be cat-calling, pulling faces, thumbing noses.

VII

The choice of *Robinson Crusoe* for Buñuel's next film would seem unpromising dramatically, temperamentally alien; Defoe's realism is humdrum and moralizing, while Buñuel's is charged and poetic. The film is as remarkable in its fidelity to Defoe as in its transmutation. After establishing the situation in a few sparse images, Buñuel follows Defoe's story-line, through Crusoe's working out of a way of life for himself, the descent of the cannibals, the rescue of Friday, the arrival of the mutineers, his outwitting of them and his final departure from the island. In style, too, Buñuel has matched Defoe's plain, direct prose; the simplicity of *Land Without Bread* is here used for an artistic purpose. Buñuel saw, as did Defoe, that Crusoe's struggle, often clumsy and inept, against conditions on the island, was fascinating on its practical, pedestrian level; he records, simply, the flat, absorbing routine of Crusoe's daily life.

Imaginatively Buñuel pierces further, looking into the heart of the man to see there the desolation and anguish of someone isolated from all human contact. Soon after his arrival, Crusoe gets drunk and imagines he hears the laughter and songs of his former companions. From an intimate close-up, the camera suddenly tracks back, as his head begins to clear, to reveal him alone in the great cave. The torment is above all sexual. Crusoe sees a woman's figure in a scare-crow momentarily billowing in a gust of wind. The sight of his dog dragging a woman's dress from a trunk inflames him with desire; determined to control himself, he rushes to a huge cliff to shout the 49th psalm. He breaks in the effort, sobbing "soul, soul, soul" in an agony that is close to insanity. This forms the climax to the first part of the film, built rhythmically from the contrast between the steady calm of Crusoe's everyday life and the passions that are lacerating him. (Both contrast and climax have now been weakened and practically destroyed by heavy front-office cutting.) From this point, Crusoe degenerates into a form of madness, subtly traced in all its gradations both by Buñuel and in Dan O'Herlihy's conscientious performance. Careless of his appearance, neglectful of his home and animals, he becomes a wayward, crazed old man, trotting along the shore under his huge goatskin umbrella, gibbering into his matted beard. Like all great dramatic poets, Buñuel has created out of a character motivated with strict psychological accuracy an immense and powerful symbol of our own times.

After the rescue of Friday, Crusoe, despite his longing for human companionship, can no longer adapt himself to another person. The first scenes between the two are gloriously funny. Crusoe's behavior is a mixture of pomposity, patronage—and fear. On the one hand, he tries to instruct Friday in the manners of his old bourgeois life (this has been brilliantly established in a dream sequence in which, while Crusoe is ill with fever, he sees his respectable old father, wearing an enormous red hat, warning him to be content with "the middle station in life," and not to go to sea). On the other hand, he lies awake at night with a gun in his hand watching for Friday, and finally in terror chains him. Only when he learns to trust Friday's affection does he return from his obsession and isolation to a new sanity. This is reflected poetically in the surface of normal life. At first the animals (always Buñuel's favorite images) had been of almost human significance to Crusoe; then they were ignored, kept for use alone; now the whole stockade becomes pastoral, abounding in bright macaws, parrots, playful coatis. Man and environment (the film was shot in the soft green jungle of Manzanillo, north of Acapulco, and the Technicolor has great delicacy) are in harmony. The film is rounded off by the excitingly handled sequence of the capture of the mutineers, and the moral is made explicit. It is a mature and beautiful work.

VIII

Most of the artists who have made the film expressive of their
unique personal visions have, at least, for a time, by fluke or
fashion, found some place within the framework of the industry.
It seems, somehow, fittingly ironic that Buñuel should have
found one in Mexico City, isolated within isolation, in an
industry pouring out its lush, Latin-American products and
helping by its prosperity to support a heartless, cosmopolitan
capital. To see Buñuel in any artistic context, one must look
beyond the cinema to the piercing, insolent seers of his own
nation, to Goya, El Greco, the Picasso of Guernica. Without
honor in his own country, he is a Spaniard first and last. How his
vision will alter is difficult to foresee. Perhaps, as with Goya or
the Mexican Orozco, it will become crueler, less supportable; but
in all his later films there are signs of a new resolution, a calmer,
though not less clear-eyed, wisdom. Pedro can at least turn on
Jaibo; Oliverio and his wife reach a truer understanding; Crusoe
returns to sanity and fellowship. It is not that Buñuel's view of
the world has changed—suffering, struggle, disease and pain are
as fierce as ever—but his belief in men seems greater; and, in that
belief, prophecy and revolt have given way to understanding and
acceptance.

IX

The moment when a myth is made flesh is always unimaginable.
I had heard the stories, of the terror in airplanes, the wild
drinking, the smashing of dishes he had cooked, in fury at the late
arrival of guests, the horror film shows organized at the Museum
of Modern Art. The setting of our first meeting, the offices of
Ultramar Films in Mexico City, could not have been more
different. They are at the end of the Avenida de la Reforma,
Maximilian's great boulevard. At the cinema next door, *El* had
just opened. Inside, in a large central office partitioned with open
desks and lined with pearl glass offices, hippy secretaries giggled

over a box of marshmallows, and thin young men with slickly
pressed suits and plastered hair joked in passing. The outer door
opened again and Buñuel came, or rather burst, in: loose jacket,
uncreased trousers, shaggy woollen open-necked shirt, middle
height, broad, muscular, a square and deeply lined face, huge
dark eyes. He was sorry he was late, he could only stay a moment.
"Je m'excuse, on est en grève au studios depuis six semaines
. . . there is a strike, perhaps you have heard, I am . . . I do
not know how to say it . . . *je suis en piquet de grève."*
We had only talked a few moments, but my image was already
firm and strong; of an immense authority, too sure of itself to
need the backing of formality; of a deep austerity and endurance
that in no way braked immediate warmth and spontaneous
response. This contradiction, the suggestion of a capacity both for
riot and for discipline, was the most emphatic of my impressions.
Later we met and talked. Though he was out of practice,
Buñuel speaks English well, only occasionally pausing for a word
or falling back on its French equivalent. I plunged straight into
the collaboration with Dali. It was like a fuse to hidden dynamite.
". . . In *Chien Andalou*, yes, we worked together, we were one.
But *L'Age d'Or*, that was my film." He went to the South of
France to work with Dali on the script, but after three days Dali,
already under the influence of the church, found collaboration
impossible.
We went on to talk about his other films: *Los Olvidados* was a
sore point in Mexico. "Many people here did not like it, they say
it is bad for Mexico, not the Mexico we want to show the world.
Some people even wrote to the papers saying that I should be
deported." Now, however, he was a Mexican citizen. It was still
very difficult to find producers to make the films he wanted. I
asked him about the other films he had made in Mexico—"not
interesting, commercial"—and mentioned *Subida al Cielo*. Instantly his eyes flamed, "Yes it *is* a nice film. I liked making that
. . . very simple, very static . . . nothing happens in it, nothing at all; no progression, but a nice film."
He asked if I had seen any other Mexican films. They were "not
interesting . . . slow, heavy, Hollywood—are you going to
that dream place?—undramatic." We talked of other directors; of

John Huston, whose *Maltese Falcon* and *Treasure of Sierra Madre* he liked; of de Sica: "Yes, I liked *Bicycle Thieves*, but even that, is it not a bit . . . a bit literary as it sees the world?" He had not heard of Max Ophuls. He had just been to see *Limelight* and asked me what I thought of it. I told him how much I disliked it and he agreed. "It is self-pitying, sentimental! That is what I have all my life wanted to attack, to fight, sentimentality, the values of the bourgeois . . . There is only one man I have ever admired . . . that is Fabre, the man who wrote about ants. You see, I would rather watch a snake than a bourgeois or a Hollywood producer."

We talked of many other things: of Mexico and my reactions to it, of his visits to London, of John Grierson, of his future plans, which include a film in France ("it is easier to make real films there"), of his present chore, and of *Robinson Crusoe*. Again his voice rumbled, his eyes glowed. "That was a film I really wanted to make. You must see that. There's nothing Hollywood about it. I start with Crusoe on the island—no ship or wreck—I have him alone for seven reels, then with Friday for three, and then the pirates just at the end as it is in the book. I just watch Robinson build his house, make pots, grow wheat . . . yes. I made it about his struggle with nature . . . and about solitude . . . and despair."

Buñuel and the Picaresque Novel

Carlos Rebolledo

. . . .

During the nineteenth century, most of Spanish literature was dominated by the naturalists, whose conscious aim it was, in the words of Pardo Bazin, "to mirror reality exactly as it is." In practice, however, most of these works reflected only the image of a frozen society, which evidently considered itself immortal. Even as the artist criticized certain aspects and details of this society, he was required to conform to a general mood of acceptance and approbation. To anyone at all familiar with Spanish naturalism, the quality that stands out immediately is a certain air of permanency in the social portrait. What emerges is a mode of realism that confuses a specific social reality with human nature as a whole; and this tendency, in turn, produces a literature devoid of depth and universality—a horizontal art, so to speak, whose descriptive content can be reduced to "landscapes and customs: the generic, immortal soul of Spain." Small wonder that Emile Zola was astonished when he learned that Pardo Bazin was a Catholic.

Luis Buñuel was born just as these ideas were beginning to crumble under a new generation of writers, the Generation of 1898. The old concepts, of course, did not die right away; they were still very much in vogue until 1920, when the followers of the Generation of 1898 began to emerge. This movement centered largely on a group of writers in residence at the University of Madrid—Alberti, Gomez de la Serna, Federico Garcia Lorca—with whom Buñuel was intimately associated. Under their influence, Buñuel, in *Un Chien Andalou*, indulged in a kind of free association against the traditions and intellectual background of the Spanish naturalism from which he came.

The venomous quality of Buñuel's first works owes as much,

From *Luis Buñuel* by Carlos Rebolledo. (Paris: Editions Universitaires, 1964). Reprinted by permission of the publisher. Translated by Sallie Iannotti.

no doubt, to the current social and political climate in Spain as to the tenets of Surrealism. For the atmosphere of moral and religious repression was reinforced by the menacing pressures the middle class had brought to bear upon the monarchy. Buñuel, then, was participating in a critical revolutionary movement which denounced the literary and social values of the nineteenth century and sought inspiration from the more distant past, the poets of the seventeenth century, from Quevedo, Gongora, and the picaresque novel. This tradition seems to have had a singular effect upon Buñuel, and I would like now to explore the picaresque theme in his work.

Before coming to Paris in 1925, Buñuel had studied under several faculties in the University of Madrid. A series of intellectual experiences, in science, literature, and philosophy, had put him in contact with a number of young poets, painters, and writers of his own age. The generation before them had sought a new definition of the Spanish character, as found, for example, in the works of Unamuno, and this had had the effect of liberating the arts from the so-called portraitism of the nineteenth century. The primary question which this generation asked itself was: What is Spain?—a question in itself reflecting an underlying reality to be explored. The loss of the last American colonies had destroyed Spain's prestige as a great empire, yet she continued to dwell bathed in this myth of the past.

At that moment, the arts in Spain reflected quite clearly the self-sufficiency that marks a decaying society. The last generation of the nineteenth century sought to rouse the country from its torpor and fix attention upon the cultural changes in Europe, which their predecessors had neglected. These artists, then, tended, on the one hand, to give a new meaning to the Spanish national character, and, on the other, to incorporate this search with recent developments in European art. Unamuno wrote: "Spain must be rediscovered. And the only ones who can rediscover her are Europeanized Spaniards." Though it was never openly expressed, the attitude of these writers reflects a profound malaise that cast a shadow upon the very moral and material foundations of the decrepit Regency society.

Buñuel's generation took up and enlarged these themes. For the little group in residence at the University, however, it was no longer merely a question of discovering the specific national character of their country, but of denouncing the establishment and opening themselves deliberately to the currents and movements from Europe. The beginning of *L'Age d'Or*, a series of shots of scorpions, contains a prologue in which Buñuel mocks and parodies the naturalists' affections, while seeming at the same time to give them a little nod of acknowledgment—homage by the very act of demonstration. A close look, however, reveals in this little prologue an echo of the dedicatory passage that the picaresque writer habitually addressed to his patrons and readers, a declaration that not infrequently surpassed the work itself in insolence and sarcasm. The prologue to *Don Quixote* is a famous example of this. Other passages, from the works of Quevedo, who is less well-known outside of Spain than Cervantes, contain subtle and vicious attacks upon his mentors and his public. "I only ask," he writes in the dedication to *Matrimonial Capitulations*, "that the benevolent reader look about him and mark what has come to pass today in the court. Then, and only then, in the light of this one task it has been my lot to perform, I may obtain some small credit among those of an inquisitive and curious nature."

Indeed, the polemical and violent character of *L'Age d'Or* is reminiscent of Quevedo in many ways. And in later films, Buñuel seems to have come progressively more under the influence of the picaresque novel, a process that can be traced through such works as *Los Olvidados*, *(The Young and the Damned)*, *El (This Strange Passion)*, and *Ensayo de un crimen (The Criminal Life of Archibaldo de La Cruz)*. For this reason, it is important to examine closely the relationship between Buñuel and the picaresque tradition.

Without any doubt, the most important change brought about by the picaresque novel was the fall of the epic hero. From antiquity to the Middle Ages, the concept of the hero reflected an extension of a human model, an ideal anchored in the imagination of the people and in a very concrete social aim. The hero embodied a human force favored by the gods, as in Homer, or an intermediary between the gods and mankind. In its major theme, this concept changed hardly at all in the centuries between those two epochs in history, encompassing as it did the idea of the exceptional.

All that man might be or should be able to accomplish in his life on earth resided in the portrait of the epic superman. At the beginning of the sixteenth century, the arts in Europe were all dominated by the heroes of ancient literature and the heroes of the *reconquista*—Achilles, Ulysses, Aeneas, and Roland, Siegfried, and El Cid, the last three coming directly from the *chansons de gestes,* which swept through Europe around the ninth century. No works, in that era, ran counter to the epic style, and not until 1557 did the first rogue, the first antihero, make his appearance in Quevedo's *Lazarillo de Tormes.* After this little novel came out, the rogue and vagabond developed rapidly and reached his peak between the end of the sixteenth and the middle of the seventeenth centuries.

The process which led to the emergence of the picaresque novel is founded upon the concept of contradiction. The new character is the deliberate negation of his traditional epic counterpart, as much in his global and cosmic personality as in the details of his adventures. Buñuel based the majority of his characters upon this formula. In *L'Age d'Or,* for example, Gaston Modot, pledged to a mission of good works and social reform, abandons his duty for Lya Lys in a classical reversal of theme. Virtue and duty are violently rejected, and thus the antihero, who refutes the ideal absolutely, assumes qualities and attributes diametrically opposite to those of the epic ideal. Not a single moral idea intervenes in Modot's relationship with the material world.

This is equally true of numerous other characters in Buñuel's films. They are endowed solely with concrete worldly desires and needs, be it the need for food in *Los Olvidados,* or the murderous and destructive urges in *Archibaldo.* Violence and the very real character of the need and stimulus in each of these films implicate a conventional society that has lost touch with humanity. Nazarin, a compensatory figure, is very like Don Quixote, defending and upholding a dead ideology. In this film, the exterior world holds the power to determine the quality of experience, while the hero is guided only by a dim mythological idea.*

Some of Buñuel's other characters, who come from a more conventional tradition, enter the picaresque obliquely, through the demands of material need. This is certainly the case with Francisco (in *El*) whose social and moral presumptions crumble under his growing lust and jealousy. As he is progressively engulfed by the single obsession to possess the woman he wants, his social life disintegrates rapidly. Lazaro, in Quevedo's novel, undergoes the same descent into moral debasement. In the second adventure, Lazaro becomes obsessed by the cask where the curé has hidden his provisions; he cannot rest until he discovers a way to satisfy his appetites. And Francisco, to get and then to keep his wife, Gloria, uses the same tricks and roguery. This character, initially so full of reserve and moral prejudice, becomes a seducer and a braggart, taking pleasure in exaggerating his riches and social position before Gloria in just the way the traditional *pícaro*, or rogue, enjoys expounding interminably on his fabulous goods and exploits to anyone who will listen.

As a final stroke, Buñuel's Francisco retreats into the church and becomes a monk to save himself from the violence of his obsession, just as Lazaro, at the end of Part II of *Lazarillo de Tormes,* retires to the church after his numerous escapades to finish out his life in a sort of moral and physical sanctuary. The great difference between them is that the true rogue of literature never hides from the triviality of his actions, never cloaks them with an idealization of any kind, but accepts them for what they are. Francisco, on the other hand, cannot extricate himself from his original ideology. In fact he uses it endlessly to try to justify himself.

The picaresque work can be recognized above all by its thematic attributes. We shall examine these themes now, and look for their counterparts in Buñuel's work.

Cruelty: The rogue first and foremost is a creature of individualistic action who accepts completely the violence inherent in

*In order to determine the precise connections between Cervantes's novel and *Nazarin*, see: Georg Lukács, *The Theory of the Novel* (M.I.T. Press, 1971), Part II, Chapter 1.

his acts. Yet at the same time, this quality is not a principle of life for him, for he has no opinions or principles. He simply makes it clear that violence exists in human relationships. Like everyone else, he serves his own interests; and this condition, based implicitly upon force, engenders the cruelty which dominates picaresque art.

The cruelty in this type of novel is linked to a particular form of humor, characteristic of Spain, that gives to events the affective value exactly opposite to what is actually expected. Another of the traits of the picaresque is to exaggerate the more harmless and inane vicissitudes in the course of the narrative, while underplaying episodes of a far greater impact. The cruelest events, the most violent, are thus forced into a singular relief by the very attitude the rogue adopts toward them. In *L'Age d'Or* Buñuel, faithful to this tradition, shows us Modot savagely kicking a blind man in the stomach. In *Lazarillo de Tormes*, Lazaro conceives a supreme revenge for all the ragging his blind master has subjected him to; he convinces his foe that at the end of a certain path there is a little brook to cross. He is lying, of course, and instead of a brook there are several wooden stakes and columns. Lazaro pretends to jump the brook and waits hidden behind the columns, while the blind man takes off in a great leap and cracks his skull upon the posts. "His head made a sound like a calabash," and he collapses half-dead. In the picaresque novel the blind are portrayed as miserly, a characteristic which provokes a certain kind of conflict. Lazaro makes a hole in his master's wine keg and secretly drinks his wine. The blind man discovers the theft and plots his revenge, waiting to catch Lazaro in the act. The blind man in *Los Olvidados*, robbed by Jaibo, waits in the same way for the incident to recur. And when the children try to steal his satchel, he makes a great public outcry and beats them with his stick.

Sometimes picaresque cruelty is tinged with a bitter irony, as in the second part of *Lazarillo de Tormes*. After vainly trying to escape from his tormentors, Lazaro falls, swooning, into a barrel; and his masters, believing him to be dead, truss him up in a sack which they load onto a donkey, intending to throw him into the river with the garbage. And in *Los Olvidados* Pedro's body is thrown over the donkey's back and he is tossed into the refuse pit. It is a powerful scene, difficult to forget. And yet it is also unlike *Lazarillo*, for here Pedro is really dead.

Lazaro is not only victimized by his blind master, the curé, and the merchants; he is also the victim of other children, who, seeing his plight, attack him and beat him in a manner recalling the cruelty of the children toward Ujo in *Nazarin*.

Most often this picaresque cruelty is brought to light in the actions of the characters; sometimes, however, it is unmasked by simple description. In *The Life of Don Gregorio de Guadanas,* by Antonio Enrique Gomez, the protagonist describes his parents. "They never ate together," he says, "because my father loathed the sight of my mother's hands, and she the sight of his eyes, which had seen the rooms and lodgings of the sick." This passage calls to mind the dark humor which Buñuel demonstrates in *La Joven (The Young One)*—the humanist priest seized with horror at the idea of sleeping in a black man's bed.

Motherhood: Lazaro's father is dead, and "his mother, with no husband to support her, had to take in wash for the stablemen. There she made the acquaintance of a swarthy dark-skinned man who worked with the others in the barn. Occasionally, coming to her door under the pretext of gathering eggs, he would come into the house." A little while after this she gives birth to a Negro baby. This is exactly what happens to Pedro's mother in *Los Olvidados.* Jaibo, the leader of the gang, comes one day to Pedro's house to look for him, and ends by sleeping with Pedro's mother. Buñuel thus shatters the myth of Woman saved and purified by maternity, and shows us the son locked in savage dependence upon the mother. This reflects a fundamental emasculation that resulted from the matriarchal basis of Spanish society. So, too, the behavior of Francisco, Archibaldo, and especially Don Jaime in *Viridiana,* is motivated by this kind of impotence.

Buñuel blames the cult of motherhood, the untouchable woman, and the projection of this archetype into adult sexual relationships for the inextricable conflicts that end in death, in suicide, or in sadistic murder for his characters. Behind this preoccupation, of course, lies the Catholic Church and its morality, which the picaresque writers denounced as fiercely as Buñuel. They sought to resolve the conflict by presenting its mythological content, and by bringing this repressed material into the conscious grasp of the masses, who no doubt engendered both the myth and the situations to which it gave rise. This is why the description of childhood takes on such enormous significance in the picaresque. In some works, the image of birth-trauma appears, dominating, for example, all the adventures of Don Gregorio de Guadanas: "Hardly was I out into the world before I tried to re-enter my mother's womb; who could have known that after nine months of imprisonment I would be let loose in a place even darker, more obscure?" And later, he says, "I began to shed the robes of life and light and clothe myself in the winding cloths of Death." All Don Gregorio's adventures are colored by this dependence upon his mother. Because of it, his contacts with women are, at first, extremely painful; they transform him into a foolish little Don Juan, a role that springs up in reaction to the opposite state of celibacy. Nor is it an accident that Lazaro experiences his first sensuous joy, after years of suffering, in a hermitage where the dying hermit leaves him his coffers filled with fabrics and cloths, and in one corner, a woman's skirts.

The blind and diseased: In *Lazarillo de Tormes,* the blind man "had a thousand ways of collecting money. He claimed to know spells and prayers for all occasions: for women who were barren, for women about to give birth, for women in all stages of pregnancy. On the subject of medicine, he declared that Galen had nothing to beat his treatment for toothache, for dropsy, fainting fits, and feminine maladies." For the first time in western literature of the Middle Ages and the Renaissance, we see the de-Christianization of the blind and diseased. Before the picaresque writers, these characters represented the model of Christian virtue and human suffering; they symbolized and prolonged the character of Christ, who suffered and died for the world. By the intervention of these sufferers, men could exercise charity and raise themselves above their ordinary human condition into the realm of mystical communion. The picaresque, however, shows that charity transforms its recipients into veritable monsters, who, falling even lower than the rogue himself, bring crisis and calamity to those about them.

We find this kind of person in *Viridiana* as well as in *Los Olvidados* and *L'Age d'Or*. And in this film the role is extended until it fills the screen with its horror and its significance. Viridiana, obsessed by charity which she can no longer practice in private, makes the beggars who come to her door into the objects of a cult. The presence of Christ is replaced by that of these miserable wretches; and the professional beggars (for in Spain begging is a vocation like any other) who habitually have to scuffle for survival, find themselves abruptly elevated into the ranks of the demi-gods. Buñuel thus unveils the origin of one of the aspects of Christian faith. But though the beggars become Christ and His disciples at the banquet, they are dispossessed of their natural, worldly life and of their social function. Viridiana makes martyrs of them, and in her turn, she becomes their victim; the sacred "last" supper is transformed into an orgy, and the characters recover their human status.

The traditional theme of the blind, the halt, and the monstrous passes, then, directly into the picaresque stream of Buñuel's work. In both cases these characters embody the rejection of a traditional moral that has outlived its time.

Hunger: Throughout all picaresque works we find hunger as a motivating force; whether in burlesque or tragedy, it is a phantasm which leads the rogue to his downfall and forms a significant part of each of his actions. The classical hero of the Greeks felt the weight of the malediction of the gods; the knight followed the vision of his lady and the hope of glorious deeds. The *pícaro* throws himself into one complicated adventure after another because he feels the rising imperatives of his starving belly.

In Buñuel's films, this theme has lost much of its vital quality; it is seldom the inescapable stimulus it was, yet it remains as an emblem in his work as a whole. The Hurdanos (in *Las Hurdes, Land Without Bread*) are motivated completely by the need for nourishment; and in *Los Olvidados*, hunger is the permanent driving force for all the characters. Pedro's dream is a concrete symbol of this primal urge, mixed though it might be with all the other drives and desires—particularly sex. In Buñuel, desire is a totality. All desires are one—the desire to survive, to reproduce, to create. And hunger, in these films, becomes a peg, a hook, upon which Buñuel hangs an apology for all the urges and needs of humanity, a society crippled and inhibited by myth. Yet it is in man himself that the sole possibility of liberation and fulfillment resides.

The picaresque novel was a popular novel, written for the entertainment of the ordinary reader. To this end, then, the episodes were as varied as possible; they followed one another without the elegant continuities of time and space, without causal reference or dramatic support. Written in the autobiographical mode, or in the form of oral reminiscence, it rested simply upon evidence, upon witness.

Perhaps by assimilation of this type of literature, Buñuel adopts most often a similarly simple style. In almost all his post-war films he presents, in a form which is exclusively suggestive, the adventures of a fictional, that is, a novelistic, hero confronted by a conventional society. As in the stories of the *pícaro*, Buñuel's adventurers rarely reach the level of the unique, and their exploits stretch out at times almost interminably.

Even though his first two films, which are really manifestos, adopt a less commercial form, and a form somewhat more constructed, we find in them once again the principal characteristics of the picaresque story: absence of dramatic causality, disregard of traditional space-time, and even the titles of different "chapters" which is the trademark of the picaresque.

This very fidelity to a past tradition, at least in so far as it dominates the work, makes Buñuel's vision lose the contemporary quality that was so valuable to the picaresque novel in its own period. By too many references to other arts, and to past epochs, the cinema of Buñuel sometimes slips from its specific domain. A part of its efficacy and its clarity is inevitably lost.

IV

The Films

. . . .

Notes on the Making of
Un Chien Andalou

Luis Buñuel

. . . .

Historically, this film represents a violent reaction against what was at that time called "avantgarde cine," which was directed exclusively to the artistic sensibility and to the reason of the spectator, with its play of light and shadow, its photographic effects, its preoccupation with rhythmic montage and technical research, and at times in the direction of the display of a perfectly conventional and reasonable mood. To this avantgarde cinema group belonged Ruttmann, Cavalcanti, Man Ray, Dziga Vertoff, Rene Clair, Dulac, Ivens, etc.

In *Un Chien Andalou*, the cinema maker takes his place for the first time on a purely POETICAL-MORAL plane. (Take MORAL in the sense of what governs dreams or parasympathetic compulsions.) In the working out of the plot every idea of a rational, esthetic or other preoccupation with technical matters was rejected as irrelevant. The result is a film deliberately anti-plastic, anti-artistic, considered by traditional canons. The plot is the result of a CONSCIOUS *psychic automatism,* and, to that extent, it does not attempt to recount a dream, although it profits by a mechanism analogous to that of dreams.

The sources from which the film draws inspiration are those of poetry, freed from the ballast of reason and tradition. Its aim is to provoke in the spectator instinctive reactions of attraction and of repulsion. (Experience has demonstrated that this objective was fully attained.)

Un Chien Andalou would not have existed if the movement

From *Art in Cinema,* edited by Frank Stauffacher (San Francisco Museum of Art, 1947; reprinted by Arno Press, Inc., 1968). Translated by Grace L. McCann Morley.

This film has no intention of attracting nor pleasing the spectator; indeed, on the contrary, it attacks him, to the degree that he belongs to a society with which surrealism is at war. (*Un Chien Andalou*)

called surrealist had not existed. For its "ideology," its psychic motivation and the systematic use of the poetic image as an arm to overthrow accepted notions corresponds to the characteristics of all authentically surrealist work. This film has no intention of attracting nor pleasing the spectator; indeed, on the contrary, it attacks him, to the degree that he belongs to a society with which surrealism is at war.

The title of the film is not arbitrary, or the product of a joke. It possesses a close subconscious relation with the theme. Among hundreds of others this title was chosen because it was the most adequate. As a curious note, it can be added here that it actually produced obsessions in certain spectators, a thing which would not have occurred had the title been arbitrary.

The producer-director of the film, Buñuel, wrote the scenario in collaboration with the painter Dali. For it, both took their point of view from a dream image, which, in its turn, probed others by the same process until the whole took form as a continuity. It should be noted that when an image or idea appeared the collaborators discarded it immediately if it was derived from remembrance, or from their cultural pattern or if, simply, it had a conscious association with another earlier idea. They accepted only those representations as valid which, though they moved them profoundly, had no possible explanation. Naturally, they dispensed with the restraints of customary morality and of reason. The motivation of the images was, or meant to be, purely irrational! They are as mysterious and inexplicable to the two collaborators as to the spectator. NOTHING, in the film, SYMBOLIZES ANYTHING. The only method of investigation of the symbols would be, perhaps, psychoanalysis.

L'Age d'Or

Ado Kyrou

. . . .

With *L'Age d'Or*, Luis Buñuel, surrealist, began a new era of film making. Actually, despite the reservations mentioned earlier, *Un Chien Andalou*, too, had been revolutionary.

On the eve of the talking picture, the break between popular cinema and the art film was already complete. The aesthetes (I use the word in its pejorative sense, although a certain aesthetic standard is always necessary) had carried the day in France. They had succeeded in making the abstract prevail.

Ballets of every kind were the rage: ballets of gypsy fairs, ballets with cubist décors, ballets about casseroles, and so on. Lights, kitchen utensils, etc., reigned supreme. The aesthetic film had banished the gag, and the colander had supplanted man. The redoubtable impressionists, or, better still, *avant-gardists* (they well deserve the military term), were working at turning the cinema into a field of maneuvers from which man was definitely excluded. Man Ray and a few Dadaists went to such maniacal extremes that they were defeated by their own excesses. A return to emotion was needed to keep the cinema from sinking into the mire in which so-called modern painting and music—as some conceive modern—find themselves at present.

Buñuel (or surrealism) is a pivot about which the cinema can veer toward genuinely felt emotion. Such a trend began with *Un Chien Andalou* and took definite form with *L'Age d'Or*.

Until 1928 the film had dealt with both reality and the dream. But it was a hobbling kind of reality because the film makers forgot to include in it certain essential elements such as imagination, and the dream was even more distorted because they forgot that it has no vigor or value unless it is rooted in reality.

From *Buñuel: An Introduction* by Ado Kyrou (New York: Simon & Schuster, 1953). Reprinted by permission of Georges Borchardt, Inc.

For Buñuel, dream is not necessarily Freudian; it is no longer set apart from the day-to-day; dream *is*. In a word, it is a matter of realism, of reality that contains surrealism just as surrealism contains reality. The images in *L'Age d'Or* are an exact reproduction of what the eye, rinsed clear of the film of habit, can behold. After di Chirico, Max Ernst, and a few other painters, Buñuel, by means of the cinema—richer than painting because it is at one and the same time movement, association, detail, and ensemble—gives us back the "savage eye" of which Breton speaks in *Le Surréalisme et la Peinture*.

With his second film Buñuel achieved perfection in free cinematic expression. Initially it was called *La Bête Andalouse* and was conceived as a sequel to *Un Chien Andalou*. In fact, Buñuel and Dali had decided to do a second film based on the gags they had not used in *Un Chien Andalou*.

Buñuel went to Spain to work with Dali, but they had only one joint work session. The two men had already grown apart. Buñuel did not recognize his friend. *L'Age d'Or* is a film by Buñuel *without* Dali, and if the latter's name still appears among the credits, it is thanks to the courtesy of Buñuel. He used only one of Dali's gags in the picture—the gentleman strolling with a stone on his head.

Dali himself wrote, in *The Secret Life of Salvador Dali:* "My idea was that the film should express the violence of the love that is impregnated by the splendid creations of Catholic myths. . . . Buñuel was filming *L'Age d'Or* alone, and I was virtually cut off. . . . Buñuel had just finished *L'Age d'Or*. I was frightfully disappointed. The film was only a caricature of my ideas. Catholicism was attacked in a primitive, quite unpoetic way. . . ."

Let us, then, forget Dali and get back to Buñuel's film.

A documentary-like opening announces that the film is an account of fact, a reportage, rather than a fictionalized story or a work of the imagination. The first subtitle reads: "The scorpion belongs to the branch of the spider family that generally lives under stones."

The insipid music that accompanies this prologue underlines

the absolute surrealism of what people like to call a "slice of life."
In the same region, and as real as the scorpions, live a band of
wretched, grotesque, horrible ruffians, the last survivors of a
vanished age. Armed with rusty swords, pitchforks, and stout
pieces of wood, these exhausted, moribund creatures draw on
their last ounce of courage as they wait to do battle with the
Majorcans. The Majorcans land after sending some archbishops
as a vanguard. Victorious without having had to fight, they found
Imperial Rome on this earth—the same earth that eventually
absorbs the corpses of its former occupants.

While the governor officially lays the first stone of the new age,
Buñuel's major theme bursts upon us: an admirable and unique
call to love. Disregarding the ceremony, "a man and woman in
fiercely lascivious embrace roll in the mud." Their mating cries
drown out the governor's inaugural address. Throughout the rest
of the film this intense love tears the prejudices, inhibitions, and
laws of society to shreds. The passage from love to revolt is
accomplished without harm to the lovers, however, for love is in
itself revolt and kills only its enemies—those who harass love and
deny life, the jackals of worldly wisdom who turn the left cheek.
There are two camps: the lovers and the others. The very structure
of a putrifying society makes it inevitable that they stand opposed. Society, outraged and terrified by love, with the dagger
thrust deep in its side, mobilizes all its poison-spewing forces—its
high functionaries, its priests, its families, its big words, its
police, its sophisticates. The lovers, torn apart as one separates
dogs in the street, each dragged to his daily dungeon, will not be
separated. Their love, their hatred, form chains that are inde-
structible.

Un Chien Andalou is, with the exception of a few sequences,
little more than filmed poetry. *L'Age d'Or*, is a film— a film that
has assimilated all cinematic tradition and speaks the true language of the film. By this time, the cinema had opened increasingly wide and deep vistas. The grammar of cinematography had
been established by Griffith, Ince, Eisenstein, and a few others.
Now Buñuel forgot all the rules and created a great cinematic
evocation of mad love. To do so, he needed to devise an infinitely
richer language than any hitherto available. Furthermore, he

scorned the technical strait jacket that hampered so many directors. He became, in brief, an innovator on every level.

His great subject demanded that all boundaries be abolished, in order to express fully the two most magnetic words in any language: love and revolt. The cinematic revolution was total. Since then, the film has been able to express everything. *L'Age d'Or* revealed it to itself.

Until *L'Age d'Or*, movie makers had not made use of repetition to hyphenate diverse themes. With Buñuel, these repeated images are so many leitmotivs that maintain the unity of dream and reality. Thus a woman's hair becomes a link between a poster that Gaston Modot sees in a hairdresser's window and Lya Lys stretched out on a divan. In the screenplay, Buñuel underlines this sequence, saying that it "must give a coincidental reality to the image the suspect has of her and reveal what, in fact, the young girl was feeling or doing at the moment the character was looking at her."

Another image that returns often is that of fingers in motion—for example, at various times the ring finger trembles on some object. "The effect of this nervous movement will be extremely disturbing since its significance is clearly masturbatory," he wrote in the shooting script. A hand on a poster, the father's hand on a bottle of iodine, the hand of the valet wiping a bottle, and, especially, the ringed finger of Lya Lys—all these images form a bond between imagination and everyday actions. Similarly, erotic desire is always expressed in the same way, i.e., teeth biting the lower lip. These details may pass unnoticed, but they are needed because they help create an atmosphere of total life.

The most perfect example of the meeting of cinema and surrealism is the mirror sequence, which I think is the most magnificently poetic sequence in the history of the film. When Lya Lys enters her bedroom and finds a cow on her bed, the animal's bell becomes the predominant sound, a sound which persists even after the cow disappears. In the next frame, we find Gaston Modot with the police, but the sound of the bell still persists, with the barking of dogs superimposed on it. As soon as we return to Lya Lys, who is leaning over her mirror, which reflects a sky with drifting clouds, the dual sound of bell and barking is enriched by the sound of the wind. This triple sound accompanies the lovers during the entire sequence, although they are miles apart. The two sounds—bell and barking—inform the spectator immediately that he is witnessing the union of two people whom distance does not separate. The wind hails the triumph of their union.

Let us not forget that *L'Age d'Or* is one of the first talking films, and that its sound effects have no technical function: they *are* the film. No one notices the "technique" of *L'Age d'Or*, which is one more argument in favor of the film's great value; it has so assimilated its own techniques as to make that technique, perfect as it is, disappear completely in the final result.

Dozens of articles have been written on the device of the interior monologues. In *L'Age d'Or*, the interior monologue, used in films for the first time, is not a trick but a primary element expressing the latent content of life.

The two lovers, revealed to themselves by love, desperately defend their union by declaring war on society, their weapons being indifference, scorn, and hatred. A man blinded in the war who might delay their meeting by so much as a moment is an enemy; an old woman, especially if she is the mother of the young girl, is slapped when her chatter separates the lovers. Love knows no *savoir-vivre* because it *is* life, and it slaps and kicks and precipitates catastrophes which lead society toward its total and desirable destruction.

But personal difficulties arise to threaten the couple, and thus we reach the noteworthy love-torture sequence in the park. Under the influence of the place, which is hostile, inhibitions, snap judgments, atavisms raise their ghostly heads. It is then that the interior monologue (or, rather, dialogue) takes place. Lya Lys and Modot, who cannot make love in the park, eliminate the place and, when we see their closed mouths, we hear: "I'm cold." "Put out the light." "No, leave it on." And a little later: "Are you sleepy?" "I want to go to sleep." "Put your head here." "The pillow is nearer." "Where is your hand?" and so on, until we come to the exultant repetition of the two words "My love, my love, my love, my love, my love . . ." Their expressions exactly mirror the words they are saying without opening their lips. They do not think, they do not imagine that they are elsewhere, where they can make love without constraint: they *are* elsewhere. Place is vanquished, and not only place but time, too, for suddenly Lya Lys, as seen by Modot, ages twenty years, although she does not change her attitude or expression. Thus it is not only a question of the interior-monologue technique, as our current fancy film cutters understand it—which would have only a scant historical value—but rather of reality made present by sound, reality that knows how to cause two characters to make a marvelous, motionless but *real* leap into space and time, to a point where they may love each other.

Confronted with this exacerbated will to love, society is shocked and scandalized and tries in every way to defend itself. Never has a portrait of society been offered us in more penetrating and implacable colors. Without mentioning all the details that expose this riffraff, let us confine ourselves to the major scene of the reception. It is worth noting that this sort of reception has been used by some of our greatest film makers to expose and denounce the hypocrisy, baseness, and cowardice of the upper classes. Chaplin was the first, in one of Mack Sennett's best comedies, *Tillie's Punctured Romance* (1914). He fired a revolver and spread panic in the midst of a social evening complete with dancing. Inkijinov, Pudovkin's hero in *Storm Over Asia* (1928), becomes aware of his revolutionary future during an official ceremony, which he interrupts with a magnificent explosion of revolt. Pabst, in *Pandora's Box* (1928), chooses a formal reception to loose a painfully sordid and hysterical drama in the midst of the strait-laced politeness of the guests. And who does not remember the extraordinary ballet-chase in Jean Renoir's *Rules of the Game* (1939), in which, linking burlesque and tragedy, he punctuates his healthfully destructive action with howls of terror and revolver shots while the poker-faced, genteel onlookers believe or pretend to believe that the spectacle was planned that way. In each of these instances, the slogan of society is the same: "Don't upset the established order."

To notice the cart on which the workers drink red wine would mean losing face for the characters in *L'Age d'Or*. Similarly, complete indifference greets the fire that breaks out in the kitchen of the big house and endangers the servants' lives. The case of the

father who kills his son in cold blood is taken somewhat more
seriously by the upper crust. But the murderer explains that the
son had dared tear the cigarette he was rolling and thus deserved
to die. The questionable explanation is unanimously accepted as
only just, everyone breathes freely, and the party continues. These
incidents serve to underline the outraged and violent reactions of
the middle-class characters when they are ready to lynch a young
man who had, with reason, slapped an ignoble old woman
because she was an obstacle to love. The wretched cart can pass;
they shut their eyes. The fire can break out in the kitchen, since
that is a part of the house unknown to them. But love threatens
them personally. It is the great enemy that can make the workers
on the cart, the denizens of the kitchen, and the murdered boy rise
against them.

Love will be defeated briefly by the lovers themselves, who are
not yet masters of their inhibitions. Shaken by despair, the
bearded orchestra leader leaves his podium and separates the
couple. This character is society's last and most efficacious
weapon. During this sequence the camera changes, not for reasons of technique but in response to a demand inherent in the
dramatic evolution of the action, and it takes the place now of the
orchestra leader, now of Lya Lys. Modot is for the moment unable
to destroy this new *loveless* couple that is formed. He suffers to
the accompaniment of an interminable roll of drums, and his
reactions can only lead him to renewed revolt. In a fury, he throws
objects—the symbols of his servitude—out the window, while at
that very moment the survivors emerge from de Selligny's Château—the inevitable conclusion to what has taken place (*The 120
Days of Sodom*, by de Sade).

This final sequence is most enigmatic when considered in
relation to the love story of Lya Lys and Modot. I believe that
Buñuel wished to acknowledge the importance of de Sade's work,
in which love must find renewed strength if it is to triumph over
itself, that is, over its inhibitions. Only then will it become the
great liberator.

It is clear that this sequence is also the apotheosis of the great
battle against religion waged in *L'Age d'Or*. In aiming at this
target, Buñuel knew that, as Karl Marx said, "criticism of Heaven

is transformed into criticism of earth, criticism of religion into criticism of law, criticism of theology into criticism of politics."

From the film's inception, the union of army and clergy is underlined in various ways: by the archbishops who come to colonize; by the monstrance that the reception guests bring with them; by the extraordinary description of "Imperial Rome, the secular seat of the Church," where "sometimes on Sundays" houses collapse as the Pope is celebrating Mass; by the Mariolater violinist. It is worth pointing out that in the scenario before shooting began, the Château de Selligny scene was conceived differently. The survivors of "the most bestial of orgies" represented by their costumes and general appearance the major religions: the Duc de Blangis wears a mustache and beard, and is dressed like the Hebrews of the first century A.D.; President Curval is dressed like a lower-class Arab—sixth century A.D.; the Bishop of K., who enters limping, is dressed like a priest of the sixteenth century. In the scenario the Duc de Blangis, who "is clearly Jesus Christ," alone manages to survive the carnage, while in the actual filming the Bishop of K. takes over this task before he has lost his beard—which turns up again in the epilogue, together with some hair on a cross, snow-covered and beaten by the wind to the accompaniment of a two-step.

In any case, the meaning of this sequence is the same, for Jesus Christ perfectly represents the spirit of religiosity and mysticism.

If religion has been harshly dealt with, other pillars of middle-class domination have not been handled with kid gloves, either. Buñuel has given the police, the family, and the army the most vigorous blows they have ever received on the screen. Thus love stands forth alone as the great and unique hope, the major revolt of man.

L'AGE D'OR CREATES A SCANDAL

In February 1930, Eisenstein's film *The General Line* (also known as *The Old and the New)* was banned. The *L'Age d'Or* scandal broke the same year. From October 2 to December 3, the film, which had been duly passed by the censors, was shown without

incident at Studio 28.* On the evening of October 3, a group of
people attending the showing waited for the right moment to
show their "superior intellectuality." On the screen, at the moment when a character places a monstrance in a stream, there were
cries of "We'll see if there are still any Christians in France!" and
"Down with the Jews!" Stink bombs exploded, spectators were
manhandled, the screen was splashed with purple ink, seats were
torn up, and pictures by Dali, Max Ernst, Man Ray, Miró, and
Tanguy which were hanging in the theater lobby were slashed.
After interrupting the showing and cutting the theater's telephone wires, the demonstrators—representatives of the Patriots'
League and of the Anti-Jewish League—fled. But stink bombs,
when weighed against a Buñuel film, amounted to no more than
senile hysteria, and the performance was resumed.

The screen that bore this mark of "Christian illiteracy" should
have been preserved so that *L'Age d'Or* could always have been
run on it. Then the priests, the Fascists, the anti-Semites, and the
superpatriots would have recognized themselves even more easily
in the parents of Lya Lys as well as in the governor, the Mario-
laters, the politicos, and the Christ of the film.

The next day, the right-wing papers featured the incident,
demanding that the most stringent measures be taken against the
film. The Patriots' League released a statement protesting against
the "immorality of this Bolshevik film," implying that an indig-
nant public had caused the outbreak. A city official, M. the
Provost de Launay, went to police headquarters and had a long
talk with the director of censorship. He had already written the
prefect of police, requesting that measures be taken against the
"offal" of surrealism. His open letter had appeared in the papers
on November 10. It contained the following splendid example of
unconscious humor: the gentleman wished to take this opportunity to protest against "other films imported from or originating
in Germany which are being or are to be shown in the Champs-
Élysées quarter, only *two steps* from the tomb of the Unknown
Soldier."

---

*A commercial film theater in Montmartre whose name stems from the fact that it
was founded in 1928.

On December 5, following de Launay's intervention with the censorship authorities, the bureau asked the management of Studio 28 to suppress "two passages dealing with bishops." The cuts were made and the screenings continued normally.

On December 7, the grand campaign of the right-wing press advocating Fascist action against "subversive" films began. The campaign was spearheaded by *Le Figaro* and *L'Ami du Peuple*. Richard-Pierre Bodin wrote in *Le Figaro* of December 7:

"A film called *L'Age d'Or*—in which I defy any qualified authority to detect the slightest artistic merit—multiplies (in public showings!) its crop of utterly obscene, repugnant, and tawdry episodes. Country, family, religion are dragged through the mire. All those who saved the grandeur of France, all those who cherish the family and the innocence of childhood, all those who have faith in the future of a race which has enlightened the whole world, all those Frenchmen who have been chosen to protect you against the poison of rotten entertainment, now ask what you think of the job our censorship is doing. . . ."

On December 8, police headquarters asked that a line in the program notes be cut: "The Duc de Blangis is clearly Jesus Christ." On the 9th, M. Mauclaire, the manager of Studio 28, was informed that a special censorship commission would review the film on the morning of the 11th. On the 10th, the morning papers received a release stating that *L'Age d'Or* was definitely banned. M. Mauclaire was so informed the same day at five-thirty in the afternoon. On the 10th, too, new articles appeared in the reactionary press.

"Let us say straight off that this production is boring. . . . This pretentious and dreary pensum has nothing to do with *avantgarde* art or with just plain art. The technical execution is so poor that it would elicit catcalls in the poorest film houses of our most provincial towns" (G. M., *Echo de Paris*, December 10, 1930). "This is a Bolshevik endeavor of a special, yes, of a truly special kind, which aims to corrupt us. Lenin's propaganda has found in certain more or less fly-by-night studios unexpected cooperation, and knows how to make use of it. . . ." (Gaëtan Sanvoisin, *Le Figaro*, December 10, 1930.)

The film was officially banned on December 11, and on the

12th, all copies were seized by the police. Here is the statement issued by police headquarters:

"In consequence of evidence verified this morning by the official commission that undertook to examine this film, shown in a theater in the Montmartre area, the prefect of police has brought charges against the manager of the theater. He will be prosecuted for an infraction of the decree of February 18, 1928, under the terms of which he may be fined up to five hundred francs and his establishment temporarily closed."

It should be noted that the damages caused by the superpatriots amounted to eight thousand francs.

Meanwhile, the Italian ambassador to France was so upset that, it seems, he remonstrated with the French government (he may have recognized his own sovereigns in the governor of the film and his wife).

The left-wing press came vigorously to the defense of *L'Age d'Or*. Especially noteworthy were the interesting appraisals by Roger Lesbats in *Le Populaire*, Lucie Derain in *Le Quotidien*, and Léon Mousinac in *L'Humanité*.

The surrealists published "A Questionnaire," in which they sought to draw some conclusions from the affair and asked themselves: "Is this intervention to be understood as an authorization given equally to those who consider religious propaganda an outrage to break up its manifestations (Roman Catholic propaganda films; pilgrimages to Lourdes and Lisieux; centers of obscurantism like *La Bonne Presse*, meetings of the Index authorities, churches, and so on; perversion of youth in charitable institutions and by military training; sermons over the radio; stores that sell crucifixes and crowns of thorns)?" by using all means at their disposal.

If I have dwelt at length on the scandal that *L'Age d'Or* provoked, it is because its manifold developments contain the most striking arguments for the importance of this work, which is even today the perfect example of the full-length surrealist film. The film was upsetting, hence necessary. Until 1930 the cinema was, with rare exceptions, bland. Therefore, it was not fulfilling its purpose. *L'Age d'Or* had the courage to show the cinema's potential. There was no longer an excuse for making insipid films in which soda pop is passed off as strong drink. It could reveal man to himself. One should always suspect films that provoke an enthusiastic response in those who have no right to like them. Buñuel, upsetting even the cynical hopes some of his enemies might have had for him, perfectly achieved his aim. He created a film that is magnetic in the highest degree for those who *love* and *live*, but murder for the living dead, the dodderers, and those who paddle in the cesspools of reaction.

Buñuel was not in Paris when the scandal over *L'Age d'Or* broke. In fact, he had been invited to Hollywood right after the first private screening.

That first private showing, prologue to the whole incident, was interesting in itself. The producer of the film, the Vicomte de Noailles, was delighted to have a film of his very own (although he knew nothing of the subject, Buñuel always having refused to tell him the details). He invited "all Paris" to the première. A liveried footman at the door called out the guests' names and the de Noailles' received amid smiles, bows, and anticipatory congratulations. It was different after the screening, which had taken place in glacial silence. With eyes averted, the guests fled, and the de Noailles', crimson with embarrassment, did not know where to hide their heads. As for Buñuel, he had never been happier—at last, the shame he had felt at the admiration of the "bourgeoisie" for *Un Chien Andalou* had been expunged.

So, in 1930, Buñuel made a quick trip to Hollywood, where, morose and aggressive, he watched the making of a Greta Garbo film. One day the M-G-M producer Irving Thalberg asked Buñuel, as a Spaniard, to give his impression of a Spanish-language film starring Lili Damita. Morose and aggressive, as always, Buñuel replied, "I don't care to listen to prostitutes." He was soon dropped by Hollywood and he returned to Spain.

The Golden Age

Henry Miller

. . . .

At present the cinema is the great popular art form, which is to say it is not an art at all. Ever since its birth we have been hearing that at last an art has been born which will reach the masses and perhaps liberate them. People profess to see in the cinema possibilities which are denied the other arts. So much the worse for the cinema!

There is not one art called the Cinema but there is, as in every art, a form of production for the many and another for the few. Since the death of avant-garde films—*Le Sang d'un Poète,* by Cocteau, was I believe the last—there remains only the mass production of Hollywood.

The few films which might justify the category of "art" that have appeared since the birth of the cinema (a matter of forty years or so) died almost at their inception. This is one of the lamentable and amazing facts in connection with the development of a new art form. Despite all effort the cinema seems incapable of establishing itself as art. Perhaps it is due to the fact that the cinema more than any other art form has become a controlled industry, a dictatorship in which the artist is dominated and silenced.

Immediately an astonishing fact asserts itself, namely, that the greatest films were produced at little expense! It does not require millions to produce an artistic film; in fact, it is almost axiomatic that the more money a film costs the worse it is apt to be. Why then does the real cinema not come into being? Why does the cinema remain in the hands of the mob or its dictators? Is it purely an economic question?

From *The Cosmological Eye* by Henry Miller. Copyright 1939 by New Directions Publishing Corporation. Reprinted by permission of New Directions Publishing Corporation.

The other arts, it should be remembered, are fostered in us. Nay, they are forced upon us almost from birth. Our taste is conditioned by centuries of inoculation. Nowadays one is almost ashamed to admit that he does not like this or that book, this or that painting, this or that piece of music. One may be bored to tears, but one dare not admit it. We have been educated to pretend to like and admire the great works of art with which, alas, we have no longer any connection.

The cinema is born and it is an art, another art—but it is born too late. The cinema is born out of a great feeling of lassitude. Indeed lassitude is too mild a word. The cinema is born just as we are dying. The cinema, like some ugly duckling, imagines that it is related in some way to the theater, that it was born perhaps to replace the theater, which is already dead. Born into a world devoid of enthusiasm, devoid of taste, the cinema functions like a eunuch: it waves a peacock-feathered fan before our drowsy eyes. The cinema believes that what we want of it is to be put to sleep. It does not know *that we are dying.* Therefore, let us not blame the cinema. Let us ask ourselves why it is that this truly marvelous art form should be allowed to perish before our very eyes. Let us ask why it is that when it makes the most heroic efforts to appeal to us its gestures are unheeded.

I am talking about the cinema as an *actuality*, a something which exists, which has validity, just as music or painting or literature. I am strenuously opposed to those who look upon the cinema as a medium to exploit the other arts or even to synthetize them. The cinema is not another form of this or that, nor is it a synthetic product of all the other this-and-thats. The cinema is the cinema and nothing but. And it is quite enough. In fact, it is magnificent.

Like any other art the cinema has in it all the possibilities for creating antagonisms, for stirring up revolt. The cinema can do for man what the other arts have done, possibly even more, but the first condition, the prerequisite in fact, is—*take it out of the hands of the mob!* I understand full well that it is not the mob which creates the films we see—not technically, at any rate. But in a deeper sense it *is* the mob which *actually* creates the films. For the first time in the history of art the mob has dictated what the

artist should do. For the first time in the history of man an art is
born which caters exclusively to the masses. Perhaps it is some
dim comprehension of this unique and deplorable fact which
accounts for the tenacity with which "the dear public" clings to
its art. The silent screen! Shadow images! Absence of color!
Spectral, phantasmal beginnings. The dumb masses visualizing
themselves in those stinking coffins which served as the first
movie houses. An abysmal curiosity to see themselves reflected in
the magic mirror of the machine age. Out of what tremendous
fear and longing was this "popular" art born?

I can well imagine the cinema never having been born. I can
imagine a race of men for whom the cinema would have been
thoroughly unnecessary. But I cannot imagine the robots of this
age being without a cinema, *some kind of cinema.* Our starved
instincts have been clamoring for centuries for more and more
substitutes. And as substitute for living the cinema is ideal. Does
one ever remark the look of these cinema hounds as they leave the
theater? That dreamy air of vacuity, that washed-out look of the
pervert who masturbates in the dark! One can hardly distinguish
them from the drug addicts: they walk out of the cinema like
somnambulists.

This of course is what they want, our worn-out, harassed beasts
of toil. Not more terror and strife, not more mystery, not more
wonder and hallucination, but peace, surcease from care, the
unreality of the dream. But *pleasant* dreams! *Soothing* dreams!
And here it is difficult not to restrain a word of consolation for the
poor devils who are put to it to quench this unslakable thirst of
the mob. It is the fashion among the intelligentsia to ridicule and
condemn the efforts, the truly herculean efforts, of the film
directors, the Hollywood dopesters particularly. Little do they
realize the invention it requires to create each day a drug that will
counteract the insomnia of the mob. There is no use condemning
the directors, nor is there any use deploring the public's lack of
taste. These are stubborn facts, and irremediable. The panderer
and the pandered must be eliminated—*both at once!* There is no
other solution.

How speak about an art which no one recognizes as *art?* I know
that a great deal has already been written about the "art of the
cinema." One can read about it most every day in the newspapers

and the magazines. But it is not the *art* of the cinema which you will find discussed therein—it is rather the dire, botched embryo as it now stands revealed before our eyes, the stillbirth which was mangled in the womb by the obstetricians of art.

For forty years now the cinema has been struggling to get properly born. Imagine the chances of a creature that has wasted forty years of its life in being born! Can it hope to be anything but a monster, an idiot?

I will admit nevertheless that I expect of this monster-idiot the most tremendous things! I expect of this monster that it will devour its own mother and father, that it will run amuck and destroy the world, that it will drive man to frenzy and desperation. I cannot see it otherwise. There is a law of compensation and this law decrees that even the monster must justify himself.

Five or six years ago I had the rare good fortune to see *L'Age d'Or*, the film made by Luis Buñuel and Salvador Dali, which created a riot at Studio 28. For the first time in my life I had the impression that I was watching a film which was pure cinema and nothing but cinema. Since then I am convinced that *L'Age d'Or* is unique and unparalleled. Before going on I should like to remark that I have been going to the cinema regularly for almost forty years; in that time I have seen several thousand films. It should be understood, therefore, that in glorifying the Buñuel-Dali film I am not unmindful of having seen such remarkable films as:

> *The Last Laugh* (Emil Jannings)
> *Berlin*
> *Le Chapeau de Paille d'Italie* (René Clair)
> *Le Chemin de la Vie*
> *La Souriante Madame Beudet* (Germaine Dulac)
> *Mann Braucht Kein Geld*
> *La Mélodie du Monde* (Walter Ruttmann)
> *Le Ballet Mécanique*
> *Of What Are the Young Films Dreaming?* (Comte de Beaumont)
> *Rocambolesque*
> *Three Comrades and One Invention*
> *Ivan the Terrible* (Emil Jannings)
> *The Cabinet of Dr. Caligari*

The Crowd (King Vidor)
La Maternelle
Othello (Krause and Jannings)
Extase (Machaty)
Grass
Eskimo
Le Maudit
Lilliane (Barbara Stanwyck)
A Nous la Liberté (René Clair)
La Tendre Ennemie (Max Ophuls)
The Trackwalker
Potemkin
Les Marins de Cronstadt
Greed (Eric von Stroheim)
Thunder over Mexico (Eisenstein)
The Beggar's Opera
Mädchen in Uniform (Dorothea Wieck)
Midsummer Night's Dream (Reinhardt)
Crime and Punishment (Pierre Blanchard)
The Student of Prague (Conrad Veidt)
Poil de Carotte
Banquier Pichler
The Informer (Victor McLaglen)
The Blue Angel (Marlene Dietrich)
L'Homme à la Barbiche
L'Affaire Est dans le Sac (Prévert)
Moana (Flaherty)
Mayerling (Charles Boyer and Danielle Darrieux)
Kriss
Variety (Krause and Jannings)
Chang
Sunrise (Murnau)

nor

three Japanese films (ancient, medieval and modern Japan) the titles
of which I have forgotten;

nor

a documentary on India

nor

a documentary on Tasmania

nor

a documentary on the death rites in Mexico, by Eisenstein

nor

a psychoanalytic dream picture, in the days of the silent film, with
Werner Krause

nor

certain films of Lon Chaney, particularly one based on a novel of
Selma Lagerlöf in which he played with Norma Shearer

nor

The Great Ziegfeld, nor *Mr. Deeds Goes to Town*

nor

The Lost Horizon (Frank Capra), the first *significant* film out of
Hollywood

nor

the very first movie I ever saw, which was a newsreel showing the
Brooklyn Bridge and a Chinese with a pigtail walking over the
bridge in the rain! I was only seven or eight years of age when I
saw this film in the basement of the old South Third Street
Presbyterian Church in Brooklyn. Subsequently I saw hundreds
of pictures in which it always seemed to be raining and in which
there were always nightmarish pursuits in which houses collapsed and people disappeared through trap doors and pies were
thrown and human life was cheap and human dignity was nil.
And after thousands of slapstick, pie-throwing Mack Sennett
films, after Charlie Chaplin had exhausted his bag of tricks, after
Fatty Arbuckle, Harold Lloyd, Harry Langdon, Buster Keaton,
each with his own special brand of monkeyshines, came the chef-
d'oeuvre of all the slapstick, pie-throwing festivals, a film the title
of which I forget, but it was among the very first films starring
Laurel and Hardy. This, in my opinion, is the greatest comic film
ever made—because it brought the pie throwing to apotheosis.
There was nothing but pie throwing in it, nothing but pies,
thousands and thousands of pies and everybody throwing them
right and left. It was the ultimate in burlesque, and it is already
forgotten.

In every art the ultimate is achieved only when the artist passes
beyond the bounds of the art he employs. This is as true of Lewis
Carroll's work as of Dante's *Divine Comedy*, as true of Lao-tse as
of Buddha or Christ. The world must be turned upside down,
ransacked, confounded in order that the miracle may be proclaimed. In *L'Age d'Or* we stand again at a miraculous frontier

which opens up before us a dazzling new world which no one has explored. *"Mon idée générale,"* wrote Salvador Dali, *"en écrivant avec Buñuel le scénario de* L'Age d'Or, *a été de présenter la ligne droite et pure de conduite d'un être qui poursuit l'amour à travers les ignorables idéaux humanitaires, patriotiques et autres misérables mécanismes de la réalité."* I am not unaware of the part which Dali played in the creation of this great film, and yet I cannot refrain from thinking of it as the peculiar product of his collaborator, the man who directed the film: Luis Buñuel. Dali's name is now familiar to the world, even to Americans and Englishmen, as the most successful of all the surrealists today. He is enjoying a temporal vogue, largely because he is not understood, largely because his work is sensational. Buñuel, on the other hand, appears to have dropped out of sight. Rumor has it that he is in Spain, that he is quietly amassing a collection of documentary films on the revolution. What these will be, if Buñuel retains any of his old vigor, promises to be nothing short of staggering. For Buñuel, like the miners of the Asturias, is a man who flings dynamite. Buñuel is obsessed by the cruelty, ignorance and superstition which prevail among men. He realizes that there is no hope for man anywhere on this earth unless a clean slate be made of it. He appears on the scene at the moment when civilization is at its nadir.

There can be no doubt about it: the plight of civilized man is a foul plight. He is singing his swan song without the joy of having been a swan. He has been sold out by his intellect, manacled, strangled and mangled by his own symbology. He is mired in his art, suffocated by his religions, paralyzed by his knowledge. That which he glorifies is not life, since he has lost the rhythm of life, but death. What he worships is decay and putrefaction. He is diseased and the whole organism of society is infected.

They have called Buñuel everything—traitor, anarchist, pervert, defamer, iconoclast. But lunatic they dare not call him. True, it is lunacy he portrays in his film, but it is not of his making. This stinking chaos which for a brief hour or so is amalgamated under his magic wand, this is the lunacy of man's achievements after ten thousand years of civilization. Buñuel, to

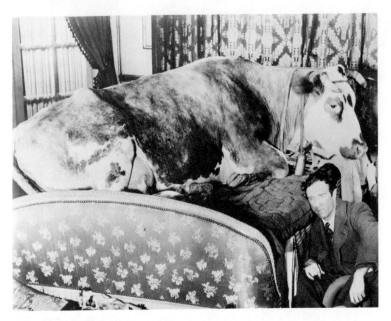

They have called Buñuel everything - traitor, anarchist, pervert, defamer, iconoclast. But lunatic they dare not call him. True, it is lunacy he portrays in his film,
but it is not of his making. (*L'Age D'Or*)

show his reverence and gratitude, puts a cow in the bed and drives
a garbage truck through the salon. The film is composed of a
succession of images without sequence, the significance of which
must be sought below the threshold of consciousness. Those who
were deceived because they could not find order or meaning in it
will find order and meaning nowhere except perhaps in the world
of the bees or the ants.

I am reminded at this point of the charming little documentary
which preceded the Buñuel film the night it was shown at Studio
28. A charming little study of the abattoir it was, altogether fitting
and significant for the weak-stomached sisters of culture who had
come to hiss the big film. Here everything was familiar and
comprehensible, though perhaps in bad taste. But there was order
and meaning in it, as there is order and meaning in a can-

nibalistic rite. And finally there was even a touch of aestheticism, for when the slaughter was finished and the decapitated bodies had gone their separate ways each little pig's head was carefully blown up by compressed air until it looked so monstrously lifelike and savory and succulent that the saliva flowed willy-nilly. (Not forgetting the shamrocks that were plugged up the assholes of each and every pig!) As I say, this was a perfectly comprehensible piece of butchery, and indeed, so well was it performed that from some of the more elegant spectators in the audience it brought forth a burst of applause.

It is five years or so ago since I saw the Buñuel film and therefore I cannot be absolutely sure, but I am almost certain that there were in this film no scenes of organized butchery between man and man, no wars, no revolutions, no inquisitions, no lynchings, no third-degree scenes. There was, to be sure, a blind man who was mistreated, there was a dog which was kicked in the stomach, there was a boy who was wantonly shot by his father, there was an old dowager who was slapped in the face at a garden party and there were scorpions who fought to the death among the rocks near the sea. Isolated little cruelties which, because they were not woven into a comprehensible little pattern, seemed to shock the spectators even more than the sight of wholesale trench slaughter. There was something which shocked their delicate sensibilities even more and that was the effect of Wagner's *Tristan and Isolde* upon one of the protagonists. Was it possible that the divine music of Wagner could so arouse the sensual appetites of a man and a woman as to make them roll in the graveled path and bite and chew one another until the blood came? Was it possible that this music could so take possession of the young woman as to make her suck the toe of a statued foot with perverted lascivi-ousness? Does music bring on orgasms, does it entrain perverse acts, does it drive people truly mad? Does this great legendary theme which Wagner immortalized have to do with such a plain vulgar physiological fact as sexual love? The film seems to suggest that it does. It seems to suggest more, for through the ramifications of the Golden Age Buñuel, like an entomologist, has studied what we call love in order to expose beneath the ideology, the mythology, the platitudes and phraseologies the complete and bloody machinery of sex. He has distinguished for us the blind metabolisms, the secret poisons, the mechanistic reflexes, the distillations of the glands, the entire plexus of forces which unite love and death in life.

Is it necessary to add that there are scenes in this film which have never been dreamed of before? The scene in the water closet, for example. I quote from the program notes:

> Il est inutile d'ajouter qu'un des points culminants de la pureté de ce film nous semble cristallisé dans la vision de l'héroïne dans les cabinets, où la puissance de l'esprit arrive à sublimer une situation généralement baroque en un élément poétique de la plus pure noblesse et solitude.

A *situation usually baroque!* Perhaps it is the baroque element in human life, or rather in the life of civilized man, which gives to Buñuel's works the aspect of cruelty and sadism. Isolated cruelty and sadism, for it is the great virtue of Buñuel that he refuses to be enmeshed in the glittering web of logic and idealism which seeks to mask from us the real nature of man. Perhaps, like Lawrence, Buñuel is only an inverted idealist. Perhaps it is his great tenderness, the great purity and poetry of his vision which forces him to reveal the abominable, the malicious, the ugly and the hypocritical falsities of man. Like his precursors he seems animated by a tremendous hatred for the lie. Being normal, instinctive, healthy, gay, unpretentious he finds himself alone in the crazy drift of social forces. Being thoroughly normal and honest he finds himself regarded as bizarre. Like Lawrence again his work divides the world into two opposite camps—those who are for him and those who are against him. There is no straddling the issue. Either you are crazy, like the rest of civilized humanity, or you are sane and healthy like Buñuel. And if you are sane and healthy you are an anarchist and you throw bombs. The great honor which was conferred upon Luis Buñuel at the showing of his film was that the citizens of France recognized him as a true anarchist. The theater was taken by assault and the street was cleared by the police. The film has never been shown again, to my knowledge, except at private performances, and then but rarely. It was brought to America, shown to a special audience, and created no impression whatever, except perplexity. Meanwhile Salvador Dali, Buñuel's collaborator, has been to America several times and created a furor there. Dali, whose work is unhealthy, though highly spectacular, highly provocative, is acclaimed as a genius. Dali makes the American public conscious of surrealism and creates a fad. Dali returns with his pockets full of dough. Dali is accepted—as another world freak. Freak for freak: there is a divine justice at work. The world which is crazy recognizes its master's voice. The yolk of the egg has split: Dali takes America, Buñuel takes the leavings.

I want to repeat: *L'Age d'Or* is the only film I know of which reveals the possibilities of the cinema! It makes its appeal neither to the intellect nor to the heart; it strikes at the solar plexus. It is like kicking a mad dog in the guts. And though it was a valiant kick in the guts and well aimed it was not enough! There will have to be other films, films even more violent than Luis Buñuel's. For the world is in a coma and the cinema is still waving a peacock-feathered plume before our eyes.

Wondering sometimes where he may be and what he may be doing, wondering what he *could* do if he were permitted, I get to thinking now and then of all that is left out of the films. Has anybody ever shown us the birth of a child, or even the birth of an animal? Insects yes, because the sexual element is weak, because there are no taboos. But even in the world of the insects have they shown us the praying mantis, the love feast which is the acme of sexual voracity? Have they shown us how our heroes won the war—and died for us? Have they shown us the gaping wounds, have they shown us the faces that have been shot away? Are they showing us now what happens in Spain every day when the bombs rain down on Madrid? Almost every week there is another newsreel theater opened up, but there is no news. Once a year we have a repertoire of the outstanding events of the world given us by the news getters. It is nothing but a series of catastrophes: railroad wrecks, explosions, floods, earthquakes, automobile accidents, airplane disasters, collisions of trains and ships, epidemics, lynchings, gangster killings, riots, strikes, incipient revolutions, *putsches,* assassinations. The world seems like a madhouse, and the world is a madhouse, but nobody dares dwell on it. When an appalling piece of insanity, already properly castrated, is about to be presented, a warning is issued to the spectators not to indulge in demonstrations. Rest impartial!—that is the edict. Don't budge from your sleep! We command you in the name of lunacy—*keep cool!* And for the most part the injunctions are heeded. They are heeded willy-nilly, for by the time the spectacle is concluded everybody has been bathed in the innocuous drama of a senti-mental couple, plain honest folks like ourselves, who are doing exactly what we are doing, with the sole difference that they are being well paid for it. This nullity and vacuity is dished up to us as the main event of the evening. The hors d'oeuvre is the newsreel, which is spiced with death and ignorance and super-stition. Between these two phases of life there is absolutely no relation unless it be the link made by the animated cartoon. For the animated cartoon is the censor which permits us to dream the most horrible nightmares, to rape and kill and bugger and plunder, without waking up. Daily life is as we see it in the big film: The newsreel is the eye of God; the animated cartoon is the soul tossing in its anguish. But none of these three is the reality which is common to all of us who think and feel. Somehow they have worked a camouflage on us, and though it is our own camouflage we accept the illusion for reality. And the reason for it is that life as we know it to be has become absolutely unbearable. We flee from it in terror and disgust. The men who come after us will read the truth beneath the camouflage. May they pity us as we who are alive and real pity those about us.

Some people think of the Golden Age as a dream of the past; others think of it as the millennium to come. But the Golden Age is the immanent reality to which all of us, by our daily living, are either contributing or failing to contribute. The world is what we make it each day, or what we fail to make it. If it is lunacy that we have on our hands today, then it is we who are the lunatics. If you accept the fact that it is a crazy world you may perhaps succeed in adapting yourself to it. But those who have a sense of creation are not keen about adapting themselves. We affect one another, whether we wish to or not. Even negatively we affect one another. In writing about Buñuel instead of writing about something else I am aware that I am going to create a certain effect—for most people an unpleasant one, I suspect. But I can no more refrain from writing this way about Buñuel than I can from washing my face tomorrow morning. My past experience of life leads up to this moment and rules it despotically. In asserting the value of Buñuel I am asserting my own values, my own faith in life. In singling out this one man I do what I am constantly doing in every realm of life—selecting and evaluating. Tomorrow is no hazardous affair, a day like any other day; tomorrow is the result of many yesterdays and comes with a potent, cumulative effect. I am tomorrow what I chose to be yesterday and the day before. It is not possible that tomorrow I may negate and nullify everything that led me to this present moment.

In the same way I wish to point out that the film *L'Age d'Or* is no accident, nor is its dismissal from the screen an accident. The world has condemned Luis Buñuel and judged him as unfit. Not the whole world, because, as I said before, the film is scarcely known outside of France—outside of Paris, in fact. Judging from the trend of affairs since this momentous event took place I cannot say that I am optimistic about the revival of this film today. Perhaps the next Buñuel film will be even more of a bombshell than was *L'Age d'Or*. I fervently hope so. But meanwhile—and here I must add that this is the first opportunity, apart from a little review which I wrote for *The New Review*, I have had to write about Buñuel publicly—meanwhile, I say, this belated tribute to Buñuel may serve to arouse the curiosity of those who have never heard the name before. Buñuel's name is not unknown to Hollywood, that I know. Indeed, like many another man of genius whom the Americans have got wind of, Luis Buñuel was invited to come to Hollywood and give of his talent. In short, he was invited to do nothing and draw his breath. So much for Hollywood.

No, it is not from that quarter that the wind will blow. But things are curiously arranged in this world. Men who have been dishonored and driven from their country sometimes return to be crowned as king. Some return as a scourge. Some leave only their name behind them, or the remembrance of their deeds, but in the name of this one and that whole epochs have been revitalized and recreated. I for one believe that, despite everything I have said against the cinema as we now know it, something wondrous and vital may yet come of it. Whether this happens or not depends entirely on us, on you who read this now. What I say is only a drop in the bucket, but it may have its consequences. The important thing is that the bucket should not have a hole in it. Well, I believe that such a bucket can be found. I believe that it is just as possible to rally men around a vital reality as it is around the false and the illusory. Luis Buñuel's effect upon me was not lost. And perhaps my words will not be lost either.

Las Hurdes: Land Without Bread

Victor Casaus

· · · · · · · · · · · · · · · · · · · ·

The Larousse dictionary is brief in its description: "HURDES: A mountainous region in Spain, to the north of the province of Cáceres, whose inhabitants have lived in deplorable backwardness."

The twenty-seven minutes of *Land Without Bread*, the documentary shot by Luis Buñuel in that region in 1932, reveal much more about the matter and end up constituting one of the most powerful documentaries in the history of cinema.

Buñuel himself once modestly described it: "A simple documentary, objective, highly objective. I didn't invent anything. Pierre Unik wrote a scientific, statistical text. We merely wished to show the most abject region of Spain."

One thing certain, however, over and above this or any other similar commentary, is that *Land Without Bread* marks an important point in Buñuel's work: all his later films, in a sense, emerge from it: his criteria on the meaning and function of cinema are concretized, and at the same time, the remarkable subversiveness of this mighty Spaniard is reaffirmed, acquiring a richer and more profound form.

Land Without Bread is Buñuel's third film and—coincidentally or significantly—his only documentary. Before making it, he had made two surrealist films—*Un Chien Andalou* (1929) and *L'Age d'Or* (1930), which had created more than one scandal in the manner typical of those years of the artistic vanguard: they were aggressions against the established order and viewed as a subversion of its values, in their evident (or seemingly) narrative incoherence, their lack of respect for, in short, what bourgeois taste had until then accepted and labeled as art.

The artistic scandal of Buñuel's first film was followed, among

From *Cine Cubano*, 71/72. Translated by Toby Talbot.

other things, by an invitation for him to come to Hollywood for six months in the role of an observer. This sort of grant, which from today's point of view seems like an effort to support or sponsor a new emerging figure, ended in a surprising, abrasive manner when Buñuel refused to attend the film shooting of a mediocre actress. "I can't waste time looking at prostitutes."

A little over a year later, he was back in Spain, to shoot *Land Without Bread*, financed, like his two previous films, by friends and relatives. The stay in Las Hurdes lasted for about four months. The shooting took almost two. He did the editing in Madrid "on a kitchen table." The following year a sort of pre-opening was held at the Press Palace in the Spanish capital. While the image was projected, the text was read directly and Buñuel did the sound from the projection booth with a record of Brahm's Symphony IV.

The real "opening" of the documentary was to take place four years later, in 1937, in Paris, during the Spanish Civil War. The circumstances of this opening provided a significant and illuminating framework for *Land Without Bread*: a civil war was being waged in Spain in which the people were defending their right to prevent all of Spain from being Las Hurdes.

Buñuel, sent by the Republic, found himself in Paris. "When the civil war broke out, I halted all my film activities and placed myself at the disposal of the government. I collaborated with the Republic during the civil war, working with the mails and serving as head of information for the Spanish embassy in Paris."

The documentary that served as debut for this diplomat of the Republic was composed of brutal images of a Spanish region "formed at the beginning of the XVIth century when some of the survivors of the Jewish expulsion and persecution, under order of the Catholic Sovereigns, went there and inhabited it."

The region is situated at least 100 kilometers from Salamanca, one of the oldest and most prominent cultural centers of the peninsula. The chief value of *Land Without Bread* consists probably in its ability to project Las Hurdes' specific condition—treated with obvious scientific and anthropological objectivity—towards a totally Spanish dimension. What we see in this moving combination—both real and hallucinatory—of misery, death, sickness, hunger, sterility and hardship (100 kilometers from

Salamanca, let us remember) is a filmic extension, a plastic synthesis of Spanish history, of the extraordinary aggregate of unresolved contradictions, untimely advances, colonial empires, economic setbacks, social protests, which left Spain bound to a feudal structure, unable to make the leap other European countries accomplished in order to undertake a new means of production and to redistribute the world, a world to which Spain no longer had access.

Land Without Bread is, in that sense, a small, modest and terrifying chronicle of the extreme consequences of that established order and, simultaneously, is a subversive call for its destruction.

Some of those who saw the documentary at its first screening in 1933 reproached Buñuel for not having focused more on the interesting architecture of La Albarca, the village at the entrance of Las Hurdes, which appears in the first part of the documentary. For Buñuel, however, those houses held no inherent beauty; they were part of a total reality towards which he strove. They could not, therefore, be treated "artistically" and outside of the film's objective. On the other hand, neither is poverty converted into a spectacle in the documentary.

Buñuel's intention is not a recreation of Las Hurdes in order to delineate its horrible features or arouse a stultifying piety. What he proposes in *Land Without Bread* is the antithesis of those cinedramas "saturated with melodramatic germs, totally infected with romantic and naturalistic bacilli." *Land Without Bread* does not strive for spectator hypnosis (despite the devastating images); on the contrary, it seeks a form of cinematic distancing, a scientific, anthropological, sociological objectivity, which allows one to reach a lucid, precise conclusion on the situation that is described and the causes that produced it. Certain elements which exemplify this quest for lucidity in the spectator can be cited: the documentary's very structure; the utilization of Brahms' music, in both an ironic and distancing fashion; the narration constructed with a simple, direct text and read in a calm tone.

As is apparent, those elements occur in intense contrast to the accompanying images: there is no possibility of connecting them for escape purposes; reality persistently imposes its hegemony; it contributes its data for the final analysis.

The structure of the documentary is simple: it resembles a travelogue: "The day of our arrival we saw the women of the village in a great ceremony." This fact imparts an air of excursion, of a pleasure trip, which will serve as an important element in the play of contrasts established by every harsh and brutal image. Such a structure turns the data over to the spectator with a seemingly naive, disinterested simplicity: the data is not even organized around related themes. But it is precisely the overwhelming sequence, the reiteration throughout the film which reveals the data to be that of a major problem. Because it is so terrible and devastating, anecdote ceases to be anecdote, and is transformed into a stated problem which demands analysis and conclusion.

Those who had viewed *Un Chien Andalou* and *L'Age d'Or* as a mere aesthetic game, another juggling act on the part of the vanguard, did not understand the significance of *Land Without Bread*. For them it was a total break with what preceded it, for others even a betrayal on the director's part.

In 1935, a journalist asked Buñuel:

"Is *Land Without Bread* a rectification or an evolution?"

And Buñuel replied:

"The film is simply a continuation of my course."

Land Without Bread definitely contains keys to his previous films, and, further, the roots of many of his subsequent works. In a sense, is not the putrified donkey who appears in *Un Chien Andalou*, the same animal who dies, devoured by the bees, in *Land Without Bread*? Is not the cow that leaves a house in a scene in *Land Without Bread* the same one we saw before in *L'Age d'Or*? Nor, in revealing these elements, has Buñuel's intention changed: subversion persists.

What is new, important, and significant in *Land Without Bread* is encountering these elements in a context which now makes them remarkable in themselves. Is not the irrationality that the surrealists sought by juxtaposing an umbrella and a sewing machine on a dissecting table likewise to be found in any of the scenes in *Land Without Bread*, with the same direct and symbolic intention?

The images which Buñuel constructed in his surrealist films now existed in *Land Without Bread* in a magical everydayness, one that was absurdly real. It is significant that Buñuel should find those everyday forms of irrationality, of unreality in the most underdeveloped zones of backward Spain, and that a Spanish-American, the Cuban novelist Alejo Carpentier, should proclaim that "the marvel of reality" could be found, intact and tangible, in our underdeveloped land of Latin America. Undoubtedly similar economic, social (and therefore cultural) conditions produced the noteworthy coincidence whereby both of these participants in the surrealist movement should reach, each via his own path, similar conclusions regarding the relationship between unreality and the surrounding world, and regarding the sources of "the marvels of reality."

In *Land Without Bread* Buñuel announces and outlines his own method of subversion: to create a crisis in our conventional criterion of a society based on economic and social inequality; to reveal the "chaste eroticism" that this society repudiates; to expose the evils of religion and of its worst practitioners. His fidelity to these principles has been notably tenacious: "The thought that continues guiding me today is the same that guided me at the age of twenty-five. It is an idea of Engels. The artist describes authentic social relations with the object of destroying the conventional ideals of these relationships, of creating a crisis in the optimism of the bourgeois world and compelling the public to doubt the perennial existence of the established order. That is the ultimate meaning of all my films: to say time and again, in case someone forgets or believes otherwise, that we do not live in the best of all possible worlds. I don't know what more I can do."

Land Without Bread is, moreover, with respect to the history of the documentary, one of the pioneering films in terms of its highly committed, lucid and analytic nature. It is a film reportage which nowadays would surely have been made with the resources of direct cinema. At the end of the documentary, the narrator adds: "Listen to what this woman says: There's nothing that preoccupies me more than thinking always of death." The narrator's voice at this point coincides with the first shot of the woman who speaks, accomplishing thereby a form of combined dubbing and narration, and clearly suggesting a direct interview.

Buñuel himself, in the aforementioned interview of 1935, explains that he made the documentary by adhering "to the limitations imposed by the footage of the film and the lack of sound equipment." In terms of its spare realization, *Land Without Bread* represents also a point of departure for the documentary view of the world which seeks to negate spectacle and tourism, in order to become an instrument of analysis and subversion decidedly in favor of the true liberation of man.

Buñuel, Citizen of Mexico

Jean Delmas

• •

In 1951, just as we were wondering, nostalgically, what could
have become of the great Buñuel, just as a dark rumor began to
circulate about his fate, an event occurred, as sudden and marvelous as a journey backward in time to the Golden Age, an event
we had not dared even to hope for: the appearance of *Los
Olvidados*. Once more we had a Buñuel, after twenty-five years,
who had been faithful, not to the formula of surrealism, but to his
own revolution in spirit.

The films which should have reached us, year after year, made
Buñuel once again the great master of the cinema, and this time
as a distinctly Mexican director. Some of the films of this period
are missing and a certain ambiguity hovers around them, as
around lost or unidentified manuscripts. (A recent, quite serious
German study, for example, places *La Hija Del Engaño* in 1935,
as an elementary exercise made in Spain.) This was an era when
Buñuel, to get his feet back in the stirrups, turned out as many as
three films in a year, films on subjects he had not chosen himself.
It would be possible to believe that some of them, perhaps, were
aimed specifically at Mexican audiences, and therefore, of little
interest to us. But Buñuel himself said: "Here in Mexico, I have
become a professional in the film world. Until I came here I made
a film the way a writer makes a book, and on my friends' money at
that. I am very grateful and happy to have lived in Mexico, and I
have been able to make my films here in a way I could not have in
any other country in the world. It is quite true that in the
beginning, caught up by necessity, I was forced to make cheap
films. But I never made a film which went against my conscience

From *Jeune Cinema*, No. 12 (February 1966). Translated by Sallie Iannotti.
Reprinted by permission of the publisher.

or my convictions. I have never made a superficial, uninteresting film."[1]

These are the Mexican films:[2] *Grand Casino* (1947), *El Gran Calavera* (1949), *La Hija Del Engaño* (1951), *La Ilusion Viaja en Tranvia* (1953), *El Rio y la Muerte* (1954). These we know to be (though we are not resigned to the fact, we might wish there were as many again) the films we needed to fill out our complete image of Luis Buñuel. They are not perhaps his finest works, what the scholars call "masterpieces," and we still lack the necessary historical perspective in order to make a final judgment. But they are, as Buñuel himself knew, worthy of the whole.

These films bring us the most moving testament; they make the director live for us; they make him seem more authentic, more complete, more immediate. Through them, we can come to understand the great, simple man who made them.

Obviously, the films chosen for presentation in France are those which conform in some way to the established image we have of the director, an image which we have held since the appearance of *L'Age d'Or*. And there is nothing wrong in that, because it makes Buñuel's return to glory easier and more assured. After all, he has been absent for twenty years. We have come to expect "hallucination," "dreaminess." And here it is, once again, in *Los Olvidados*, woven into a realistic tale. This quality is less easily recognized in *On a Volé un Tram* because everything in this film is dreamlike, it is even indicated in the original title: *La Ilusion Viaja en Tranvia*. Yet even here, each detail is completely realistic. Another basic ingredient is "cruelty." *Los Olvidados* was surely the last word on a cruel world. Another is "eroticism." This, too, is present in *Los Olvidados*, and again, almost extravagantly, in *Susana* (1950), which opened in France soon after it was produced. This film is somewhat less good, it seems to me, than the five films released today. The other necessities: "anti-clericalism," "atheism," and a confrontation with religion, such as we find in *El*, are equally good here. (Sometimes, too, the distribution of these pictures depends upon the prestige of a well-

[1]Interview with Wilfried Berghahn, *Filmkritik*, no. 5, 1963.
[2]These films were introduced in France by "Great Classic Films," produced by Studio 43.

known earlier work, such as the very fine *Robinson Crusoe* or the more questionable *Wuthering Heights;* but this is another question entirely.)

The Buñuel who comes to us in these five new films is a Buñuel without "isms"—a Buñuel evidently content to have a camera in his hands once more, a laughing Buñuel, a bantering, mocking Buñuel. And a Mexican Buñuel, who accepts the conventions of the Mexican cinema. He makes a game of them, at times, yes. But tenderly, ironically. I am reminded of Picasso the day of his bull-fight, offering to the victor the little traditional statue of the bull, and not *the* Picasso, burning with genius. This is, then, a Mexican Buñuel, who is willing, above all, to be moderately useful to his adopted country in the difficult process of creating a better future (or one at least less evil), after all the revolutions have failed—as Mayakovsky was willing to forget his private ambitions in order to be modestly useful to his own land and his revolution. But still, aside from the banter, aside from the educational necessities and the conventions—the "edifications" which are not really part of his nature, Luís Buñuel, as always, repudiates the foolishness of the "think-no-evils," the clear conscience of the "do-gooders."

El Gran Calavera is the second film in Buñuel's new career.[3] It opens with a tangle of legs, then a little knot of men, attached to these legs, in a prison cell. Then there is a shot of the bewildered reveler who politely makes his excuses when he disturbs his companions so that he will have room to scratch himself. He is invited to leave the cell with the reverence accorded to the very rich, and already, in these first few shots, the mark of the master is recognizable. It remains, in that subtle touch, in the humor, as strong as it was twenty years ago.

The drunken reveler is Don Ramiro, financier and millionaire. Since his wife's death, he has taken to drink, and his family has stuffed themselves unscrupulously, making good use of the money the drunk is stupidly wasting. Life is good for Don Ramiro's brother, Ladislov, his sister-in-law, and his son. Don Ramiro is aware of the situation, but he lets it go on. His drunken lucidity ends, however, in a great revolt when the "clod" arrives (and

[3]When this article was finished, the first of these films, *Grand Casino* (1947), had not yet appeared in France.

Buñuel gives this character a magnificent idiot's face) and wants to marry Don Ramiro's daughter, Virginia, for her money. Without the slightest regard for social conventions, this usually sweet-tempered gentleman makes mincemeat of the fiancé and his dignified parents.

Another brother, a doctor, informed of Ramiro's misbehavior, imposes a "treatment," aimed at curing what in his eyes is a malady of the moral sense. Following his instructions, Ramiro's drunken sleep is prolonged by an injection; he wakes up in a mean hovel of a boarding house in the suburbs where his family, dressed in rags, has crowded together. Ladislov has become a carpenter, his wife a laundress, the son a shoe-shine boy. They make Ramiro believe that his business has failed. They fabricate papers to prove it. But the convincing proof, for Ramiro, is the sight of these loafers going to work. He believes them and is overcome by remorse. "Operation good-deed" is so effective, in fact, that Ramiro tries to commit suicide. This incident uncovers the trick. But Ramiro decides to turn the tables, to teach his family a lesson in their turn. The laugh is now on the do-gooders.

New information, also forged, reveals to the family that in the interval Ramiro has really gone bankrupt. The lazy brother will have to continue being a carpenter (and later will find he cannot stop himself), and the sister-in-law will have to stop playing the hypochondriac and become a laundress in earnest. Don Ramiro, himself, who complains about his morally more degrading employment as undertaker, spends his supposed work-hours smoking cigars in the old mansion which he secretly still owns. But he stops drinking. Malice restores his will to live and gives meaning to his existence.

Pablo, a young electrician who was brought in to foil the suicide, has become the unhappy family's benefactor. He procures work for Ladislov and his wife, though they do not really want him to. He is also in love with Virginia, who loves him in return. Then one day, the former fiancé returns. Pablo is at first enraged, but puts up no resistance. After all, he is poor and the other man is rich—Pablo and Buñuel are under no illusions. Love can be lost through want of money. So there is the brave young girl at the altar about to say "I do" to her clod.

But Don Ramiro will have none of this. For one thing, she does

not love the man. For another, he says, "I refuse my consent."
Pablo too has come to his senses. Earlier in the film, he had
declared his love for Virginia in a very peculiar manner. To
augment his salary, Pablo drives through the streets of the city in
an old car, fitted out with a loud-speaker system, shouting out
advertising slogans. One day he takes Virginia with him, and in
his excitement, he forgets to turn off the microphone, so that the
whole street rocks with their lovers' duet, sandwiched between
two slogans. On Virginia's wedding day, he comes to the door of
the church and interrupts the service with his ear-splitting an-
nouncements. Don Ramiro responds.

I have concentrated on this film more than the others because,
coming as it does at the onset of his second career, it shows clearly
that Buñuel has not changed. This film is a very moving allusion,
an inversion really, like a negative print, of the themes in *L'Age
d'Or*. Good deeds lead to evil, suicide. Work redeems other
people, rather than the worker. Love conquers money, but only
because an old drunkard intervenes in the normal functioning of
the mechanism that the lovers themselves accept. Here, once
more, we find *l'amour fou*, but proclaimed, this time, to the
world at large through a loud-speaker. The predicaments in
which Buñuel places both his characters and himself make us
tremble, not for the characters, of course, but for him. How can he
ever get himself out of this one? He does, invariably, get himself
out. And when all is said and done, we see him laughing as he
peers at us through the veil of his images.

La Ilusion Viaja en Tranvia, however, is a more mature work,
produced by an artist who has more freedom in his materials. It is
a rather foolish tale of a trolley conductor and a driver who are
not resigned to giving up their old car, now consigned to the
scrap heap. They take it out one fine night for a last spin, and
have to keep this cumbersome toy for a whole day in order to
sneak it into the depot the following evening. In some ways this
film is similar to Polanski's *Two Men and a Wardrobe*. But the
choice of the trolley is a stroke of genius, infusing the story with
new meaning. The car runs on rails. ("The company's car runs on
the company's rails," as the old company man says in the film.)
Of all objects in the world, it is the least suited to anarchy. And

yet this particular trolley becomes anarchistic. It is difficult to keep it for a day. Along the routes there are ordinary people waiting for their regular car, and the two kidnappers cannot convince them that this is a phantom trolley. Above all, when the riders get aboard, the conductor cannot allow them to pay, or he will be open to charges of theft. And this, for the paying public, is a most suspect development.

Thus, the phantom trolley becomes the vehicle for a startling journey through a full-fleshed Mexico. Poultry hangs from the luggage racks, quarters of beef are brought aboard by butchers. Even a Saint-Sulpice madonna is carried on by two bigots who ask its protection against an impure world where the trolley fare is free. Yet behind these characters who pass by in silhouette, there is a solid, whole-cloth society, which is not a silhouette.

Buñuel lays all about him to waste with a vengeance. The trolley company is embued with divine rights, linking the directors to the least of their employees, a retired flunky who chases the two runaways and the stolen car. The delinquents are saved by the director's belief in the infallibility of the technocracy, and the punctuality of the flunky all but ensnares them. Above them all is the established power of money, portrayed as a fetish, which explodes in the trolley service offered by the two scoundrels: "extraordinary and free." All the riders insist on paying, each for his own personal reason, and each resents the fact that in the society they live in, nothing can be free without being suspect. At this level, comedy becomes philosophy. It is plain that this marvelously tricky little celebration of a trolley ride is not a game of chance but a "mystery play," ironic and popular, about original sin.

El Rio y la Muerte and *La Hija Del Engaño* are a little less direct in their impact because they were made for a Mexican audience, and they deal, for the most part, with Mexican traditions. In Latin America, everyone has a soft spot in his heart for "the soaps," in our parlance. And in the screenplay for *La Hija Del Engaño* you will find all the elements of traditional melodrama. "Don Quintin, an honest little white-collar worker, is betrayed by his wife. He kicks her out and she tells him their daughter is not his child. He abandons the child on Lencho's

doorstep, a drunkard who already has a daughter, Jovita. . . ."
This is the script published by the distributor. It is exact; not
another word could be added. But what does not appear in the
script is the humor with which these words are spoken. The way,
for example, Buñuel handles this very "Hector Malot" theme of
the foundling, the infant martyr, who becomes a young woman
seeking the alleviation of her miseries through love. First we are
shown shots of the child in the drunkard's house. Then there is a
long black-out, during which we hear the sound of blows. Then
the child reappears on the screen, this time as a grown woman.
Her conversation with Jovita indicates that her step-father still
beats her. Throughout the film, humor plays the role of healer in
the melodrama (without destroying the melodramatic elements).

El Rio y la Muerte is also very Mexican—a film about a bloody
feud between two families in a village. It portrays the near-
impossibility of escaping from an outmoded law based upon an
equally outmoded sense of honor. The net closes about everyone,
even the mother, who originally wants to keep her son out of the
murderous game, and even, too, about the son, who becomes a
doctor, and knows that his role is to save lives rather than destroy
them. It is probably true that in France this film will be interpreted as a game, a sort of parody of a Western. But I think that
Buñuel was not playing a game. He was preaching. To the
Mexican audience, the repeated revolver shots are meant to say:
"Look. You draw your gun at the drop of a hat. See how foolish
this is!" It is a mistake to view this respect for science as naïve; the
contrast between the doctor, who saves lives, and the prejudiced
people, who cause death, is a very real consideration for a
Mexican audience. We live a different life, but Mexico is a country
where murder is rampant, and mass-murder is not unknown. And
yet, this same Mexico is the only country that wanted an artist of
the people. Here even a foreign director (and I think, too, of the
men who made *Forgotten Village)* accepts his duty as village
teacher. Mexico saved Buñuel and gave him back to us, and for
that alone we owe it our gratitude.

I am well aware that Buñuel is at his best when he limits
himself to the interpretation of reality. But I like to think he has
agreed to make himself useful in a country which took him in. I

respect the "international citizen" Buñuel, the Sunday-best Buñuel, whom we have known so well in the past. But I love this everyday Buñuel who comes to us today. And when, indeed, we can have our Buñuels one a day every day of the week, then I thank the beneficent gods who are smiling. And when there are only five Buñuels, and none for Saturday and Sunday, I am bored stiff and find my faith in the gods slipping.

Los Olvidados

André Bazin

• • • • • • • • • • • • • • • • • • •

Luis Buñuel is one of the most curious figures in the history of the cinema. Between 1928 and 1936 he made only three pictures, and of these, only one, *L'Age d'Or*, can be considered a full-length film. Yet these few strips of celluloid are undoubtedly among the classics of the cinema, and certainly, along with *Blood of a Poet*, among the few avant-garde works to have aged gracefully. And they are among the rare films of major importance to emerge from the surrealist movement.

Land Without Bread, Buñuel's semi-documentary on the miserable people of Las Hurdes, carried on the ideas set forth in *Un Chien Andalou*; indeed, the impassive objectivity of the journalistic approach far surpassed the horror and force of the mere dream-world. The donkey stung to death by bees achieves that nobility of vision found in the old barbarous mythology from the Mediterranean, every bit as well as the dead donkey on the piano. In this kind of boldness, Buñuel resembles one of the grand old men of the transition era between the end of the silent and the emergence of the talking film. Only Vigo, in spite of the small body of his work, can be compared to Buñuel. And yet, for a space of 18 years, Buñuel virtually vanished from the cinema. Unlike Vigo, death did not cut short his career. As far as we knew he had simply been swallowed up by commercial work in the new world, or perhaps in order to make a living, he was grinding out obscure third-rate pictures in Mexico.

Now, suddenly, here is a new film, signed by Buñuel. Oh, yes, a grade B film, a production ground out in a month on a short budget. But a film, at last, in which Buñuel has had a free hand in developing his own screenplay, his own directing and editing. It

From *Qu'est-ce que le Cinéma?* III: Cinéma et Sociologie (Paris: Editions du Cerf), 1961. Translated by Sallie Iannotti.

is like a miracle. After 18 years, and from the other side of the world, the old Buñuel sends us a message, faithful to *L'Age d'Or* and *Land Without Bread*, a message that lashes the spirit with its red-hot wires, and leaves the conscience no room to draw a breath.

The theme, on the surface anyway, is the same that, since the appearance of *Chemin de la vie*, has served as a model for all films dealing with juvenile delinquency: misery makes an evil counselor, and redemption comes through love, trust, and hard work. The fundamental optimism of this theme is, first of all, a moral optimism, on the order of Rousseau's, which proposes an innate goodness in man and a paradise of innocence in childhood, laid waste before it is ripe by an adult world. But it is also a social optimism, which suggests that society can repair the evil it has done through reeducation. In the rehabilitation center, a social microcosm founded on the trust, order, and brotherhood from which the young delinquent was too early weaned, the adolescent can be reestablished in his original innocence. In some ways this system works not so much to reeducate as to exorcise and convert. Psychological truth, garnered by experience, is not the main point. The static thesis on ravaged childhood, from *Le Chemin de la vie* and *Le Carrefour des enfants perdus* to *L'Ecole buissonière* (the character of the dunce, in particular) indicates that the central idea is the creation of a moral myth, a sort of social parable whose message is intangible.

But now *Los Olvidados* injects a new element; it warps the unfolding of this myth. Pedro, a difficult inmate of a model farm, is given the opportunity to prove himself worthy of trust. He is given a pack of cigarettes and money to buy sausages, like Mustapha in *Chemin de la vie*. But Pedro does not return to his open cage, not because he wants to steal the money and run away, but because he allows himself to be robbed by Jaibo, the evil companion.

You will notice that the myth is not contradicted ideologically, from within. It cannot be. If Pedro had broken faith, the director of the farm would still have been able to tempt him to right action. It is, objectively, much more grave that the experience strikes from without, and against Pedro's will, because in that case society is saddled with full responsibility—first, for having corrupted Pedro to begin with, and second, for having endangered his well-being. It is a good thing, the film seems to say, to set up model farms where justice, work, and brotherhood reign. But as long as injustice and sorrow remain unchanged in the environment, the evil persists. It is the evil of the objective cruelty of the world.

These references to films about wayward youth, however, illuminate only the most superficial aspect of a film that is, at base, fundamentally different. This is not the time to unravel the conflicts between the explicit thesis and the more profound ones; it is enough to point out that the first of these is significant only as a painter's subject is significant. For beyond the conventions (which he often takes up only to destroy) the artist perceives a transcendental truth, both moral and sociological—the metaphysical reality, if you will, of the cruelty of the human condition.

Los Olvidados is a great film precisely because it does not depend upon moral absolutes. There is no trace of Manichaeism in the characters; their guilt is fortuitous; their destinies cross like swords. Certainly, on the psychological and moral levels, Pedro is basically good and fundamentally pure. He is the only character who crosses this sea of filth without being sullied by it. But even Jaibo, the bad boy, who is sadistic, cruel, perverse, and treacherous, does not inspire repugnance so much as a kind of horror that is not incompatible with love and pity. He is like Genêt's protagonists, except that the author of *The Miracle of the Rose* deals with an inversion of values that we do not find in Buñuel's film. Buñuel's children are beautiful, not because they are good or bad, but simply because they are children, in crime as in death. Pedro is brother-in-youth to Jaibo, who betrays him and beats him to death. And although each becomes what his childhood experiences make of him, they are equal in death. Their dreams are the measure of their destinies. Buñuel performs the remarkable feat of recreating two dreams in the worst tradition of Freudian-Hollywood surrealism. And yet he brings us to horror and pity. Pedro runs away because his mother refuses to give him a piece of meat when he asks for it. Then he dreams that she gets up in the night and offers him a whole quarter of beef, raw and dripping blood, but that Jaibo, hidden under the bed, snatches it away. We can never forget this piece of meat, palpitating like

some ghastly sea creature, offered by a mother who smiles like a
madonna. Neither can we forget the miserable, mangy mongrel
who crosses and recrosses Jaibo's consciousness as he lies dying in
a shadowy no-man's land, his forehead crowned in blood. Buñuel
has furnished us with the only contemporary aesthetic expression
of Freudian symbolism that works. The surrealists used it too self-
consciously; we cannot respond to symbols too obviously and
arbitrarily chosen. By contrast, in *Un Chien Andalou*, *L'Age
d'Or*, and *Los Olvidados* these psychological situations are presented in all their profound and irrefutable truth. Whatever the
plastic form Buñuel gives to the dream (and in this case, it is
highly ambiguous) his images pulse with the life and feeling of
dreams. The dark, thick blood of the unconscious circulates in
these scenes, and drenches us, as if an artery had been opened into
the soul.

With both children and adults, Buñuel avoids making judgments. If adults are more generally wicked, it is because they are
more entrenched in misfortune. No doubt the most shocking
aspect of this film is that it dares to show the lame and halt
without making them pathetic. The blind beggar, tormented by
the children, avenges himself by turning Jaibo over to the police.
A legless cripple who refuses the children cigarettes is robbed and
left to lie on the pavement at some distance from his cart, and yet
he is clearly no better than his tormentors. In this world where
misery reigns, where everyone scuffles for life however he can,
there is no scale of misfortune. We are taken beyond good and
evil, and even further beyond happiness and pity. The moral
sense which some of the characters seem to possess is only, at
bottom, another accident of fate, a drop of purity and integrity
which the others do not happen to have. It does not occur to the
privileged ones to reproach the others for their evil ways any more
than they try to defend them. These people have no reference
except life itself, this life we think we could domesticate with our
moral and social order, if only the social disorder of misery would
cease to exist. We live in a sort of infernal earthly paradise, its
exits blocked by swords of fire.

It is absurd to reproach Buñuel for having a perverse taste for
cruelty. True, he does seem to choose situations for their par-
oxysms of horror. What more awful sight can be imagined than a

child stoning a blind man, unless it be a blind man revenging himself upon a child. After Pedro is slain by Jaibo, his body is tossed into a nameless ravine along with a spill of garbage and wastes, dead cats, and empty cans. And the people who get rid of him by throwing him there are among the few who have cared for him, a little girl and her father. But the cruelty is not Buñuel's. He is only revealing the cruelty that exists in the world. If he has chosen the most horrible examples, it is because the real problem is not whether good exists, but how deep into the sphere of misery human life can go. He probes the cruelty of creation itself. This theme was already evident in *Land Without Bread*. It makes little difference whether or not the miserable Hurdanos were truly representative of the Spanish peasant. They undoubtedly were. But they represent, first of all, the misery of all mankind. Thus it is possible, between Paris and Madrid, to measure the very limits of human degradation. Not in Tibet or Alaska or South Africa, but right in the Pyrenees, men like you and me, heirs of the same civilization, members of the same race, have become degraded, cretinous goatherds, subsisting on green cherries, and too brutish to brush the flies from their faces. It does not matter that they are an exception. It is enough that it is possible. Buñuel's surrealism reaches to the bottom of reality. We feel it. It knocks the breath out of us, like a diver weighted down with lead, who panics because he might never again feel solid earth beneath his feet. The dreamlike nature of *Un Chien Andalou* plunges us into the human soul. In *Land Without Bread* and *Los Olvidados* we explore man in society.

Yet the cruelty in Buñuel's work is entirely objective; it is nothing more than lucidity, nothing less than despair. And though pity is absent from the aesthetics of his films, compassion is a basic ingredient of his work as a whole. At least this is true of *Los Olvidados*, for it seems to me that this film represents a change of concept and a development since the appearance of *Land Without Bread*. The documentary on the Hurdanos was not devoid of a certain cynicism, a complacency that lacked objectivity; and in it the absence of pity becomes an aesthetic provocation. *Los Olvidados*, however, is a film of love, and it demands love. Nothing could be more unlike existential pessimism than

Because it evades nothing, concedes nothing, because it dares with surgical obscenity to make an incision in the corpus of reality, his cruelty can rediscover humanity in all its grandeur, and compel us, by a kind of Pascalian dialectic, to love and admiration. (*Los Olvidados*)

Buñuel's cruelty. Because it evades nothing, concedes nothing, because it dares with surgical obscenity to make an incision in the corpus of reality, his cruelty can rediscover humanity in all its grandeur, and compel us, by a kind of Pascalian dialectic, to love and admiration. Paradoxically, the predominant feeling that emerges from both *Land Without Bread* and *Los Olvidados* is the impression of an incorruptible human dignity. In *Land Without Bread*, a mother sits, immobile, holding on her lap the body of her dead child. And the face of this peasant woman, coarsened by poverty and sorrow, has all the beauty of a Spanish Pietà, in which nobility and harmony combine. In the same way, the most hideous faces in *Los Olvidados* never fail to be human. The presence of this beauty in horror (and it is not simply the beauty *of* horror), the sublime endurance of human nobility in the midst of decadence, transform that cruelty into acts of love and compassion. And it is for this reason that *Los Olvidados* does not affect us adversely, with either sadistic complacency or false indignation.

It is not possible to avoid touching on the surrealism in Buñuel's films. He is, indeed, one of the rare valuable representatives of this mode. But it would be a mistake to accord it too great a place in his work. His surrealism is a part of the rich and fortunate influence of a totally Spanish tradition. His taste for the horrible, his sense of brutality, his tendency to delve into the utmost extremes of humanity—these are all the heritage of Goya, Zurbaran, Ribera. And above all, it reflects a tragic sense of life, which these painters expressed through the ultimate human degradations: war, sickness, misery and decay. But their cruelty, too, served only as a measure of their trust in mankind itself, and in their art.

On *Nazarin*

FOOD FOR THOUGHT . . .   P.-L. Thírard

The priest in *Nazarin* is a continuation of the priest in *La Mort en ce Jardin*. They both raise the same questions. To avoid being accused of anti-clericalism and to continue his "profession of nonfaith," Buñuel took as his hero a priest who is not a hypocritical bastard (as for example was the priest in *El*), but who is, rather, clearly a "man of goodwill." This hero is weakened and diminished by his belief in God and religion. He is capable of surmounting this "disgrace" and of becoming human. But to the extent that he becomes a man, he will be that much less a "priest" and a "Christian."

Let us examine the unfolding of the padre's story, played by Michel Piccoli. At the outset of *La Mort en ce Jardin* he joins hands with the oppressors of the people. He is led, however, to hide a rebel sought by the police. He lets it be thought that he is sleeping with a prostitute rather than betray the fugitive. He follows a small hounded group into the jungle and sheds, little by little, through exhaustion and hunger, the persona of the priest, permitting, for example, his companions to drink from the sacred chalice, and ripping up the pages of his breviary to make a fire. But when old Castin becomes insane and dangerous, the padre gets himself killed trying to reason with him. Each of the padre's enterprises fails; each time he trusts someone, it turns out badly. His opposite is Chark, the outlaw, the tough man who kills first and thinks later. It is he who is right, not the padre.

This is how Buñuel seems to present the issue, and how Kyrou also has interpreted it. Yet the following points must be noted:* when the padre acts "like a man," he does not cease to act as a

From *Positif*, No. 38 (March 1961). Reprinted by permission of Editions Opta. Translated by Danielle Salti.
*See *Luis Buñuel e la religione*, in *Inquadrature*, 2–3.

Christian. He refuses to betray, to deliver the fugitive to the police; but hagiographic collections are full of accounts of priests martyred because of the secrecy of confession. He tears up his breviary to make a fire and offers drink from a chalice; these are acts of simple humanity, the blasphemous character of which is more symbolic than real. I believe that Buñuel indeed meant to say what Kyrou has construed. But I find it terribly unconvincing. I am likewise unable to muster much enthusiasm for the character of Chark, presented as a "positive hero."

Enter Nazarin. This time the priest is the main character. The opposition of the "true Christian" to "the hierarchy"—the latter representing hypocrisy and self-righteousness—does not imply that the pure Nazarin represents an ideal. We find that his series of attempts to live as a "true Christian" meet regularly with failure. The priest comes in conflict with love (the scene of the dying woman's rejection); he refuses solidarity with the exploited (the scene of the twig plucked during the shooting). But there again the ambiguity persists, particularly in the final scene. It is the one, summary objection to such unresolved cinema that where it leads nobody knows (like Cabiria at the end of Fellini's film, the hero of *Racines du Ciel,* or that of *l'homme aux colts d'or*). There can be no doubt, on the other hand, as to the final destination of Charlie Chaplin or Shane.

Everything unfolds as if Buñuel were torn between two perspectives: one, a poetic, nonrational, surrealistic perspective—that of *L'Age d'Or,* where it is not a matter of demonstration but of blasphemy (the Duke of Blangis was obviously Jesus Christ)—and the other, a perspective of reason and evidence. For the latter, Buñuel does not allow himself to show an ignoble priest (in the optical *L'Age d'Or* a priest is necessarily ignoble, in the style of Uruffe's priests) but rather a real priest, one of those to be cherished by the most irreproachable Christians, a saint. But Buñuel cannot conceal the correspondence which exists between a Christian and a human view of life; he will therefore have to build his story dangling between these two perspectives, relying alternately upon symbol and the demonstrations of objective reality.

And he must shift from one method to the other according to the argument brought to bear. Thus the famous scene of the priest plucking a twig during shooting: everything that precedes it invites consideration as an empirical demonstration. But it is a symbol. Here is why: it would have been just as logical upon hearing the shots for the priest to rush back to where they came from (a little later he puts into practice the parable of the Good Samaritan), even without it being a question of "solidarity with the exploited." It is therefore an arbitrary symbol. And the incident in the prison where Nazarin allows a hoodlum to beat him without a word and then wins him over by his dignity alone is also ambivalent. It can be viewed as proof of the absurdity of "turning the other cheek," but it also brings to mind all those similar scenes in which a weak man, as opposed to the strong, is saved by his dignity alone (*Tant qu'il y aura des hommes, Le bal des maudits, Les fiorettis de Francois d'Assise, Destin d'un homme,* etc.)—which always provides good dramatic effect, but is not necessarily Christian or anti-Christian.

The fact that Buñuel has slipped hints into the film (Clovis Trouille's sneering Christ, the drums of *L'Age d'Or*) only indicates the same ambiguity. Those who can understand, understand. If it is, as we are told, a film of combat, it is a farce: it is intelligible, by definition, only to those who are already convinced.

It must be obvious by now that my purpose is to challenge Buñuel. His position is untenable. One cannot play on both levels. Only talent and poetry will be demanded if, using symbolism, even blasphemy, Buñuel chooses to take a particular hero, to tell a story for its own sake. If, on the other hand, he is creating a model, then one has the right to demand rigor as well. In *El*, Francisco is obviously an exceptional man. The ordinary man in *El* is Raul, the engineer, a man of our times with a modern conception of love, to whom "fighting for a woman" seems absurd, since he refuses to view her as an object. He is, naturally, totally uninteresting. If Buñuel had wanted to make a polemical film, he would have wondered whether or not Raul was a Christian, what the consequences of this might be, etc. Buñuel has preferred Francisco, quite rightly, and the film is all the better for it.

Because Nazarin, after all, could easily be as evangelical and yet react differently; because the material failure of his enterprises proves absolutely nothing (no more than the failure of the priest in *La Mort en ce Jardin:* see the journal in *Diary of a Country Priest);* because this film is only "diaphanous" for a very small minority, those who, no doubt as a matter of predestination, have not received Grace—those who are not in possession of the Buñuelian patent of interpretation—are quite excused for erring in the night.

IN THREE POINTS . . .   Louis Seguin

·   ·   ·   ·   ·   ·   ·   ·   ·   ·   ·   ·   ·   ·   ·   ·   ·   ·   ·   ·

The interpretive attempts of some, the more or less feigned surprise of others regarding its supposed ambiguity, and the snickering of both when they are told of the absence in *Nazarin* of any opacity and of the uselessness of any interpretation, are all due to a serious confusion. Buñuel, they believe, intended to describe objectively, in order to draw a lesson, the life and times of a *good* priest. Well, Nazarin is not strictly that for anyone: not for the Church, not for his brothers, and not for himself.

I

It was not in vain that Saint Thomas Aquinas insisted on the union of Wisdom and Prudence, that prudence incapable of comprehending sublimities yet so necessary when a circumspect path must be drawn in the World. Nothing displeases the Church more than the untimely initiatives of its overzealous servants. Franciscanism, evangelical simplicity, the return to the love of God and of His creatures—the Church appreciates these some-times, when a vanguard can flatter certain souls in collision with an overly tyrannical authority during certain times of temporal weakness. But it always considers them with a restless and vigilant eye, as prompt to condemn William of Occam's extreme propositions and to discuss Fénelon's pure love, as it is to bring back to the fold the worker priests—congratulating itself not on their uncertain evangelic successes but on their perfect submission.

By taking the disdain of worldly goods to the ultimate—taking in an injured, condemned prostitute, wandering on the roads to dispense perfect love, by the excessiveness of his vocation and the scandal he arouses, Nazarin can be for Christians only an object of painful astonishment. From the point of view of the Roman Catholic Church, this repulsion is perfectly logical and justified. From *The City of God* to the encyclical *Diu satis*, passing through the *Rule* of Saint Benoît, Catholicism strongly praises the virtue of humility, but promptly canalizes the masochism thus encouraged by subordinating it to a precise obedience to God through the obligatory path of Hierarchy. Saint Francis of Assisi himself had guarded against presumptions of the individual regarding reforms. "Blessed," he said, "be the servant of God who places his trust in the clergymen . . . and woe unto those who scorn them." When he neglects the advice of his personal priest in Torcy, when he judges with one glance a "bad" priest he finds on the road, and above all as he pursues his solitary search for the truth of an authentic Christian life, Nazarin is proud, a rebel, and one can understand why OCIC, despite certain impulsive inclinations, refrained from bestowing its prize upon the auteur of *L'Age d'Or* whom some, with more or less certain good faith and muddle-headed haste, would have wanted to believe had been, if not converted, at least sobered, or, better yet, diminished in his recalcitrance.

II

The cliché, according to which the Church, disdainful of the temporal world, is as a matter of principle solely concerned with the spirit, can only impress the simple-minded or those avid for facile moral comfort. The Church could not be insensitive to the

perpetual material failures suffered by one of its pastors, justi-
fying them with a mystical "No matter, all is Grace." Following
Bernanos, Bresson surrounded himself in *Diary of a Country
Priest* with great precautions to dissipate the smell of heresy
which threatened to spread around his hero. The country priest
never exceeds certain limits; his conflict remains, above all,
internal; his mistakes do not go beyond a dramatically obtained
confession or the somewhat too timidly rejected insistence of an
adolescent girl.

Buñuel has no such scruples. He gives rein fully to his un-
frocked priest in the certainty that, rejected by the Church, but
always inhabited by a desperate love of God and men, he can only
do what he does: sow fire and murder in his wake. The intention
of *Nazarin* is not to show that even when he is sincere a priest
cannot escape error—if this were the case, all the travesties, all the
distortions, would be legitimate. Rather, it is that a priest, because
he believes in God and wants to be a dispenser of things sacred, a
mediator among men as the representative of a supposed deity, is
all the more harmful for his desire to be honest: Savonarola is more
contemptible than Alexander VI. It is no longer a pact signed by an
opium seller and a despotic society; the very nature of relations
among men is vitiated. The more the priest will try to be close to his
fellow men, to dissipate the screen of duplicity with which some of
his kind surround themselves, the more catastrophes he will
unleash. From *El* to *Nazarin* the progression is as clear as it is
logical. A man's madness (*El*), the hypocrisy in the face of violence
(*Cela s'appelle l'aurore*), murderous blunder (*La Mort en ce
Jardin*), and systematic devastation (*Nazarin*) form the logical
chain which, far from moving toward appeasement, manifests a
growing violence in Buñuel, a growing desire to destroy the very
principles of Catholicism. *Nazarin* goes well beyond *l'Auberge
rouge*; with Lara, the final catastrophe was the derisive consecration of the monk's efforts. With Buñuel it is the man of God
himself who unleashes catastrophe by the impetuosity of his faith.
The priest who, with the alibi of a supposed love, performs egoistic
activities is a wretched individual. But this one believes in the
purity of his intentions and acts with the help of actual Grace. The
bitterly derisive "little flowers" which Nazarin plucks amidst

resounding gunshots of a conflict to which his evangelic goodwill has just given birth, are bitter proof of his unredeemed injuriousness.

In his halting and unfailingly clumsy search for a truth and a love which elude him only to be metamorphosed under his bewildered gaze into violence, Nazarin appears like the Mother Courage of Christianity. He protests, but is unable to change anything because he uses inefficient yet dangerous weapons. In wanting to soften men's suffering by way of charity, he only aggravates those situations into which he intrudes, much like Mother Courage who, by dint of outwitting an abstract war, ends by causing the deaths of her children.

The comparison with Brecht is far from fortuitous. *Nazarin* is also a film about non-intervention, whose worst aspect, Christianism, the hero is out to denounce. The priest never has, can never have in what is for him the best of cases, more than that submissive gesture regarding which the worker in *Les Fusils de Mère Carrar* tells the priest: "The attitude one adopts to forbid oneself from accepting something is terribly similar to capitulation."

III

But, it will be said, all that is nothing. Nazarin may be awkward; he is scoffed at, useless, and scorned—we agree. But his harmfulness is only accidental. When Grace shines by its absence upon the fluid field of actuality, it is only to reappear all the better, all the more habitual upon the sky over which it reigns incontestably, spread over all people and things. It can be shown with ease that Nazarin receives Grace, in spite of his errors and even, with some added rhetoric, because of them. Is this not the case in those two films comparable to *Nazarin*—the Bresson-Bernanos *Diary of a Country Priest* and Rossellini's *The Little Flowers of Saint Francis?*

Yet that quality of grace would still have to manifest itself through some sign, the lack of which is particularly felt in Buñuel's film. Without going into the details of Norberto Del Prado's *De Divina Gracia,* since the catechism is sufficient, it can be assured that habitual Grace is bestowed upon he who is able to accept its presence. The Christian senses an acute feeling of his own dignity, yet feels that it is an appeasement, the announcement of assistance toward sanctification. It must reveal itself all the more to the priest, through highly concrete psychological expression. This sense of grace illuminates *The Little Flowers of Saint Francis* throughout, penetrates the denouement of *Diary of a Country Priest* and may be disclosed to any communicant with a little talent in Fellini's work.

For the Franciscans, this presence is Joy. "When," said Thomas of Celano, "the Devil has been able to ravish the soul's joy from one of God's servants, he is at the height of his wishes . . . but when the heart is full of spiritual joy, it is in vain that the serpent spreads its mortal poison." Saint Francis of Assisi and his brothers will therefore be shown by Rossellini to be always gay and happy, walking triumphantly into the worst misfortunes. This happens to such an extent that the ridiculous panoramic scenes rising toward the heavens, used for "spiritual effect," are quite unnecessary. As to the famous last words of the country priest, who would be more drawn toward some somber Jansenist humor, they are uttered with a newfound serenity: "His countenance was calm and he even smiled."

Nazarin is far from such a reckoning. From the beginning to the last scenes of the film, he can parade only his unhappy consciousness laced with a rather unorthodox morose delectation. Avid for the spark, for the sign that will justify him in his own eyes, which will give him, if not a peace which he rejects, at least a certain spiritual tranquility—not only does he find nothing, but he seems to reject even the possibility. He can only escape. He escapes from a plague-stricken village when the doctors arrive; he escapes from the woman's sickbed, chased away by human love; he escapes from the battlefield he has himself unleashed; and he even escapes from the responsibility for the "miracle" of which he may be the cause. The expressionless face of Francisco Rabal, astutely chosen by Buñuel, can only reflect a dismal astonishment, a lack of trust in God's assistance which should seem at least peculiar to the more intelligent moviegoer. Might God not also be dead there? And this priest, might he not be a far more repulsive monster than the brutal and cynical lover of Beatriz? Might not the dwarf, compared to such a deformed spirit, seem full of earnestness and nobility?

There is nothing more to see in *Nazarin* than what is shown, and that is why Benayoun speaks of a "diaphanous" film. Nazarin's "interpreters" are the kind souls who seek by force to detect a transcendence, whereas the film refuses God and His Grace any role. There are also the clever who, with a hardly more subtle ill-will, would disclose the flaws through which this transcendence might penetrate a film. This amounts to nothing more than a warped manner of interpreting the film.

Obviously one can still say that white is black, that the pine-apple-bearing Christ laced with drum-rolling in the denouement is an edifying image. Rabal, after having vainly attempted to practice the love of God, to discover human solidarity, looks like what he is: an idiot. No doubt he is aware of this idiocy and one might believe that he will be able to find himself, without god, "proud as a man."

THE PRIEST AND THE MAN   Marcel Martin

. . . .

It is presumptuous to claim to master a film as difficult as *Nazarin* after having seen it only once. At the time of its presentation in Cannes, it perplexed a good number of Buñuel's partisans, while the Catholic critics slyly pretended to see in it a Christian film; it is even said that the representatives of the International Catholic Office of Cinematography had considered for a moment awarding it their prize. Yet I have it from a good source that Buñuel learned with bewilderment that *Nazarin* could be viewed as a Christian message. In spite of what the Catholic critics say, and they have a well-known tendency to "incorporate"

Buñuel, *Nazarin* cannot fail to receive the worst moral grade from the Catholic Central.

This said, it must be recognized that the film is very complicated and that many details discourage its exegesis. It would be absurd to pretend to explain everything. Buñuel has been and remains a surrealist, and it would be in vain to attempt to provide a rational explanation for all his images.

The character of Nazarin appears to be a development of the priest in *La Mort en ce Jardin*, Father Lizzardi. One is brought to remember the cavalry he suffered in the company of a small group of fugitives across the virgin forest, and how he ceased being the odious little priest of the beginning to become a man. Faced with the problem of violence in society, Lizzardi placed himself instinctively and naively on the side of "order" against justice. He began to understand when injustice and violence affected him in the flesh, and ended up by perishing as uselessly as he had lived, but rehabilitated.

The character of padre Nazario is placed in the same perspective, but at a higher level. Likewise faced with the problems of justice and violence, he seems to find himself immediately on the side of the victims. Living in poverty, he refuses all compromise with the Pharisees who are his superiors and his colleagues (the refused breakfast) and takes a stand against the established order (he shelters a prostitute). While all the conformist (or "official") priests in the film are perfectly odious, he appeals to us through his purity, his altruism and his unselfishness, although these virtues are founded upon a mistaken conception of society, namely, upon a belief in the efficacy of non-violence.

It is important to note that he fails in all his attempts to improve mankind because his action is placed in the context of a given social setting which he has no mind to challenge. Men are corrupted by the social structure, and any effort at improvement which does not first come to grips with the social order (the "established disorder," as it has been called by Mounier) is nothing but vanity and reveals one to be no more than a dupe.

Thus his good works do not prevent his meager belongings from being stolen; the lesson in dignity which he gives the colonel who forces a peasant to make an about-turn to salute him

. . . he fails in all his attempts to improve mankind because his action is placed in the context of a given social setting which he has no mind to challenge. (*Nazarin*)

almost ends in tragedy for Nazarin; he thinks that the two women follow him out of contrition, whereas they are only in love with him; the plague-stricken woman he takes care of has her husband chase him away; and the prisoner he attempts to convert to a better life only thinks of asking him for money. In sum, it seems that the Christian morality preached by Nazario turns out to be totally inadequate in a society which is nothing but a jungle.

Yet if he is ineffective and useless, Nazario is far from being ridiculous or odious. He is not odious because he practices a true Christian morality and because he refuses to give in to the Pharisees and the compromises of Church officialdom. Thus he rejects the "miracle" as the fruit of ignorance, superstition, and witchcraft, while the Church exploits it (Lourdes). He is not ridiculous because his dignity and courage grant him respect: the lesson he gives the colonel can only arouse admiration, even if its mad uselessness almost inspires derision.

Such a gesture may redeem another detail in the film which is difficult to explain and which is the only incident which might lead one to imagine that Buñuel scorns his hero: Nazario negligently plucks a twig from a bush while we hear the shooting between the foreman and the workers. I see this not as cowardice, but as an example of Nazario's total incapacity to understand or even imagine social problems such as unemployment. In a clear-cut situation, such as in the quarrel with the colonel, his reaction is immediate and just.

Until the end, Nazario's inadequacy in the world remains total. Yet he is going to discover certain feelings unknown to him until this point. He thus notices that a dying woman prefers to call upon the man she loves rather than upon God's assistance; he realizes that "there is no justice for the humble"; he discovers after being harshly beaten by a fellow prisoner that anger and contempt can take the place of resignation; and finally the pineapple he is offered allows him to know true compassion and charity in others (in the past, the rich had given him alms only to prevent his poverty from causing a scandal).

Unencumbered by his cassock, a "uniform" which disqualified him by making him an unwitting accomplice of the established order, Nazario discovers values which change him into a different man, as was the case with Father Lizzardi before him. Only a ridiculous sectarianism would deprive him, merely because he is a priest, of the benefit of his generous acts: hiding the prostitute from the police is an act as noble as that of the protagonist of *Cela s'appelle l'aurore*, who hid his murderer friend. Nazarin, therefore, deserves our respect because he behaves like a man. His priesthood and the limits of his social conscience cannot be held against him.

What is important is that Nazario is respectable as a human being. The fact of his priesthood is secondary, since it is when he practically ceases to be a priest that he becomes truly and fully a man. I thus arrive at the heart of my analysis: Buñuel ascribes

divinity to humanity; he brings his character from mysticism to
humanism—which forbids any comparison with Fellini, a comparison which might provoke a naive or sly identification of the
pebble in *La Strada* with the pineapple in *Nazarin*. But the
symbolism of the road is diametrically opposite in these two
films.

It is clear that for Buñuel it matters little whether a man is a
believer or not. By the end of the film, Nazario has been relieved
of his cassock and his priestly functions, if not of his faith. The
divine metaphysics which had determined his behavior have
proven to be totally ineffective. The morals which he puts into
practice, founded upon non-violence, charity, love of one's fellow
man and a concern for his dignity, are no more specifically
Christian than those of a Gandhi or of any lay humanist. He is a
sort of free-floating hero, ineffective and ultimately useless, but
still a hero because he is solitary, rebellious, and deserving of
respect.

The final images of the film present a new problem: Has
Nazario gone insane? Does he take himself for Christ, as might be
suggested by the drum-rolling, directly borrowed from the ending
of *L'Age d'Or*, where Christ came out from the castle of Sadeian
orgies? Cannot one just as well assume that he is on the road to
unfrocking, to renouncing the Christian solutions and consolations of whose vanity and impotence he is at last conscious?

Nazario became a man by ceasing to be a priest. Since *L'Age
d'Or* Buñuel has always struck heavy blows against priests, in
whom the surrealists saw the symbol of that opiate which is
religion. Now that the surrealists of yesteryear attend mass or
belong to the Communist Party, one cannot reasonably blame
Buñuel for his present position. If the Catholic critics are so
tempted to "incorporate" him, is it not because he has never
scorned the man in the priest?

In this film Buñuel confirms, with greater depths and more
detours than ever, his conviction that priests can also be men and
that their rank does not authorize us to doubt their qualities *a
priori*. "You are a saint," says the prostitute to Nazario. By
discovering humanity, he may be simply becoming a man.

MONSTERS   Ado Kyrou

.   .   .   .

There is nothing more painful than to have to explain the
clearest, simplest things; but since for some time now obscurantism has become the Christians' second weapon (the first
being modernism), we must travel that path, and if we seem to be
smashing open doors, too bad! In any event, poisonous spiders
spin their webs on those open doors, making it necessary to break
them open in order to destroy the spiders.

I naturally agree with Benayoun and Seguin on the substance
of *Nazarin*, and will therefore not dwell upon the abundant
proofs of their thesis, namely that Nazarin is more an atheist
than anti-clerical.

On the other hand, there is an issue which has not been
analyzed. Buñuel is Spanish and a surrealist. He is therefore
attracted to monsters, to those beings behind the walls of di
Chirico's paintings and who haunt Goya's. In all of Buñuel's
work the unusual, that is to say the monstrous (I do not consider
this word as necessarily pejorative) enjoys an open house. Physical (the blind, lame, goitrous, etc.) and moral monstrosity (the
demented, neurotic, mystical, etc.) are the solid basis upon which
Buñuel's world is built. Since he is also a moralist, he does not
fail to take a position regarding those monsters and to declare his
love or hatred toward them. Even in the worst of cases, any
monster, however hateful, is much more interesting to Buñuel
than petits bourgeois of the kind in *Umberto D.*

A man who is young, attractive and healthy, who is a trans-
vestite, swears to abdicate his greatest joys (love, for example), and
who purports to believe in myths, is certainly a monster. This
man is, in fact, doubly a monster. He is part of a monstrous whole
called the Church and he behaves in such an unusual manner that
he fools the naïve and participates in the worst coercions. For he
sincerely believes in the very idiotic nonsense his companions

only pretend to believe, and in this sense he is at the least similar to them. What an admirable field for investigation!

Buñuel, then, sometimes amused, sometimes outraged, sets loose this double monster and watches him live and act in contradiction with his superiors and with life itself. What would the Christians who found the film "confusing" have wanted? Should Buñuel clamor, "This monster is ugly?" But, after all, he calms him, since he shows Nazarin dressed as a woman, unaware of the perturbations he provokes, and useless, atrociously useless and maleficent. If one does not see this man as a monster, and Buñuel addresses himself to healthy people, let them see Cloche's films!

Certain secondary characters in the film, even if they are physically monstrous, enjoy Buñuel's entire sympathy: the dwarf in love with the prostitute, the prostitute in love with the priest in whom she sees only a man, the dying woman who rejects the comforts of religion and demands the presence of the man she loves, etc.

This film places love and its Christian caricature in confrontation. Buñuel contrasts those who love with a man who adores a non-existent being, a "God," and wants to "do good" while eliminating any sexual or social context. "Love your neighbor," says the man of the Christian myth. "Love women and your companions," says Buñuel. The first precept leads to ideological wails, to resignation; the second, to love and rebellion. The choice is ours.

Thank you once again, Luis, for having given us a film full of flamboyant images, charged with dynamite, hope, love and certainty—a film addressed to mankind.

On *Viridiana*

ON *VIRIDIANA*   *Luis Buñuel*

. . . . .

Viridiana follows most closely my personal traditions in film-
making since I made *L'Age d'Or* thirty years ago. In all my work,
these are the two films which I directed with the greatest feeling of
freedom. I have been more or less successful with my films, some
of which, to be sure, have been banal. For myself I must say that I
made them just to make a living. Equally, however, I must say,
also, that I have always refused to make concessions and I have
fought for the principles which were dear to me.

I went back to Spain from Mexico because that is my country
and I could work there with total freedom. I did work there on
Viridiana with that freedom. What followed was one of those
pieces of nonsense that time will take care of.

We do not live in the best of all possible worlds. I would like to
continue to make films which, apart from entertaining the audience, convey to people the absolute certainty of this idea. In
making such films I believe that my intentions would be highly
constructive. Today movies, including the so-called neo-realistic,
do not make it clear that we do not live in the best of all possible
worlds.

How is it possible to hope for an improvement in the audiences—and consequently in the producers—when consistently we
are told in these films, including even the most insipid comedies,
that our social institutions, our concepts of country, religion,
love, etc., are, while perhaps imperfect, unique and necessary?
The true "opium of the audience" is conformity.

In none of the traditional arts exists such a wide gap between
the possibilities of what can be done and the facts of what is being
done, as in the cinema. Motion pictures act directly upon the

From *Film Culture*, No. 24 (Spring 1962). Reprinted by permission of the
publisher.

spectator. To the spectator, persons and things on the screen become concrete.

In the darkness they isolate him from his usual psychic atmosphere. Because of this the cinema is capable of stirring the spectator as perhaps no other art. But as no other art can, it is also capable of stupefying him. The great majority of today's films seem to have exactly that purpose. They thrive in an intellectual and moral vacuum. They imitate the novel. Films repeat over and over the same stories.

However, for myself, looking across the years I must insist that I have not tried to prove anything and that I do not use the cinema as a pulpit from which I should like to preach. I realize that perhaps I will be disappointing a great many with this statement. But I know that people will draw from *Viridiana* and from my other films many symbols and many meanings.

I want to make some comments about my film *Viridiana*. I feel that it is very Spanish, and it must be understood that *Viridiana* was a little-known saint who lived in the period of St. Francis of Assisi. The story is born of this situation: a young woman, drugged by an old man, is at his mercy, whereas in other circumstances he could never be able to hold her in his arms. I thought that this woman had to be pure and so I made her a novice preparing to take the final vows.

I know I have been criticized for having shown a knife in the shape of a crucifix. One finds them everywhere in Spain and I saw many of them in Albacete. I didn't invent them. It is the photography which stresses the malice and the surrealistic character of an object fabricated innocently and put into mass production. I am also reproached for my cruelty. Where is it in the film? The novice proves her humanity. The old man, a complicated human being, is capable of kindness toward human beings and toward a lowly bee whose life he does not hesitate to rescue.

In reality, *Viridiana* is a picture of black humor, without doubt corrosive, but unplanned and spontaneous, in which I express certain erotic and religious obsessions of my childhood. I belong to a very Catholic family and from the age of 8 to 15 I was brought up by Jesuits. However, for me, religious education and surrealism have left their marks all through my life.

Viridiana is a picture of black humor, without doubt corrosive, but unplanned and spontaneous, in which I express certain erotic and religious obsessions of my childhood.

Concerning *Viridiana* once again: I think that it has in it most of the themes which are closest to me and which are my most cherished interests.

VIRIDIANA   Emilio G. Riera

· ·

I have had the good fortune to see *Viridiana* and once again I find myself confronted with a number of problems regarding the man

From *Film Culture*, No. 24 (Spring 1962). Reprinted by permission of the publisher. Translated by Toby Talbot.

Luis Buñuel and what he represents. At first viewing of this profoundly Buñuelian film—the most Buñuelian in fact to date— it might seem sufficient to repeat some of the things which have already been noted about its creator and to add a few specific points. Curiously, however, although there is an apparent continuity of style and vision of the world in Buñuel's work, each of his new films demands a fresh reappraisal, particularly in the light of *Viridiana*. It is evident that Buñuel has not attained a coherent body of work through mere repetition but rather by a perpetual pursuit of self-discovery. *Viridiana* is a work of genius, and as such has accomplished much more than it set out to. In it Buñuel offers his audience a splendid opportunity for exploring his creative universe and finding enrichment in a fresh point of view, a new outlook on reality. If one can judge a film by the degree to which it serves as a lived experience for the viewer, *Viridiana* is without doubt exceptional and will, I predict, become a milestone in film history. Without further preliminaries, I shall attempt to set forth my impressions of the film.

Buñuel is not a believer to be overlooked. He obviously believes in the miraculous or, rather, in the liberating force of the irrational and in the poetry of instinct. Religion, however, as commonly understood, is, paradoxically, merely an attempt to rationalize the miraculous. It holds that God's existence can explain everything, whereas in reality the miraculous ceases being so the moment an argument, albeit an argument based on a supreme being, claims to endow it with logical meaning. This is the function of dogma. And of one thing I am certain—Buñuel is utterly free of dogmatism. He likewise instinctively opposes a secular form of rationalism which endows man with the ability to attain absolute knowledge, which is another form of dogmatism, one which gives man divine powers.

On the other hand, Buñuel is not an agnostic. Like any true artist, he explores the furthest stretches of reality, which does not necessarily mean that he refutes the validity of objective, scientific knowledge. On the contrary, knowledge is scientific only when it is cognisant of the miraculous and the futility of arriving at the absolute. (Buñuel's respect for science and systematized knowledge can be clearly appreciated, for example, in *El*.) Precisely because he extracts the entire substance of his art from the miraculous and the irrational indicates that he is antidogmatic and, therefore, an atheist—at least as far as his films show. Yet his atheism is unrelated to the sort of atheism which tries to reduce the real world to the dimensions of its own necessarily limited idea of reality.

Because Buñuel is an atheist, for that very reason he is not really blasphemous. His attitude is devoid of all diabolism. Not once does this movie-maker deride or insult God, which would be tantamount to acknowledging His existence. Buñuel never discusses God. What he discusses is man's conception of God, thereby revealing the strange, unpredictable role that religion plays in the subconscious of his characters. In *Viridiana*, Buñuel does not group the beggars in an arrangement similar to the figures in Da Vinci's "Last Supper" in order to belittle Christ and his apostles

In *Viridiana*, Buñuel does not group the beggars in an arrangement similar to the figures in Da Vinci's "Last Supper" in order to belittle Christ and his apostles by comparing them to some drunkards. What he is doing in this instance is reducing representation of the divine to the human scale.

by comparing them to some drunkards. What he is doing in this instance is reducing representation of the divine to the human scale. If indeed he is mocking anything, it is not Christ himself, but the manner in which Christ's image is worshipped. By the same token a crucifix serves doubly as a pocketknife, and the protagonist's objects of worship (a cross and a crown of thorns) are subconscious symbols of erotic impulses. Idolizing or insulting Christ are polar aspects of a similar dogmatic attitude, whereas incorporating religion and making it function within the characters' innermost unfathomable lives is something else again. A crucifix does not lose its mystical aura if someone spits on it, but it does if it is subjected to a use for which it was not intended. And it is noteworthy that although objects of worship lose their mystical qualities, they retain for Buñuel their miraculous qualities. Every atheist knows this, although he would not admit it.

Buñuel can neither prevent nor ignore the fact that his work is an outgrowth of the broad symbolism of a Catholic conception of the world. This is a question of perspective. An Egyptian author, even if he were an atheist, would produce a markedly Islamic work, whose nature would become increasingly evident as time went by. The Buñuelian trinity of eroticism–religion–death, a constant theme in his films, is conceivable only within the specific limits of Catholicism and, more concretely, of Spanish Catholicism. *Viridiana* has confirmed what we might have always suspected: Buñuel, the apotheosis of anti-patriotism, has never ceased being profoundly Spanish. The characters of this, his most recent film, have the authenticity which those of his Mexican films never had, not even those of *Los Olvidados*. *Viridiana*'s authenticity springs from Buñuel's intimate identification with Spain. Neither praise nor reproach is implicit in this fact, of course. One is Spanish, just as one belongs to one of the two sexes, or one is tall or stocky.

Buñuel's Spanishness explains to a great extent the persistence of the religious theme in his films. Spain has never completely abandoned the Inquisitorial spirit which couples the notion of sin with physical chastisement. Buñuel's films depict carnal flagellation and laceration and how it leads to the wild extremes of abnormal eroticism, masochism and fetishism. In *Viridiana* we watch Fernando Rey squeezing his feet into a pair of women's shoes and putting on a woman's corset, another form of physical oppression. Necrophilia, too, is clearly suggested when the fore-mentioned character goes into ecstasy over Silvia Pinal's inert body, a replica of his long deceased wife. Death and love are associated as forms of absolute possession.

Thus the trinity eroticism–religion–death are founded upon the concept of physical profanation. The beggars are monstrous because of their depraved profanity. Once and for all, Buñuel destroys the myth of purity cloaked in rags (which clearly iden-tifies him with a Marxist line of thought). His beggars are like lepers eager to contaminate others with the curse of their disease. This is what *they* have to give, and their simple presence serves to point out the essential absurdity of the notion of misguided charity. These people force Viridiana (Silvia Pinal) to face stark human reality. Viridiana is a feminine counterpart of *Nazarin*. Whereas *Nazarin*, however, was profaned by a thief's wrathful utterance, Viridiana is ravaged by one of the beggars. Through such profanation, revolt and utter nonconformity, man's true nature is revealed.

While Viridiana is another Nazarin, the elderly Spanish gentle-man, portrayed by Fernando Rey, is a reincarnation of Arturo de Cordova in *El*. Once again we have a social parasite who allows his lands to lie fallow and who is torn by the conflict between his prejudices, fantasies and religious impulses as, for example, after having drugged Viridiana, he implores his servant: "Don't mis-understand what I'm doing, Ramona." This man is represent-ative of the spirit of Spanish Catholicism, which has been nur-tured on the pursuit of death, due to the impossibility of attaining the absolute in life. The quest for the absolute is his distinctive trait, as it is Viridiana's, Nazarin's, and as it is likewise prominent in *El* and in *Ensayo de un Crimen*. It is the distinctive trait of poets.

In portraying each of his characters, their confrontation with reality and their personal inadequacy, Buñuel shows in each instance the failure of old Spanish dogmatism. There is here an unmistakable connection with a long literary tradition ("Don Quixote", the picaresque novel, Quevedo and Galdos) and therefore any attempt to regard *Viridiana* as merely a comment on Spain's present-day political and social situation is obviously too facile an interpretation. Actually, the film reflects a perennial picture of Spain (although, I hope, not of its future).

In short, all of Buñuel's work reveals a moral position towards a society to which, wittingly or unwittingly, he belongs, and which plays a determining role in his life. *Viridiana's* extraordinary richness and density is a result of its having been filmed in Spain which means that it is not lacking in the essence of Spanishness and concrete significance for Buñuel. We can realize now why some of his Mexican films might have left the impression of disorientation and conventionalism. Buñuel was attempting to depict Spain while employing Mexican faces and backgrounds. That is the simple truth and any chauvinistic reaction of injured pride is sheer stupidity.

An entire book could be written about *Viridiana* without exhausting its subtle meanings and implications. I have discussed the characters played by Silvia Pinal and Fernando Rey, but a great deal could also be said about the character portrayed by Francisco Rabal, who typifies a mongrel, commonsense Spain, stripped of poetry, to which Buñuel ironically concedes possible victory at the end of the film, when Viridiana winds up playing cards. And then there is Ramona, the servant, another participant in the card game, who, by sleeping with her employer, gains the right to eat at the same table with him, and who seems to foreshadow the future downfall of traditional hierarchies. The beggars, those excruciatingly human characters, enable Buñuel to achieve one of the most hallucinatory scenes that has ever been seen on the screen. It is straight out of Goya.

We already know that Buñuel despises the deliberate use of symbols, as *The Young One* bears out. Yet, he intuitively endows his characters with such powerful symbolical force that one may easily be led to detect symbols everywhere. However, there is nothing illegitimate about them. As a matter of fact, Buñuel never falls into a preconceived abusive symbolism which might jeopardize the concrete, human nature of his characters. A symbol should emerge from the cinematographic material itself, and never overshadow it.

I doubt whether the script itself of *Viridiana* has a fraction of the film's richness. The dialogue, indeed, is excellent, so much so that one could say it is the first authentic Spanish dialogue in any film, and that does not mean that it is academic Spanish. One must suppose, however, that some of the dialogue emerged from the actual production. For in experimenting with his actors, Buñuel used an actual beggar to play a beggar's role. And while every moviemaker knows the value of working with a well-defined script, the talented ones realize that making a movie means a constant re-discovery of its elements.

Buñuel proves in *Viridiana* that his much commented-upon technical shortcomings are a myth. Naturally, Buñuel does not think in terms of technique, but any movie-maker who knows how to move his camera about without ever being enslaved to a false notion of style, and who can provide us with an impressive succession of scenes, is certainly one who thinks in cinematic terms. And therein lies the secret of all cinematographic technique. Likewise, there was no need for Buñuel to continually bear in mind Eisenstein's and Prokofiev's illuminating essays on the role of music in films in order to dispense with music when he considered it unnecessary and to play Handel's "Messiah" during certain passages of *Viridiana*, using music for dramatic effect rather then reiteratively. In other words, Buñuel does not conceive of music as a mere adornment, but as an element of counterpoint, to be used integrally rather than as a superfluity. This reveals exceptional realistic integrity, although other movie-makers, who do not share Buñuel's views, may legitimately choose to incorporate music into their films.

This movie has thoroughly excited my imagination, and yet my review may seem inconclusive. *Viridiana* must be seen several times to be appreciated fully. Meanwhile, however, it has accomplished the miracle of arousing the enthusiasm of all those who have seen it, something which *El, Nazarin,* and *The Young One* did not succeed in doing, although I will not discount these films and I am willing to argue endlessly with people who agree with me about almost everything except this. I must confess, however, that, unlike Buñuel's previous films, *Viridiana* has the great advantage in that there can be no confusion between the ambiguity of the physical reality and any ambiguity in its creator's moral position.

Viridiana, as everyone knows, has been censured by the Franco government and by the most reactionary element of the clergy. Defense of the film however should not be limited to Buñuel's political adversaries who would certainly like to see the last vestige of his work destroyed. The freedom to exhibit *Viridiana* ought to be defended by all those who wish to see it and judge for themselves. As for the potential intrigues and pettiness of the so-called "defenders of national industry," the pocketbook patriots, they must be staunchly opposed by those who, convinced that *Viridiana* is the work of a sincere man, feel it their duty to listen to him.

VIRIDIANA AND THE CRITICS   Louis Seguin

. . . .

Viridiana has many virtues, and the greatest of these, as in almost all of Buñuel's films, is its power to disturb. We have only to read the critics to be convinced of this, for most of them, confronted by this film, have scurried for cover. Time and again they try, very gingerly, to diffuse its power, partly because that is the thing to do, and partly because they are afraid to admit their ignorance of what they evidently believe is a mysterious and fascinating conspiracy. And so they chatter on in order to avoid the first basic principle in Buñuel's works—the first basic principle, indeed, for

From *Positif,* No. 47 (July 1962). Reprinted by permission of Editions Opta. Translated by Sallie Iannotti.

all self-respecting thinkers—that God can be only incomprehensible to man.

This, as I said, is the first clear assumption we can make when we look at Buñuel's films. But it is not the major one, nor is it as facile as the Reverend Father Bro, O.P., would have us believe; for although he is careful to mask his intentions, he protests too much. Such, too, is the aim of Mardore's provincial subtleties and Jean Carta's elementary tricks in *Témoignage chrétien*.

After expostulating for three or four paragraphs, Mardore can no longer restrain himself from the pleasures of slander:

> Long ago, it is said, the man who later created *L'Age d'Or*—goaded by ambition and the sort of snobbery that is excusable in the very young—wanted more than anything in the world to shine in the high society of Saragossa. To this end, or so the story goes, he cultivated the friendship of a man whose appetite for fame was equally insatiable—the future General Franco, then Director of the Military Academy in Saragossa. Now, years later, did the dictator remember that gay young blade who hung around his old circle, when, responding to the scandal unleashed by the Vatican, he virtually insured the popularity of *Viridiana*? I am not privy to his thoughts, so I find it difficult to understand how "reasons of state," or, better yet, the absence of a sense of humor, or, best of all, a particularly subtle form of humor, could have incited him to ban Buñuel's film. And to extend this censorship from one end of his country to the other. By this act, backed by his absolute authority, he has forever secured the reputation of its being subversive for this film, and rendered the director the invaluable service of spreading his fame. Perhaps he remembers being present at its birth.*

By such ringing rhetoric, fraught with alliteration ("absence of a sense of humor") and chance neologisms ("thematic subversity") Mardore has sought to perpetuate an irksome and rarefied misconception. He has, however, merely proved his own banal taste for gossip. After this initial salvo, he surrenders, for those who might still dare to doubt, the last shred of his critical integrity:

> I envy the innocence and self-assurance of the neo-, crypto-, or para-surrealists who believe that Buñuel was merely referring to "imbeciles" and not to them in his interview with Georges Sadoul (*Les Lettres Françaises*, no. 878).

Cahiers du Cinéma, no. 127, p. 49.

A vision of Buñuel's disavowing his friends of long standing would indeed be an occasion for his enemies to celebrate. But these friends might open that copy of *Lettres* and see for themselves; what they read will reassure them. Buñuel said: "Certain imbeciles have written that I have made a *film noir*. To hell with dirty films. I detest them." Of surrealists—neo, crypto, or para— not a word. Buñuel is saying, once more and with good reason, how he distrusts anything which degrades mankind. He bluntly and vigorously expresses the hope that he will not be confused with Yves Allégret. *"Noir"* in this context can have no other meaning, above all, historically and artistically, in the mouth of a man who has long dreamed of filming *The Monk*. The surrealists, among whom Mardore no doubt once counted himself (until he realized his most cherished ambition, writing for *Les Cahiers)* have never believed otherwise.

These minor deceptions, however, do serve a purpose. They prepare the way, at some length—for fully half the article, in fact—for Mardore's "illuminations" of Buñuel's metaphysics.

The error of the "Buñuelian activists and extremists" is that they never "glance, it seems, at more than one side of their favorite planet." Mardore, himself, is of the exactly opposite opinion from Moullet. If Buñuel, good atheist and anarchist that he seems to be, appears to attack society and religion, "this position of attack" only seeks to "correct the abuses of the system from the vantage point of 'alienation' [*étrangeté*], from which the almost impalpable shifting of reality can be observed." He enjoys "a dialectic that ponders the infinite, at once affirming and destroying the possibility of understanding." In brief, then, going from one extreme to another, from a position of "with" to one of "against," from the inside to the out, Buñuel's film is "as complex as the mystery of life." This charming fluctuation, from dialectic of love to all-embracing mystery is, in its very elasticity, capable of pardoning the fuzzy analyses of men like Mardore and the lack of assurance in their convictions.

Mardore, interpreting in his own way Buñuel's "universal duality" (he is perhaps alluding here to Descartes' "universal doubt," though one is never quite sure), develops a Prisunic philosophy which he generously attributes to Buñuel. First, he sets aside the thorny question of blasphemy. This, he says, is strictly a matter of style. *Viridiana's* heresies and blasphemies spring from the imprecision of the Spanish tongue, a language which, no doubt in comparison to his own jargon, Mardore judges to be of little significative importance. For the most part, it is merely a question of a pious reaction against idolatry, which Mardore calls "decanting the routine." In actuality, of course, this takes in most of the film.

As for the rest of the film, the "spiritual adventures" of Viridiana, Mardore, like the last of the little quails, is torn between belittling it, a course which, on reflection, he abandons, and christianizing it (in a dull reduction of Buñuel's Christian connections) as a criticism of pride. The most that can be said of these reflections and conclusions is that they are neither very new nor richly imaginative. Mardore extends them, however, by tossing out labels which obviously enchant him, all the more as they are, for him, words without meaning. Like Moullet, he speaks of "materialism," of "truth" and "reality." He spouts formulae, such as "if one does not intend to play god . . ." which, strictly speaking, say nothing. A good professor of philosophy (though Mardore, of course, affects a distrust of professors, no doubt because these specialists know their own language) would surely have marked the margins of this manuscript with signs of his irritation and perplexity.

Such an overriding desire to see himself as a scrupulous dialectician leads any writer (especially when his cultural level is as summary as Mardore's) only to promulgate confusion. Meaning is lost among "vague and impure things" which damned beyond recall the preface to *Monsieur Teste.* And the worst of it is that the misapplication of technique reflects upon the subject the writer was thought to be defending. This, without a doubt, is the most heinous crime a critic can commit, and one which he must avoid at all costs; he may condemn, explain, curse, exalt, or complain. But he must never reduce what he is discussing to the level of its occasional confusion. Nevertheless, Mardore lost a magnificent opportunity. If he was up on his Plato, he would have been able to couple the word "alienation," which he flung out completely at random, to "exile," to the *aetheia* of Thales, in Plato's *Theaetetus,*

which makes a mockery of the masses. If Mardore had read
Nietzsche instead of talking aimlessly of "the exacerbation of
Nietzschian individualism"—a phrase devoid of any sense—he
might have seen that the exile, the aberration, was blood-brother
to the Madman in *Joyful Wisdom* who, taunted even by "those
who do not believe in God," poses the final question of Nazarin
and Viridiana: "God is dead. God is dead and it is we who have
killed him. . . . The magnitude of this act is too great for us.
Are we, too, not forced to become gods, to seem worthy of the
gods? Never before has there been such a grandiose act, and those
who come after us will, because of our act, become part of a
history more noble than any that has gone before." If Mardore
had read Heidegger, at least, he could have contemplated the
conclusion of the commentaries: "And thought commences only
when we learn that Reason,* which reigned most gloriously for
centuries, is the greatest, deadliest enemy of Thought."

For Buñuel, God is an infantile malady in metaphysics, which
man must suffer through, and learn to overcome. True humanism
begins only afterward—beyond the alienation.

Buñuel knows the significance of the thing he fights as well as
he knows its anatomy. In his struggle with the Angel, he emerges
victorious, but only after understanding that what he has fought
is a distorted reflection, inconsistent with himself. He has recounted this battle time and again since *L'Age d'Or* because he
sees it as an example; he has learned, precisely, where and how to
deliver his blows.

As an illustration of this, we turn now to the Reverend Father
Bro, Dominican, who was invited by *Figaro Littéraire* to discuss
the question: "Is Buñuel's *Viridiana* a wicked film?" When Bro's
interlocutors—Dominique Rolin at the helm—do their utmost,
with unparalleled stupidity, to make Buñuel's message "reas-

---

*With a capital R. This becomes a transcendental word, or name; it denotes the
absolute, the divine, if you will, to which our ideas must refer if we are to compre-
hend the world. This condemnation includes the layman's "Reason" also. "It is
not enough," said Crevel, "to substitute one priest with another. We must suppress all priests."

suring" (having, indeed, insulted Buñuel in passing, declaring that he possesses "the fanaticism of his race," for example), Reverend Bro will not let them get away with it:

> Priest that I am, I am very aware of what is foremost in Buñuel's mind—that is, the struggle between shadow and light, good and evil. I am aware, too, of his desire to eliminate any easy solutions. This is a question of too much importance to pass over lightly.
>
> But I cannot help being shaken by the deliberately shocking elements Buñuel has chosen to put in *Viridiana*.
>
> In the first place, he parodies the suffering of the innocent, even the suffering of Christ. He profanes the ritual which I perform each morning when I celebrate the Mass. He slips in thousands upon thousands of allusions to the Passion of our Lord. In one scene, he alludes to Jesus in the Garden of Gethsemane; in another, to the Immaculate Conception; in a third, the head of Jesus washed by Veronica. It is at this point that I am forced to ask myself if the public ought to see all the impieties Buñuel inflicts upon us.
>
> Another element of shock goes much deeper than the mere will to commit sacrilege. Buñuel leaves mankind no alternatives. No hope in the goodness of man, no belief, is tolerated. If childhood is the subject, it is shown to be corrupt, contaminated. Love also, and parenthood in particular, suffer the same fate. Buñuel does not allow the presence of children ("what an affliction of kids . . .") or human endeavor to compensate for suffering. And the film ends in a vision of a love triangle which is quite obviously sordid.
>
> Yes, this wickedness scandalously throws the whole value of man into doubt.*

In other words, a battle line is drawn up; it is him or us. Beyond the fact that this discussion opens up new perspectives in the argument (the theological seminary of *Positif* has given us a complete history of the censored impieties of *Viridiana*) Reverend Bro's feeling of revulsion has at least the merit of a perfect internal logic.

For the true believer, Buñuel's world can only be an object of fear and loathing. It is not only because of its heresies and its immoralities; for the curses, even in Spanish, the *ménage à trois*, and the irritation that comes in response to the scathing purity of childhood, have always been condemned by the Church. Rather, it is because Buñuel confirms what Reverend Bro and all true Christians abominate: the idea that humanity is sufficient unto itself. That there is no need whatever for hope. This, the second of the three cardinal virtues is what led St. John to say: "Rabbi, we

*Le Figaro Littéraire, 14–4, 1962, p. 25.

know that thou art a teacher come from God; for no one can interpret these signs unless God be with him."* And Jesus himself promises "Blessed are the poor in spirit, for theirs is the kingdom of heaven."†

One point, which Bro, in his preoccupation with other matters, merely hints at—Buñuel's impassivity before "the human effort to compensate for suffering"—has been covered quite fully and almost simultaneously, by a layman, Jean Carta, in the April 13 issue of *Témoignage chrétien*.

Carta, although he denies it ("Let us not seek to convert him, that would be ridiculous") reverts quite naturally to the classic argument: Buñuel, he says, is "anguished" and "obsessed"; he is marked—and Carta is very careful to tell us exactly how—by his Catholic upbringing: "In his attitudes, some obscure and incessant battle against the Angel can be discerned." Buñuel commits certain heresies, which Carta, by a neat turn of phrase, is pleased to define as "laborious." Let us by-pass the question of whether Carta could, in the improbable case that he might want to, define in *Témoignage chrétien* "easy" sacrilege, and go on to the more subtle points, which Carta calls the "message" of the film.

Viridiana, he says, "tells the story of a virtuous woman who wants to perform good deeds. Believing, with Saint Paul, that charity forgives all, believes all, supports all, she gathers about her a handful of repulsive and cynical beggars, with the pious intention of taking care of them and saving their souls. But these beggars repay her with ingratitude and violence. In the meantime, in the same setting—a country estate—her cousin succeeds in running a profitable business."

Several paragraphs later, Carta concludes:

> Buñuel's anti-Christian arguments might carry some weight if he did not resort to trickery. Whether the spectator is Catholic or not, he will be hard put to recognize the social doctrine of the Church in the actions of these illuminated creatures, whom the artist presents as his finest children, the most advanced, the most "committed." It will be even harder if one is aware of the immense current of social Christianity which has come into being and daily grown stronger during the last several decades. *Témoignage chrétien* is

*John I, 3, 2.
†Matthew V, 3.

one of the voices of this movement. And in this movement, a spirit of charity without lucidity, without the value of a collective perspective, without political commitment, cannot suffice. The half-blind bigotry, the absence of common sense which Buñuel attributes to his "good" priest Nazarin, as well as to the "devout" Viridiana, reign still, perhaps, in certain sectors of the Spanish Church, the most archaic in Europe, but it certainly does not pertain to the militant Church around us, in the syndicates, for example, of the French Mission, or even in the prisons of the Gaullists.

Viridiana, and I say this not in a spirit of contention, comes too late to convince us. The film expresses—and herein lies its value—the anguish and obsessions of a man, an artist. But in the very design of the message we see only a "Spanish" criticism, a hundred years behind the times, hopelessly provincial. Buñuel has chosen a crippled adversary, too easily overthrown.

Before going any further, it might be useful to explain that the reservations expressed in *Témoignage chrétien* come from the progressive Catholics. Even in *Positif,* alas, Paul-Louis Thírard has developed a similar argument around *Nazarin,* but it can be easily transposed to *Viridiana.* According to this theory, Buñuel's priest and his novice are two loveable idiots, and by presenting them in this way, in reducing them to this level, the director has overplayed his hand.

But, returning to our text, Carta (out of either divine idiocy or laborious humor) next mistakes orthopedics for sexual deviation. He is under the illusion that in *Viridiana* love, de Sade style, is mingled inextricably with a fascination with rape and degradation. Carta makes an error in interpretation rather surprising, at first glance, in one who involves himself in cinematographic theology in a Catholic journal. Saint Paul's Charity, the third of the cardinal virtues, has little in common with the gestures of Buñuel's priest and his young girl who give their goods to the poor. Those "highest mandates" are theological virtues; they have God as their prime object, in contrast to the moral virtues. On the presence or absence of this theological Virtue, Charity, hangs the definition of the Christian character. As Saint Paul said in Chapter 13 of the First Letter to the Corinthians: "And if I bestow all my goods to feed the poor, and if I give my body to be burned, but have not Charity, it profiteth me nothing."

This misinterpretation, so common today, is not a gratuitous one. It permits Carta to pretend to believe that Buñuel concerns himself only with the social doctrine of the Church. Yet actually this director's goal in *Viridiana* is to demonstrate that since God does not exist, man, when he awaits the divine consecration of his works, hopes in vain. It is not fitting to seek an absent God in his creatures, but to bestow on these creatures an immediate, practical love, and above all a physical love. Pedophilia and the *ménage à trois* fulfill these needs and answer these creatures' desires, no matter how much this might be shocking to Jean Carta. Buñuel is satisfied to be counted among those men who, like the Madman in *Joyful Wisdom,* have "plied the sponge and erased the horizon." In contrast to the men who attack the effect in order to cure the cause, Buñuel shows himself to be a man who is thoroughly familiar with the united, powerful Church he fights, while he calmly strikes at its vitals.

In the light of these salient points, Carta proves his criticism once more to be of questionable value. From Albert de Mun to Georges Suffert, including Leo XIII and the evils of Marc Sangnier, the Catholic Church has carefully provided itself with a strong position "on the left." The Church knows, because it is wise, that times are hard; it acts in accordance with this knowledge. To *Das Kapital* the Church replies with the encyclical *Rerum Novarum;* it pardons, within exacting limits, a man like Bishop Davezies when it sees the Free School in France menaced by a proposed change of regimen.

But the social activities of the Church have always had certain limitations. When Albert de Mun proclaimed his love for the masses and put his new beliefs into practice, he thought no less of the Church: "By its very essence, socialism is condemned to fail, or to instigate violence. Probably both. . . . It is necessarily left to those who attribute their passions to the most audacious of origins. . . . All that is good, just, and truly fruitful in its aspirations derive from Christian influences. In rejecting them, the socialist condemns himself to sterility." Like Marx, Buñuel declares for the opposite view, and he goes on to prove his case.

Furthermore, and here Carta's game appears particularly dishonest, the hidden tactic cloaks, however imperfectly, the desire for further conquests. The pendulum swings, in stately rhythm: the Pope on the "left" is succeeded by a Pope on the "right."

Rerum Novarum is followed by the *Syllabus*. Everywhere that the Church continues in power, or regains its hold on power, the use it makes of that authority is deeply reactionary. One has only to recall events in Colombia, Italy, western France, and Spain, where the story of the recent strike by the Basque and Austrian Episcopates, which—stripped of all its political character—was condemned to failure, to know that this is true. When he assures his audience that the naïve evangelicism of Nazarin or Viridiana is "perhaps" only the earmark of "certain remote sectors of the Spanish Church," Carta is adding hypocrisy to dishonesty. This charity (with a lower-case c) is, in the eyes of the Church, at least equal to another kind of Charity. It is a Charity, more social in nature, which the hierarchy has the most solid reasons for distrusting, since it still smarts under the memory of the worker-priests who came to the logical conclusions of their apostleship and defrocked themselves.

When the critical moment arrives, the Church hastily folds up its advanced elements. The vise clamps shut upon any little fingers which remain in the way. And the idiots on both sides of the struggle who have invested themselves up to their necks in this point of view are likely to find themselves suddenly arm-less. They have no choice, then, but to believe, to obey, and to pray in unison with the Reverend Father Delarue.

Oh, yes, Buñuel knows what he is doing when he dismisses Charity. He is striking at the very root of our alienation, of our exile. His thesis in *Viridiana* is limited, it is true, but he is all the more honest for that. Only the Church pretends to pass from the individual to the universal. Buñuel keeps himself to a precise, concrete situation, to a social category. It is evident that another sort of film could be made about the worker-priests. Its pace would be different, but its end would be similar, and neither Carta, alas, nor Thírard would find the truth in it.

A final point. It is not pleasant to see critics like Jean Carta enjoy harassing (and in such an underhanded way) a man they would never confront in the open. It is equally unpleasant to see a reputable journal like *Positif** implicated in their endeavors.

---

*Carta quotes a line by Marcel Oms, taken from "the excellent collection recently devoted to Buñuel by the review, *Positif.*"

"Thank God—I am still an atheist":
LUIS BUÑUEL AND
VIRIDIANA   David Robinson

. . . .

> *Viridiana* is a direct continuation of my personal tradition from *L'Age d'Or*. With thirty years between them, they are the two films I have made with the most freedom.

The wonder is not that Buñuel, who is one of the greatest artists the cinema has produced, should have spent fifteen years in the wilderness. Between *Las Hurdes* (1932) and *El Gran Calavera* (1947)—though properly speaking it was *Los Olvidados* in 1950 which marked his return—he was virtually inactive, confined to unproductive administrative jobs in the studios or driven to refuge in the Museum of Modern Art, from which he was hounded by the first anti-Communist witch-hunts. (Not that he was known as a Communist; but as director of *L'Age d'Or* he was fair game for the Red-hunters.) The wonder is rather that in the wilderness he was never tempted; never once, before or since, compromised; so that *Viridiana* still speaks as loud and as clear and with the same voice as *L'Age d'Or*, still asserting sanity and cleanliness in a world whose nature is to be mad and filthy. If there has been a change in the thirty years between, it is that the Swiftian fury of *L'Age d'Or* has given place to a calmer philosophic clowning, as cool and therefore as deadly as Voltaire.

> It was not my intention to blaspheme, but of course Pope John XXIII knows more than I do about these things. . . .

The story of how *Viridiana* came to be made is now well known. Gustavo Alatriste proposed that Buñuel should make a film exactly as he wished. Then it was decided that the film should be shot in Spain, in co-production with the two most

From *Sight and Sound,* Vol. 31, No. 3 (Summer 1962). Reprinted by permission of the publisher.

advanced new companies there. UNINCI began production with *Welcome Mr. Marshall* and recently produced Torre-Nilsson's *The Hand in the Trap*; Films 59 enjoyed considerable international success with their first features, *Los Golfos* and *El Cochecito*. Buñuel can hardly have been reluctant to identify himself with this renascence in the Spanish cinema; and the Spanish authorities were rashly delighted to welcome him home. They had, of course, underestimated their wandering son.

Somehow the script of *Viridiana* was put over on the censor, who requested only one slight change to the ending—a proposal which Buñuel gratefully accepted as a distinct improvement over the conclusion he had himself devised. The film was finished, and almost before anyone was the wiser, arrived in Cannes. The story goes that the censors never saw the film complete: it was barely ready in time for Cannes, so that with due apology it was submitted for appraisal in short sections, whose piecemeal effect must have seemed more or less innocuous.

At Cannes, of course, the film was a triumph, and the official Spanish representative proudly but incautiously stepped on to the platform to collect the Palme d'Or. The horse had bolted and the stable doors began to slam. The authorities were appalled: the Pope himself was said to have given voice to his disapproval. Officials were dismissed. A hue and cry was begun to find and destroy the negative. Trade agreements were invoked to prevent the film from being shown in France. The Spanish press was forbidden even to print its title. At 61, Buñuel was still as scandalous as he had been at 29, when *L'Age d'Or* provoked riots and bomb-throwing in Paris.

> I don't see why people complain. My heroine is more of a virgin at the dénouement than she was at the start.

The form of the story is comparable to *Candide* or *A Cool Million,* in that it is the progress of an innocent and her discovery of life in all its carnal and surreal monstrosity. On the eve of taking her final vows, Viridiana is bidden to visit her sole relative, Don Jaime. Her reluctance, her fear of facing the outside world, proves to be a foreboding. She finds that her uncle is a devout and gentle old patriarch who plays sacred music on the organ and does not acknowledge his only son because he was born outside the church's grace. The old man's strange pleasures include squeezing his plump body into the wedding garments of the wife who died on the night of their marriage, watching his housekeeper's little girl skipping, and caressing the phallic handles of the rope he has given her. Spying on Viridiana through a keyhole, the housekeeper, Ramona, discovers that the girl sleeps on the floor and that her luggage consists of a wooden cross, some nails and a crown of thorns.

Viridiana resembles Don Jaime's dead wife, and he asks her to put on the wedding dress. She does so; but when her uncle goes on to ask her to marry him, Viridiana angrily refuses. With Ramona's assistance, Don Jaime drugs the girl and carries her to bed. First laying her out like a corpse, he passionately kisses her, but stops short of worse assaults. Next morning, however, he tells Viridiana that she cannot return to her convent, for he has possessed her while she slept. She leaves the house notwithstanding;* but Don Jaime has one last trick to outwit her. He hangs himself with the child's skipping-rope. His heirs are Viridiana and his natural son, Jorge.

The second part of the film opens with the Mother Superior's visit to the errant novice; and there is a characteristic Buñuel observation when the old lady puts on her spectacles, to transform her ascetic face into that of a fat old gossip, indecently curious to know Viridiana's motives for leaving the convent. Viridiana tells her that she intends to pursue Christianity independently and alone. This purpose she carries out by surrounding herself with a group of disciples—fearful old thieves and beggars and whores whom she feeds and clothes and teaches to pray. Her disciples quarrel viciously among themselves and cast out one of their number who is diseased. They are grandly, monstrously ungrateful: "The string beans were a little bitter today." But Viridiana blithely harvests virtue's own reward.

Meanwhile Jorge, Don Jaime's son, sets himself to build up the decayed estates; and a comic but clumsy sequence of cross-cutting contrasts vigorous, insolent images of manual work with the

---

*Actually, Don Jaime immediately confesses that he was lying, that nothing happened between them. But an angry Viridiana leaves the house anyway. [Ed.]

effete hypocrisy of Viridiana's beggars at their *angelus*. Jorge himself is normal and average and without complication. He dismisses the silly mistress he had brought to the mansion with him; and when the devout Viridiana promises to be a difficult lay, he turns quite easily to the lovelorn Ramona.

One day masters and servants must all go to town, and the beggars are left in charge. Their good intentions easily collapse and they mischievously break into the house to organize an orgiastic feast. They gorge, drink, swear, blaspheme and copulate. The blind leader of the beggars tells tales of robbery in churches, of betrayal and informing. At the height of their merrymaking they pose around the table in the exact attitudes of the Last Supper; the cock crows, and a whore pretends to photograph them, using as a camera the chief instrument of her trade. The orgy mounts, the beggars perform a mad *jota* to the "Hallelujah Chorus". Suddenly the merrymaking comes to an end as the blind man flies into a fearful rage on learning that his woman is with another beggar. He lays furiously about him with his stick; and over the destruction the gramophone sings triumphantly "And He shall reign for ever and ever." The beggars discreetly but tipsily take their leave as the proprietors return.

When Jorge and Viridiana enter the scene of chaos, he is overpowered by one beggar while another—his trousers supported by the self-same phallic skipping-rope—rapes Viridiana. Jorge bribes the second beggar to kill the rapist, just at the moment that the police, called by Ramona, arrive at the house.

The epilogue is not so tense or furious as the ending of *L'Age d'Or* or of *Nazarin*. Viridiana sits, evidently sadder and probably wiser, in her room. Outside in the garden her religio-masochistic paraphernalia—the cross, the nails, the crown of thorns—burns on a bonfire. Ramona's little daughter curiously fishes the crown out of the fire, and it lies there flaming on the ground: the image recalls the last image—the hair blowing on the cross—of *L'Age d'Or*. There, however, the feeling was of putrefaction, here of purification. Indoors, Jorge plays at cards with Ramona, who is evidently his mistress; and the gramophone is now playing a crazy pop song, "Shake, shakemedown, shake," which dominates the whole of this last section of the film. There is a knock at the door: it is Viridiana, who is at last pleading for human companionship. Ramona makes to leave, but Jorge stops her and has her sit down with Viridiana. "All cats," he says, "are grey in the dark." (This was the censor's invention: Buñuel's script had Jorge and Viridiana left alone.) And so Viridiana is dealt a hand of cards. The camera rapidly draws back from the little group at the table. "I knew," says Jorge, "that one day my cousin would play cards with me."

> It's no good telling people that all's for the best in this best of all possible worlds. . . . I believe that you must look for God in man. It's a very simple attitude.

Viridiana's picture of mankind does not present a very flattering image of God. Buñuel depicts men's viciousness in terms that are no less direct and no more amiable than those of *L'Age d'Or*. If there is a hero at all, it is Jorge, who lives positively and (as a good surrealist) according to the dictates of desire. Yet one feels that Buñuel does not prefer him to the others—even to Don Ezekiel, the vicious little clown always good for a laugh and ready to cause trouble, or to the odious man with diseased hands (has he really venereal disease, or is it just the fallacy of the good that disease is the visitation of the wicked?) who repays Viridiana's kindness by abetting her rape.

The film's total effect is invigorating rather than depressing because Buñuel values them all alike as men, and likes them all because they are funny and human. If there is one whom he does not like, it is Don Amalio, the blind leader of the beggars. Buñuel has never liked blind men, linked as they are with false sentimental associations. In *L'Age d'Or* Modot kicked a blind man to the ground. Don Amalio can hardly be distinguished from the vile blind beggar in *Los Olvidados*. Don Amalio is Christ at the Last Supper; Don Amalio has been an informer; among the beggars it is Don Amalio who looks for all the world like a true bourgeois when he puts on the clothing Viridiana gives him. On the other hand, if there is one character whom Buñuel really admires, it must be that insolently proud beggar who rejects Viridiana and spits on her piety; and in the same breath demands alms from her. This is a noble independence.

Other men might be affected to pity by this picture of rot and corruption. But for Buñuel pity implies resignation, and resignation defeat. In a way the irresistible moral degradation of the beggars recalls the hysterical litany of woes that beset the Hurdes. It was not the viper that bit them that was deadly, but their efforts to cure the wound. In the same way it is Viridiana's piety and goodness which corrupt. In *Las Hurdes* too there was no pity, only the clear gaze of a man who is prepared to recognize the world for what it is, and in doing so makes the first and vital step to therapy.

> If Christ came back, they'd crucify Him all over again. You can be *relatively* Christian but to try to be *absolutely* Christian is an attempt doomed to failure from the start. I'm *sure* that if Christ came back the High Priests and the Church would condemn Him.

Buñuel admits no pity; and no panaceas. Nor does he accept the panaceas that are offered elsewhere. He is set, as he has always been set, against the soporifics of conventional morality and conventional sentimentality. "I am against conventional morals, traditional phantasms, sentimentalism and all that moral uncleanliness that sentimentalism introduces into society. . . . Bourgeois morality is for me immoral, and to be fought. The morality founded on our most unjust social institutions, like religion, patriotism, the family, culture: briefly, what are called the 'pillars of society'." The true answer is to live in the world and to seek God in man. The Christian virtues are unexceptionable in their argument, but in their application they are unreal, for the world is what it is.

In recent years Buñuel has become more and more interested in the figure and the failure of the perfect Christian. Dr. Lizzardi in *La Mort en ce Jardin* is a prototype. *Nazarin* really was Christ in modern dress. His attempts to practice Christ's principles invariably led to disaster. His mere presence among road-workers resulted in slaughter. Society being organized as it is, his martyrdom was inevitable. In the last shot, to the sound of the tambour of Calanda, he walks towards the camera like the other Christ at the end of *L'Age d'Or*, although this time he is victim instead of tormentor. In the final sublime moment when Nazarin receives human—not divine—charity, there seems to be an atone-

"I am against conventional morals, traditional phantasms, sentimentalism and all that moral uncleanliness that sentimentalism introduces into society. . . . Bourgeois morality is for me immoral, and to be fought. The morality founded on our most unjust social institutions, like religion, patriotism, the family, culture: briefly, what are called the 'pillars of society'." (*Viridiana*)

ment of some kind. Like Lizzardi and Nazarin, Viridiana's Christianity is destined to failure. Paradoxically it is her very piety which corrupts corruption. As in *Nazarin*, one feels at the end that there has been an atonement of man to man: Viridiana seems nearer salvation in human contact than in divine service.

But *Viridiana*, like all Buñuel's films, defies a simple interpretation. It is meant healthily to shock and disturb, and not to answer questions. Buñuel's statements are of their nature ambiguous and paradoxical. "If the meaning of a film is clear, then it can no longer interest me," he says.

> The film seems an involuntary imitation of dreams. The cinema might have
> been invented to express the life of the subconscious, whose roots penetrate so
> deeply into poetry . . .

The critic of *The Times* wrote: ". . . the film itself is a
masterpiece, perhaps one of the last, and undoubtedly one of the
most unexpected, in the chequered history of surrealist art."
Buñuel is still the surrealist of 1929:

> *les objets bouleversants,*
> *le cassage de gueules,*
> *la peinture fantastique* . . .
> *l'écriture automatique,*
> *l'anticléricalisme primaire,*
> *l'exhibitionisme,*
> *les plaisanteries pas drôles.*

By his own account his conception of the film was a matter of
association. The story was built up from unrelated images: "It
was born out of one image . . . a young girl drugged by an old
man. . . . Then I thought that this girl should be pure and I
made her a novice. . . . The idea of the beggars came later."

The film's rich atmosphere is built out of images which are
nothing if not surrealist: Viridiana's sleep-walking, ashes on the
bed, dreams of black bulls and so on. Buñuel gives free play to his
own private fetishisms. He admitted in an interview that the only
image he recalled from *Les Anges du Péché* was the scene in
which the nuns kiss the feet of one of their dead sisters. *Viridiana*
is full of feet—Rita's skipping feet; Don Jaime's grotesque boots
and the novice's square-toed shoes marching side by side; the
striptease of Viridiana's lower limbs. For no reason at all Francisco Rabal (Jorge) is seen washing his feet. (One naïvely polite
English critic guessed that this was because feet are the natural
focus for a nun's downcast eyes.) Only briefly does Buñuel
indulge his entomological preoccupations, when Don Jaime
carefully rescues a nasty little fly which has fallen into a water
butt. Phallic references proliferate, however: a richly comic and
vulgar scene has Viridiana innocently, instinctively recoiling
from contact with a cow's teat.

> Technique has no problems for me. I've a horror of films *de cadrages*. I detest
> unusual angles. I sometimes work out a marvelously clever shot with my

cameraman. Everything is all beautifully prepared, and we just burst out
laughing and scrap the whole thing to shoot quite straightforwardly with no
camera effects.

The real marvel of Buñuel is that he has the technical mastery
to fulfil his ideas and his poetry. Technically *Viridiana* is un-
usually elaborate for its director. The camera moves a good deal;
there's a tendency to show people in vistas seen through several
rooms. The cameraman, José F. Aguayo, has the same sort of
pictorial vigor as Figueroa, and the same ability to visualize the
anti-beautiful beauty of Buñuel's conceptions.

With Buñuel, one never feels that technique is something
interposed between conception and execution. Problems of *mise
en scène* seem to have no more existence for him than do problems of technique in a sketch by Picasso or Goya. Grandly
independent of conventional techniques as of conventional ideas,
Buñuel seems to have the ability simply to put pictures on the
screen with the accuracy and certainty of a good paperhanger
sticking up paper. Largely this is due to the assurance and
precision of his conceptions. "If I plan and shoot two hundred
and fifty shots, then two hundred and fifty shots appear in the
finished film." A friend described his work on *Viridiana* thus:
"Before each shot he would wander about with a viewer, all by
himself, for half-an-hour, lining up and planning the shot while
the crew sat drinking. Then he'd go over and say 'Right: this is
what I want.' Then they'd go and get the shot, while he sat
drinking."

Thank God—I am still an atheist.*

If Buñuel's creative life had ceased with *L'Age d'Or*, he would
have had a safe place in film history. That film revealed unfore-
seen possibilities in the cinema for surrealism, for anarchy, for
philosophy, for anger. Succeeding works in Mexico and in France
represent a body of work which few directors have paralleled, but
never excelled the first, extraordinary feature film. Now Buñuel
has made his second masterpiece, his most authoritative work:
"The second pole," in the words of Ado Kyrou, his most fervent
admirer, "which sustains the wonderful Buñuel edifice."

*The quotations from Buñuel are taken from a number of magazine interviews.

On *The Exterminating Angel*

THE EXTERMINATING ANGEL: NO EXIT FROM THE HUMAN CONDITION Michel Estève

. . . .

Free, at last, of financial worries, and sufficiently known and appreciated to impose his own views upon his productions, Luis Buñuel has become the grand master of the cinema he could never have been in the era of silent films. In releasing three fine pictures one after another, *Nazarin, Viridiana,* and *The Exterminating Angel,* he has shown himself indisputably an artist of the first rank.

The Exterminating Angel (the name, if I remember rightly, given Green's protagonist in Moïra who was obsessed by a false purity, and the title of the unpublished play by José Bergamin[1]) is not Buñuel's most satisfactory film. But the richness of its inspiration makes it a key film which throws his other works into a profound relief.

Luis Buñuel is by nature, almost by instinct, a visionary, a poet of the screen. Like a novelist, who uses an association of images, both real and imaginary, to create a flow of action and to breathe life into his characters, the author of *Un Chien Andalou* bases his films on the unfolding of an image, or the memory of a landscape. Of *Viridiana* Buñuel himself once said: "I thought of the story for the film in Mexico; it came from an image. This is the way I proceed every time, and the whole work gushes forth like a

From *Études Cinématographiques*, 22–3 (Spring 1963). Translated by Sallie Iannotti.

[1]The adaptation of this play, entitled "Los Naufragos," is signed by Buñuel and Luis Alcoriza. Buñuel's title evokes the biblical "exterminating angel." See, in particular, *Samuel* II, 24, verses 16ff; *Kings* II, 19, verse 35; *Exodus*, 12, verse 23; *Psalm* 78, verse 49.

fountain. . . ."[2] According to Buñuel's son, Juan, the idea for *The Exterminating Angel* originated in the famous painting by Géricault, "The Raft of Medusa."[3]

The reader may well ask what possible connection can be established between the two tattered creatures, prisoners of the sea tormented by hunger and thirst, and Nobile's elegant guests, gathered together in a luxurious manor house after an evening at the opera. Indeed, the connection is at first surprising, but it is completely justified, as a close examination of the progression of sequences will show. For these elite aristocrats—nobles, generals, magistrates of the court—find themselves, once dinner is over, quite unable to leave the salon. No apparent reason is given; in fact, the doors remain wide open, yet not one of them can bring himself to cross the room and step over the threshold. Cutaways wilt, ball gowns rumple, paint and coiffure little by little shift and fade, until the elegance of dress and manner has given way entirely to a vulgarity of mien and attitude. Hunger and thirst become progressively more insistent. So, by the end of the first evening, the midnight guests and Géricault's castaways have become recognizable companions in distress.

The Exterminating Angel, however, is not simply a cinematic transposition of Géricault's canvas. Nobile's salon, a latter-day raft of Medusa, is also the Second Empire drawing room of *No Exit;* indeed, Buñuel's film suggests Sartre's hell much more forcefully than Jacqueline Audrey's mediocre production.

The connections between *No Exit* and *The Exterminating Angel* are numerous and significant. In both, the basic story is quite simple, the setting and the action equally symbolic. In Sartre and in Buñuel, we are given a parable that points an accusing finger at the basic state of human life. In the opening scenes of the film, the ponderous gates swinging shut upon Nobile's posh estate, 1109 Providence Street (an ironic twist typical of Buñuel), hint to the spectator of the sequestering that awaits the characters. With the exception of the very last sequence, the action takes place in a single setting: Nobile's modern

---

[2] *Les Lettres françaises*, 878, June 1, 1961.
[3] *Les Lettres françaises*, 928, May 24, 1962.

Mexican salon of 1962, which corresponds to the 1860 salon in *No Exit*.[4] Both artists choose details for their overt symbolism. The bronze on the mantel obviously represents the "pure" object, the "self" as Sartre conceived it, deprived of consciousness. The presence of a letter opener and the absence of books implies a dissolution of cultural values. In *The Exterminating Angel*, art itself is reduced to nothingness, when the pianist can extract from her instrument nothing more than plaintive monotones, and again when the elegant company breaks up the cellos to build a fire. In Sartre's drawing room, with the door bolted on the outside and the bell broken, help from without is inconceivable. In Buñuel, the characters, as if held in by an invisible force, cannot leave in spite of the open doors, and the curious bystanders who wait outside cannot be of any service whatsoever. In both Sartre and Buñuel, the one room becomes a closed universe, with no passage to the exterior world.

Several years ago, Buñuel made this statement: "On the screen time and space become flexible; they expand and contract at will. Chronological order and the relative value of duration no longer correspond to reality."[5] Seen in this light, Buñuel's use of cinematic space and time is quite remarkable. It is fascinating that in a single setting, a bounded, limited space, the characters can be inexorably hounded and entrenched. And as this room is imperceptibly transformed into a "prison," so Nobile's reception becomes progressively an "abominable eternity," where the orderly fluctuation of time has been abolished.

It goes without saying that the business of a director is to produce a filmic space, a specific duration, playing upon the double chords of psychological time (the subjective unfolding of time perceived through the consciousness of the hero) and imaginary time (dreams and hallucinations). But it seems that in this film Buñuel is even more concerned with the representation of time than in most of his other films.

For the prisoners of Providence Street, lived time is oppressive. The rhythm of the film, a calculated languor (and a careful study

---

[4]In the first sequences of the film, there are shots of the kitchen, stairways, and dining room, but the principal setting is incontestably Nobile's salon.
[5]See "Poesie et Cinéma," quoted by Ado Kyrou in *Luis Buñuel* (Seghers, 1962).

of the editing reveals how extraordinarily long the sequences are) traces the subjective perception of time: if space is collapsed, time is lengthened. In *No Exit*, Sartre projected an imaginary future, eternity, into the present, in order to give us an insight into reality, conceived as a hell. In *The Exterminating Angel*, Buñuel goes even further; without recourse to the hypothesis of an imaginary eternity, even an atheist one, he projects, not in the future, but in our present daily lives the reality of our human fate. And though, at the end of the film, the characters have a fleeting illusion of having escaped their horrible destiny by effacing time (the guests take up the initial conversation and the places they occupied at the beginning of the party, hoping by some miracle to escape from the salon[6]), they very quickly find themselves captive once more, this time forever, in the Cathedral. The circle has opened only to snap shut again, more firmly, inexorably, upon their mediocrity.

Through this use of space and time, Buñuel displays many of his characteristic themes of reflection and mirror imagery. For Inez, Estelle, and Garçin, who think they are dead, the absence of mirrors symbolizes the impossibility of contemplating the superficial "self," the impossibility of retrieving a flattering image of themselves. With death, according to Sartre, comes the end of "bad faith."

The characters in *The Exterminating Angel* live on in our world, but they live under the sentence of death, with greater or lesser reprieve. In Nobile's salon, acts of bad faith can be given only so much free rein. As the hours pass, and day follows night in a rigorous, implacable monotony, the masks fall, one by one, reduced to ashes in the fire of truth. And this, man's truth, as it is presented by Buñuel, reveals, little by little, its fundamental ferocity. By a violence as subtle as it is insistent, *The Exterminating Angel* underscores the conflict between the essence of the individual and his mask. Abandoning their coats, shedding their gowns, the guests—prisoners now in their own hell—cast

---

[6]The camera avoids defining windows as "openings" onto the outside world. In fact, there is only one shot of a window, when a guest deliberately breaks one. This permits Buñuel to deliver a little salvo against racism, for another guest says: "A Jew going by, no doubt."

off their facades. Seen in this perspective, Buñuel's film is the antithesis to his *Robinson Crusoe*. As opposed to the sound man "in a state of nature,"[7] the "social" man, elegant, sophisticated, distinguished in diplomatic or military circles, becomes, in the face of peril, "a wolf of a man."

Three major aspects of Sartrean existentialism can be traced through this film: the theme of the absurd, the failure of communication, and the conception of the Other as executioner. Absurdity appears in situations (Nobile returns home with a dozen guests and finds all his servants, except for the butler, have gone); in events (the succulent main dish is spilt on the floor the very moment the hostess announces it); and in the characters themselves, thrashing about in their foolishness.

Communication breaks down within the group of characters; this is first suggested by a ridiculous series of introductions, a misfiring, if you will, of a basic ritual (one character, responding to an introduction, replies: "It's all Greek to me."). Communications break down between one class and another (the guests are addressed, in vain, by the crowd of spectators, among them several of Nobile's servants who have gathered at the doors). And finally, there is the failure between the individual and the authorities (the officers who come to the manor cannot make contact with the people within).

In this film, as in *No Exit*,[8] the Other is conceived as executioner. He is a shackle, a hindrance to the individual's desires by the very fact of his existence. He is, by definition, "excess baggage" (for example, the lovers have to wait for nightfall so that they can make love in the closet). In relationships with one another, each of us is in the position of the "misunderstood," and quarrels are inevitable. In the process of our lives, the Other becomes our judge. Here, the majority of the guests end by condemning Nobile to death, simply because his sumptuous home has become their prison.

---

[7]Here Buñuel is following the tradition of Thomas Hobbes *(Leviathan)*, John Locke *(Essay on Civil Government)*, and Rousseau *(The Social Contract)*.
[8]See Pierre-Henri Simon, "L'Autre dans le théâtre de J.-P. Sartre," in *Théâtre et Destin*, (A. Colin, 1959).

Faced with the Other and his power as executioner, each character reveals his hideous afflictions: egoism, cowardice, cruelty. In *The Exterminating Angel*, acts of brutality are legion: a piano, slammed shut on the player's fingers, a comb deliberately broken to humiliate a woman still concerned with her appearance, as if beauty might survive the destruction of the mask, as if beauty might resist the test of truth. Characters slap one another. The colonel knocks a woman to the floor. Someone tosses a sick man's pills out of the room. It is impossible not to recall Sartre's words: "This, then, is hell. I would never have believed it. You know how it goes: the sulphur, the stake, the rack. . . . Oh what a joke! We don't need a rack. Hell is other people."[9]

The undeniable presence of these three themes, however, is not enough to make us define *The Exterminating Angel* as a totally existential work. While Buñuel meets Sartre on a number of points, he diverges profoundly on others. To understand the purpose of the artist, it is necessary to examine two other perspectives, political and social satire, and, of course, surrealism.

Explicit or covert, satire is present in most of Buñuel's films. We see it in certain details: the salon in *L'Age d'Or*, which opens onto a kitchen where a serving girl is on fire; the choice of protagonist in *El*; the choice of all the protagonists in *Archibaldo de la Cruz*; criticism of dictatorship in *La Fièvre Monte á El Pao*. Absent from *No Exit*, satire is very much present in *The Exterminating Angel*. In the guise of an evening's gala, from which the servants have taken the precaution to flee[10] (the butler who stays is, in the final analysis, nothing more than a papier-maché figure), Buñuel castigates the aristocracy. He makes these nobles—aristocrats in name, wealth, or power—prisoners of their own habits and rules, and the taboos of their society. The guests leave the salon at last, but they can only understand the Te Deum as a new call to the old social structure, and they quickly don their masks of respectability and go on as before. (Their self-complacency is picked up in a long, lateral tracking shot.) The church becomes their definitive prison, and in the concentric circles of

[9]J.-P. Sartre, *Huis Clos* (Gallimard, 1954), p. 167.
[10]At the beginning of the film, one of the servants confides to the others, "I can't stand it, I've got to get out of here."

. . . Buñuel castigates the aristocracy. He makes these nobles—aristocrats in name, wealth, or power—prisoners of their own habits and rules, and the taboos of their society. (*The Exterminating Angel*)

light, the cloistering goes on, and is extended in the course of the final shots, to include all members of that social class.

Here *The Exterminating Angel* resembles *Land Without Bread*. The tone changes at the end, and is applied to a new domain. Yet nothing has really changed at all; the same general plan persists. Buñuel has a passion for clinical examinations, which he uses to evoke a feeling of "distance." Several of his films open with a documentary: the treatise on scorpions in *L'Age d'Or;* the sugar cane in *Subida al Cielo;* the meager resources of the poor in *La Fièvre Monte á El Pao.* This documentary form is present in *The Exterminating Angel,* when the rites and customs of a particular class are forced through the sieve of satire.

The Exterminating Angel, like *Land Without Bread,* focuses upon a micro-society, whose foundations the artist undermines by denunciation. The micro-society in *Land Without Bread* is that of the poor, the disinherited victims of the world. In *The Exterminating Angel*, it is that of the powerful, the rich, the opulent. In the one, the tone is rightly pathetic, in spite of the rigor and aridity of the commentary. In *The Exterminating Angel*, it is full of bite and humor; in both, the micro-societies are examined without self-righteousness, in their own terms, and in their internal conflicts. For in both films, Buñuel is denouncing a single crime.

That crime is the human condition itself, in which poor and rich alike are fragmented and alienated. The major difference between Sartre and Buñuel lies in this point. For in Sartre man is a prisoner in the sight of others only when he refuses to assume responsibility for his own destiny. And for Buñuel, man is kept captive by society, no matter whether he controls power in that society or is a helpless victim of it. *No Exit* suggests a metaphysical alienation; *The Exterminating Angel* is about the alienation imposed by a specific social order. In this film, Buñuel makes a powerful statement, which also appeared in *L'Age d'Or*, that man is split apart and crippled by everything that diverts him from himself—that is to say, by all forms of esoteric doctrine and rule (in this film, freemasonry, for example), of religious creed (Catholicism), and primitive, instinctive belief (magic).

This is the point of view of the surrealist, for whom liberty itself is only a hypothesis, and difficult if not impossible to acquire in reality. And here is a second point of Buñuel's divergence from Sartre's thought, for the author of *No Exit* and *The Flies* identifies himself with his freedom. "I am my freedom," says Orestes,[11] and this liberty makes him the peer of the gods. So Sartre's character is condemned to be free by assuming responsibility for his actions; Buñuel's hero knows how to approach this ambivalent liberty only by attacking it, by attacking the ideological structures of society.

In 1954, in an interview with André Bazin and J. Doniol-Valcrose, Buñuel said:

[11] J.-P. Sartre, *Les Mouches* (Gallimard, 1954), p. 100.

Surrealism has taught me that life has a moral significance that man cannot
afford to ignore. Through surrealism I also discovered for the first time that
man is not free. I used to believe our freedom was unlimited, but I have found
in surrealism, a discipline that must be followed. This has been one of the
great lessons in my life, a marvelous and poetic step.[12]

In the final analysis, *The Exterminating Angel* cannot be fully
understood outside the perspective of surrealism. To deliberately
ignore it would be to rob the content and form of the film of their
full significance. In his *First Manifesto*, André Breton wrote: "the
marvelous is always beautiful; it doesn't matter what specific
marvel is beautiful; it is enough that it is marvelous for it to be
beautiful."

The plot of *The Exterminating Angel* testifies to the presence
of the marvelous, or of "mystery," to use Buñuel's word. Recently
he said, "It is mystery that interests me. Mystery is the essential
element in any work of art."[13] The obscure and dream-like
sequences in *The Exterminating Angel* can, of course, be explained as the effects of prolonged confinement. But they are,
more than that, elements necessary to the very form of surrealism.
This is true in most of Buñuel's films. The same interpretation
can be applied to the presence of the menagerie, which also
functions on more than one level. For if the bear, for example,
affirms, in the words of Philippe Durand, "a lost paradise for a
corrupt class, or a rising force parallel yet incomprehensible to
that class,"[13] it also functions as a symbol of the animal world
itself, as the quintessential non-conformist by the very fact that it
has never lived in a society.

The real content of *The Exterminating Angel* is not ordered
politically, but metaphysically. "I want an integral vision of
reality," Buñuel has said. This vision implies, surely, the negation of all social conformities; but the surrealist revolt always
takes place on the moral plane, not the political one. Beginning
with *Un Chien Andalou*, Luis Buñuel has never ceased to incite
us to revolt. This call to revolution, however, is not in the Marxist
vein, because the director of *Viridiana* believes that reformation of

[12]*Cahiers du Cinéma*, 36, June 1954.
[13]Interview with the *Revista de la Universidad de Mexico*, January 1961, reprinted
in A. Kyrou, op. cit., pp. 111–12.

social and political structures can neither remove nor change the facts of life. Nor can it transform the human heart. Buñuel's revolution is a surrealist one, and the surrealist spirit rises up once more in *The Exterminating Angel,* in the "absolute non-conformity" which Breton spoke of, in the taste for blasphemy (for example, the dream sequence in which the Pope stands trial), and in the quest of man to go beyond the face of despair.

In this film, seemingly so despairing, mankind is nonetheless passionately cherished. One social class goes to its doom, envying the servants who have escaped. But I am not so sure Buñuel saves the domestics entirely because they belong to an oppressed class. He saves them because they are simple men, sane and healthy, close to their feelings and instincts. The beggars in *Viridiana* were much more repulsive than Don Jaime or Jorge or the young novice, and ordinarily Buñuel shows man alienated by society no matter what his social status may be. Among the captives in the salon in *The Exterminating Angel,* Nobile possesses an undeniable nobility, for he is willing to sacrifice himself in an attempt to deliver his guests. And in the suicides of the lovers, there is possibly a tinge of hope that true love, separated from the conditions of human life, can be realized. Actually, *The Exterminating Angel* suggests a nostalgia not so much for "impassioned love" (which was the theme of *Un Chien Andalou* and *L'Age d'Or*) but for that "passion for immortality" invoked by Breton in his comments on Monk Lewis's *The Monk.*[14]

Realism is always present in Buñuel's aesthetics. In *The Exterminating Angel,* man's ghastly wounds are not those of the flesh, as they were for the poor creatures in *Land Without Bread,* the blind and legless beggars in *Los Olvidados,* the dwarf in *Nazarin,* and the beggars in *Viridiana.* They are wounds which show in behavior and actions; horror, filth and misery give way to a leprosy of the soul. The brutal reality is the same. This is in the Spanish tradition, of course, and in his choice of details Buñuel can be thought of as a modern Goya. But the brunt of realism in Buñuel is carried not so much by his aesthetics as by his metaphysics. Over the ugliness, cruelty, and horror, a voice may be heard which bears witness to love among men, and repudiates the

[14] J.-J. Pauvert, ed., *Premier Manifeste du Surréalisme,* 1962, p. 28.

evil which is a natural part of life. The will to denounce despair soars above the despair itself. In the violence of his protestation, Buñuel achieves a caustic blasphemy, and yet there is evidence, too, of a sacred devotion. Because the sacred is ambivalent, linked to the quest of the atheist as well as to the passion of the faithful, it affirms in both, according to the poet Jean-Claude Renard, "something inviolable in man, a point of purity, a center of life that neither degradation nor despair and constraint can ever totally consume."[15]

[15]"Retour au sacré," *La Nef,* June-July 1951.

A LETTER ON
THE EXTERMINATING ANGEL   Juan Buñuel

• • • • • • • • • • • • • • • • • • •

16 August 1963

Dear Mr. Weinberg,
Chére Gretchen,

As to the *Angel Exterminador,* there is not much to explain. I'll just give you some comments and thoughts about it which I had asked my father, others which he simply dropped when I did the sound mixing with him.

The *Angel* is probably just a repetition of themes which he has used in all of his films . . . *obsessions* would be the correct word. As to symbolic interpretations, I think there are none. The film, to me, is essentially a comic film, but with a very strong corrosive interior. Corrosive in a social and surrealist sense. He

From *Film Culture,* No. 41 (Summer 1966). Reprinted by permission of the publisher.

has always liked the idea of people being separated from the rest of society and how they would react in this new "ambiance." For example, he wanted very much to make Golding's *Lord of the Flies.* Therefore, the problem of why these people are caught in this room is of no importance. We see that the doors are wide open, that there is no reason why they can't leave, or why the people outside cannot go in. We never know if they cannot leave because they cannot . . . or because they don't want to. It is not important. The fact is that they are there.

Once this is established, then the film can go on in its development. The people are then shipwrecked. Without food or water, they react in a normal way. He has his satirical moments towards human beings and their societies. As to the repetition of events . . . there are some twenty identical repetitions (The guests enter twice, people meet themselves or are introduced three times, the same toast is given twice, the beginning of the film or of the soirée ends as it started, with the piano music and everyone congratulating the piano player, etc.) is just an idea he had. He says, "In everyday life we repeat ourselves every day. Every morning we get up, we brush our teeth with the same brush and with the same hand and movements, we sit at the same breakfast table, we go to the same office, meet the same people . . . and how many times has it happened in a party where we say hello to someone and an hour later we again shake hands, say hello, and then exclaim, "Oh, what are we doing, we just said hello a minute ago."

One thing which many people have commented upon, have discovered a symbolic interpretation, is the sequence in which the women leave the closet which has been used as a WC. One says, "When I lifted the lid, I saw an eagle flying below me," and the other answers, "I saw a rushing torrent and the wind blew leaves into my face." That is explained by the toilets of the town of Cuenca. This Spanish village is built on the top of a mountain, an ancient town, and many of the houses are constructed on the side of cliffs. The toilets, therefore, since modern plumbing still does not exist, hang from the house, like the old-fashioned outhouses. Yet, when one lifts the lid, one sees several hundred feet down the face of the cliff (an effect that Hitchcock could use) to the river. Most Spanish farm houses have this but the toilet opens onto the barnyard where the chickens are scratching around . . . in the filth we make.

As to the ending, there is really no logical explanation. *The Exterminating Angel* is like a plague; first it starts with a small group of people, then a whole church full, then on to the rest of society. The revolution is just a mass outburst of the society which the forces of "order" try to put down. But the fact is that, whether they wanted to or not, the society is in a fix. I guess that is about the only "symbolic" interpretation one could give. Has it to do with the menace of atomic war? I personally think that it is not that direct but that it is a *feeling* or an abstracted statement that he has felt about the situation of modern man. We've gotten ourselves into the mess, and whether we are staying in it because we want to or because we have to is the problem.

Many have tried to interpret the significance of the sheep, the bear and the sheep at the church. These he sets up in his story line very logically. He once knew, in New York, of a woman who would pull the same joke with the waiter who spilled all the food at a dinner party, to which she had invited very distinguished and important people. Taking it a step further, he introduced a bear and sheep. This, later on, gives the shipwrecks a chance to eat when the escaped bear scares the sheep into the room. Now, at the end, what is more logical, he asks, than to have some 30 sheep enter the church because there are a greater number of people to be fed. 3 sheep for 20 persons, 30 sheep for 300 persons. No interpretation of: the Bear is Russia who sends food to the starving, or: The sheep is the Christian sheep symbol, man caught in his own religion, Christianity, etc., etc.

That's about the best I can do. There are many little incidents, like everyone taking and chewing the opium, which the head of the house had for wild parties, as a sedative for their hunger and their pains. The dreams they have are mostly recollections of his childhood in Calanda, the bells, the screams of a mother who has lost her child. . . .

I hope to see you soon and if you plan a trip to Paris, please write and if we can do anything for you, just ask. Joyce sends her regards and we both send a big "abrazo" to you both.

Juan

The Two Chambermaids

Tom Milne

• • • • • • • • • • • • • • • • • • • •

Le Journal d'Une Femme de Chambre* ends with a stunning *coup de Buñuel* after the main action (in which the chambermaid, Célestine, secures the arrest for rape and murder of her brutal lover, the militantly anti-semitic coachman, Joseph) has been concluded. In two swift final sequences, Célestine sells out to bourgeois comfort by marrying the crazy Captain from next door, while Joseph, having got away with his crimes, settles down in his little café in Cherbourg where he happily watches a Fascist demonstration parading the streets. As the demonstrators disappear round the corner, Buñuel lifts his camera from the empty street to a stormy sky, suddenly riven by a flash of lightning as the word "Fin" appears on the screen. Given the fact that the action is set in 1930, this is a brilliantly ominous evocation, not only of the imminent rise of Hitler, but of the reverberations which still smolder under the surface today.

But it can also be read in another way, as a barbed private joke. For, as the chanting demonstrators file past him, Joseph starts a cry of "Vive Chiappe! Vive Chiappe!" which the demonstrators take up blindly; and Chiappe, of course, was the Prefect of Police who, in 1930, banned *L'Age d'Or.* By cutting into and thus speeding up the footage of the "Vive Chiappe-ists" marching away, Buñuel turns them into absurd automata, literally whisks them out of sight, then lifts his camera to call on that avenging blast of lightning. Here Buñuel is at his brilliant best, and yet the sequence leaves one a trifle uneasy, as though someone apparently aiming at a range target had instead killed a passing bird. "Only connect . . ." *Le Journal d'Une Femme de Chambre* is a beautiful film,

From *Sight and Sound,* Vol. 33, No. 4 (Autumn 1964). Reprinted by permission of the publisher.

*The French title is used here for Buñuel's film and the English for Renoir's.

impeccably photographed, impeccably acted, impeccably directed; yet somewhere, its connections grow hazy.

The trouble seems to lie partly in an awkward indecisiveness about the character of Célestine, whose ambiguity tends to shadow the film, and partly in the fact that Octave Mirbeau's novel is almost *too* tailor-made for Buñuel. Jokingly, when it was announced that he was to make this film—and remembering bizarre details like the skewered goose and slaughtered squirrel from Renoir's version—one said that he was going to have the time of his life. And he has. Buñueliana (mostly culled from Mirbeau) abounds in the film, from the elderly foot fetishist to the lady with the bathroom full of test-tubes and syringes, from the ants crawling over the greenhouse frame to the snails crawling over the murdered child's leg, the butterfly being blown to pieces by a bullet, the absurd priest toddling along the street, or that same slowly and painfully skewered goose. Buñuel himself has remarked à propos of *Viridiana* that he originally intended Don Jaime's son (the character played by Francisco Rabal) to be a dwarf, but changed his mind because people would have said it was "too Buñuel." One's complaint in *Le Journal d'Une Femme de Chambre* is not so much that it is too Buñuel, as that most of the Buñueliana is simply superb decoration.

Take the foot fetishism, for instance: played by Jeanne Moreau with a delicious mixture of wide-eyed curiosity and yawning boredom, these scenes are exquisitely funny, but superficial. In Mirbeau, as the old man excitedly watches Célestine lacing up her boots, he cries, "Why don't you walk? Walk a little so I can see them move . . . see them live." Buñuel uses the same dialogue, but shoots the scene primarily for comedy (close-ups of Célestine wobbling along on the high heels), thus missing the suggestion that in the old man's eyes the boots are living things. Consequently the next scene, where the old man is found dead in bed, naked and clutching the boots, is robbed of most of its disquieting overtones. Both sequences, in fact, tend to be greeted with complaisant amusement by audiences. The opening sequence of *El*, on the other hand, where the camera follows Francisco's fascinated gaze down the row of naked feet while the old priest lovingly washes and kisses them, then moves to a pair of neatly shod feminine feet and up the shapely body of the girl on whom he is to lavish his desperate obsession, inextricably mingles piety and sexual attraction in a single movement of the camera, to evoke the exact sensation of crawling revulsion which Mirbeau was after, and which Buñuel's *Journal* hardly attempts.

It is possible, of course, to see the film as a masterpiece in a minor genre, simply as a collection of sharply incisive sketches illustrating the corruptions and perversions of the French bourgeoisie. On this level it certainly works beautifully. *"La campagne, c'est toujours un peu triste,"* says Célestine almost as soon as she arrives at La Prieuré, and Roger Fellous' camera records a beautiful, mournful landscape of fields, parks and forests from which life seems to be alien, to have retreated into warmly fetid burrows like the gloomy Monteil mansion, stuffed to bursting point with *objets d'art*, and with a grand salon where visitors are obliged to take off their shoes in case they soil it. It is against this grey, joyless background that Buñuel unfolds his tableau of decadence and depravity, which is perfect of its kind: in a room where a massive bible stands open on a lectern and a Pre-Raphaelite angel simpers from a wall, old M. Rabour leafs through his album of Victorian girlie postcards; the frigid Madame Monteil interviews a fascinated curé about the theological implications of *"certaines caresses,"* or concocts weird potions in the privacy of the bathroom which Célestine is forbidden to clean; and an elderly, virginal and tolerably hideous kitchen-maid weeps with tearful joy when coaxed into the steamy damp of her laundry by the furtively desperate M. Monteil. Buñuel, however, has tried to push a little further, not entirely successfully, through the character of Célestine herself.

Mirbeau's novel, written in 1900, is a first person narrative in which Célestine describes her life as a housemaid in the country home of a wealthy bourgeois couple, the Lanlaires (in Buñuel, the Monteils); her flirtation with the crazy, flower-eating Captain next door; her affair with the coachman, Joseph, whom she knows to have raped and killed a little girl; her marriage to him and departure to open a café in Cherbourg after he has stolen the family silver. Round this central narrative is woven a fairly shapeless mass of incidents recollected by Célestine from her previous employments, notably her engagements by an old lady to keep her tubercular grandson happy (incorporated by Renoir), and by an elderly foot fetishist (incorporated by Buñuel). The purpose of both central narrative and surrounding incident is to show the depravity of *les maitres,* the abominable conditions of life below stairs, and the inevitable corruption of the servants by their masters. Célestine's unhypocritical, diamond-sharp eye does not exclude herself from the general condemnation. In one of the most striking chapters of the novel, she describes her first meeting with the prancing Captain next door, who demonstrates his taste for eating flowers, proudly explains that he will eat *anything,* then rushes her off to meet his beloved pet ferret, Kléber. Célestine, with deliberate malice ("Then a diabolical idea crossed my mind"), observes that of course he wouldn't eat Kléber. Confused by this unexpected challenge, the poor, unbalanced Captain immediately breaks the ferret's back and drifts away towards his kitchen. Significantly, Célestine has nothing to do with the killing of the Captain's squirrel in Renoir's version, while the episode does not figure at all in Buñuel's: for in both films Célestine is transformed from the dispassionate observer of Mirbeau's novel into a heroine.

With *The Diary of a Chambermaid,* this is not particularly surprising, not only because the film was made in Hollywood, or because Renoir's conception demanded a hero and heroine to unite the two worlds of masters and servants in revolution, but also because his characters are never conceived in acid. Mirbeau's Célestine must have been totally alien to Renoir. Though by no means unsympathetic—her clear-eyed honesty is a distinct saving grace—she has the kind of cruelty and strength of will which enable her to confront her opponents head on. For the most part, Renoir's characters act savagely only when driven to it, like Legrand in *La Chienne,* Lange in *Le Crime de Monsieur Lange,* Lantier in *La Bête Humaine.* Normally they tend to treat other people's lives and beliefs, however unjustifiable, with a kind of respect, preferring to slip away to their own world rather than have things out. Boudu (in *Boudu sauvé des eaux*) spits on M. Lestingois' floors, cleans his shoes on the bedclothes and sleeps with his wife, but dives quietly back into the river rather than have to tell his benefactor that he would prefer not to be the object of his well-meaning charity.

For Buñuel, the savage, uncompromising iconoclasm of *L'Age d'Or* still holds good, and his characters tend therefore to be much tougher (in both directions, good and bad), more certain that their path is the right one. The difficulty, as Buñuel is well aware, is to know which path leads where: and this is why so many Buñuel heroes, apparently on the right road, come a moral cropper (Father Lizzardi in *La Mort en ce Jardin*, Nazarin, Viridiana), or learn the hard way (Robinson Crusoe, Ramon Vasquez in *La Fièvre Monte à El Pao*, Dr. Valerio in *Cela S'Appelle L'Aurore*). Mirbeau's Célestine, in fact, is a complete Buñuel character, who could slip unaltered into any of his films, whether her role was to explode the pretensions of a Nazarin or a Viridiana, or whether she herself was to cut a path through her own frailties to true humanity like Crusoe or Dr. Valerio.

In the first half of the film, Buñuel's Célestine (Jeanne Moreau) is a more or less conventional soubrette-heroine, very similar in behavior and reactions to Paulette Goddard in *Diary of a Chambermaid*: refusing to be overawed by Madame's fussy severity, mockingly parrying the amorous advances of Monsieur, boldly challenging Joseph's sullen authority, flirting gaily with the Captain, tenderly protecting the lonely little girl (the timid kitchen-maid in *Diary*), and in general reacting with vigorous honesty to the various turpitudes and injustices which she witnesses. By the halfway mark, however, the films (and the novel) begin to diverge. Renoir concentrates on the love affair between Célestine and Georges, the Lanlaires' tubercular son, while Buñuel moves to Célestine's affair with Joseph. Secretly attracted by Joseph's brooding, animal power, she is further fascinated when she discovers that it is almost certainly he who has murdered the little girl. It is never made clear (and probably isn't to Célestine herself) how much her determined efforts to get to bed with Joseph owe to love, and how much to her belief that there he may be persuaded to reveal the truth about his guilt. At all events, as soon as she is certain Joseph is guilty, she manufactures evidence against him and secures his arrest. Whatever her earlier motives,

It is never made clear (and probably isn't to Célestine herself) how much her determined efforts to get to bed with Joseph owe to love, and how much to her belief that there he may be persuaded to reveal the truth about his guilt. (*Diary of a Chambermaid*)

in the brilliant sequence of Joseph's arrest Buñuel makes it quite clear that she does love him after a fashion. "We are alike, you and I," Joseph has surprised her by saying, "not to look at, of course, but deep down inside"; and as Joseph is led away by the gendarmes, Célestine meticulously arranges the glasses in the center of the table with Joseph's exact gesture, then expressionlessly traces the word "Salaud!" with her thimble. The abuse is addressed to Joseph, but Buñuel leaves us in no doubt that Célestine is aware that it also refers to herself. She has done the world a service by ridding it of Joseph, but as with Viridiana, motives, acts and consequences are very different things.

This is a superb sequence—as fine as anything Buñuel has done—but the rupture in tone with what has gone before is excessive. It is as if the world of the first half of the film were being viewed objectively, and the second subjectively, without any adequate transition or character motivation. One sees what Buñuel is trying to do, of course. Mirbeau's Célestine does not betray Joseph, but marries him. She agrees to go to Cherbourg although she knows about the murder, and it is then that Joseph says, with complete truth, "We are alike, you and I." Buñuel places this remark earlier, when Célestine only suspects about the murder: in a sense he is trying to have his cake and eat it by making Célestine *unlike* Joseph in that she rejects his crime, but *becoming* like him when she commits a crime of her own by betraying him. There is no reason why this should not work, as *Nazarin* and *Viridiana* work, but here the two crimes seem unevenly balanced because Célestine has been presented earlier as a perfectly justified avenging angel.

Further, when Viridiana sits over the final game of cards, the rock-and-roll song blares out, and Jorge tells her "All cats are grey in the dark," one feels that her whole world has collapsed, that retribution is complete. With *Le Journal d'Une Femme de Chambre* one feels nothing of the sort. Buñuel cuts directly from the scene of Joseph's arrest to Célestine's wedding to the Captain. Obviously, by its placing in the film between Joseph's arrest and his acquittal (to go to Cherbourg to promote Fascist ideals), this marriage should carry forebodings of disaster. The Captain (played by Daniel Ivernel), however, comes over as a mainly likeable character. Presented with much less fantasy than by Renoir, shorn of his flower-eating, gay prancing, and the sudden maniac killing of his pet squirrel (which makes him a real homicidal threat in *Diary of a Chambermaid*), he seems a reasonable catch for Célestine: eccentric certainly, but otherwise an amiable, rather stolid country gentleman. Admittedly he is a liar, and has deceived his previous housekeeper into thinking she will inherit his money. In the context of the corruptions and deceits manifested by almost everybody else, however, the Captain seems

comparatively harmless. And when we last see Célestine, comfortably breakfasting in bed with the Captain dancing attendance
and a maid busy with the housework downstairs, one can't help
feeling that even if she has sold out to *les maîtres*, she has done
remarkably well for herself. All cats are Siamese in Célestine's
dark.

Mirbeau, presenting the two worlds of rich and poor, masters and
servants, through the dispassionate eyes of Célestine, observes
with cynicism that they are in effect one world, united by sex and
depravity. Buñuel, never a cynic, has done his best to change
Célestine's role from a passive to an active one, and has left her
broken-backed as a result. This problem never arises in *Diary of
a Chambermaid*, where Renoir presents her unequivocally as a
heroine: the two worlds are quite distinct (with M. Lanlaire a
good master, and Joseph an evil servant), and it is the purity of
her love for Georges Lanlaire which finally unites both masters
and servants in revolution. Renoir's film has suffered a good deal
of abuse in the past, being accused of phoniness, incompetence
and worse. Although it has now been rehabilitated, and its
extraordinary parallels noted with the acknowledged masterpiece
La Règle du Jeu, an air of apologetic reservation still tends to
creep in, so that it is usually pictured as an engaging fantasy, a
Règle du Jeu in minor key. It would be more accurate, in fact, to
describe it as a *Règle du Jeu* on a wider register. Everything is
carried to greater extremes: on the one hand, the fantasy and
artificial comedy, on the other, the paroxysmal cry of anger.
Rather as Franju, in *Hôtel des Invalides*, used an *hommage* to
militarism to present a violent attack on it, so Renoir presents a
bitter call to revolution in the guise of a romantic charade. The
extraordinary final sequence (which is not in Mirbeau's novel,
nor in Renoir's script—it was improvised on the set), in which
Joseph tries to cut his way with a whip through a Quatorze
Juillet carnival and is lynched, while Georges frenetically distributes his family silver to the crowd, is probably one of the finest
and most uncompromising in Renoir's whole work.

In itself, of course, an artificial charade, as *Diary of a Chamber-*

maid would appear to be on the surface, could not carry this weight of meaning. But, as always with Renoir, it is the texture that counts; exactly as in *La Règle du Jeu,* he constantly undercuts the charade element by twisting his puppets to reveal flesh and blood. In particular, the film arouses one's sympathies with extreme care and cunning so that one feels not only for Georges and Célestine, or for M. Lanlaire, so downtrodden by his wife, or for the Captain, so cruelly driven to kill the squirrel which is the only thing he really loves, but even for the eminently un-pleasant Joseph. Renoir, even when he dislikes a character, as he obviously dislikes Joseph, can always understand him, and in two striking scenes he allows us to penetrate Joseph's sullenly hostile exterior. One is the visit to the Lanlaire cellars, when Joseph shows Célestine the family silver, hidden away like Aladdin's treasure in glittering, useless heaps, literally begging to be taken out and put into circulation; the other, the strangely touching moment when Joseph confides in Célestine his dream of retire-ment to the café in Cherbourg.

The corresponding scene in Buñuel's film goes for very little, not so much because his Joseph is more ruthless or evil (in fact, Renoir's Joseph is much more sinisterly terrifying), as because there is little nostalgia or desire in Buñuel for *le paradis perdu* of simple little sensuous pleasures like the springtime sun, the sweep of the countryside, or the return to a native village. At the end of *Boudu sauvé des eaux,* when Boudu falls out of the punt into the river, he forgets everything to wallow delightedly in the warm, gently flowing water; and it would probably never occur to Buñuel that one could express a sense of complete liberty by that joyous 360 degree pan round the hill and riverbank as Boudu settles down to share his sandwich with a goat. *The Criminal Life of Archibaldo de la Cruz,* for instance, ends with Archibaldo, the homicidal maniac, curing himself by hurling the music box which is at the source of all his troubles into the river, and walking gaily away down a verdant, tree-lined path. But it is not Archibaldo's emergence into this world of fresh, unoppressive landscape so much as the grasshopper which he now refrains from killing which, for Buñuel, indicates his release. The same intellectual, rather than sensuous, method can be seen in *Nazarin,* where the priest's defeat is not indicated by the endless dusty road along which he wearily trudges, but by the pineapple which the old peasant woman humbly offers him. The most striking example of all, perhaps, comes in what might be called Buñuel's most Renoiresque film, *Robinson Crusoe*. Here, even though the story concerns a man coming to terms with himself and his environment through enforced solitude, Buñuel's vision is entirely interior and intellectual. In the beautiful scene when Crusoe runs wildly to the mountain top to shout the words of a psalm across the depths of the valley, all that he receives is emptiness— the hollow echo of his own voice and an intensified awareness of his barren isolation.

With Renoir, landscape invariably evokes a lyric response. Even in *La Bête Humaine*, when Lantier nearly strangles his cousin Flore in an epileptic fit, one remains keenly aware of the beauty of the grassy bank where only a moment before they had been quietly talking; in *The Southerner*, the opening tracking shots through the cotton fields convey at once the terrible, backbreaking drudge of the pickers, and the blinding beauty of the sea of cotton balls in the bright sun. Renoir's work is full of this regret that man is not more free to enjoy the beauty which offers itself so freely. And *Diary of a Chambermaid*, in spite of being exceptional among Renoir's films in that it was shot entirely in studio sets, has this same quality. In theory, the village sets are quaint France *à la* Hollywood; in practice, beautifully lit and photographed (art director, Lourié; camera, Lucien Andriot), they have an impressionistic enchantment, nowhere more evident than in the shimmering radiance of the scene in which Célestine, in white dress and parasol, trysts with Georges under the great oak in the middle of the village square. The scenes in the Lanlaire garden, too, have the same sunlit beauty, so that one feels real regret when the Captain slashes furiously at the flowers, or hurls stones through the neatly ranged rows of greenhouses (characteristically, Buñuel has the Captain hurling an unsavory mixture of old boots, cans and garbage). For Renoir, the Lanlaire house and park, like their silver, is too precious to allow one selfish, tyrannical woman to keep to herself.

Visually, *Le Journal d'Une Femme de Chambre* is just as

striking, if not more so, but Buñuel draws a totally different quality from his landscape. Here the overriding impression is not of spring, but of the encroaching gloom of autumn. *"La campagne, c'est toujours un peu triste,"* Célestine observes bitterly, and outside a grey mist wavers uncertainly through the great vistas of silent trees, while inside, the rooms are lined with protective layers of tables, chairs, lamps, books, statues, plants and ornaments of every description, all huddled close together. Everything offers an intangible threat of hostility: as we watch Célestine arrive at La Prieuré, a hand stealthily draws aside the foliage which partly screens her from view, and proves to belong to the harmless M. Rabour, out for a stroll in his park; a butterfly settling lazily on a flower in the apparently empty garden is suddenly blown to bits; the little girl, Claire, lies dead in a sunlit patch of forest beside the bush of ripe wild berries which she has been picking. Even the loveliest single composition in the film, a tranquil long shot of Joseph quietly raking a bonfire while the smoke drifts across the front of the house, takes on a savage disquiet by being placed immediately after the rape scene. For Buñuel, in fact, landscape is a chameleon, indistinguishable from its inhabitants. And if the corrupt society of La Prieuré were swept away, the place would be reborn: *autres moeurs, autres pays.*

Having said this, where next? Originally, this article started out from the idea that here was a unique opportunity to draw a direct comparison between the work of two great directors. As it progressed, it became increasingly apparent that the task was only feasible up to a point. How can one make any valid comparison that neatly sums up two films which, despite their common origin, are so different from each other, and in any case operate on entirely different levels? For me, *Diary of a Chambermaid* is a complete success, *Le Journal d'Une Femme de Chambre* isn't; and yet, what does that mean? Not necessarily that Renoir's film is greater than Buñuel's, certainly not that Buñuel's is any less remarkable, but simply that in a Renoir context his film works, while in a Buñuel context *Le Journal* doesn't.

Here, perhaps, one is at the crux of the problem. It is impossible to dissociate either film from one's knowledge of the director's other work: they come to us as part of a private world, ringed by an aura of hints, cross-references, even aspirations which may not be apparent from the films themselves. One's feelings about *Diary of a Chambermaid* must be colored by recollections of *La Règle du Jeu* and the echoes between the two films which illuminate Renoir's conscious attempt to transpose his theme on a wider register (or, as Bazin put it, much more neatly, to compose a variation on his *drame gai* as a *tragédie burlesque*). Considered in isolation, it might be perfectly possible to find *Le Journal d'Une Femme de Chambre* not only a brilliant realisation of Mirbeau's novel, but a completely successful film. But *Viridiana* remains in the background as a reminder that, through the character of Célestine, Buñuel is reaching beyond Mirbeau, and that his conception does not, finally, come off.

There are, though, tangents which one can seize fleetingly, such as the fact that in adapting a minor, often rather unpleasant novel, Renoir and Buñuel have made major films which so transform the original material that neither emerges as unpleasant. The undiscriminating mass of incident in the novel, which often reads like an anthology of Sunday newspaper revelations, is shaped by both directors through their vision of what the world might be into sharp attack on the inhibitions and deprivations forced on humanity by a corrupt, meaningless social structure. Again, the novel has a strong streak of repellent cruelty (notably Mirbeau's gloating description of Célestine's despairing attempt to die with Georges by mingling her kisses with the blood he coughs up), which is harnessed by Renoir and Buñuel into a strong undercurrent of violence.

Curiously, therefore, *Diary of a Chambermaid* becomes one of the normally gentle Renoir's most violent films (the brutal fight in the greenhouse; the killing of the squirrel; the episode of the goose; Joseph's whip; the murder of the Captain; the lynching); while the normally savage Buñuel scales down to meet Renoir in reticence. There is very little that shocks as the slashed eye in *Chien Andalou*, say, or much of *Los Olvidados* shocks. Instead, the sequence of Claire's murder is skirted in shots of a wild boar and a rabbit, the sound of beating wings, of a train rushing past, of a whistle screaming, to the almost elegiac tenderness of the shot of Claire lying half-hidden behind a bush while two snails crawl gently across her leg; the discovery of the old foot fetishist, in an exquisite arabesque of the camera down from the bed canopy, backed by a graceful earlier quotation of the music box from *Archibaldo de la Cruz*, lifts to a hint that he has at last found peace.

And there the tangent divides again. For Renoir, with his optimistic faith in man, the revolution can come now; for Buñuel, with his pessimistic faith (his bitter realism, if you like), it only must.

For Renoir, with his optimistic faith in man, the revolution can come now; for Buñuel, with his pessimistic faith (his bitter realism, if you like), it only must. (*Diary of a Chambermaid*)

Saintliness

Pauline Kael

We are so often bathed in emotion at the movies by all those directors whose highest ambition is to make us feel feelings that aren't worth feeling that the cool detachment of Luis Buñuel has a surprising edge. Buñuel doesn't make full contact with us, and the distance can be fun; it can result in the pleasure of irony, though it can also result in the dissatisfaction of feeling excluded. His indifference to whether we understand him or not can seem insolent, and yet this is part of what makes him fascinating. Indifference can be tantalizing in art, as in romance, and by keeping us at a distance in a medium with which most directors try to involve us he deliberately undermines certain concepts that are almost axiomatic in drama and movies—especially drama and movies in their mass-culture form. Buñuel, who regards all that tender involvement as "bourgeois morality," deliberately assaults us for being so emotional. His most distinctive quality as a movie-maker is the lack of certainty he inflicts on us about how we should feel toward his characters. Buñuel shoots a story simply and directly, to make just the points he wants to make, though if he fails to make them or doesn't make them clearly he doesn't seem to give a damn. He leaves in miscalculations, and fragments that don't work—like the wheelchair on the sidewalk in "Belle de Jour." He's a remarkably fast, economical, and careless movie-maker and the carelessness no doubt accounts for some of the ambiguity in the films, such as the unresolved trick endings that leave us dangling. From the casting and the listless acting in many of his movies, one can conclude only that he's unconcerned about such matters; often he doesn't seem to bother

From *Going Steady* by Pauline Kael (where it appears under the title "Simon of the Desert"). Copyright © 1969 by Pauline Kael. Reprinted by permission of Little, Brown and Co. in association with The Atlantic Monthly Press. This material also appeared in *The New Yorker*.

even to cast for type, and one can't easily tell if the characters are meant to be what they appear to be. He uses actors in such an indifferent way that they scarcely even stand for the characters. Rather than allow the bad Mexican actors that he generally works with to act, he seems to dispense with acting by just rushing them through their roles without giving them time to understand what they're doing. Clearly, he prefers no acting to bad acting. The mixture of calculation and carelessness in his ambiguity can be maddening, as in some of *Viridiana* (1961) and in most of the slackly directed *The Exterminating Angel* (1962). But sometimes what makes an artist great and original is that in his lack of interest in (or lack of talent for) what other artists have been concerned with he helps us see things differently and develops the medium in new ways. Like Borges, who won't even bother to write a book, Buñuel probably doesn't think casting or acting is important enough to bother about. And casting without worrying about whether the actors suit the role—casting almost *against* type and not allowing the actors to work up characterizations can give movies a new kind of tone. Without the conventional emotional resonances that actors acting provide, his movies have a thinner texture that begins to become a new kind of integrity, and they affect us as fables. Most movies are full of actors trying to appeal to us, and the movies themselves try so hard to win us over that the screen is practically kissing us. When Buñuel is at his most indifferent, he is sometimes at his best and most original, as in parts of *Nazarin* (1958), which opened here last summer, and in almost all of his newly released—and peculiarly exhilarating— *Simon of the Desert.*

Other movie directors tell us how we should feel; they want our approval for being such good guys, and most of them are proudest when they can demonstrate their commitment to humanitarian principles. Buñuel makes the charitable the butt of humor and shows the lechery and mendacity of the poor and misbegotten. As a movie-making comedian, he is a critic of mankind. One can generally define even a critic's position, but there is no way to get a hold on what Buñuel believes in. There is no characteristic Buñuel hero or heroine, and there is no kind of behavior that escapes his ridicule. His movies are full of little sadistic jokes that we can't quite tell how to take. The movie director most influenced by de Sade, and the only one still at work who had close ties to the Surrealist movement, Buñuel has gone on using the techniques of the Surrealists in the medium that once seemed their natural habitat. We may not really like his jokes, yet they make us laugh. A perturbing example that comes all too readily to mind: When Jorge, in *Viridiana*, frees a mistreated dog that has been tied to a cart and then we see another cart coming from the opposite direction with another dog tied to it, is Buñuel saying that Jorge is a realist who does what he can, or does Buñuel really mean what the audience, by its laughter, clearly takes the scene to mean—that Jorge's action was useless, since there are so many mistreated dogs? This "joke" could be extended to the "comedy" of saving one Jew from the ovens or one Biafran baby from starvation, and I think we are aware of the obscenity in the humor even as we laugh—we laugh at the recognition that we are capable of participating in the obscenity. His jokes are perverse and irrational and blasphemous, and it may feel liberating to laugh at them just because they are a return to a kind of primitive folk comedy—the earliest form of black comedy, enjoyed by those who laugh at deformity and guffaw when a man kicks a goat or squeezes an udder too hard. Buñuel reminds us of the cruelty that he feels sentimental art tries to hide, and we respond by laughing at horrors. This is partly, I think, because we are conscious of the anti-sentimentality of his technique—of his toughness and his willingness to look things in the eye.

Some of his recurrent jokes are really rather private jokes—the udders and little torture kits and objects turned into fetishes—and Buñuel throwing his whammies can seem no more than a gigantic, Spanish Terry Southern. Bad Buñuel is like good Terry Southern—a putdown and a crackle. Sometimes when we laugh at a Buñuel film we probably want to sound more knowledgeable than we are; we just know it's "dirty." Yet this is the vindication of the Surrealist idea of the power of subjective images: we *do* feel certain things to be "dirty" and some kinds of violence to be funny, and we laugh at them without being able to explain why. Buñuel gets at material we've buried, and it's a release to laugh this impolite laughter, which is like laughter from out of nowhere, at jokes we didn't know we knew.

Once, in Berkeley, after a lecture by LeRoi Jones, as the audience got up to leave, I asked an elderly white couple next to me how they could applaud when Jones said that all whites should be killed. And the little gray-haired woman replied, "But that was just a metaphor. He's a wonderful speaker." I think we're inclined to react similarly to Buñuel—who once referred to some of those who praised *Un Chien Andalou* as "that crowd of imbeciles who find the film beautiful or poetic when it is fundamentally a desperate and passionate call to murder." To be blind to Buñuel's meanings as a way of being open to "art" is a variant of the very sentimentality that he satirizes. The moviegoers apply the same piousness to "art" that his mock saints do to humanity: both groups would rather swallow insults than be tough-minded. Buñuel is the opposite of a flower child.

Simon of the Desert, a short (forty-five minute) feature made in Mexico in 1965, just before he made *Belle de Jour*, is a playful little travesty on the temptations of St. Simeon Stylites, the fifth-century desert anchorite who spent thirty-seven years preaching to pilgrims from his perch on top of a column. It is, in both a literal and a figurative sense, a shaggy-saint story, and (unlike much of Buñuel's work) it is charming. The narrative style of *Simon* is so straightforward and ascetically simple that it may be easier to see what he is saying in this film than in his more elaborate divertissements about saintliness turning into foolishness—*Nazarin* and the complicated, allusive *Viridiana*, which was cluttered with Freudian symbols. Buñuel seems to have a grudging respect for Nazarin and Simon that he didn't show for Viridiana, whom he made sickly, chaste, and priggish. *Viridiana* seemed dramatically out of focus because Buñuel didn't even dignify her desire to do good, and so the film had to depend on the pleasures and shocks of blasphemy—probably not inconsiderable for insiders, but insufficient for others. The tone of *Simon* is almost jovial, though the style is direct—just one incident after another—and as bare and objective as if he were documenting a scientific demonstration; even the Surreal details (like a coffin skittering over the ground) are presented in a matter-of-fact way. Buñuel has himself in the past given in to temptation: with more money than he was accustomed to, he fell for the fanciness of all that French *mise-en-scène* that made his *Diary of a Chambermaid* so revoltingly "beautiful." But there's very little money in *Simon*, and there was, apparently, none to finish it; the bummer of an ending was just a way to wind it up.

Simon (Claudio Brook) performs his miracles, and the crowds evaluate them like a bunch of New York cabdrivers discussing a parade: whatever it was, it wasn't much. He restores hands to a thief whose hands have been chopped off; the crowds rate the miracle "not bad," and the thief's first act with his new hands is to slap his own child. The Devil, in the female form of Silvia Pinal (much more amusing as the Devil than she was in her guises in other Buñuel films), tempts him, and, at one point, frames him in front of the local priests, who are more than willing to believe the worst of him. Simon is a saint, and yet not only are his miracles worthless—they can't change men's natures—but even he is dragged down by his instincts. Buñuel is saying that saintliness is sentimentality, that, as the platitude has it, human nature doesn't change. This is not, God knows, a very interesting point, nor do I think it has the slightest validity; the theme is an odd mixture—a Spanish schoolboy's view of life joined to an adult atheist's disbelief in redemption. This outlook creates some problems when it comes to responding to Buñuel's work.

There are probably many lapsed Catholics who still believe in sin though they no longer believe in redemption, who have the disease though they have lost faith in the cure. In this they are not much different from the Socialists who still accept the general Socialist analysis of capitalism without having much confidence in the Socialist solutions. But psychologically there is an enormous difference between those who regard man as the victim of violent instinctual drives and those who live by a belief in justice and decency, even without any real conviction that society will ever be better. The pessimistic view can be so offensive to our ameliorative, reforming disposition that it's almost inconceivable to us that an artist whose work we respond to on many levels can disagree with us at such a fundamental level. And so with Luis

Buñuel in films, as, in literature, with D. H. Lawrence and T. S. Eliot and Pound, we often contrive to overlook what the artist is saying that is alien to us. Because Buñuel is anti-Church and is a Spaniard at odds with Franco, because he satirizes bourgeois hypocrisy, there is, I think, a tendency to applaud his work as if this were all it encompassed. At the movies, when we see horrors we expect the reformer's zeal; that is the convention in democratic art, and perhaps we project some of our outraged virtue onto Buñuel's films. We feel free to enjoy his anarchic humor—which is often funniest when it is cruelest—because we can feel we're laughing at Fascism and at the human stupidity that reinforces Fascism. But though his work is a series of arguments against the Grand Inquisitor's policies, his basic view of man is the Grand Inquisitor's. Buñuel attacks the Church as the perverter and frustrater of man—the power trying to hold down sexuality, animality, irrationality, man's "instinctual nature." He sees bourgeois hypocrisy as the deceptions that men practice to deny the truth of their urges. His movies satirize the blindness of the spiritual; his would-be saints are fools—denying the instinctive demands not only in others but in themselves. Surrealism is both a belief in the irrationality of man and a technique for demonstrating it. In his *Land Without Bread*, Spain itself—that country that seems to be left over from something we don't understand— was a Surreal joke, a country where the only smiling faces were those of cretins. Like other passionate artists who fling horrors at us, Buñuel is an outraged lover of man, a disenchanted idealist; being a Spaniard, he makes comedy of his own disgust. He can't let go of the Church; he's an anti-Catholic the way Bogart was an anti-hero. He wants man to be purged of inhibitions, yet the people in his movies become grotesque when they're uninhibited. And when his saintly characters wise up and lose their faith, he can't show us that they're useful or better off, or even happier. He is overtly anti-romantic and anti-religious, yet he is obsessed with romantic, religious fools. He has never made a movie of *Don Quixote*, but he keeps pecking away at the theme of *Don Quixote*, and gets himself so enraged by the unfulfillment of ideals that he despises dreamers who can't make their dreams come true. In

Buñuel attacks the Church as the perverter and frustrater of man - the power trying to hold down sexuality, animality, irrationality, man's "instinctual nature" . . . his would-be saints are fools - denying the instinctive demands not only in others but in themselves. (*Simon Of The Desert*)

Viridiana, he twisted the theme into knots—turning in on himself so far that he came out the other end.

How can Buñuel in *Simon of the Desert* make a comedy out of a demonstration of what liberals have always denied and yet make liberals (rather than conservatives) laugh at it? It's as if someone made a comedy demonstrating that if you divided the world's wealth equally, it would all be back in the hands of the same people in a year, and this comedy became a big hit in Communist countries—which, however, it might very well do if the style of the comedy and the characters and details were the kind that the Communists responded to. And it might become an underground hit if it had jokes that brought something hidden out into the open: Buñuel's Freudian symbols and blasphemous gags alienate

the conservatives and, of course, please the liberals. And then
there is the matter of style. Buñuel doesn't pour on the prettiness,
he doesn't turn a movie into a catered affair. There is such a thing
as mass bourgeois movie sentimentality; we are surrounded by it,
inundated by it, sinking in it, and Buñuel pulls us out of this
muck. "Simon" is so palpably clean that it's an aesthetic assault
on conservative taste. It's hard to love man; Hollywood movies
pretend it's easy, but every detail gives the show away. Buñuel's
style tells the truth of his feelings; the Spanish stance is too strong
for soft emotions like pity. Though, as in *Diary of a Chambermaid*, he can be so coldly unpleasant that we are repelled (and
happy to be excluded), he never makes people pitiable lumps.
And though he may turn Quixote into a cold green girl or a
dithering man, in his films the quixotic gestures of the simple
peasants are the only truly human gestures. A dwarf gives his
inamorata an apple and his total love; a woman offers Nazarin a
pineapple and her blessing. Nazarin is so stubbornly proud that
it's a struggle for him to accept, and Buñuel himself is so proud
that he will hardly give in to the gesture. Humility is so difficult
for him that he just tosses in the pinapple ambiguously—he's so
determined not to give in to the folly of tenderness that he cops
out.

At the end of *Simon of the Desert* Simon is transported to the
modern world, and we see him, a lost soul, in a Greenwich
Village discothèque full of dancing teen-agers. This is a disas-
trous finish for the movie—a finish of the careless kind that
Buñuel is prone to. The primitive Mexican desert setting situates
the story plausibly, but New York is outside the movie frame of
reference, nor does this discothèque conceivably represent what
Simon's temptation might be. What Buñuel intended as another
little joke is instead a joke on his gloomy view. "It's the last
dance," the Devil says, though what is presented to us as a vision
of a mad, decaying world in its final orgy looks like a nice little
platter party.

Buñuel's Golden Bowl

* *

Most of all, Buñuel wanted to go back to work in Spain again. He had been encouraged by reports that the brouhaha over *Viridiana* had calmed, that censorship there had been relaxed. He returned. Then, after months of preparation, in the summer of 1963, Franco's government refused the shooting authorization for his version of Galdos' *Tristana*. Later that year, in France, he made one of his finest films, *Le Journal d'Une Femme de Chambre*. When shown in Paris, in 1964, it was coolly received. A year later, one of his old pet projects, an adaptation of Lewis's *The Monk*, was finally about to take shape. At the last minute the production company was dissolved, and it too had to be written off. The Hakim Brothers then approached Buñuel to ask him to consider a screen version of Joseph Kessel's novel, *Belle de Jour*. He accepted, and cloistered himself in an ultra-modern building in Madrid with Jean-Claude Carrière (co-scenarist on *Le Journal* and *The Monk*). They finished the script in five weeks. The shooting schedule for this, Buñuel's twenty-seventh film, was ten weeks. He brought it in in eight.

Belle de Jour is a masterpiece, technically Buñuel's most accomplished, free-flowing work. It is unique, the only one of his films in which his obsessions, his purity, and his convulsive spirit have all been fully, satisfactorily organized into an architectonic whole. It unfolds so smoothly, with such sustained legato, that there is no chance to catch a breath. *Viridiana* was a step in this direction, the underrated *Journal* a near-arrival. *Belle* is the many-faceted and perfect Golden Bowl, which crowns a life's work. When released in Paris recently, it was greeted with shock, reticence and disappointment by most of the critics for the daily

From the Lorimer Modern film Scripts Edition of *Belle de Jour* by Luis Buñuel. Reprinted by permission of Lorimer Publishing Ltd., England.

and weekly papers. The great man, tired, deaf, sixty-seven years old and alcoholic (his own admission), now only wants to return to Mexico and rest.

Joseph Kessel's novel, published in 1929, whipped up a fair *succès de scandale* at the time. Although Buñuel has said of it: "La novela no me gusta nada," it is a far from uninteresting book, firmly in the tradition of the French *roman psychologique*, and a precursor of the post-war but already classic *Histoire d'O*. It concerns a beautiful young *grande bourgeoise*, Séverine Sérizy, wife of a handsome young surgeon (Pierre) whom she deeply loves. She has every reason to be happy, but of course isn't. She learns that an acquaintance, a woman of her own class, is working in a brothel. Séverine gradually becomes obsessed by the thought of such a situation, finds out the address of one of these bagnios, and applies for a job there. She only works afternoons from two to five—thus her sobriquet, Belle de Jour. Frigid in the arms of her kindly, well-behaved husband, she is impelled by a masochistic urge for humiliation which leads her to seek out "rough trade." Marcel, a doting young gangster, falls in love with her; she soon becomes very fond of him. The devoted hoodlum attempts to kill a friend of her husband who is about to inform Pierre of Séverine's double life. The murder misfires when Pierre intervenes, and it is *he* who is seriously wounded. He recovers, but is paralyzed, condemned to a wheelchair. Overcome by guilt, Séverine confesses everything. Pierre never speaks to her again.

Kessel elevated this novelettish plot through a convincing portrayal of the frightening divorce between the heart and the senses. In 1936, Philippe Hériat adapted the book for the stage. The play was rejected by sixteen theatre directors and as many actresses. It has never been performed; with luck, it never will be.

Although Buñuel does not fancy the novel (he didn't like Defoe's *Robinson Crusoe* much either), he stated: "I found it interesting to try to make something I would like, starting from something I didn't. . . . I enjoyed complete freedom during the shooting of *Belle*, and consider myself entirely responsible for the result." He took pains with the editing, modifying several sequences in the process—a procedure rare for him. Hindered often in the past by tight budgets, his only inconvenience here was the producers' insidious auto-censorship; several cuts were made by them before *Belle* was sent to the censors.

Buñuel's last great film is close in spirit to his first great film, *L'Age d'Or*. Indeed, one of the things in *Belle de Jour* which seems to have bothered people is its fidelity to what can only be called the true spirit of surrealism: not the tacky Surrealism to be found in the moth-eaten commemorative art shows which have popped up from time to time in Paris, London or New York art galleries since the war, but the invigorating, positive, liberating surrealism which marked *L'Age d'Or*, caused riots when that film was first shown, and resulted in its being banned for a generation. The result is more mellow, less overtly aggressive than *L'Age d'Or*, even calm. But it is all there.

Buñuel: *"Belle de Jour* is a pornographic film . . . by that I mean chaste eroticism."

Buñuel: *"Belle de Jour* is a pornographic film . . . by that I mean chaste eroticism."

The film contains threads of events from Kessel's book. But Buñuel has turned the book inside out, ripped the surface from it, and stitched inside to outside with such invisible mending that much of the time the heroine's real life, her fantasies and child-hood memories, are integrated as a fluent story in which past, present, and the merely possible form a solid block of narrative. With her, we fall through trapdoors of consciousness, and then, with relief, fall out of them—but only into new ones.

Buñuel did not like the novel's ending, "because morality is saved." The climax of his film is simply the most astonishing "open ending" in the history of the cinema. It is the meanest trapdoor of them all (half open?—half shut?), a renewal of the beginning; but once seen, it fastens the entire film into a writhing subliminal image, that of an admirable circular serpent, forever catching its own tail in its own mouth.

The film's motifs are not those of the book. Kessel tells the story of a woman who loves one man with her heart, and a few dozen others with her body—and feels badly about it. Buñuel sidesteps sin and guilt; for him they are obviously luxuries the human race has been burdened with for too long. His film (the theme is far from new to him) tells the story of a liberation from the moral handcuffs of social caste by means of a personal *sacerdoce,* a self-fulfilment.

During the main credit titles, an open landau trots down a pleasant country lane towards the camera. Inside it, Pierre (Jean Sorel) and Séverine (Catherine Deneuve) are cosily enlaced. She tells her husband that she loves him more each day. Suddenly, he orders the coachman to stop and his wife to descend. The lackeys drag her through the woods. At Pierre's command, she is gagged, bound to a tree, whipped, etc., by the servants. "What are you thinking about, Séverine?" an off-screen voice asks. "About us," Séverine replies to Pierre. "We were driving in a landau." They are in the bedroom of their Paris apartment.

A few days later, at a mountain ski resort, they meet Pierre's friend (Father Lizzardi from *La Mort en ce Jardin* and Monteil from *Le Journal d'Une Femme de Chambre*), here called Husson (Michel Piccoli). "He's rich and idle. They're his two main illnesses," a woman friend remarks. Returning from her holidays,

Séverine learns that a young married woman of her "group" works in a clandestine brothel. (Clandestine because Kessel's novel, like France, has been modernized, and *maisons de rendezvous* are no longer legal.) Husson, met one day at the country club, insists on supplying her with details about "the houses" he has known. After days of hesitation spent obsessed by troublesome thoughts, Séverine goes *chez* Madame Anaïs (Geneviève Page), and as she climbs the stairs to the brothel for the first time, we come upon a little girl in church (Séverine as a child?) refusing the host. The priest is impatient: "Get it down you!" Séverine does get herself enrolled in the brothel, and returns that very afternoon to begin work—all gleaming patent-leather shoes Buñuelian style on the stairs.

She is recalcitrant with her first customer, an obese bonbon magnate, but when he and Anaïs get tough with her, she becomes joyfully submissive. One busy day, her list of clients includes a truckling gynaecologist, who has come *chez* Anaïs for the same reason as Séverine—to be humiliated. She cannot cope with him, but is pleased to be manhandled by a huge Japanese who tries to pay with a Geisha Diner's Card. We then see her seated demurely, enjoying the fresh air in an elegant outdoor café near the Cascade in the Bois de Boulogne, where Bresson's *Dames* were wont to meet. (At the next table, too thin to be Hitchcock, is a Spanish tourist, Señor Buñuel, talking business with one of the Hakim Brothers.) She is approached by the one-time leading man of *La Mort en ce Jardin* and *Cela s'appelle l'Aurore* (Georges Marchal). He is wearing no make-up and looks like a weird old French Duke. He asks Séverine if she likes money, and tells her that, indeed, he is a rich Duke. He invites her home for "a very moving religious ceremony." They are driven to his château by the two footmen who had whipped her at Pierre's command right after the main credit titles. The Duke dresses her up as his dead daughter, covers her with asphodels, mutters something about "the inebriating odor of dead flowers," then disappears under the coffin for a part of the service which the producers removed before submitting the film to General de Gaulle's censor board. When the ceremony is terminated, she is paid for her pains and kicked out into the rain.

She . . . is pleased to be manhandled by a huge Japanese who tries to pay with a Geisha Diner's Card. (*Belle de Jour*)

One day at the brothel, the Nazarin (Francisco Rabal), who has become a Bolivian gangster, arrives with a young protégé, Marcel (Pierre Clementi). They have just robbed a bank messenger (bringing the profits from the latest Vadim film?) in the lift leading to the Hakim Brothers' office, 79 Champs-Elysées, and are loaded with money to spend on pretty women. Marcel falls in love with Séverine and returns often to see her. She develops a strong physical passion for the hysterical punk, although she still loves her husband.

Marcel discovers Belle's secret identity, invades her home, shoots her husband, and is pursued and killed by the police. Pierre recovers. He is paralyzed, has lost the power of speech and will spend the rest of his days in a wheelchair. One beautiful autumn afternoon, Séverine is seen giving her husband his medicine. Then, looking out of the window of her splendid Paris apartment, she sees in the pane the reflection of the pleasant country lane (leading to the Duke's château?) where the landau was driving in the opening sequence. "I haven't had any more dreams—since your accident," she lies to Pierre lovingly. She then hears Buñuelian cowbells (first heard in 1930 in *L'Age d'Or* when Lya Lys, on discovering a huge cow on the bed of her splendid Paris apartment, chased the *vache* off the *lit*, looked into a mirror, and saw moving clouds and a vision of *her* lover). Pierre rises from his wheelchair. He is no longer a cripple, he can speak, he pours a drink. "Let's take a vacation, go to the mountains." "Do you hear?" she replies, and looking out of her Paris window we see the open landau in the country landscape. The coachmen from the opening scene are driving it down the country lane, towards Pierre and Séverine. Has it come to take them to the château?

This summary does even less than skeletal justice to the complex enchantments of *Belle de Jour*. Before moving on to a discussion of the reaction it provoked, here, at random, is a brief of particulars which after three viewings of the film stand out strongly:

—Geneviève Page as Madame Anaïs: one of the great performances of the screen in recent years; and most uncanny it is, since the role, as written, is rather one-dimensional.

—None of the film's "fantasies" are in the book—the girl refusing the host is of course plumb Buñuel. He discards, however, a ferociously Buñuelian item which occurs at the beginning of Kessel's novel. During the last days at winter sports, Séverine falls ill; by the time she returns to her Paris home, a near-fatal case of pneumonia has developed. And it is at *this* point that she begins to be aware of her disquieting sensuality, after the doctors "have delivered her body to the bites of leeches."

—When the bonbon magnate (Francis Blanche) invites the girls at the house to drink a bottle of champagne with him, the sequence is so superbly articulated, although unostentatiously edited, that its climax, as the cork pops (a miraculously "right" placed high-angle group shot), physically imposes itself as a major moment in the film, even though the scene itself is of relatively little importance. There is no precedent in Buñuel's work for such a purely formal "state of grace."

—It is early in the film. Séverine returns home, after the disturbing taxi ride during which brothels were discussed. Flowers are brought in, sent by Husson. She drops the vase. "What's the matter with me today?" she mutters. Until this point, color in the film has been cool and non-committal. Now, the visual shock of the red roses sprawled on the floor is tremendous—out of all proportion to the apparent seriousness of the incident. A chromatic premonition. As if she had opened a tin of sardines and a live cobra had popped out.

A few years ago, when another masterpiece, Dreyer's *Gertrud,* had its world première in Paris, kilometers of indignation, abuse, and downright foolishness were spat out into print. History has repeated itself with *Belle de Jour*—right down to *Cahiers du Cinéma* belatedly tipping the scales back to sanity again (*Cahiers* 191, 192) with articles more cogent and perceptive; above all, less concerned with protecting Paris concierges from the mischievous productions of dirty old Danish and Spanish cinéastes.

Positif, in its July issue, also counter-attacks with a first page editorial: "The brilliant brains of our critics manifested in chorus the disappointment caused them by *Belle de Jour* . . . thus proving the softening of their own cortexes. This united front of mediocrities was just the most recent attack on one of Buñuel's best films. The producers had already taken up the censor's shears themselves and adulterated it. In our next number we will run the articles the film deserves, but as of now, we would like to assure all of the above gentlemen of our hearty scorn."

What had the "above gentlemen" said? Here are a few pearls:

Garson in *L'Aurore:* "The ensemble is indecorous."

Baroncelli in *Le Monde:* ". . . prosaic . . . mediocrity . . . platitude. . . . One can't believe that such bad dreams could go on inside Catherine Deneuve's pretty head." [It is precisely because Buñuel knows better than anyone else what *can* go on inside pretty heads that his casting of the part is perfect. Deneuve's glacial in-gazing is a wondrous sight. She often looks as impressively opaque as Ingres' "La Grande Odalisque"; sometimes like *Marnie* reading between the lines in *Alice in Wonderland.* The more Séverine the *grande bourgeoise* "degrades" herself, the more beautiful and blooming the actress becomes. Her finest role.]

Mohrt in *Carrefour:* "The average moviegoer's disappointment is justified." [The average moviegoer has made *Belle de Jour* into one of the biggest box-office successes of the year. It has just entered its third month of unbroken first run showings at three of Paris's largest cinemas.]

Marcabru in *Arts:* "A radical-socialist film . . . short of breath and heart. . . . The director has benefited from a sympathy from the critics so excessive that it's close to blindness. . . . Buñuel has fallen on his face two times out of three for many years. He has been given the benefit of the doubt because of his age . . . he shouldn't take advantage of it."

Henry Chapier in *Combat:* "Buñuel has lost Kessel's generous sentimentality, the marvelous way Kessel knows how to make vice sympathetic." [Buñuel needs sentimentality like Titian needed color-blindness. He has never been concerned with vice as such—he may not even know what it is. If he has read Chapier, he may know now: pushing sentimentality is vice.]

M. Chapier again: "Upper middle-class Parisian women are no longer restrained by sexual taboos, and we could only believe such a story if it were taking place in Spain . . . or at most in Bordeaux or Rouen." [Is French Puritanism such a thing of the past? Far from it. It is merely something foreign tourists, their eyes filled with postcard visions of Pigalle *filles de joie*, can't be expected to know about, and something most Frenchmen, *their* eyes filled with Fifth Republic State TV homilies, prefer to ignore. It was, after all, only a few weeks ago—in 1967—that a French law dating from 1922, making it a criminal offence to disseminate any information in favor of birth control, was finally abrogated. It was under the current Gaullist régime, and while the far side of the moon was being photographed, that the hoary works of Havelock Ellis were banned in France. If all the excellent books outlawed under "Aunt Yvonne's" reign of public morality were put on shelves, they would constitute a rich modern library. Where does M. Chapier find his unrestrained upper-class Parisian women? He may have been seeing too many old Lubitsch films laid in Paris.]

All of the boys had a really hard time finding their way out of the last reel. Georges Sadoul is an old friend of the director, and don't get him wrong, he does *like* the film, but it's certainly a good thing "Buñuel put a lot of humor in it . . . otherwise certain sequences would be nauseating." Sadoul thinks that Séverine's husband just gets well at the end. Aubriant in *Candide* tells us that Pierre was only pretending to be wounded—in a dream. And Marcel Martin, in *Cinéma 67*, strains at an imaginary gnat and swallows ten camels. For him much of the film is dream, but since Buñuel is satirizing bourgeois characters, the dialogue is banal on purpose and the color is mediocre (in truth Sacha Vierny's autumnal Eastmancolor camerawork is superb), because naughty Séverine must have been looking at some faded old blue films before the story started. This "colored" her thoughts!

Only one strong sensible voice has so far been heard in this wilderness of obfuscation: Jean-André Fieschi, in a refreshingly sane piece in *Cahiers* which presents a well-reasoned argument against "a unilateral reading of the film."

Indeed, it is impossible and unnecessary to decide whether the end of *Belle de Jour* conveys a shift from fantasy to reality or vice versa. The ambiguity is as immanent in the film, as deliberately Buñuel's, as the tranquil nobility of his point of view—a decent neutrality which condemns no one. He does not side with Séverine, nor can he regard her as a pervert. She has her reasons; but so does everyone else. Neither he nor his heroine wastes a minute worrying about Divine punishment. In accepting herself, Séverine liberates herself. She is no longer *une grande bourgeoise,* but a human being who has undergone a shattering *and* enchanting apprenticeship. But instead of a Hollywood-style clinch at fade-out time, we and she can content ourselves with visions of Séverine, joyful handmaiden at her husband's wheelchair-side *and* (or) riding with Pierre in the magic lantern of her mind down a beautiful country lane, where at any moment he may stop the carriage and deal her the merely divinely human punishment which to her is another name for love.

On *Belle de Jour*

THE BEAUTY OF *BELLE DE JOUR*

Andrew Sarris

. . . .

Luis Buñuel's *Belle de Jour* has evoked in many critiques that all-purpose adjective "beautiful." Catherine Deneuve is undeniably beautiful, never more so than in this context of Buñuelian perversity, and almost any meaningfully designed color film seems beautiful if only because the vast subconscious sea of the cinema is safely gelatinized within the frames of an academic painting. Describing a film as beautiful is unfortunately too often a device to end discussion, particularly nowadays when irrationality and hysteria have become institutionalized as life styles. *Elvira Madigan* is beautiful in the way flowery poems are poetical, not through functional expressiveness but through lyrical excessiveness. *Bonnie and Clyde* is beautiful when its luminously lyrical close-ups involve the audience with the killers, but the film is equally beautiful when its concluding slow-motion ballet of death and transfiguration takes the audience off the hook by distancing the characters back into legend and fantasy. The fact that the close-ups contradict the distancing is immaterial to the film's admirers. *Bonnie and Clyde* is beautiful, and consistency is the hobgoblin of little minds.

I would argue that *Belle de Jour* is indeed a beautiful film, but not because of any anaesthetizing aesthetic of benevolently mindless lyricism. Nor is the film beautiful because its director's visual style transcends its sordid subject. The beauty of *Belle de Jour* is the beauty of artistic rigor and adaptable intelligence. Given what Buñuel is at sixty-seven and what he has done in forty years and twenty-seven projects of film-making and what and whom he had to work with and for, *Belle de Jour* reverberates with the cruel

From *The Village Voice*, May 2 and 9, 1968. Copyright © 1968 by *The Village Voice*, Inc. Reprinted by permission of *The Village Voice* and the author.

logic of formal necessity. From the opening shot of an open carriage approaching the camera at an oblique ground-level angle to the closing shot of an open carriage passing the camera at an oblique overhead angle, the film progresses inexorably upward, an ascent of assent, from the reverie of suppressed desires to the revelation of fulfilled fantasies. But whose desires and whose fantasies? Buñuel's? His heroine's? Actually a bit of both. The exact proportion of subjective contemplation to objective correlative can best be calculated by comparing Joseph Kessel's basic anecdotal material with what appears on the screen.

In his preface to *Belle de Jour*, Kessel writes: "The subject of *Belle de Jour* is not Séverine's sensual aberration; it is her love for Pierre independent of that aberration, and it is the tragedy of that love." Kessel concludes his preface with a reprovingly rhetorical question for those critics who dismissed *Belle de Jour* as a piece of pathological observation: "Shall I be the only one to pity Séverine, and to love her?"

The "sensual aberration" of which Kessel writes undoubtedly seemed more shocking in 1929, when the first French edition was published, than it would seem in the current period of erotic escalation. Séverine Sérizy, happily married to a handsome young surgeon, goes to work in a house of ill-repute, actually less a house than an intimate apartment. The money involved is less the motivation than the pretext for her action. Pierre, her husband, provides for her material needs handsomely, but his respectfully temporizing caresses fail to satisfy her psychic need for brutal degradation, a need first awakened by a malodorous molester when she was a child of eight. To preserve a façade of marital respectability, Séverine works at her obsessive profession only afternoons from two to five, the mystery of her matinée schedule causing her to be christened Belle de Jour. Kessel's novel, like his heroine, is fatally divided between clinical observations on sexual psychology and novelistic contrivances to overcome the innate lethargy of a woman of leisure. Husson, a weary sensualist in her husband's circle of friends, is a particularly intricate contrivance in that he triggers much of the novel's intrigue. It is Husson who first alerts Séverine to her own frustrations by his unwelcome advances. It is he who inadvertently supplies her with the address of her sensual destiny, and who, discovering her double life, poses such a threat to her non-Belle-de-Jour existence that he precipitates, almost innocently, the final catastrophe.

Marcel, a gold-toothed gangster infatuated with Belle de Jour, provides a violently melodramatic climax to the novel, by agreeing to murder Husson to preserve Séverine's secret and Belle de Jour's respect. Irony is piled upon irony as Marcel's assault on Husson is deflected by Pierre, who is so grievously wounded that he is confined for life to helpless paralysis in a wheelchair. Marcel and Husson remain silent about Belle de Jour, thus enabling Séverine to escape a public scandal and even prosecution, but, perverse to the end, she confesses everything to Pierre, and is rewarded not with his forgiveness but with stern silence.

Buñuel and his co-scenarist Jean-Claude Carrière retained most of the characters of the novel. Séverine goes to work for Madame Anaïs in both novel and film, and Belle de Jour's colleagues are Charlotte and Mathilde in both versions. The most striking variation between novel and film is in the elaborately structured dream apparatus of the film. Kessel's Séverine never dreams the concrete images of Buñuel's surreal reveries of feminine masochism. There are no floggings in the book as there are in the film, no binding of hands with ropes, no sealing of mouths, no splattering with mud. Kessel's Séverine never really dreams at all; she merely recollects the past and anticipates the future. If the novel had been filmed in the thirties or the forties by a French director trained in the Tradition of Quality, a Marcel Carné or Claude Autant-Lara perhaps, Séverine would probably have been played with many shimmering close-ups to dramatize the desperate conflict between her feelings and her senses. The background music would have been exquisitely sentimental. Except for the bells that signal the movement of the horse-drawn carriage, Buñuel uses no music whatsoever. No Simon and Garfunkel, no Beatles, no Donovan, not even the realistically based music of radios and record players. There is no radio or television in the modern world of Belle de Jour, but there is a Geisha Club credit card. Buñuel has stripped modernity of its specificity. Thus we are not bothered so much by the suspicion that horse-drawn carriages are not as likely to figure in the reveries of Séverine's (or

Catherine Deneuve's) generation as in the memories of Buñuel's. The fact that Buñuel does not employ music in *Belle de Jour* is not significant as a matter of general aesthetic policy. Buñuel himself has derived ironic counterpoint from the musical backgrounds of such recent films as *Viridiana* and *Simon of the Desert*. He must have felt that he didn't need music to underscore the fundamental irony implicit in a woman with the face of an angel and the lusts of a devil. Still, *Belle de Jour* overcomes an awesome handicap of affect by disdaining the facile frissons of music.

Many of the script changes were dictated by the differences in the media. Pierre emerges through Jean Sorel as a much duller character than in the book, but it is difficult to see what any director can do with the character of the Noble Husband in such a grotesque context. The changes in Husson's character are more meaningful. Kessel's Husson was more mannered in his ennui, but he takes advantage of Séverine's degraded status as Belle de Jour to possess her body. Buñuel's Husson (Michel Piccoli) is more fastidious; he loses interest in Séverine at precisely the instant she becomes available to him as Belle de Jour. But it is Buñuel's Husson who tells Pierre of Belle de Jour after the accident; Kessel's Husson never seriously contemplated such a course of action before or after.

Kessel wants us to love Séverine by identifying with her; Buñuel wants us to understand Séverine by contemplating the nature of her obsession. Instead of indulging in Kessel's sentimental psychology by staring into Catherine Deneuve's eyes, Buñuel fragments Deneuve's body into its erotic constituents. His shots of feet, hands, legs, shoes, stockings, undergarments, etc., are the shots not only of a fetishist, but of a cubist, a director concerned simultaneously with the parts and their effect on the whole. Buñuel's graceful camera movements convey Deneuve to her sensual destiny through her black patent-leather shoes, and to her final reverie through her ringed fingers feeling their way along the furniture with the tactile tenderness of a mystical sensuality, Séverine's, Deneuve's or Buñuel's, it makes little difference.

The beauty of the filmed version of *Belle de Jour* arises from its

Buñuel fragments Deneuve's body into its erotic constituents. His shots of feet, hands, legs, shoes, stockings, undergarments, etc., are the shots not only of a fetishist, but of a cubist, a director concerned simultaneously with the parts and their effect on the whole. (*Belle de Jour*)

implication of Buñuel in its vision of the world. It is Buñuel himself who is the most devoted patron of *chez* Madame Anaïs, and the most pathetic admirer of Catherine Deneuve's Séverine-Belle de Jour. Never before has Buñuel's view of the spectacle seemed so obliquely Ophulsian in its shy gaze from behind curtains, windows, and even peepholes. Buñuel's love of Séverine is greater than Kessel's, simply because Buñuel sees Belle de Jour as Séverine's liberator. The sensuality of *Belle de Jour* is not metaphorical like Genêt's in *The Balcony* or Albee's in *Everything in the Garden*. Most writers, even the most radical, treat prostitution as a symptom of a social malaise and not as a concrete manifestation of a universal impulse. Buñuel reminds us once again in *Belle de Jour* that he is one of the few men of the left not afflicted by puritanism and bourgeois notions of chastity and fidelity. The difference between Buñuel and, say, Genêt is not entirely a difference between a man of images and a man of words. What distinguishes *Belle de Jour* from most movies is the impression it gives of having been seen in its director's mind long before it was shot. There is a preconceived exactness to its images that · will inevitably disconcert middlebrow film critics, especially those who are highbrows in other cultural sectors. It is only the specialist in film who can fully appreciate the directness of Buñuel's image above and beyond the novelistic nuances he sacrifices on the altars of shock and laughter.

The ending of *Belle de Jour* is tantalizingly open as narrative. Husson has told Pierre about Belle de Jour, or at least we presume so. Buñuel does not show the scene, and we are not obliged to believe anything we do not see, but there is no particular reason to believe that Husson has not carried out his stated intention. Buñuel does not cast his audience adrift in a sea of ambiguity at every opportunity; he is simply not that interested in dramatic suspense. Séverine enters Pierre's room, and for the first time in the film Buñuel's technique obscures the flow of action. Buñuel breaks up the spatial unity of the scene with alternative sights and sounds to indicate a range of possibilities. Cut to Jean Sorel's tear-stained face. Pierre Knows All and Feels Betrayed. Cut to his crumpled upturned hand. Pierre is Dead from the Shock of His Grief. Cut on the sound track to the bells of a carriage, and to Sorel's voice asking of Deneuve's pensive face what Séverine is thinking. Everything Turns Back to Fantasy.

Or does it? Some critics have suggested that Séverine has been cured of her masochistic obsession by becoming Belle de Jour. Hence the empty carriage at the end of the film. She will no longer take *that* trip. One French critic has argued that the entire film is a dream, but the big problem with such an argument is Buñuel's visually explicit brand of surrealism. Earlier in the film, Husson calls on Séverine at her home and is rudely rebuffed. Buñuel cuts immediately to a shockingly "cute" Boy-Girl-profile two-shot of Séverine and Husson at the ski lodge. As the camera pulls back, we see Jean Sorel and Macha Meril at the same table. It must be a dream, we assure ourselves, while Séverine and Husson slip out of sight under the table to perform some unspeakable act of sacrilege against bourgeois society. The table begins to bump up and down, but the deserted partners, Sorel and Meril, are only mildly concerned. Buñuel has transported *Belle de Jour* back to *L'Age d'Or*, but the effect of the scene is unsettling if we accept it as occurring in Séverine's mind. Here I think Buñuel slipped into a sadistic attitude of his own toward Pierre, since this is the only scene in the film in which Pierre is made to look completely ridiculous. The key to the scene, however, is not Séverine's characterization but Buñuel's satiric attitude toward Hollywood sentimentality. The profile shot more than the table-bumping gives the show away, but audiences would never "get" the joke without the table-bumping, and Buñuel does not disdain vulgarity as one of the strategies of surrealism.

Actually we are such Puritans that we talk of surrealism almost exclusively in the solemn terms of social defiance. Humor is only a means to an end, but not an end in itself. No, never? Well, hardly ever. And in Buñuel's case laughter serves to disinfect libertinism of its satanic aura. If we can laugh at the prissiness of perversion and the fastidiousness of fetishism, not with smug superiority, but with carnal complicity, we become too impli-cated to remain indifferent. Buñuel's masochist, unlike Genêt's in *The Balcony*, satisfies his devious lechery by stroking the thighs of his professionally cruel mistress. Buñuel's brothel is a brothel and not one of Genêt's microcosms, and Buñuel's sensuality turns in upon itself as an enclosed experience devoid of allegorical significance.

Similarly, the entire film turns in upon itself by ending with the same question with which it began: "Séverine, what are you thinking about?" And Séverine tells the truth in her fashion. She thinks of places and conveyances and trips and herds of Spanish bulls named Remorse except one named Expiation. At the end, she is still dreaming, and who is to say that the dream is any less real or vivid than the reality it accompanies? Certainly not Buñuel's probing but compassionate camera. There are several possible interpretations of Buñuel's ending, but the formal sym-metry of the film makes the debate academic. Buñuel is ultimately ambiguous so as not to moralize about his subject. He wishes neither to punish Séverine nor to reward her. He prefers to contemplate the grace with which she accepts her fate, and

Buñuel is nothing if not fatalistic. Even the hapless husband is granted a mystical premonition when he sees an empty wheelchair in the street. It is destined for him, and the concreteness of Buñuel's visual imagery is so intense that we feel that the wheelchair is destined for Pierre as Pierre is destined for the wheelchair.

Buñuel's fatalism actually undercuts the suspense of the narrative to the extent that there is no intellectual pressure for a resolved ending. Between the fatalism and the formal symmetry, *Belle de Jour* seems completely articulated as a Buñuelian statement. We do not have to know what we are not meant to know, and Buñuel establishes a precedent within his film for the ambiguity of his ending. This precedent involves Madame Anaïs, after Séverine the most absorbing character in the film. Alone of all the characters, Madame Anaïs is the truth-seeker, and she is inevitably far from the mark. She misunderstands the motivations of Belle de Jour from the outset, and she misinterprets Belle de Jour's departure. Still, she is always staring at Belle de Jour as if it were possible to peel away layers of lacquered flesh to the raw impulses underneath. The scenes in which Geneviève Page's Madame Anaïs gazes with loving curiosity at Catherine Deneuve's Belle de Jour gleam with a psychological insight not customary with Buñuel, or, as rigorously empirical aestheticians would have it, the scenes gleam with the appearance of a psychological insight, the very beautiful appearance derived from two extraordinary screen incarnations.

The great irony of *Belle de Jour* is that a sixty-seven-year-old Spanish surrealist has set out to liberate humanity of its bourgeois sentimentality only to collide with the most sentimental generation of flowery feelings in human history.

Tristana

Joan Mellen

. . . .

On the surface, *Tristana* is about a pure young girl who is seduced by her guardian. It takes place in Toledo, Spain, long a stronghold of the double standard guaranteeing the man sexual license and the woman the choice of falling from grace or repressing her sexuality beneath a guise of sanctimonious innocence. Most of the women in Tristana's world choose the latter; she, however, has courage enough to flee from the house of her guardian, Don Lope, who calls himself her father or husband, "whichever I choose." She elopes with a handsome young artist who wishes to marry her. Two years later, still unmarried and afflicted with what seems to be a fatal illness, Tristana returns to the house of the guardian she despises. Bearing for the rest of her life the mark of her illness, an amputated leg, she murders Don Lope years later by allowing him to die of a heart attack without calling a doctor.

But within the confines of this rather melodramatic if morally resonant plot, which always borders on the perverse, as do all of the director's films, Buñuel has managed to interweave meanings that go far beyond the Electra theme. Throughout the film, Buñuel comments on the psychological effects of social dependance. Tristana quickly hates Don Lope because he watches her every move and refuses to allow her even to go for a walk unless she is in the company of the maid, Saturna. As the film begins, over the credits church bells peal, enclosing within their power the two women in black, Tristana and Saturna, who walk toward the camera. The church bells represent the authority of the male over the female in patriarchal Spain. Left an orphan by the death of her mother, Tristana is at the mercy of Don Lope. That no man

From *Film Quarterly*, Vol. 24, No. 2 (Winter 1970–71). Reprinted by permission of the publisher.

is to be trusted by a woman is expressed in Saturna's first words in the film which are a confirmation of the injustices suffered by her sex: "May my dead husband rot in hell."

Don Lope is the "good man" of his time, a liberal aristocrat. Yet when we first see him, he is soliciting a vivacious girl on the street. His overwhelming concern with matters of honor and morality does not pertain to his amorous relations with women. Don Lope strips Tristana of all her possessions except a few musical scores, and of her ideas as well. "I'll manage to clear your head of superstitions," he tells her at this first meeting. Her mother (who was also his lover), he asserts, "had no brains." Later, Tristana begins to have the nightmare that will pursue her throughout her life: she sees the head of Don Lope transferred into the phallic bell clapper at the church tower. This terrifying image of the ghoulish head of Don Lope represents at once her desire and repulsion for the lascivious, aging guardian. Tristana's fear of him is the fear of being smothered, her identity obliterated both psychologically and sexually. It is a fear confirmed by the authoritarianism of the man. "The only way to keep a woman honest," says Don Lope, quoting a Spanish folk saying, "is to break her leg and keep her at home," a prophecy of what will happen to Tristana.

Buñuel carefully develops the means by which Don Lope molds and shapes the young Tristana's mind to conform to his own plan to make her his life-long dependent. Out for a promenade, they see a young couple, and Don Lope sneers: "the sickly odor of marital bliss." Marriage, he tells Tristana, means a farewell to love; for love to be free, no official blessings should intervene. By seeming to allow her total freedom, Don Lope hopes to bind her to him in more subtle and binding ways than the legal. Only apparently sceptical, Tristana, whose goals are to be "free" and "to work," absorbs the lesson.

Buñuel's psychology is impeccable. Her mind a *tabula rasa*, it is logical that Tristana would become whatever her surroundings provide, that her psychic impulses would be directed by the will of her domineering guardian. The teachings of Don Lope prove to be deadly for both. By having Tristana persistently refuse to marry her young artist lover, Don Horacio, Buñuel illustrates how deeply the unconscious of Tristana has accepted Don Lope's half-baked notions about "free love." But this in turn increases her dependence upon Don Lope himself, filling her with a despair and self-hatred that culminates in his murder. Cleverly, Don Lope kisses Tristana for the first time right after he has spoken against marriage. Her defenses weakened, with a giggle she admits that she does indeed care for him.

Ultimately, this dependency leads her to become simply perverse. She takes delight in the presence of the half-witted, deafmute son of Saturna who at the end pushes her wheelchair for her because he is dependent upon *her*. She shuts him out of her room only to expose her body to him gloatingly from the balcony. Like Don Lope, Tristana needs a victim. As Saturno rushes off into the bushes, the boy provides an analogue for Tristana's own youthful reaction to the aging Don Lope with its simultaneous fascination and repulsion.

Sexually, Tristana, after her initiation by Don Lope, becomes the sister of Belle de Jour. It is no accident that both parts are played by Catherine Deneuve, whose perfect blonde beauty has the quality of ice, of emotion repressed, a trait utilized as well by François Truffaut in *La Sirène du Mississippi*. Like Belle de Jour, Tristana is a woman whose sexuality has been perverted by a fear of seduction by an older, forbidding father figure, and who can now respond only to the brutal and the perverse. Thus Tristana leaves her young lover to return to the sombre house of Don Lope.

The archaic, gradually decaying quality of Don Lope's world is expressed in the golds and browns, the colors of autumn, which dominate the *mise en scène*. This mood is enhanced by Deneuve's being dressed throughout the film only in combinations of brown, white and black, reflecting a sensibility tamed by the norms of its world. Toledo's narrow winding medieval streets provide a real labyrinth to echo Tristana's unconscious imprisonment. (A panorama of Toledo both opens and closes the film.)

Tristana's tie with the force that corrupted her is epitomized by her return to the house of Don Lope. It is the force of his repulsive-attractive presence upon her sexuality, the equivalent of the desire of the daughter for her father. Don Horacio is logically repelled by Tristana's perversity, expressed in her refusal to marry

him and her rejection of his love for that of Don Lope. In alliance
with the corrupt and the unnatural are the priests who describe
Tristana's refusal to marry Don Lope as "irrationality" and who
would legalize her psychological, social, and sexual imprisonment.

Until the fantasized wish-fulfillment at the end, the murder of
the oppressive father-lover, the hatred of Tristana for Don Lope
can express itself only in the small victories of the oppressed. She
toys with and then devours two testicle-like chick peas. She
throws in the trash his motheaten carpet slippers, for which he
has a more than rational attachment. The final expression of her
perversity is her gesture at the end of the film of opening the
window and letting the snow and cold engulf the dying Don
Lope. For the perverse in the world of Don Lope has always been
treated as the natural. (He even tells her that she would be more
appealing to some people with her amputated leg.) He is delighted
with the conjunction between her return to absolute dependence
as a cripple and his lifelong perverse feelings toward the sexual
and women. It is, of course, perfect justice that Don Lope should
fall victim at the end to his own perversion. Tristana responds in
the manner he has taught her. "The kinder he is," she says, "the
less I love him." She expresses the psychological damage done to
women in her culture—the same damage expressed by Belle de
Jour, who could be awakened sexually only in a brothel.

Tristana reflects as well Buñuel's preoccupation with the decay
of Spain. He explores its obsession with an old order, represented
by Don Lope and his cronies who meet every day in a café filled
with indolent former aristocrats. It is a world defined by norms
and relationships which have outlived their time and have now
become dangerous. *Tristana* takes place in the twenties after the
fall of the first republic which presaged the invasion of the fascists
in the next decade. It conveys the image of a Spain that is already
amputated. The crippled Tristana represents in her person the
generation to be maimed by the Civil War, embodying as she does
the frequent image in Franco's Spain of the amputee.

Buñuel creates an image of the defeat of liberty. In one scene
workers are being chased by some Guardia Civil on horseback,
while others pursue them with swords. The precarious existence

She expresses the psychological damage done to women in her culture - the same damage expressed by Belle de Jour, who could be awakened sexually only in a brothel. (*Tristana*)

of the worker, the man on the street, is meant to be viewed in opposition to Don Lope's impotent reactions to the horror of work. While the men in the machine shop from which Saturno runs away must work long hours, Don Lope is free to decide to live in genteel poverty until the death of his wealthy sister, Josefina. Don Lope's attitude toward the workers reveals the self-righteous *noblesse oblige* of the aristocrat. Pointing the police in another direction, he allows a thief to escape because "he was weak and needed protection . . . the police stand for power." His gesture on behalf of "justice" is, characteristically, an act in which he does not have to participate. For Don Lope "money is vile"; for the workers in the metal shop, on the streets, and omnipresent in the scenario, it means survival. Buñuel clinches the decadence of Don Lope by rapidly cutting from Don Lope

and Tristana going to bed for the first time to the scene of the
police chasing workers down the street.

Don Lope stands thus for the impotence and historical amnesia
of Spain, a role defined as well by Carlos Saura in *The Garden of
Delights* through the character of Antonio. And Don Lope's
impotence is far from innocent. Hypocrisy defines his very sensibility. It is expressed in his self-conscious and superficial rejection
of religion as well as in the ridiculousness of his code of honor
which decrees that he live by all the ten commandments except
those having to do with sex, by which he means seduction. Don
Lope has the arrogance to argue that he takes a girl only if she
consents. He proudly maintains that he would exclude the wife of
a friend or "the flower blooming in innocence." With no dialogue needed, Buñuel cuts to the innocent Tristana reading
musical scores, soon to be the victim of Don Lope's lust.

Don Lope's impotence is far from innocent. Hypocrisy defines his very sensibility. (*Tristana*)

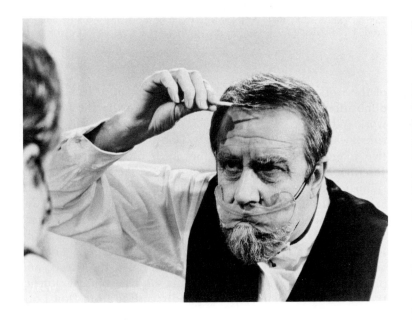

Don Lope refuses to judge a duel because the participants have agreed to fight only "until the first sign of blood," and he hates "circuses." He won't be the arbiter at so cheap a price. His morality is thus expressed in limbo, devoid of any real content. It is couched in terms that will not touch upon his life: a duel, a harmless denunciation of priests, the contempt for the degradation of work by a man who is kept all his life by a private income, the rejection of marriage by a man who savors sex more with a mistress, particularly if she is innocent and thirty years younger than he. It is the almost psychotic sense of honor of the hidalgo who would rather starve to death than work, although he must sell everything he owns. In Don Lope's case it is the honor of a man who has debauched a girl destined to live with him as his daughter.

The essential frivolity of such a code, the hypocrisy of a morality which exacts no sacrifices, is nowhere better expressed than in one of the last sequences of the film in which the now aged Don Lope, bespectacled and grey, with his beard no longer dyed black, has coffee with three grasping priests on the eve of his death. The priests are waiting in eager anticipation for his death, which they hope will mean bequests to them. They savor his rich, creamy coffee and cakes, stuffing themselves as snow falls outside the window. Taking shelter with the rich, they are shielded from the harsh aspects of life. Don Lope has forgotten his atheism, his heretical cry, "long live the living," after the funeral of that intractable dowager, his sister Josefina. He has forgotten that he refused to call a priest when Tristana was deathly ill on the ground that "the only true priests are those who defend the innocent." After Tristana returns to the house where she was dishonored, ironically but with precise realism, the priests return also. They have been enlisted to convince Tristana to marry Don Lope and end her life of "sin."

Nowhere is the "honor" of Don Lope better satirized than in Buñuel's cutting back to Tristana's days of innocence, before she entered the house of Don Lope. The film ends on the image it began with: the innocent Tristana walking pleasantly with Saturna, beautifully under-played by Lola Gaos. The repetition of the view of Toledo now expresses the world which has buried her. The resounding church bells are no longer nostalgic but have become painful symbols of hypocrisy.

Spain, like Tristana, its "sadness," has been destroyed by a cruel code of honor, defiled and left amputated by hypocrisy. And it can summon nothing with which to replace the old code. Tristana is left in the house (Spain) of Don Lope with no new values to heal and revitalize her internal and external habitation. *Tristana* belongs with *Belle de Jour* in the Buñuel *oeuvre*. It is post-*Viridiana* and post-*Nazarin* in its sensibility, refusing even the illusion of a messianic figure equivalent to Viridiana, Nazarin or Simon of the Desert come to heal the poor. The political has been transformed back into the sociology of a callous aristocracy struggling with its death throes in an unrelieved homeland. Buñuel no longer can offer the deception of the character with Christian impulses whose hopes will come to nothing because his dedication to the poor as a single individual is painfully inadequate. The religious motif appears now only in burlesque, in the begging priests hovering around Don Lope on the eve of his death.

Tristana briefly shares the innocent hope of a figure like Viridiana, but she is too soon engulfed by a world which denies a woman any outlet for her creative energies. Tristana must sell her beloved piano soon after her mother's death, and it is only after her leg is amputated, when she is once more under his reign, that Don Lope buys her a new one. By this time Tristana sees her amputation as defining her condition and her future. Paradoxically, although he does not live to see it, Don Lope was right when he demoniacally said that the sick Tristana would never leave his house alive. Her loud piano playing during the last visit of Don Horacio is symbolic of her repression of all healthy impulse. Transforming tender feeling into harsh aggression, it is meant to drown out what remains in her of hope and possibility. Don Horacio, as Tristana guesses, will never return. She is left amidst the furniture of decadence to live out her future. Her youthful sexuality has been reduced to a semi-demented exhibitionism before the frightened deafmute, Saturno.

The circular structure of the imagery, the rapid repetition of the images of Tristana's life until we return to the first sequence of the film, reflects the hopelessness Buñuel feels, both toward Spain and toward its victims. Buñuel has relentlessly and brilliantly exposed the destruction of the individual by a corrupt, hypocritical moral code which makes no pretense of improving a society in which class animosities are deepening and brutality is growing.

The Milky Way

THE MILKY WAY   Oswaldo Capriles

. . . .

Luis Buñuel's endless monologue on the religious theme has
always been a converging point for critics; and it has been the
source wherein they sought the secret to the uniquely Buñuelesque style. The psychologist-high priests, the exegetes of the old
anarchistic surrealism by which Buñuel has always been labeled,
and the critics of the left, have all coincided in an interpretation
of Buñuel which has acquired the status of dogma: Buñuel is, for
them all, an inveterate atheist, an executor in cinema of Freudian
surrealism, incessantly dedicated to a battle unto death with
Christian dogma, which has obsessed and fascinated him since
childhood. Hence, one such priest invokes Buñuel's well-known
statement: "I am still an atheist, thank God" as the tacit confession of a rebel's abiding faith, albeit that of an agreeable,
willful rebel.

The statement's unique, clear sense of the renegade, which is
very Spanish, is totally ignored. Buñuel, in fact, is fundamentally
a man of scandal, an individual whose public polemic does not
run parallel to his presumed "secret" polemic, whose proposals
are more modest than most people are wont to believe. The
essential Buñuelesque ambiguity, continually intertwined and
with the utmost transparent clarity, is merely the discursive turn
of phrase, the "brilliant" remark, the pirouette made by the idea
within his aggressive but highly orthodox cinematographic imagery.

Buñuel is the Hatter in *Alice in Wonderland*, amiably convincing the little girl that Time is a living being; speech in his
films likewise is perpetually interrupted by the twists and turns of
his unique pattern of thought. Speech flaunts the same convic-

From *Cine Cubano* 71/72. Translated by Toby Talbot.

tion of the Hatter that time has voluntarily stood still. Dating back to *Land Without Bread*, the critical interpretation of reality appears consistently as a preoccupying theme for Buñuel; and with *Un Chien Andalou* speech turns into aggressiveness—at times gratuitously—in order that he may achieve a strange synthesis of disorder and homogeneity. For pro-Buñuelesque exegetes, it is an expressive stylistic disorder, with an inherent homogeneity; for the "anti" interpreters it is the contrary. In reality, if reality can be discussed with respect to the absurd task of exegesis, Buñuel is an uneven filmmaker, who has done purely commercial jobs (in which his genius crops up with abundant frequency), and who has concerned himself with certain themes, not always so interconnected as it would seem; and who, above all, works with cinema the way an artisan would with oral narrative.

Buñuel cannot disengage himself from the story; anecdote is always one step ahead of reflection. And his themes are manifested by *narrative* images. The group of rebels who shoot the Pope in *The Milky Way* have walked a long stretch from that street where *Diary of a Chambermaid* ends. The solitude of Simon the Stylite continues—and sharpens—the contradiction between Nazarin's saintliness, as a life style, and the fall from grace. *Viridiana* treats the impossibility of charity, with that same masochistic energy with which the heroine of *Belle de Jour* abandons herself to fantasies of her continual deflowering. And the plumber who for the first time excites the tender sexuality of Belle is the same old man who collects buttons in *Diary*, and hence, the same gentleman who engages in inoffensive contortions under the coffin where Belle de Jour lies, the same one who lovingly watches the youthful apparition of Viridiana in her bridal robes.

A catalogue could be drawn up, which would be of no importance, however, based on the repetition of various characters in the body of work generally regarded as typically Buñuelesque. Such a catalogue would merely allow one to illustrate the pervasiveness of certain gestures, of moral prototypes, when, in fact, what is truly interesting in Buñuel is to follow the continuity of

his *story*. And that story involves nothing particularly transcendental or spiritual. It is a trivial, modest story which concerns
itself with concrete events, a whole series of important acts, just as
the good Fellini's baroque images of people are placed in a
personal story, his own modest but probing autobiography.

The comparison between Buñuel and Bergman has proven
tempting for many critics. Bergman has involved himself in a
long, rich monologue which is fundamentally a personal preoccupation, an interpretation of the world and of existence,
which includes the question of the artist's intervention as intermediary; the artist becomes a conscience which is both judge and
participant, which sees and is merged with the object of his
vision. The *moral* consequence in Bergman is inevitable. With
Buñuel the monologue is more subjective, more elemental and
realistic, his purpose much less ambitious; Buñuel's "religious"
preoccupation is basically, and simply, the necessity to reproduce
a rich, inhabited world, an assumed and conscious reality, which
for him, however, constitutes a favorite sphere of play, an *affective*
need.

There is no apparent moral anguish in Buñuel, but rather a
need for dispute, at its essence the typical Spanish resentment
against *dogma*, a form of combat against the repression of free
thought. Buñuel's battle against dogma is the principal theme of
Nazarin, *Viridiana* and *Simon of the Desert*, although it would be
an error to think that this was his sole expressive purpose. The
logical destruction of a non-temporal, immaterial dogma is accomplished by way of the temporal and material, through a banal
story, through irrefutable anecdote, without the story, however,
becoming secondary.

Rather, the anecdotal aspect in Buñuel is fundamental and
indispensable to any proper reading of his work. The underlying
reason for his probing into concrete reality is to deposit therein
with the utmost naturalness, the germ of corruption, of fermen-
tation which reality asserts when it is faced with the immanent,
the sublime, and which secular destiny ultimately reduces to
biblical dust. It is not anti-dogma explained, but reality demonstrated, the fruit of an image serene in its development. If it is

chaotic in form, and in its accumulation of events, it is only because the disputants of dogma are revealed to be successively and hence, absurdly, triumphant.

Buñuel's sincerity lies, on the one hand, in his relative humility of purpose, and on the other, in the ingenuity of his traps and ruses. Never confessing his intentions, he is nonetheless perfectly direct in his execution. He never resorts to cunning deceit, although occasionally he does rely upon euphemism. *The Milky Way* fulfills its intention, this time stated, to make a film about heresies, or rather, a work on dogma and its consequences, the dogmas of the Catholic Church and the degradations of those dogmas, which are "heresies." This dialectical relationship between dogma and heresy is clearly explained by Buñuel in *The Milky Way*. The prologue, intended for the film but abandoned in the final version, stated:

> Everything in this film concerning the Catholic religion and the heresies it has provoked, especially from the dogmatic point of view, is rigorously exact, except for error on our part. The texts and citations are taken from the Scriptures, modern and ancient works on theology and ecclesiastical history. . . . Throughout the film, apparitions, miracles and accounts of miracles will be treated with the utmost seriousness, in accordance with the traditional representations given by the Church, without any spirit of deformation. . . . This is in no way a polemical or thesis film but rather a picaresque type tale, which recounts the adventures of two pilgrims who one day took the road for Santiago de Compostela. . . .

The foregoing leads one to deduce that Buñuel tried to be forthright and to "play it clean"; in actuality, the film deals with the six great Christian themes which have given rise to most of the chief heresies: the first is the problem of the Eucharist, particularly the dogma of transsubstantiation, affirmed at the Council of Letran in 1215; the second is the theme of the origin of evil in the world; the third is the famous dogma of the dual nature of Christ, word and man; the fourth is the theme of the Trinity, a dogma which caused much blood to flow after its birth in the year 325 during the Council of Nice, with the declaration of the consubstantiality of the three beings: Father, Son and Holy Ghost; the fifth theme is the conflict between grace and freedom, in other words, the resistance to grace, or free will; and finally, the appearance of the great theme of the Virgin Mary, the meaning of her virginity and the absence of original sin, which at this point relates to "Mystery," in the dogmatic sense conferred upon it by religion. The name of the film derives from the identification in many countries between the Milky Way and the road to Santiago de Compostela.

We accede therefore to a kind of enormous "collage" of the great themes of dogmatic Christianity. Through a continual interpolation of a variety of temporal and spatial elements, we roam through the entire history of Christianity, constantly confronted by that dialectical struggle between dogma and heresy, while the central adventure, the thread of continuity, continues being the adventure of the two "pilgrims." The element of anecdote is introduced by a scene where the two heroes meet a sort of devil who predicts their arrival at Compostela and their meeting with a prostitute who will give them two sons, whom they will call, respectively, "You are not my people" and "No more compassion." A dwarf then appears who allows a dove to escape, and the two pilgrims continue their journey, leaving behind a sort of ominous Trinity. There is an interpolated scene on the possibility of a shaven Christ, a possibility which Mary, with a clear sense of her historical responsibility, avoids by preventing Nazarin from shaving. The pilgrims, meanwhile, encounter a child-Jesus, who obtains a ride for them in a luxurious automobile, only to be expelled from it by taking the name of God in vain.

The arrival of Pierre and Jean, as the chief characters are named (John and Peter, the apostles), at an inn situated near the highway, allows them to attend a debate on transubstantiation held between a mad priest and a police officer. Here Buñuel deliciously extracts the absurd element through an impeccable monologue delivered by François Maitre on the role of the priest. Following this, the pilgrims meet a shepherd who leads them to a place where a ceremony is held under the direction of the famous Bishop Priscillian, follower of the same doctrine which made the Manicheans famous, that of the existence of two distinct, separate principles, good and evil, lodged respectively in the soul and body of human beings. The followers of Priscillian considered it necessary to destroy evil by forcing the body towards pleasure; sensuality, employed as a religious obligation, ought to lead to the liberation of the soul over the body. "To humiliate the body, to subject it unceasingly to pleasures of the flesh" was the motto of the Priscillianites. This is followed by an orgy of a fanatic, impersonal nature, actually one of the best scenes in the film. Afterwards, one of the pilgrims decides to confront God by making a profession of belief in atheism (though not of heresy). In reply, he receives a bolt of lightning, which falls from the sky and burns a nearby bush. When his companion rebukes him for having defied God, Jean responds that the bolt of lightning, after all, *did not fall on him.* Whereupon the other says: "Imbecile! Do you think that God is at your disposal?"

The problem of atheism is thus summarized in an insoluble antithesis. The anecdote is a fine reply to those tormented by Buñuel, the atheist "despite himself." Following this scene is the sequence with the maitre d'hotel, who explains the dogma of Christ's dual nature. Interspersed afterwards are scenes out of Christ's life, depicted always with the same color and imagery as in traditional Catholic representations. These are of Canaan's wedding, which establishes a vivid imagery, halfway between sheer orthodoxy and the absurd, of a carefree, cursing, joyous Christ, who produces the miracle of the wine with the insouciance of a hippie. Following this is a dreamlike sequence of the shooting of the Pope, alternating with a celebration held at an institution of charity. Another of the great themes then appears, that of hell and purgatory. A heretic is tortured for denying their existence, whereupon a priest asks himself if the cause of bloodshed and violence is a consequence, not so much of heresies as of the dogmatic, intransigent attitude of the established Church.

And thus it continues; Buñuel alternates between one "grand theme" and another, veering between the most trivial adventures of the protagonists and reflections on an allegorical level, based on the successive appearances of Christ and his disciples. The next theme to appear is that of a debate on the adequacy of grace, enacted by a Jesuit and a Jansenist, who fight a duel in front of a chapel inside of which a convulsive nun has had herself crucified by her companions. Jean and Pierre attend the duel as seconds and witness its resolution in an endless dispute between the doctrine of free will and that of irresistible grace. The presence of the nun's sacrifice suffuses the duel sequence, which is highly intellectual, with an emotional-anecdotal parallel.

The famous problem of the Trinity now arises through a confrontation between two Protestant students and religious authorities during the disinterment of the body of a bishop discovered to be heretical during his lifetime. From this point on, there is a structural variation in the film, for the protagonist-pilgrims are abandoned for a while in order that we may follow François and Rudolph, the Protestant students, transformed into modern hunters who at twilight arrive at a Spanish inn, after having witnessed an apparition of the Virgin who hands them a rosary, identical to another which they had destroyed during practice. We are in the modern period, and the students come to an inn where a Spanish priest recounts the curious miracle of the Virgin and then holds forth on her maternity, while in the room of one of the students, a beautiful girl passionately defends the priest's statements as she lies chastely on a bed near Rudolph's.

Our two pilgrims are also at the inn. As they are leaving, holding a ham, they are arrested by the Civil Guard and finally, in full daylight, reach Santiago de Compostela. The prostitute whose appearance was predicted at the beginning awaits them, and when the three go to make love, Christ appears, performing the cure of two blind men. When Jesus departs, the apostles follow him and the blind men, presumably cured, walk behind. Only their hesitant feet are visible and their canes tapping the ground so that they might not fall. . . .

Clearly Buñuel is not simply attempting, as he declares, to create a story in the style of the picaresque novel, although, as was previously stated, *The Milky Way* marks the first time that Buñuel "announces" his intentions at the beginning of a film. A further reason to be distrustful . . .

What is involved, in addition to an examination of the dogmas and their respective heresies, is a devastating analysis of the pillars of "historical" Christianity. The scenes with Christ, which are continually interpolated, are clearly meant to demystify the traditional image; in the first place, the image itself (a beard or no beard?), then the personality of the character (Canaan's wedding), and finally the miracle as seen by the apostles—dogma as opposed to reality, for the blind men remain as blind as before.

The Marquis de Sade, who appears in another brief inserted scene, represents the quest for the sensual absolute, the absolute without God, affirming what one of the pilgrims gleans while defying God in the midst of the storm. The humorous effect of most of the "anecdotal" scenes combines with the level of the "comic lack of transcendence" in the scenes about Christ. These are to be viewed in contrast to the sequences on the dogmas, which are treated with absolute fidelity to the texts and with utter seriousness in their action. In the latter type of scene, the absurd departs from the setting (for example, the duel), or from contrast with the context (the de luxe restaurant where the maitre d'hotel pontificates on the nature of Christ), or through the character's personality (the mad priest who poses the dogma of the Eucharist). Thus, there is no "good faith" (understood as impartiality) in our inveterate Buñuel with respect to his treatment of the famed "picaresque novel."

It is clear that there is a thesis and an argument in *The Milky Way*. One might hold, as do many naïve viewers, that Buñuel actually takes the polemic about religion seriously. In this respect, we refer to the comment made at the onset of these remarks: Buñuel is probably less distressed by the religious problem than some good souls wish to believe. With all the detachment and coldness one could desire, Buñuel has achieved a highly explicit, single-minded, coherent compendium of the devastating reasons for opposing religion as an historical phenomenon, as rational thought, and as providing transcendence. Indeed, the narrative oscillation in time and space enables us to see more clearly the anachronism of established religious institutions, not only with regard to their unbending dogmatism but with respect to the liturgy whose rhetoric can only contrive and fail to make substance rather than form of the dogma itself.

Buñuel judges religiosity, but that judgment is never a metaphysical one. It is a judgment arrived at through a constant confrontation with reality: hence, the previous remarks on "reality" in Buñuel's films.

Christ himself, however, despite everything, is saved from destruction. Preserved as a hippie symbol, incapable of taking his own role seriously, his similarity with Nazarin is clear. The affectionate, sad respect with which Buñuel treats his Nazarin has shifted to a gay, open complicity. But Buñuel perhaps would not admit that he has his own secret Christ, for his own particular use.

THE MILKY WAY   Derek Malcolm

· · · · · · · · · · · · · · · · · · ·

In *La Ilusion Viaja en Tranvia,* a tramcar, overdue for honorable retirement, is taken for a last and suitably anarchic spin by a crew who have apparently been over-inspired (but of course, since this is a Buñuel film) by indulgence at a religious festival. It is not entirely fanciful to suppose that *La Voie Lactée* (Planet) is Buñuel's last spin, a final and plausibly anarchic assault on man's capacity to forget his humanity when face to face with what he judges to be immortal.

This detailed and exhaustive history of heresy in 19 sequences has certainly been received in France as if it were a testament, but, to be sure, the "living cathedral" still breathes and we have learned before to be wary of farewell appearances. By all accounts he looked somewhat frail when receiving his special award at the Venice Festival, yet hardly a man without a last surprise or two up his sleeve. The question is—does he supply them here? Well, yes and no. There are times when *La Voie Lactée* looks pretty frail

From *Sight and Sound,* Vol. 39, No. 1 (Winter 1969–70). Reprinted by permission of the publisher.

too beside the severity of *Nazarin* or *Viridiana*, or even *Simon of the Desert*. One is never quite sure whether it is Buñuel defying God as usual, or the Almighty getting His own back for the first time.

There is somehow an unfamiliar softness behind the irony, even behind that wickedly impious portrayal of Jesus which has Bernard Verley, pastel-robed and rather sheepish, stopped in the act of shaving (with a cut-throat vaguely reminiscent of *Un Chien Andalou*) by the Virgin's remark: "*Mon fils, ne te rase pas. Tu es beaucoup mieux avec ta barbe.*" It is not for nothing, one feels, that a Catholic critic remarked with indelible certainty after the first London showing: "Ah, he has RC written right across his heart." Perhaps it is just that we like to hedge our bets a bit when the possibility of a final confrontation approaches. Whatever it is, the film is quintessential, but rarely vintage Buñuel.

The plain and perfect method, with its slightly self-denying reliance on *le plan Americain* and its aesthetic refusal to make anything look too pretty, is totally unravaged by time—it looks better and better, in fact, beside much of today's prodigious tastelessness. There is still also the capacity to emerge now and then from behind the various masks (surrealist, showman, humanitarian and practical joker) with an expression that would wipe the complacency off the face of either the most spiritual or the completest materialist. To the former he is again saying: "If God exists, how I hate Him." This time the latter get: "My hatred of science and technology will perhaps bring me to the absurdity of a belief in God." Each statement is of course highly ambivalent. He has never been concerned to demythologize art with clear answers to cloudy questions. There is too much at stake for that.

But he has, in another way, never been more precise. His many months of collaboration with Jean-Claude Carrière on a project long mulled over has prompted him to note, with uncharacteristic emphasis over the final credits, that everything in the film which concerns Catholicism and the heresies to which it has given rise is rigorously exact. The texts and citations are either taken from the Scriptures or from works of theology, which is perhaps why it has already been dubbed a theological Western. Yet one does not always feel, as his two tramps (Paul Frankeur and Laurent Terzieff, very much waiting for Godot) make their pilgrimage to the shrine of St. James at Santiago de Compostela (Campus Stella, the road to the stars, hence The Milky Way), that the same rigor has been applied to the metaphysics of the film as to the delineation of the heresies themselves.

When we reach the problem of transubstantiation, for instance, an innkeeper says that for him the Host is both wafer and body of Christ, in the same way as paté is both itself and hare. Whereupon a curé, who is afterwards gently taken off to an asylum, complains bitterly that this is precisely the heresy of the 16th century Pateliers. Good history no doubt, and amusingly done. But when we have finished smiling at the scene's absurdity, what have we really got left? Not perhaps much more than a paté.

And so it goes on, and it does go on rather. Our two puzzled combatants wander not only along the route to the shrine but through space and time as well. They witness a duel between a Jansenist and a Jesuit who insult each other (before walking off arm in arm) with statements that are extracted, word for blessed word, from 17th century texts. They watch as children recite some of the more lunatic canons of the Church at a summer picnic-cum-pantomime, the scene crosscut with visions of young revolutionaries shooting the Holy Father with unholy zeal. They dream uncomfortably of Priscillian, the heretic bishop of Avila (the only way to liberate the soul from the body is to exhaust the body of its pleasures), and later meet a whore (Delphine Seyrig, somewhat uncertain) with whom they cavort in the bushes in an unconscious travesty of the aforesaid heresy—particularly apt, it turns out, since there's a rumor that the body of St. James is, in fact, that of Priscillian after all. Finally we meet Jesus again, who uncompromisingly underlines that He has come to earth to divide as well as to unite.

The film encompasses all six major heresy-inducing dogmas—Christ at once both God and Man, the Trinity, Transubstantiation, the Immaculate Conception, Free Will and God's prescience, and the Origins of Evil. It is an unprecedented primer for Catholics, an ammunition dump for unbelievers, an amusement for filmgoers, and for Buñuel possibly a necessary exorcism. Like most surrealists, he has been totally hypnotized by the super-

It is an unprecedented primer for Catholics, an ammunition dump for unbelievers, an amusement for filmgoers, and for Buñuel possibly a necessary
exorcism. (*The Milky Way*)

structure of religion and bewitched by man's attempt to mold that
edifice so that it conforms to the baser and/or more foolish
instincts of his own nature. The result, he seems to say (but things
are not often what they seem with Buñuel), ends not only in the
corruption of religion but, much more important, of man himself. Though *La Voie Lactée* ultimately seems too much of an
entertainment for the proper underlining of its more deadly
purposes, one thing is patently clear. He is still after "shaking the
optimism of the bourgeois world." One just wishes that his latest
attempt to do so wasn't quite so easy to be taken up and cherished
by that world. Once we start overtly patting him on the head, he is
sunk.

The Phantom of Liberty:
Further Investigations Into The Discreet Charm of the Bourgeoisie

Joan Mellen

. . . .

The title of Buñuel's *The Phantom of Liberty* borrows from the opening line of Karl Marx's *Communist Manifesto:* "A specter is haunting Europe—the specter of Communism." But with a combination of sadness and caustic parody, Buñuel notes that the specter which strikes fear into the heart of the bourgeoisie today is not a dethronement of its ruling class but the opposite—the possibility of its own freedom unburdened by the dead ends of sexual license, willful irrationality, and the liberty to go beyond the self-indulgent eccentricities of the individual ego.

"It is no longer possible to scandalize people as we did in 1930," Buñuel has remarked, comparing *The Phantom of Liberty* to *L'Age d'Or*, its closest ancestor in his work. "Today you have to do it with sweet subversion." And this is what he has done, never sacrificing his bitterly ironic distance from the panoply of human folly he so mercilessly depicts. He refuses, as always, to allow his performers to act, to be anything more than human instruments illustrating our collective escape from meaningful freedom of choice. We feel close to but identify with none of them. They exist, even stars like Jean-Claude Brialy and Monica Vitti, as phantasms, embodiments of the patterns of behavior by which, every day, we demean liberty by limiting it to our own paltry desires.

This article is published here for the first time by arrangement with the author. Copyright © 1978 by Joan Mellen.

"It is no longer possible to scandalize people as we did in 1930," Buñuel has remarked . . . "today you have to do it with sweet subversion." (*The Phantom of Liberty*)

Buñuel finds that we have substituted arbitrary willfulness for freedom, like the parents in one episode of this film who insist on declaring their daughter a missing person, although she is sitting plainly before them. This exercise in willfulness, in its extravagance, reveals the timidity, caution, and enslavement to repressive convention of these nominal practitioners of personal assertion.

Freedom as license is all we can accept. The "we" is, once

again, the bourgeoisie, the ruling order of our time. *The Phantom of Liberty* functions as a sequel to *The Discreet Charm of the Bourgeoisie*, exploring anew those distortions of consciousness and cowardly irrationality which for Buñuel presage the downfall of this class, its values, and its social order. The episodes, structured, like those of *L'Age d'Or*, in relation (like the mind itself) to the free association of ideas, reveal how the bourgeoisie engineers its own destruction. This anticipated and certain fate has been signaled by Buñuel through the clap of thunder at the close of *Diary of a Chambermaid*, through the spiritual paralysis and cannibalism of *The Exterminating Angel*, and by the nightmare of random assassination reflecting the dissolution of a divided, competing class which haunts *The Discreet Charm of the Bourgeoisie*.

With each film, Buñuel grows even more uncompromising in his excoriation of the ruling bourgeoisie. So pervasive is its degenerative influence in shaping our psyches that even those who would dethrone it, if they are from bourgeois backgrounds, have assimilated its values and sensibility. In *The Phantom of Liberty* the Spanish revolutionaries about to be shot in 1808 during the Napoleonic occupation by French soldiers are not on the side of freedom. "Down with liberty," they yell in a typically surreal Buñuel touch. "Long live the chains!" For it is a perverse triumph of bourgeois values that the revolution, which would replace the power of this class, perpetuates its mode of rule and hence the ill use of the people it supposedly wishes to free. "Down with France," cry the Spanish insurgents, for if, in 1789 France was the emblem of revolutionary freedom, it was a bourgeois revolution which in its Bonapartist decline makes them prefer the chains they have. French conquest invokes the revolutionary freedom that had been reversed in France itself. Bonaparte, like Stalin later, claims for himself the libertarian impulse of the revolution he has reversed. The betrayal of revolutions and the growth of "revolutionary" societies more repressive than those they replaced have made a mockery of revolution as a quest for liberty—Buñuel's first point in this film.

Socially, historically, and psychologically, Buñuel unveils our real alienation from any meaningful appreciation of freedom. Behind the incident we see depicted in *The Phantom of Liberty* stand these facts of which Buñuel expects his audience to be aware. When in 1814 Napoleon's armies were driven from Spain after a bloody guerrilla war, the Spaniards restored to the throne Fernando VII, the monarch deposed by the French in 1808. The rebellion was negated as the Spanish indeed sacrificed their liberty for the old chains. This incident underlies the opening sequence of Buñuel's film. It is his comment on the pain and suffering depicted in Goya's "El Tres de Mayo," the painting which greets us as the film opens.

Even those who would call themselves revolutionaries are about to substitute one tyranny for another. Freedom, which Buñuel associates with personal liberation, rationality (in a direct reversal of the attack on rationality in *Un Chien Andalou* and *L'Age d'Or*), and a better world slip further and further from our grasp, a perception which causes the director to remain as coldly distant from his characters as ever. It would be preposterous, given its theme, for *The Phantom of Liberty* to have a hero. Buñuel follows each character only to discard him when one more promising—that is, revelatory of bourgeois intransigence— happens along.

The image which pervades *The Phantom of Liberty* is that of Goya's "El Tres de Mayo," depicting a firing squad mercilessly butchering a group of men at close range. Lying in a heap are the bloody bodies of those already exterminated. The most important revolutionary is illuminated and wears a flowing white blouse; he becomes a spot of brightness in an otherwise bleak and dark scene. Standing with his arms raised, he faces his tormentors, his eyebrows slanted to suggest the bewilderment of defeat. His eyes are wide open in terror. The painter's passions are totally with him, as are Buñuel's. Or so it seems.

For as the film, set at first in 1808, opens, the victims in Buñuel's enactment of the painting, including a monk, shout "Down with liberty." The juxtaposition with the Goya painting immediately undercuts its powerful effect. This will be no simple glorification of revolutionaries and vilification of the bourgeoisie. Buñuel laments that people have been so thoroughly imbued with the culture's disdain for liberty that even when they rebel against its abuse, they emulate its ways. The predilection for authoritarian rule affects the most rebellious no less than their oppressors. The future in the hands of such militants, who value freedom less than the triumph of their cause, who confuse power with liberation, seems unlikely to improve upon the past.

The sound overlaps which pervade this film seem equally to suggest a cyclical view of human experience. In this sense, *The Phantom of Liberty* may be Buñuel's most pessimistic film. But if history repeats itself, it is the direct consequence of our failure to insist upon freedom, even in a society of which we approve. Without this, we do not merely fail to advance. We regress.

So totally have we failed to supply the concept of liberty with any substance that we are left merely with license, and a relative license at that. Margaret Mead is mentioned at one point in *The Phantom of Liberty* to suggest the relative values of cultures. This notion Buñuel both accepts and finds irrelevant to the concerns of our civilization, since it evades defining the substance and desirability of each set of values, apart from whether or not they are relative to each other.

In an early episode, two little girls playing in the park are shown presumably dirty pictures by a man who appears to be perverse. He takes out his "pretty pictures" and the little girls laugh. In a startling reversal, Buñuel suggests that *he* cannot corrupt *them*. By about the age of ten, they are already corrupted.

But more. The postcards turn out to be only scenes of the monuments of Europe: each to his own fetish. One girl's parents "ooh" and "ah" over them, as if they were indeed titillating. Of a picture of Sâcré Cœur they salivate, "This is going too far." They fall into a passionate embrace, perhaps fueled by memories of their experiences at Notre Dame, the Arc de Triomphe, and Sâcré Cœur. Pleasure, relative and personal, is fueled as much by the past as by the present.

Yet, having sacrificed our freedom, we can be manipulated into arousal by anything deemed forbidden, even by a postcard of Sâcré Cœur. Having abandoned our autonomy before a valueless culture, we have condemned ourselves to being puppets who can feel enthusiasm for the inane, shame before what we have been arbitrarily taught is shameful, whatever it is. The motif is reiterated in a later episode where excretion is performed in company

The postcards turn out to be only scenes of the monuments of Europe: each to his own fetish . . . Pleasure, relative and personal, is fueled as much by the past as the present. (*The Phantom of Liberty*)

amidst polite social chatter, while eating, treated as obscene, takes place in closed little rooms and is considered dirty, unmentionable, and a function unworthy of taking place in public. The toilet-table conversation dwells on how many billion tons of excrement people eliminate each day, perfectly acceptable talk, while the "foul smell of food," a taboo subject, may be mentioned only with disdain, as off-color humor, as an insult, or in passing. Thus does Buñuel, here as in *The Discreet Charm of the Bourgeoisie*, satirize the bourgeois obsession with food as an escape from concern for the liberty it once invoked against absolutism, but of which it is now the antithesis. Indeed, so degenerate has bourgeois culture become, relative to its revolutionary and libertarian origins, that through its indulgence and obsession with cuisine it ignores its own imminent demise.

What have we done with our freedom? We have placed tarantulas and spiders under glass, like the husband, played by Jean-Claude Brialy, who lusts over the postcards of Parisian landmarks. (Thus does Buñuel comment simultaneously on his own lifelong fascination with entomology.) Or we make meaningless choices which we confuse with freedom, like this same husband "fed up with symmetry," who then changes the arrangements of objects on his mantel.

For Buñuel, the unconscious remains the only arena in which real feelings abide, however we may be cut off from them during our "waking" moments. At night—after a series of zooms and diagonal dollies, Buñuel's means of letting us know that we are descending into the unconscious—the man dreams of a rooster, a woman with a crutch (recalling Pierre's obsession with wheelchairs in *Belle de Jour*—a vagary of perception which foreshadows his own fate), an ostrich (which will reappear later in the film), and a postman who bicycles into the bedroom and tosses him a letter. Was it all a dream? The next day, he shows the actual letter to his doctor. Buñuel insists that the distortions of the unconscious contain a hidden truth more real than the "objective" events of our lives.

This doctor's nurse now becomes the focus of the film as we follow her journey home to visit her sick father. The "plot" and the particular people Buñuel chooses to highlight, are based purely on chance. One would do as well as another. All will reveal what little value we grant to liberty.

Driving along, the woman passes a gigantic army tank whose occupants ask her if she has seen any foxes. With the freedom they have, Buñuel muses, people can conceive of nothing better to do than to hunt foxes. They trap animals on whom they vent frustrations as full-blown through repression as the tank itself.

The nurse stops in the rain at an inn at which are stranded a variety of Buñuelesque personalities. The downpour is a reminder that liberty is not always at our disposal. The freedom men squander so profligately may be taken from them by mere chance, by fortuitous circumstances of nature beyond their control, like famine, drought, flood, earthquake, or—a storm. Liberty is circumscribed as well by the presence of others, who compulsively act out their own fantasies and obsessive needs. A flamenco dancer and her husband bang their door closed; the liberty of others undermines their own by intruding on their solitude and privacy. They represent humanity in a repressive society and are an image of Spain itself, anxious, frustrated, irritable, and isolated.

A passel of monks is present, one of whom has invoked his religion to denounce the "hellish weather." The monks appear to wish only to console the woman worried about her sick father. One remarks that "if everyone prayed to St. Joseph, peace would prevail," a sentiment in which none of them seems particularly to believe. A dolly in to the image of a man and child, a religious artifact, gives way to the poker game which the woman and monks have lost no time in setting up. It becomes apparent that their real, underlying motive in entering this attractive, now scantily clad, woman's room was actually to pursue the card game. That the woman is so sensual at night and so demure by day is another of the ambivalences in which Buñuel delights. It reveals the degree to which our surface behavior disguises needs una-vowed in daylight, a further barrier to our freedom because our very identity and sense of self is rooted in impulses which compel that behavior. And in a condition of compulsion, we cannot be sure about anything.

The monks use their holy medallions in the game and smoke like chimneys, the things of this world appealing to them most. The game itself proceeds in religious terms. "I open with a Virgin," says one; another plays a "Father." Religion is revealed to be a screen for hidden urges now brought to light under the cover of darkness and the raging storm. The monks reveal that few are left who believe, just as liberty is devoid of content, reduced to a ridiculous virginal aunt in her fifties seducing in another room her twenty-year-old nephew. Liberty is thus defined by the absurd: a nephew demanding to see his virgin aunt naked.

Or it may be a staid, prim couple who are suddenly shown to be equipped for an orgy with black leather costumes cut out to expose naked buttocks while whips are wielded. A monk asks the man if they have ever met in the Congo, a mysterious part of the globe where, as with that colonial exploitation which enriched the bourgeoisie, each might have carried on his dirty work unimpeded, pace Conrad's *Heart of Darkness*. When the sado-

Religion is revealed to be a screen for hidden urges now brought to light under the cover of darkness and the raging storm. (*The Phantom of Liberty*)

masochistic couple's visitors move to depart, the man cries, "At least let the monks stay!" For our religion is itself a sexual fetish and equally fueled by repression and perverse excess. Out of this revelation, members of religious orders become the most sexually desirable of all and the most attuned to the dynamics of sexual frenzy burst loose. The oldest monk gains his audience's sympathy by punctuating the scene with the down-to-earth humor so enjoyed by Buñuel: "He likes to be hit, *I'll* hit him!"

We have mistaken our perversions for freedom, having failed to locate values which would not pander to our unwholesome need to be debased and humiliated out of deep self-hatred and loathing. Buñuel has often spoken out against pornography as the antithesis of either sensuality or freedom. He includes this corrective lest anyone mistake his paean to free love in *L'Age d'Or* for an endorsement of compulsive sexual excess, which is as driven as it is joyless.

The plot moves along by chance—the sole liberty we have allowed ourselves and hence no liberty at all, because every area of control or choice has been removed. The next morning, the woman picks up an instructor of the gendarmerie whose students, confusing childish defiance with freedom, have written "The colonel is a cuckold; the captain is a fag" on the blackboard. The lecture on law, and its purpose in maintaining the social order (in whose survival Buñuel has no interest whatsoever), is interrupted by a call to target practice. Militarism and its attendant bloodshed have supplanted rationality and purpose in our culture. An accident calls more pupils away. Those who remain read a Trotskyist publication at their desks. It speaks of workers sounding the alarm, Buñuel's portent of events more promising and redeeming perhaps than those he is condemned to depict as a chronicler of the last days of the bourgeoisie, while we remain haunted by those false prophets and pseudo-revolutionaries shouting "Long live the chains." A military leader enters to assist the Professor, who cannot control his unruly students. The lecture concerns the consequences of general upheaval; even in the lair of the police, rebellion is inevitably and forever in the air.

We shift to a doctor using every euphemism at his command to avoid telling a man that he has cancer. Liberty has degenerated to obfuscation. What he calls a "neoplasm" finally becomes "cancer of the liver . . . in a fairly advanced state." What he calls a small operation which might be done at any time proves to be scheduled for the next morning. The doctor offers his victim a cigarette; the man slaps him across the face in a futile gesture of rebellion and fury at being humiliated by the doctor's cowardice. The slap may take place in fantasy or actually occur. It no longer matters. For we are dying in this condition, and whether the circumstance is concealed or not cannot alter it. Moreover, the longer we are deceived, the more outraged we are upon finding it out. Hence the patient's bitterness is validated, even if he were actually to slap the doctor. But having momentarily confronted hypocrisy, the patient goes home to announce to his wife that it "was nothing." Even when victimized, we are too conditioned in the ways of hypocrisy to surmount them easily in our relations with those dependent upon *us*.

It is this man's small daughter who is "kidnapped" and "disappears" from school. The man and his wife are so fixated on the notion of her absence that they have sacrificed the freedom of perception, which would have told them as they sat in the police station that she was right there beside them. The prefect of police, in a wild display of our willful blindness to the reality staring us in the face, asks the child herself for her vital statistics and how she came to disappear!

On the wall in this prefect's office is a reproduction of Goya's "Tres de Mayo," an emblem of the prefect's own role on behalf of repressive authority. It reflects as well the painter's angry comment on the unspeakable slaughter that has been the hallmark of the bourgeoisie and its agents. By hanging this painting, the prefect condemns himself, serving Buñuel's purpose without a word of rhetoric or polemicizing dialogue. The *mise-en-scène* of a Buñuel film, the ambiance of the shot, contains the director's point of view. This is especially necessary for Buñuel, who, seeing clearly our entrapment in this decaying culture, refuses to create even a remotely sympathetic character. And this daring approach is all the more remarkable since Buñuel rarely requires more than two or three takes for a shot. His people in *The Phantom of Liberty* are both frail individuals and representatives of their class. This fact alone, in a film about the decadence of the bourgeoisie, precludes our sympathizing with them.

A sniper enters the scene, a man first seen petting the dog of a shoeshine man. He inveighs against cruelty to animals ("Those who mistreat animals should be shot") but feels no such compassion for the human beings he is soon to mow down from the thirtieth floor of a nearby skyscraper. He might be a descendant of Viridiana's cousin, Jorge. The man is tall, quiet, and intellectual in appearance. He wears glasses and a tweed sportcoat, conveying scholarly detachment (and is played by Pierre Lary, Buñuel's long-time assistant).

Appearances always deceive in Buñuel. The man appears to be the opposite of what in fact he is—a lunatic killer on a senseless rampage. This lover of animals also kills a bird. He is able, in fact, to make no distinction between men and animals, even as our butchery of the animal kingdom makes our slaughter of human beings both explicable and psychologically inevitable.

Freedom in our time has been frequently conceived as unhindered destruction, the only passion with which we seem truly at home. And whatever liberty we could hope to have is always circumscribed by the existence of such madmen. In a world where anything can happen to anyone at any time, what liberty remains, phantom as it is, should be all the more cherished. As a young surrealist, Buñuel deployed violence in his early films to suggest a revolutionary impulse; recall the memorable opening image of his first film, *Un Chien Andalou*: a man slitting a woman's eyeball with a razor. "We used violence as a weapon against the establishment," Buñuel remembers. "Now society itself has become so violent that it is hard to use violence to make an artistic comment." In a period when social degeneration has brought mass murder, Buñuel sees violence as the artist's enemy, along with "the fetishes that cause cruelty and perversion." The free love exalted in *L'Age d'Or* has in this social order become distorted into self-destructive incest, painful perversity, and lust without the possibility of gratification.

Convicted of first-degree murder without extenuating circumstances and condemned to death, the sniper leaves the courtroom a free man, shaking the hands of well-wishers, including the judge and his prison guards. He is a celebrity, a hero. People clamor for his autograph. Like the trials of our time, his has been a theatrical event with the murderer as the star, having nothing whatsoever to do with the pursuit of justice, and emblematic of the will to destroy which is cultivated and rewarded today. Perhaps for the first time in his life, the sniper is valued as an individual, like those Watergate "celebrities" making fortunes out of their disgrace and iniquity.

Later, on the anniversary of her death, the sister of the prefect of police phones him with a request that they meet in the mausaleum. In a flashback, we observe him listening raptly while she plays the piano for him stark naked, her breasts violently shaking, her only garments black stockings and shoes. These are variations on the fetishes of Buñuel characters from the hero of *El* to the old man who fondled women's boots in *Diary of a Chambermaid*. Freedom for the prefect proves to be the freedom of his incestuous feelings, which, repressed yet secretly nurtured, led to the sister's death of "iliac passion," in which she vomited excrement. This disease, seemingly invented by Buñuel, suggests the disruptive, self-destructive, frustrating nature of her relationship with her brother and the sickness a repressive society makes of pleasurable and innocent sensation.

Four years after her death, the brother remains so obsessed with her that he believes her to be alive. But before he can enter his sister's tomb to learn "the mystery of death" which she has promised to divulge, he is arrested as a lunatic, "a bum who claims he is the police commissioner." Buñuel is showing us that all commissioners are in fact moral vagrants and madmen vested with power. The prefect and a now materialized other commissioner, his social double, are in fact colleagues, and they meet in the police station. In a world bereft of logic and purpose, each can be the "real" commissioner. The two begin to plot, comrades in arms, with their own store of secrets and conspiracies. Buñuel leaves them without unraveling the tedious details of their identity or telling us which is the "real" commissioner—an irrelevant detail. By now, director and spectator are each sufficiently distanced from the charades of everyday life behind which repressed and oppressed people hide and lie to themselves and others.

The last sequence of *The Phantom of Liberty* finds us at a demonstration staged at the zoo. It begins with a disorienting montage of close-ups of animals: seal, hippopotamus, elephant, and lioness. Buñuel, challenging our species chauvinism, forces us to ask ourselves whether we are in fact better than—or even different from—these supposedly lower forms of creation. The two commissioners arrive and enter the zoo, and we suddenly realize that they are its most appropriate inhabitants. Shouts of a crowd come up on the soundtrack: "Down with freedom," "Down with freedom!" The police fire, and instructions of "Charge" and "Hit hard" are discernible on the soundtrack amidst the chaos.

A 360-degree swish pan leads us not to a shot of the demonstrators we expect to see, but to an ostrich that looks straight into the camera, fixing us with its gaze, challenging us as to who is the more caged or pathetic, while the guns, asynchronously, rage on. As the gunfire continues, Buñuel freezes the frame out of focus, while the cries are still heard. The police have been forced to fire on those denouncing freedom, a stinging critique of an ineffectual left which, in identifying liberty with authoritarianism, is so bereft of humane values that it is replaced by an ostrich! The shooting continues over the end titles.

Liberty has become a phantom through our distorted consciousness, so deformed that we can't tell the difference between reality and our psychic configurations. Seemingly sane people treat as missing a little girl seated among them. We are impotent before our biology; this girl's father can only slap the doctor who informs him that he has cancer of the liver. The omnipresence of death should make us cherish freedom all the more, but, prisoners as we are, it doesn't. We can't tell the difference between past and present, burdening ourselves with two prefects of police, as if one weren't enough, or between dream and reality, as with the materialized letter delivered by a phantom postman. Goya's "El Tres de Mayo" hangs on the wall of a police station; revolutionary fervor is now usurped and in the hands of a repressive enemy. Confused, we are more imprisoned than the animals in the zoo. And worse, unlike them, we *delight in* our bondage, recalling the revolutionaries in the opening sequence who shout "Long live the chains." We have been rendered unwittingly comfortable within our psychic cages to the point where we prefer them to liberty, an experience and aspiration we neither understand nor desire.

Having built our lives upon contradictions, we have prevented ourselves from discovering liberty. This term itself has been undermined through misuse by revolutionaries who are the mirror-image of the tyrants they seem to defy. Buñuel despairs for us, doubting not so much the possibility of redemption as its likelihood. His faith lies in the passion and wit of the film itself, a human triumph over our failure, to date, to want sufficiently to be free. The act of making films about this dilemma for the past half century has been Buñuel's real declaration of confidence in a human race dominated by a bourgeoisie given to hypocrisy, sadism and, above all, a disrespect even for its own capacity to live differently and better.

"A Magnificent and Dangerous Weapon": The Politics of Luis Buñuel's Later Films

Randall Conrad

•   •   •   •   •   •   •   •   •   •   •   •   •   •   •   •   •   •   •

"In the hands of a free spirit," Luis Buñuel told an audience in 1953, "the cinema is a magnificent and dangerous weapon."[1] He was not necessarily speaking of film as a surrealist explosion or as a weapon in the class struggle. For Buñuel even the commercial cinema could become a weapon both surrealist and political, a weapon against bourgeois society.

Buñuel's consciously held politics have moved back and forth between the positive class consciousness of *Cela s'Appelle l'Aurore* and the anarchist pessimism of *Los Olvidados,* between Marxism and the Freudian politics of surrealism. Although perhaps Buñuel aims to obtain a permanent dialectic between the two ideologies, a Buñuel film typically has a firm surrealist basis that is overlaid with a deliberate Marxist slant—Buñuel's caution that his message of revolt will advance revolution, not reaction. In another article, I have discussed the relation between surrealism and Marxism in Buñuel's formative period.[2] We shall here examine that relation in Buñuel's commercial output of the past three decades.

Los Olvidados is a drama about delinquent boys in Mexico

This article has been revised from the original, which appeared in *Cineaste*, Vol. VII, No. 4 (1977). Reprinted by permission of the publisher and the author.
[1]Buñuel, "Cinema, Instrument of Poetry" (1953), in Ado Kyrou, *Luis Buñuel* (New York, 1960), p. 110.
[2]"The Minister of the Interior is on the Telephone: The Early Films of Luis Buñuel," *Cineaste*, Vol. VII, no. 3 (1976).

City. The innocent Pedro becomes an accomplice to the murder of another boy by the gang's leader, Jaibo, because Jaibo intimidates him into keeping silent. Buñuel's intricate scenario intertwines the boys' stories as they are variously affected by developments, chiefly the stories of Jaibo, who is guilty, and Pedro, who is innocent yet compromised. (A third child, Ochitos, represents pure innocence, an utter humility in the face of fate. Ironically, he is instrumental in finally denouncing Jaibo to the law.)

The boys are fatherless and transfer their longing for parents onto the environment, the authorities and each other, in relationships of dependency and acts of savage violence. When Jaibo begins an affair with Pedro's mother, he becomes in effect a father to Pedro, but a father with one role only, that of the intimidating rival whom the son would like to kill. The benevolent paternal role is filled by the director of Pedro's reform school. Pedro is not fated to make his way safely between the extremes; Jaibo kills him, then is killed by the police.

Buñuel displays a consistent preference for melodrama, most obviously in his film's many horrifying scenes, but also in its abundance of coincidence (Jaibo reappears just as Pedro is let out on good behavior) and in its intercutting of different characters' episodes so as to afford us a superior dramatic vantage. Thus, for example, we are in the objective position of knowing Jaibo committed the theft for which Pedro gets sent away. We are also in a position to appreciate the whole complex of motives for Pedro's final courageous attack upon Jaibo. Their fight incidentally clears Pedro of the theft, yet the dramatic importance of this bit of poetic justice consists in binding together the inner determinism (Pedro's guilt and repression) and the external forces (theft and survival, the inevitability of brutality) which Buñuel sees as mutually reflective and reinforcing. Melodrama enables us to see the whole picture, heightened. *Los Olvidados* stands nearly alone even among Buñuel's films in achieving a synthesis of inner and outer realities in the guise of realism.

By the same token, however, *Los Olvidados* is by no means a politically encouraging work. The poor are amoral and vicious, and every character is the plaything of destructive forces as inescapable as destiny in ancient tragedy. What for Buñuel is ultimate realism (perhaps the true test of our compassion) might simply be pessimism, a concession to bourgeois ideology. Georges Sadoul, Buñuel's ex-surrealist friend whose film criticism reflects the orthodox line (and later the revisionism) of the French communists, recounts this conversation with Buñuel:

> When Luis came to the opening of his film in Paris in the spring of 1951, I personally had disliked *Los Olvidados*. For the wrong reasons (in which I had an iron belief). I told myself: this is a pessimistic film, people will be disgusted with their own humanity, they'll see atomic annihilation as a blessing. I was so deeply persuaded of this that I couldn't conceal it from my very dear friend. Embarrassed and sad, I resolved to tell him shortly before he left Paris.
>
> He replied that I was wrong, that one must show life in all its facets, and that the atrocious poverty of children in Latin America is one of those aspects. And he said if I was right, if it could be proved to him, he'd cut off his—what separates a bull from an ox.[3]

Sadoul adds that he later changed his mind. One would conclude that Buñuel got the better of the exchange. Actually Sadoul had put his finger on what separates Buñuel from a Marxist, a sore spot harking back to the Communist repudiation of surrealism twenty years before.

Buñuel covered himself politically in the lecture of 1953 already cited, suggesting he has done his revolutionary duty by dealing a blow to bourgeois optimism. As if the intervening years of bitter debate over socialist realism had never complicated the issue, Buñuel cited with approval Engels' 1885 dictum on realism:

> I will let Friedrich Engels speak for me. He defines the function of the novelist (and here read film maker) thus: "The novelist will have acquitted himself honorably of his task when, by means of an accurate portrait of authentic social relations, he will have destroyed the conventional view of the nature of those relations, shattered the optimism of the bourgeois world, and forced the reader to question the permanency of the prevailing order, and this even if the author does not offer us any solutions, even if he does not clearly take sides."[4]

[3]Georges Sadoul, Preface, in Buñuel, *Viridiana* (Paris, 1962), p. 22.
[4]Kyrou, p. 112. Engels' letter to Minna Kautsky (1885) appears in Craig, ed., *Marxists on Literature* (1975); Solomon, *Marxism and Art* (1973); and other volumes.

For Buñuel, passing beyond the pure surrealism of *Los Olvidados* would have meant adopting a positive ideology upon which even neorealism is finally predicated.

Nevertheless, Buñuel was not immune to criticism like Sadoul's. *Cela s'Appelle l'Aurore* is plainly about class allegiances, freedom and responsibility. Doctor Valerio, a humanitarian who cares for the poor on an island like Corsica, conceals his friend Sandro, a worker wanted for murder, from the police. Distraught at the death of his wife, Sandro aimed his pistol at the loathesome capitalist who oppresses the laborers of the island, believing him responsible for the woman's death. The murderer had his reasons, and Valerio now implicitly condones them by hiding Sandro from the law.

Pressure on Valerio is compounded by the fact that during his wife's absence he has fallen in love with another woman, Clara, who shares his compassion and encourages him to make the right decisions, even though concealing Sandro might call attention to their illicit affair. In any case, Sandro is discovered prematurely, but kills himself before the police get to him. Sandro's death obliges Valerio to side more consciously with the oppressed, and sanctions his love for Clara.

Sandro has no freedom in Buñuel's view; it is the petty bourgeois, Valerio, who changes sides. *Cela s'Appelle l'Aurore* belongs to what I might call a tradition on the left—the drama of class consciousness expressed through the options of a petty bourgeois character obliged to decide between a life of compromise and a moral stand which in this case is not strictly political but entails a shift of class sympathy nevertheless.

The class spectrum in *Cela s'Appelle l'Aurore* is actually a simple one. It is impossible not to hate the sinister capitalist Sandro kills, while, quite to the contrary of *Los Olvidados*, we sympathize easily with workers like Sandro. Similarly, the peasants are decent and victimized. Buñuel depicts only one of them as an amoral exception, in an incidental scene.

However, Buñuel's placement of Valerio's consuming love for Clara in a parallel relationship to his quasi-political gesture in hiding Sandro is intended to complicate as well as heighten the moral choice Valerio makes, beyond the canon acceptable to a positive realism. Valerio is an adulterer and Sandro a murderer. And yet we never doubt they are good men. The inverse of Jaibo, Sandro is a positive character in spite of his committing a murder.

Buñuel's deliberate complications notwithstanding, *Cela s'Appelle l'Aurore* approaches an optimist rhetoric. Buñuel virtually puts a cinema of identification in the service of a class typology. The final shot, in which Valerio and Clara walk into the sunrise with their new allies, the workers, is the closest Buñuel comes to suggesting any positive resolution.

Many of Buñuel's films of the early 1950s are domestic comedies or melodramas. Buñuel exploits the archetypes which are the stuff of melodrama; at the same time he abolishes the sentimentality, the bourgeois esthetic of "identification" that usually conceals the real social content of those archetypes. Thus we watch Francisco, the protagonist of *El*, behave as the specimen of a particular pathology and at the same time as a specimen of his social class, the bourgeoisie.

In Buñuel's properly surrealist works (not only *L'Age d'Or* but also *Wuthering Heights,* Buñuel's throwback to surrealism's heroic depiction of obsessive love), the archetypal conflict pits the lover against society. In *L'Age d'Or*, a cocktail reception symbolizes bourgeois society as the monolith opposed to the lover. In *El,* on the other hand, the conflict takes place entirely within Francisco; he is at once the mad lover and the repressive bourgeois. Francisco himself stages a dinner party expressly to be near the object of his desire, taking pains to invite his confessor and his future mother-in-law as well—the very social and familial influences that inhibit him.

Buñuel uses melodramatic coincidence to symbolize fate, which really is the expression of subconscious impulse. This is clear at the end of *El*, when Francisco's paranoia weaves his random experiences (noises, faces glimpsed) into an obsessive hallucination. It is no coincidence that Francisco deliriously attacks the priest in the very church which has stifled his emotional and sexual happiness in the guise of protecting it. Yet one speculates about the subconsciously willed quality of the film's coincidences only in retrospect; what is striking on the screen is their absurdity.

The Criminal Life of Archibaldo de la Cruz is built humorously along the same lines as *El*. It has the same subject—a man's destructive complex about women—and it has a similar ironic relationship to Buñuel's early surrealism, recalling *Un Chien Andalou* (as *El* recalls *L'Age d'Or*). Buñuel's handling of melodrama is even more burlesque than in *El*. Flashbacks and reality-versus-fantasy juxtapositions interlock and form one subjective world in *The Criminal Life of Archibaldo de la Cruz*.

In his fantasy, Archibaldo is convinced he holds the power of death over women; in everyday life he feels contempt for those who attract him, except his fianceé whom he worships as an angel. Like the destructive Francisco, who remains a prisoner of his fetishism while believing he is sane and free, Archibaldo sees no discrepancy between his inner and outer worlds. But unlike Francisco, Archibaldo is naïvely convinced that his harmless fantasies have led to actual crimes—that he has murdered a series of women. Finally, Archibaldo unwittingly begins to liberate himself by confessing to a judge. Like a psychiatrist, the judge matter-of-factly separates inner and outer reality, acknowledging the normality of Archibaldo's aggressive fantasies. "We can't put you on trial for wishing someone's death. We can't prosecute a person's imagination. Thinking isn't a crime!" In Buñuel's exaggerated happy ending—an instant self-therapy which only makes Buñuel's pessimism in such matters more obvious—Archibaldo rids himself of his obsessions and goes off to enjoy a normal relationship with a mature woman, having finally grown into the tender yet aggressive creature that males are supposed to become.

In many films Buñuel surreptitiously undermines the normal authority of the family, reminding us of its original perversity, exclusion of passion, and inhibition of children. Sexual and parental roles in *La Hija del Engaño* are cruel and repressive, far more charged erotically than society admits. Yet Buñuel's film is a broad farce; with ironic distance we observe the heroine (all of whose problems are caused by her father) exclaim to the suitor who will take her away that he is like a father to her. In *Susana* a respectable household is reduced to erotic chaos by the intrusion of a seductive visitor; father and son become unwitting rivals for the same woman. *Una Mujer Sin Amor* is nominally a defense of love regardless of consequence, but Buñuel's emphasis is on the unspoken attractions and hatreds that lie beneath the surface of domestic accord. The social significance of family morality is hinted at in *El Gran Calavera*, wherein a bourgeois is obliged to try living by the work ethic he supposedly raised his family in.

Buñuel's technique is to exaggerate normal family roles in order to hint more plainly at the sexuality and aggression which condition them. Thus of the two brothers in *Una Mujer Sin Amor*, one is legitimate and one illegitimate; their rivalry is that between any siblings smarting under parental unfairness. The desire of an old man for a virgin has aspects of a father's incestuous desire in *Viridiana* and *Tristana*. The old man is an uncle in *Viridiana* and a guardian in *Tristana*, but they virtually summon up a taboo.

The authority for Buñuel's oblique, pessimistic studies of "authentic social relations" in the family is, of course, Freud. Yet Buñuel could have defended himself from accusations of reactionary idealism, if anyone were accusing him, by citing Marxist authorities. After all, he is not treating human relations in the abstract; he is portraying the bourgeois family, in which natural conflicts are not resolved but aggravated. As Engels affirms, hypocrisy itself is socially conditioned.

The class consciousness of *El Bruto* deals with a crisis of class allegiance in the hero. This is "the brute," a crude, powerful slaughterhouse worker named Pedro whom the owner of the packinghouse hand-picks to serve as his thug in breaking up a militant rent strike by impoverished tenants of a slum block he owns.

Pedro performs his reactionary work of intimidation faithfully and without remorse, going so far as to kill the leader of the strike; he also enjoys the sexual company of the capitalist's wife.

Soon, however, things go badly. Hunted for the murder, Pedro takes refuge with an innocent young woman. By a twist of fate she is the daughter of the murdered striker, though she doesn't know Pedro is the killer. They live together, and Pedro knows tenderness for the first time. He also begins to side with the oppressed masses he had brutalized before. But the capitalist's wife, jealous of Pedro's new love, betrays him. Pedro kills the capitalist in a rage, thus amending his previous wrongs in a primitive way, and is in turn tracked and shot down—like a brute—by the police.

What animates the class conflict in *El Bruto* is Buñuel's parallel between Pedro's dawning class consciousness and his archetypal progression from brutality to humanity through his new love. With this parallel, Buñuel is able to say two things at once. First, the capitalist form of society we live in is not civilization at all, but a brutal state preceding it. It is Pedro's new-found class consciousness, simultaneously with his new tenderness, that represents civilization. Second, however, Buñuel implies through specific themes of father-killing that Pedro's violence, while finally revolutionary, inescapably revives the archetypal murder. Revolution itself, without necessarily losing its positive value, is thus assimilated to the irrational rebellion which underlies civilization permanently and generates its conflicts.

El Bruto further contains this crucial paradox: remorse of conscience, that Christian invention which enabled civilization to develop historically, is both the source of Pedro's capacity for love and the reason for Pedro's undoing at the hands of a society that denies love.

Two minor comedies based on virtually identical ideas form a pair of complements. Buñuel seems simply to have rendered the same theme once in an apolitical context and once in a class-conscious one. A bus in *Subida al Cielo* and a trolley in *La Ilusion Viaja en Tranvia* carry their passengers toward unknown explorations. Bus and streetcar symbolize everyday social routine and at the same time the possibility of escaping it. Both comedies are predicated on the idea that the hero's courtship must be interrupted by his initiation into certain mysteries of life before it can be consummated. In *Subida al Cielo*, however, the archetypal mysteries are largely moral, while in *La Ilusion Viaja en Tranvia* they consist in a knowledge of the political realities of capitalism.

Without departing from broad comedy, *La Ilusion Viaja en Tranvia* adds up to a demystification of capitalist relations. The hero is a motorman obliged to take his trolley on two illicit runs before his problems regarding his job and woman friend can be resolved.

The story might have proceeded from Buñuel's curiosity about the psychology of work. How do people who ought to know better nevertheless get sentimentally attached to the habit of working, to the very tools and machines from which they make an inadequate living and a frustrating contribution to a dubious society? The motorman and his conductor friend, for instance, get drunk and wax sentimental over "their" streetcar, which is being retired from service, even though they have just been abused by the company and are in danger of being laid off (for being too efficient!). The story proceeds also from a materialist's curiosity about the hidden social context of alienated labor. What contradictions and what individual power relationships really make up a public company? Or by what chain of circumstance is there poverty in one part of town and a surplus of products in another?

The motorman and his friend, inebriated and uninhibited, decide to take their cherished streetcar for one last illegal midnight run, though it will get them in trouble. The sneak run seems a compensation for their years in the service of capitalism. The entire sampling of society whom they pick up—night laborers and late revellers,—get to ride for free in a utopian togetherness. ("Sounds like communism to me," an American tourist complains.)

The two workers are then obliged to make a far less comfortable run in daylight to try to get their trolley back to its garage without being detected. Their experiences on this trip reveal the class-divided society which stands in the way of realizing the preceding utopia. They pass a mob about to get violent over the high prices set by the local food store. Later the streetcar comes across mobsters who are stockpiling grain in a warehouse, creating a shortage; this touches off another riot. Meanwhile in town a watchman gets drunk with a friend and comically tries to explain inflation and exploitation to him. When normal barriers are down, everyone's "natural" class consciousness comes out.

A retired motorman who pesters the two exemplary adventurers represents the false consciousness they might have had in other circumstances. Even though the old man has spent his life and health in the service of an ungrateful company, he persists in taking the side of the bosses against his fellow workers. He keeps trying to get the two drivers discovered and fired during their excursion, but ironically the management never takes the old man's alarm seriously and the film ends happily for the workers. (On the archetypal level, the old man also represents parental authority, or the Freudian superego—precisely because his vigilance is ineffectual.)

With the important exceptions of *El Bruto* and *La Ilusion Viaja en Tranvia* (two films explicitly about workers' class consciousness), workers in Buñuel's films nevertheless occupy their conventional place in bourgeois art, the background. (So do the servants and waiters, who have different symbolic functions however.) Curiously, urban industrial workers are usually absent from Buñuel's world. Yet their occasional presence in the background of scenes—sullen, absorbed, mysterious in a way—lends a social resonance to Buñuel's bourgeois dramas. The surveyors and masons in *Viridiana*, the railroad workers in *Nazarin*, and the construction workers at the dam site in *El* all have an importance extending beyond their brief appearances on screen.

By the same token, however, Buñuel is chiefly interested in labor and artifact as signs of the sublimated drives he finds at the basis of civilization. Explosions, the erection of buildings, and digging the earth for treasure (oilwell workers in *Gran Casino* and diamond miners in *La Mort en Ce Jarden)* are important as collective projections of the sexual impulse. Civilization viewed as the product of instinct has no more manifest purpose than the societies of ants and termites, Buñuel implies. The dam site workers in *El* are filmed as tiny figures moving in organized teams, mastering the terrain through an apparently efficient division of labor.

Undermining this efficiency, however, are counterproductive instincts as well as progressive ideals, both evidently unknown among insects. Humans evolve morals and ideals, rationalizing and improving the societies they are born into; yet, they can scarcely contain antisocial impulses which threaten to undo the work of civilization. Buñuel apportions the ideals to his bourgeois humanitarians, and the instincts to his bourgeois madmen. The first category is typified in *El* by Francisco's rival in love, a sane and reasonable engineer. The second is embodied in the compulsive Francisco himself, who looks down at the crowd from his tower (again a perspective upon the insect colony) and cries, "Worms I could crush in an instant!" Even an irrational reaction is socially conditioned, and Buñuel ironically identifies Francisco's position as the expression of a class ideology (the bourgeoisie having usurped the nobility). "Egotism," Francisco explains after his outburst, "is the essence of a noble soul."

El Rio y la Muerte, Buñuel's chronicle of a feud to the death between generations of two macho families, explores the relation between violence and civilization through the mediation of family roles. The two families are reconciled—but only after innumerable murders—by the selfless efforts of the one family member enlightened by education, a doctor who comes home to his village. Doctor Anguiano is a positive hero such as Buñuel rarely portrays. He is civilized, non-violent and courageous—the opposite of the brutes he must oppose. It is characteristic of Buñuel's dialectical humor (and his view of the price of civilization—a symbolic castration) that Buñuel makes Anguiano a cripple, first in an iron lung and later in a wheelchair from which he delivers a declaration of faith in life's possibilities to his nurse-fianceé. Buñuel's schematic polarity between the cripple who loves life and the virile types who answer violence with violence applies in subtler form to his other films.

Buñuel's survival stories set in jungles or on islands are case studies of civilization's conflicts. Buñuel lifts his characters from their normal immersion in the decadent society to which they were more or less adapted and drops them into a primitive context: they must struggle against an indifferent natural environment and recreate civilization.

A handful of outcasts bound to each other only by bad faith and hostility are forced to keep company as they escape from a riot-torn mining town through an impenetrable rain forest in *La Mort en Ce Jardin.* Once the dubious protection of civilization is left behind, Buñuel reverses the conventional scale of values. The only outcast equipped for survival is one violent man who has a practical and thoroughgoing contempt for society, yet also has an unrealized capacity for tenderness. He is one of Buñuel's negative heroes, though not as criminal as the irredeemable Jaibo. The other castaways are crippled by the delusions to which they cling. What finally condemns most of them is their dependency, whether they realize it or not, upon the very civilization which has cast them out and which they are unable to reestablish in miniature even for their own safety.

Most survival movies glorify reactionary social myths under the cover of apolitical entertainment. On the contrary, Buñuel adds a pointed political setting to *La Mort en Ce Jardin*. The fictitious Latin American country from which the outcasts escape is torn by a recognizable agony, the violent installation of fascism. A workers' rebellion is met with armed repression; a jailbreak fans the flames of the abortive revolution. By the time Buñuel's characters are making their escape, the somber archways of the Spanish-style capital are half in ruins and the streets are swarming with uniformed troops who pry into every cranny like the red ants in the jungle.

Buñuel thus obtains a political perspective upon the survival theme. The refugees all believe they have no connection with this society. But the religion, venality, and bourgeois ambition which are their undoing originate precisely in this near-fascist society and bind them to it even as they seek freedom.

Buñuel's retelling of a castaway's singlehanded reinvention of civilization to keep himself from savagery, *Robinson Crusoe*, contains a more ambitious yet ambivalent effort to integrate the study of civilization with a specific political critique. Crusoe painfully masters nature, although he cannot abolish his own solitude, which nearly drives him mad. Buñuel contrasts Crusoe's hard-won material treasures (bread, clothing, etc.) with his spiritual consolation, the Bible. The latter proves to be useless, though Crusoe realizes it only in times of crisis. With the arrival of Friday, Crusoe's civilization reveals itself as a hostile defense against the unknown, against other men. Although Crusoe declares with a hypocrisy that may be unconscious that he and Friday are to be friends, he must enslave Friday because he cannot afford to trust the mysterious cannibal.

Buñuel is exploring two things at the same time. Friday stands for a taboo, cannibalism, which Crusoe must overcome anew if his civilization's promise of friendship is to be realized. At the same

time Buñuel is out to expose the arbitrariness—the racist imperi-
alism—with which Crusoe's civilization asserts superiority over
that of Friday. (For example, Buñuel allows Friday the last laugh
when Crusoe tries to convert Friday to his faith, forgetting how
useless the superstitions of Christianity were when he was alone.
Why doesn't God just kill the Devil, Friday wants to know—and
put an end to sin? And since God does allow the Devil to tempt us,
why is he angry when we fall into temptation?)

The character of Friday must thus do double duty, symbolizing
both a pre-civilized way of life which must be domesticated
and a way of life which just happens to be alien to Crusoe and so
reveals Crusoe's unconscious norms. The barbarity of Crusoe's
civilization is fully visible when Crusoe ends up teaching the
former savage, once his potential enemy, to use firearms. The
happy ending—Robinson secures the rescue of himself and "his
man"—is presumably undercut by the ironic prospect that the two
men who have learned to be brothers will inevitably resume the
relations of master and servant under the cover of civilization.

Buñuel makes castaways of a group of refined bourgeois in *The
Exterminating Angel*, not by lifting them out of their decadent
society, but by imprisoning them right inside it. An unknown
force confines the group to their townhouse. As food and water
run out, they spend an unknown number of days attempting to
free themselves with a variety of religious and superstitious
exercises culminating in mass hysteria.

Incarcerated in the midst of their own urbanity, the bourgeois
are as cut off from sustenance as the castaways in the midst of
nature in *La Mort en Ce Jardin* and *Robinson Crusoe*. But
where the castaways must recreate the ways of civilization, the
bourgeois drop the cover of sophistication only to reveal plain
hostility. Where the castaways must be amoral, violent, murderous in order to lay the basis for civilization, the characters who
survive the longest in *The Exterminating Angel* are those whose
roles in life are disciplined by professional dedication with an
element of resignation: the doctor, the head servant (who "studied
with the Jesuits"), and the host himself, who alone among the
bourgeois has consciously assimilated the civilized proprieties as
a necessity, not a convenience.

As the bourgeois' imprisonment shifts from the townhouse (lay society, trapped between bourgeois reason and superstition) to the house of God (the ultimate explanation or superstition), so the outside context expands. The police cordon in earlier scenes, which quite normally keeps curiosity-seekers at a distance from the quarantined townhouse, escalates in the final sequence into officers on horseback firing into a screaming crowd on a public square, a metaphor of fascism.

La Fièvre Monte à El Pao is one of Buñuel's openly political melodramas. El Pao is a fictitious Latin American dictatorship where political prisoners are worked to death in the governor's slave camps. The government attracts the masses to the national holiday assembly only because it distributes raw meat free to the famished crowd. First, however, the crowd must wait out the speechmaking, kept at gunpoint from attacking the meat trucks.

Vasquez, a liberal functionary with irresolute ambitions, believes he can open channels of reform in the fascist regime he works for. He discovers too late that the political system is infinitely more vicious than he imagined. His naïvete brings death to the woman he loves and enslavement to the guerrillas and political prisoners he hoped to protect. He survives a round of murderous power struggles only to see his bids for reform nullified or turned into their opposite—sacrificed in the tradeoff of bourgeois politics. At length, having unwittingly handed over his love, his honor and his own ambition, the token liberal administrator is left with the most insidious consolation of all, bad faith. Vasquez derives a short-lived meaningless pride from the one purely symbolic gesture he finally accomplishes—authorizing the unshackling of the political prisoners against his superior's orders. As Buñuel's final shot of Vasquez among the convicts suggests, he is his own political prisoner for the rest of his life. His freedom depends upon the servitude of others.

Although on the surface this film is a demonstration of the impossibility of political reform under fascism, Buñuel does not pause to consider Vasquez's politics in any detail. Buñuel's real aim is to demonstrate that a moral code, a responsibility to freedom, is affirmed or denied in every choice; halfway measures like Vasquez's are denials compounded. Yet this issue does not come alive in Buñuel's scenario. Vasquez never really has the freedom to affirm or deny. The reason is that Buñuel has tried to invest his character with a contradictory dimension, a pure passivity. Vasquez is only the creature of his consuming affair with a symbolic woman who is older, more passionate and less scrupulous than he, the widow of the preceding tyrant, embodying the inescapable seductions of El Pao's corrupt system. Buñuel's symbolic parallel between Vasquez's love and his political destiny is the negative equivalent of the parallel between Valerio's love and his movement toward liberation in *Cela s'Appelle l'Aurore*.

Buñuel's political triumph is probably *Diary of a Chambermaid*, a harsh caricature of France's provincial bourgeoisie set in 1929, when the fascist movement was gaining strength in France. Célestine, a chambermaid, suspects rightly that the head servant in the same household is guilty of having raped and killed a little girl from the neighborhood, though no one else connects Joseph with the crime. She attempts to bring Joseph to justice in a devious way of her own. She compromises her own integrity voluntarily, first sleeping with Joseph to extort a private confession, then planting false evidence of Joseph's crime as the only way to incriminate him. (Like the young man at the end of *Subida al Cielo*, Célestine acts dishonestly to achieve a higher justice.)

Ironically, the case against Joseph does not hold up in court. In Buñuel's ending, Joseph goes free and prospers as a shady cafe owner, an aggressive supporter of the antisemitic nationalist movement. Célestine languishes in a marriage of convenience to a conservative retired colonel, her spirited effort to secure justice having been only a prelude to the larger injustice, the political reality of fascism.

Knowing Joseph is guilty, we gladly see him arrested; we can probably overlook Célestine's private amorality if it serves a greater justice. But Joseph is freed by a court which is biased toward the fascists anyhow. Célestine's effort to nudge the wheels of justice is doomed to fail, Buñuel suggests, because individual morality is powerless against the organized amorality of the state. On the contrary, morality is compromised, contaminated and reversed by the social organism.

Buñuel allows us to glimpse the larger political world—the

fascists' demonstration in Cherbourg—only in a fragmentary sequence at the very end of *Diary of a Chambermaid*. He simply thrusts the demonstration upon us; the political references (to Chiappe, notably) are actual, but not explained. If Buñuel draws no tighter connection between Célestine's private drama and the political developments, it is because the real theme of *Diary of a Chambermaid* is precisely the disproportion between the private and public dramas:

> The private story, the individual drama, cannot in my view interest anyone worthy of living in his times. . . . I do not consider man in isolation, as a particular case, but in his relationship to other men.[5]

In 1953, when he spoke these words, Buñuel might have seemed to be calling plainly for a social realism opposed to individualist ideology and bourgeois sentimentality. As we have seen, however, much as Marxism has influenced his work, realism is no solution for Buñuel. At best it is a partial instead of a "total vision." Buñuel has conducted his own search for a political cinema, a cinema that accounts for the individual *and* society—and the tension between the two—rather than simply describing one systematically in terms of the other.

Perhaps *Diary of a Chambermaid* best represents that political cinema. Buñuel offers no positive image of freedom, political or moral; he demonstrates what freedom is not. *Diary of a Chambermaid* can be taken as a class-conscious demonstration of the proposition that individual freedom is a bourgeois illusion, and worse, an illusion that conceals and perpetuates oppression. It can just as readily be taken as a bourgeois statement of pessimism, a closed universe. The stronger Célestine's effort to get rid of Joseph, the more she is unwittingly his accomplice, for that effort itself is vitiated by the impossibility of morality. It is Buñuel's denunciation of fascism itself which is the ambivalent element in *Diary of a Chambermaid*. It makes the film one of Buñuel's strongest politically, yet at the same time—seeing that this fascism has no effective opponents as it flexes its muscles—it makes it a global expression of the political pessimism which is inherent in Buñuel's vision.

In *Cet Obscur Objet du Désir*, public or political reality is

[5]Kyrou, p. 110.

but the mirror of private reality, and presents only its irrational, violent side. Hijackings, explosions and sabotage rock the protagonist's world from first to last. Armed hoods (who double as musicians, ironically) take his billfold; terrorists take his car. Buñuel's hero pursues his heart's desire across a real world that is rocked by violence and death, yet he ignores that world—tossing away the evening headlines, turning off the morning broadcast. His private universe, though it is no more peaceful (or comprehensible) than the reality he journeys through, is all that matters. Politics right *and* left are the object of a chilling contempt in Buñuel's most recent film.

In contrast, Buñuel charges *The Discreet Charm of the Bourgeoisie* with an accessible left-wing polemic.

The four bourgeois heroes get away with murder, dope smuggling and other crimes in seeming immunity, until finally they are arrested in a surprise raid by a dutiful police inspector and his efficient staff. It is a pleasure to see them get their deserts (like watching Joseph's arrest in *Diary of a Chambermaid*). However, no sooner are they languishing behind bars than the poor inspector receives orders from high places (a phone call from the minister of the interior) to let them go immediately. The degenerates get off scot-free, thanks to the intervention of a corrupt government. (In case we admire the police for doing their duty, Buñuel catches us short by showing another scene in which they torture a young man accused of revolutionary terrorism.) Buñuel's polemic against the charade of bourgeois justice is plain.

Buñuel subjects even his own Freudian pessimism to political perspective. The following scene implies it is the bourgeoisie themselves who separate politics and psychology into virtual antagonists and give priority to the latter—in order to prolong a violent domination of society by their own class. Rafael has foiled a Mirandan freedom fighter in her attempt on his life. Holding her at gunpoint, he permits himself the luxury of a theoretical disputation. His concluding line is: "No, if Mao said that, it's because he didn't understand Freud!" Of course, Rafael can permit himself this superior assertion because he has absolute power of execution over the woman at that moment (and a frustrated desire for her); he will shortly terminate all discussion by sending her cruelly to her death.

The Discreet Charm of the Bourgeoisie and *The Phantom of Liberty* form a pair of complements—a treatment of the same theme. *The Phantom of Liberty* treats violence and obsession with death as something fundamental—society's paradoxical reason for existing. The class aspect of that society is identified but not emphasized. Each scene is originally some commonplace of melodrama, bourgeois society's self-image. But some discordant element enters the picture, makes nonsense of the conventional content, and uncovers the archetypal meaning of the commonplace, which always has to do with a latent fear of death.

The world of *The Phantom of Liberty* is one of materialism without transcendence. History brings no lessons or progress. *The Phantom of Liberty* deceptively begins with historical episodes—first the execution of Spaniards in 1808 by Napoleon's occupying militia, then a French captain's desecration of Queen Elvira's tomb. The whole edifice of history crumbles to the

A French Police Chief takes aim against invisible menaces in Luis Bunuel's surrealistic comic masterpiece. (*The Phantom of Liberty*)

ground, however, as Buñuel cuts unexpectedly to presentday France, where the remainder of the film takes place.

History vanishes like a disturbing dream in daylight. The murky tale of death and lust operates as a premonition, an archetype, not as interpreted reality. Bourgeois society, a Marxist may say, does not produce real history, only necrophiliac fables for the nursemaids of the bourgeoisie. Yet Buñuel himself views the historical incident, the executions of 1808, without transcendence. The Spanish partisans' perverse cry of *Vivan las cadenas* ("Long live chains," or "Down with freedom" as the titles translate it) before they are shot leaves no room for freedom's positive form. Buñuel insists, whether dialectically or pessimistically, on seeing freedom and life only in terms of oppression and death. Death, as it flits among the unconnected lives in Buñuel's film, may be the only form in which we glimpse the phantom of freedom.

Society in Buñuel's past films dispatched its criminals as threats. Today society tolerates and even condones the "killer poet," the ambassador of Miranda, or Joseph the fascist child-rapist. One can argue that Buñuel is redefining the political enemy in our own time; the new liberal capitalism promotes violence in the guise of tolerance. But that equation is probably too simple. In *Cet Obscur Objet du Désir* notably, Buñuel has expressly erased the old lines of battle, both politically and psychologically. Society in this newest film does not symbolize only the monolithic enemy of rebellion (the superego, say) as in Buñuel's earlier films. Rebellion is a permanent convulsion in the social order itself, and its manifestations are not inherently heroic.

With its unusual effort to treat political and psychological realities as parts of an indissoluble whole, Buñuel's work not only reflects, but responds to the struggle between idealism and materialism. Buñuel is a materialist who nevertheless insists on subjective reality, an idealist who is dialectical, a determinist who exalts the will to freedom. Buñuel sees social revolution as one avatar of an archetypal rebellion which can take other valid forms as well. Yet he respects Marxism and he very often deliberately opens his films to the left while closing them to the right.

It is significant that *Gran Casino*, the first of Buñuel's commercial films, opens like several others with a jailbreak. It is no less significant that the hero's escape is accompanied by a sardonic discussion among the cellmates as to whether it's better to break out or to stay in. Buñuel rejected the label "pessimist" at the time of *Los Olvidados*, yet volunteered it at the time of *The Discreet Charm of the Bourgeoisie*: "I'm pessimistic; but I hope to be a good pessimist. In any society, the artist has a responsibility."[6] Ultimately for this "good pessimist," society is founded on a basis so conflicted that its essential injustice cannot perhaps be eradicated; yet it is nothing other than the constant effort to eradicate it which defines humanity. "Surrealism taught me that man is never free yet fights for what he can never be," Buñuel has said, "that is tragic."

[6]Quoted by Carlos Fuentes in *The New York Times Magazine*, March 11, 1973.

That Obscure Object of Desire

BUÑUEL'S TRIUMPH, BERTOLUCCI'S FLOP

Vincent Canby

. . . .

Little things keep interrupting Mathieu (Fernando Rey), the charming, urbane, 50-ish French businessman who's the hero of Luis Buñuel's effervescent new comedy, *That Obscure Object of Desire*. While Mathieu is in his elegant library in Paris, in the middle of some delicate negotiations with the mother of Conchita, the maddeningly fickle, changeably beautiful, 18-year-old Spanish dancer he wants to make his mistress, there is a sudden, very loud "snap," just offscreen. Mathieu's eyes betray the tiniest flicker of impatience as his ever-ready valet, Martin, enters the room and, most discreetly, without a word, removes the body of the mouse that's just been trapped while Mathieu was talking solemnly of love, respect and financial security.

Some time earlier, when Mathieu was in his limousine en route to the railroad station in Seville, a booby-trapped automobile had exploded in the street ahead, forcing Mathieu's chauffeur to make a detour. In a fancy Paris restaurant a fly plummets into Mathieu's gently stirred, certainly not bruised martini. One serene morning in Seville, Mathieu is strolling in the courtyard of an ancient church. Two black-robed peasant women stop him, one carrying an infant in her arms. The mother pulls back the blanket to show Mathieu her baby—a small, pink-snouted white pig.

One of the aspects of the film that makes *That Obscure Object of Desire* simultaneously so cockeyed funny and so mysterious is the manner in which the outside world keeps impinging on the

From *The New York Times*, October 16, 1977. © 1977 by the New York Times Company. Reprinted by permission.

consciousness of Mathieu, whose only wish is to possess, now and forever, the willful, headstrong Conchita. The object of his obsession is so unknown to Mathieu that Buñuel has two ac- tresses—the serene Carole Bouquet and the equally beautiful but more earthy Angela Molina—alternate in playing the role, though not in any schematic way. The two faces of Conchita simply indicate Mathieu's mounting confusion and frustration as he pursues his love through a contemporary world in which a fly in a martini is scarcely any more or less momentous than the attempted assassination of the Archbishop of Sienna, reportedly the work of a guerrilla group called the Revolutionary Army of the Infant Jesus.

What is the extraordinary Buñuel telling us in *That Obscure Object of Desire*, the 77-year-old master's 30th feature since *L'Age d'Or* (1930) and a comedy to match the best of his recent work, including *The Exterminating Angel* and *The Discreet Charm of the Bourgeoisie*? Almost as many things, I suspect, as there are people who see the film, but mainly he is sharing with us a view of life as seen by an artist who's as old as our century and whose creative impulse has not, as usually happens with filmmakers, been dampened by the years. Instead, it has been refined to an easy control and a perfection more often seen in painters and writers than among people who make movies in the furious hustle of the market place.

It was no more than an accident of programming by which the final two films at the recently concluded 15th New York Film Festival were this new masterpiece by Buñuel, which runs a speedy 100 minutes, and Bernardo Bertolucci's semi-controver- sial, 245-minute epic about 70 years of Italian political and social life told in the stories of three generations of two families, one landowners and the other serfs. *1900*, the would-be magnum opus by the 37-year-old Bertolucci, is the grandiose flop of a very young, very talented man who has sought to capture truth by marshalling what looks to be a large portion of the physical resources of the Italian movie industry and employing the best actors of three countries and two continents. Truth, though, is not so cheaply and easily captured.

1900 is virtually an anthology of various kinds of indecisions.
When Bertolucci showed it at the 1976 Cannes Film Festival, it
ran almost five and one-half hours. When it was subsequently
released in Europe, Bertolucci had cut it to five hours and 10
minutes, and it was shown in two parts as if it were two separate
films. At one point Bertolucci was editing it down to a 4 1/2-hour
version while his producer, Alberto Grimaldi, was trying to peddle
his own 3 1/4-hour version to Paramount Pictures against Bertolucci's protests (as well as those of a number of film critics who
signed a petition on behalf of Bertolucci's artistic integrity and
the director's civil rights).

I refused to sign that petition, not because I had seen the film or
had anything against Bertolucci, whose work I've long admired,
but because it seemed to be an intramural fight of the sort that
makes the movie business go around (and forever separates it
from any identification with the fine arts). After all that fuss the
Bertolucci-approved version we are now seeing here runs four
hours and five minutes and has been dubbed into a sort of opera-
libretto English that numbs the mind in a way that not even four
hours of adequate English subtitles would.

1900, which started off with a budget of something over
$3,000,000 and went over $8,000,000, would probably never have
seen the light of day, at least in this form, if Bertolucci's previous
film hadn't been such a huge financial success. It would have
been a tough producer who could deny the director of *Last Tango
in Paris* everything he wanted for his next picture, and it would
have taken a director of more modesty and self-doubts than
Bertolucci apparently has not to believe that he could make the
epic he wanted of *1900.* The reviews of *Last Tango* and the
balance sheets must have been heady reading.

Backed by these reassurances, Bertolucci plowed ahead with his
major work that, had it succeeded, might have been a Marxist
War and Peace. As it is, it's a mixed-up, Marxist romance that's
soft at the core, full of outrageously operatic touches of the kind
that only the late Luchino Visconti ever got away with, and then
only once, in *The Damned.* It's also full (toward the end) of
highly stylized, group-movement choreography that's already

been taken to its cinematic dead-end by Hungarian director Miklos Jancso.

1900 starts off quite nicely and conventionally as the inter-woven story of the aristocratic Berlinghieri family and the Dalco family, who are serfs on the Berlinghieris' estates. Two sons born into the families on the same day in 1901 grow up side by side, as friends, competitors and, ultimately, points of view. Alfredo, played by Robert De Niro with a kind of Lower East Side charm that hasn't much to do with the movie he's in, is the Berlinghieri scion, a man with too much taste and humanity to embrace Mussolini's Fascists but not enough guts to fight them. Olmo, played by Gerard Depardieu in the film's only consistently good performance, is the peasant who becomes transformed by his social conscience and a proud, banner-waving, Marxist-psalm-singing revolutionary.

Between these two men is a third, Attila (Donald Sutherland), who isn't a Hun but might as well be, a prototypical Fascist who works for the Berlinghieris as their foreman and who, when he's not insulting the help, is squashing cats with a butt of his head, sodomizing little boys and dropping helpless widows atop spiked fences.

Decadence in Bertolucci movies can be terrifically cinematic and rather perversely beautiful, as he demonstrated in *The Conformist.* In *1900* it is virtually set decoration and is so overdone as to be ludicrous.

Until now Bertolucci's fondness for excess has always been part of the method rather than the point. In *1900* it's almost all there is. Even in this four-hour and five-minute version there's too much of everything—too many pretty pictures of broad land-scapes, too many scenes of peasants behaving in the hearty, ribald manner that movie peasants affect, too many easy juxtapositions of upper-class decadence and lower-class strength, too much (at the end) red-flag waving that isn't meant to be realistic but impressionistic, though that switch in style comes too late.

In addition to Depardieu's, there are some other good per-formances, especially by Burt Lancaster as the Berlinghieri patri-arch, but the rest are quite bad, including Donald Sutherland (whose role, admittedly, is an impossible one), and Dominique Sanda as De Niro's French wife, a lady who takes to drink because she's turned off by her husband's lack of political bone.

Bertolucci takes over four hours to show us more than we need to know about his characters, more than we want to know about his politics (which is passionate in a theoretical way) but not as much as we might have liked to know about specific political events that mark the 70 years covered by the movie. Though the film spans a lot of time, its view is short and narrow.

That Obscure Object of Desire tells what seems to be a small, rather special story about one man's mad obsession with a woman he can't possess, but Buñuel being Buñuel (a man whose politics, I suspect, are not too different from Bertolucci's), is incapable of limiting himself to the short view. *That Obscure Object of Desire* is not only about sex and manners but politics, religion, physics, you-name-it, about almost everything that touches us in our daily lives. Though his film is a model of efficient narrative, there's hardly a scene in it that doesn't evoke the manifold mysteries that—Buñuel knows—lie just beyond the film-frame.

Though he's now 77 and made his first films when in his twenties, Buñuel did not begin to earn a living from films until he was 47. He's never had a box-office hit to equal that of *Last Tango*. Because he came late to commercial movies (in Mexico), he appears to be frugal about the way he shoots, getting as much as possible from every image, with the least waste of motion. This is why—when his films work as *That Obscure Object* does—the images have the effect of exploding in a continuing flow of odd, contradictory associations. They are the bubbles in his champagne. It's ironic that Buñuel, whose age is more than twice Bertolucci's, should make a film that looks so fresh, modern and tough, while Bertolucci's is sentimental, downright old-fashioned.

THAT OBSCURE OBJECT OF DESIRE: AN APPRECIATION. BUÑUEL AT SEVENTY-SEVEN, OR *L'AMOUR FOU* FIFTY YEARS LATER

Antonin Liehm

. . . .

The scriptwriter of all of Buñuel's later films, and also of *That Obscure Object of Desire*, Jean-Claude Carrière, had commented upon Buñuel's method of work: "You can provoke images. Imagination is a capacity you can develop. What is needed is meditation, concentration, a great calm of the soul and of the body and, of course, a privileged location. In Buñuel's case this is a bar. Not every bar. It must be dark enough, very comfortable and, as much as possible, deserted. For the fourteen years that we have been working together, Buñuel has been selecting hotels mostly for their bars. He goes there first. I leave him alone for some twenty minutes. When I join him, he tells me what he has "invented." Sometimes it is just an image or a series of images, but it may also be an entire sequence. I listen.

"Often this has little to do with the script. It is more a kind of ritual training, like an athlete preparing for a bout—a call for images which begin closing in on him. They emerge from the darkest corners of the bar—as, for instance, did the potato sack of *That Obscure Object of Desire*, which we schlepp along, full of our worn-out desires and the obstacles we ourselves place before them. Yet, if we were to penetrate to the bottom of our inner self, what would we find but a piece of old lace covered with blood?"

The lights were extinguished; the film was about to begin. The old Pierre Louys story with its dusty images of bourgeois erotic fantasies and obsessions was to emerge on the screen, as it did in

This article is here published for the first time by arrangement with the author.
Copyright © 1978 by Antonin Liehm.

other adaptations of this novel, *La Femme et Le Pantin:* an eternal myth for an eternal remake.

But Buñuel's world is not that of the turn of the century. It is our world with its violence, bombs, and killing. His characters pretend that they can ignore this world. The old bourgeois game of pretending to oneself and to others that nothing unusual is happening has always been one of Buñuel's favorite themes. In *That Obscure Object of Desire*, Buñuel's hero pretends that the violence of his society does not concern him until the very moment when he finds himself facing the knife—or the owner of the knife—under the bed of the obscure object of his desire.

Buñuel laughs and makes us laugh, but his is not the frivolous laughter of commercial surrealism, which has become as fashionable today as it was intolerable at the time of *L'Age d'Or*. In *That Obscure Object of Desire* we discover not the amusing wit of *The Phantom of Liberty*, but the wise, ironic, sad smile of a man who has long understood the world without ever having to give up anything in which he believed. Nor has he relinquished what he has always loathed as he continues to celebrate the *amour fou* of his younger years.

In *That Obscure Object of Desire* you can find Buñuel's Spain—a train compartment transformed into a Spanish tavern where strange visitors tell strange stories with children always present in this school of odd, bizarre dreams come to life. Buñuel's surrealist dimension is equally present not only in the potato sack but in the mouse trapped at the most inappropriate moment, in the fly, in the priest, and in the gypsies carrying a pig instead of a baby—the last suggesting Goya as well.

There is, however, something not entirely different, but nevertheless new, on the level of Buñuel's cinematic inventiveness. The idea of replacing the unsatisfactory Maria Schneider with two different actresses (Carole Bouquet and Angela Molina) came to Buñuel only when he found himself without a leading lady after shooting had already begun. But a stroke of genius it was nonetheless, an improvisation of monumental consequence for the whole enterprise by an artist who, at seventy-seven, is in full command of his creative capacities.

What is it that is so overpowering in this rather conventional story of an aging rich man who becomes a prisoner of the obscure object of his desire, the saint and the whore in one female body— or two? More and more, we understand that what is significant is the perspective which Buñuel grants the tale and the comments he makes. There was always perspective in Buñuel: an irony, a system of references. Never did he express it better than in a recent talk with Michel Delain: "I only ask myself simple questions. Eroticism and religion, for instance. Well, had it not been for the second, the first could not exist." Buñuel always places things in context; his dreams always explore the complex relationship between the social and the private, the rational and the sensual. Sometimes his fantasies are critical, sometimes satirical; always they are surreal. But this time, more than ever, an ironic perspective dominates the entire film. The wisdom of distance, the love-hate relationship between the author and his Pierre Louys characters, the almost grotesque double angle, both subjective and objective—all these lift Buñuel's film far above the average. There are no formal discoveries, no special effects, no fireworks. Rather, we are offered a constant, uninterrupted search for greater depth, for more ironic perspective—which are one and the same.

It is all very funny, but humor is the perspective of true art. Buñuel and Jean Claude Carrière know it well. They always laugh when things are dead serious. But so did Cervantes. The lights go on. The film is over; *L'Amour fou* fifty years later: wise, trivial, understanding, sad, tragic, ironic, funny—not the only possible attitude toward the world, but the world as a whole.

V

A Debate on
The Discreet Charm of the Bourgeoisie

. . . .

The Discreet Charm of the Bourgeoisie

WHY IS THE CO-EATUS ALWAYS INTERRUPTUS?   John Simon

• • • • • • • • • • • • • • • • • • •

Luis Buñuel's *The Discreet Charm of the Bourgeoisie* presents me with a critical poser. Here is a film that has received rave notices from all reviewers, top to bottom, and is doing well with local audiences; yet I consider it absolutely worthless. Why?

The film operates on two levels: as an essentially realistic yet satirical portrait of the French bourgeoisie, and as a series of dreams and visions constituting a surreal plane. Not only does the film strike me as a failure on each of these levels, it does not even manage to benefit from contrasting or dovetailing the two. I submit that Buñuel, who has made some splendid and some dismal films, is now an old, exhausted filmmaker, and that his besetting sins of lack of discipline and indulgence in private obsessions have gotten quite out of hand.

To begin with the satirical-realistic level: satire must, at the very least, be funny. But *Bourgeoisie* is either groaning under old, obvious jokes or coasting along barren stretches of mirthless nastiness. A sextet of rich and decadent bourgeois, including one ambassador from the imaginary Latin American country of Miranda, enjoy eating copiously and well. Yet, for one reason or another, their meals get interrupted. Let's call this the co-eatus interruptus theme.

For example, they come to dinner at their friend's house on the wrong day and must leave. They go, instead, to a country inn, but find in an adjoining alcove the dead proprietor's body awaiting the undertaker, and so decide to leave. Or they go, of an after-

From *The New York Times*, February 25, 1973. © 1973 by The New York Times Company. Reprinted by permission.

noon, to a fashionable café-restaurant in Paris and, successively ordering tea, coffee and hot chocolate, are told by the returning waiter that the place is out of each. So they leave.

Where is the joke or satire in that? No decent restaurant is ever out of all beverages, so the scene does not correspond to some ludicrous reality. But what about satiric-comical heightening? Does the scene, by indirection or hyperbole, succeed in ridiculing fancy restaurants? Or their waiters? Or their clientele? None of the above. Does it, then, make some sardonic point about French society? Not at all. Is it funny? No, only preposterous. In another scene the group sits down to dinner only to be interrupted by some officers, who are to be billeted with them and whose maneuvers have unexpectedly been moved ahead. Dinner is de-layed while the hostess improvises additional food and tables, and the meal is about to start again. But now the other mock army attacks prematurely, the officers must leave, and we get an inter-ruptus within an interruptus. Absurd, yes; funny, no.

And not meaningful either. What do these and other such scenes tell us? That the French bourgeoisie likes its food and takes it seriously, and hates to be thwarted in its enjoyment of it. So what? The Italian bourgeoisie is just as keen on eating, and so is the German and Austrian, and any other you are to name, with the possible exception of the English and American. But is this telling us anything new or enlightening or needful of iteration? What is so hilarious about people rattling off names of dishes or holding forth on the best way to make dry martinis? Nothing; yet from the way audiences are laughing you'd think the ushers were passing out laughing gas.

With interrupted eating comes also interrupted sex, the arche-typal interruptus. A husband discovers his wife on the verge of adultery with his good friend the ambassador; or guests arrive for lunch just as the host and hostess feel so amorous that they must have instant intercourse—so they must climb out of the window and have it in the bushes. This is not only juvenile prurience, it does not even make satirical sense: if these solidly married bour-geois can still pant for each other so at high noon, all is not lost. Where the blood stirs, there is hope.

But where is the satire, where the joke? Two people greedily pawing each other at an inopportune moment? Compared to that, a man slipping on a banana peel is Wildean wit and Swiftian satire.

On the surreal plane, the equivalent to the interruptus is the shaggy-dog story. In a sense, a dream is always over too soon, before the punchline of fulfillment can set in. But Buñuel shaggy-dogifies his dream or fantasy sequences in every possible way. A young lieutenant pops up from nowhere and relates a childhood vision in which his dead mother and her murdered lover appeared to the boy. They tell him that the dead and bloody man is his real father, and that the evil man he lives with is merely the killer of that true father. At the ghosts' urging, the boy poisons his pseudo-progenitor. He has had an unhappy childhood, says the lieutenant, and departs, never to be seen again.

Another man, a sergeant, is brought on to recount a dream of his. It is full of weird goings-on in a necropolis photographed and edited as in cheap horror movies; the events signify nothing meaningful or related to anything else in the film. The sergeant is asked to tell also his "train dream," but there is no more time for this. He has to leave, and we are left with a shaggy dog within a shaggy dog.

Again, a police commissioner we neither know nor care about has a dream about a bloody sergeant, allowing Buñuel to bring on yet another bloody corpse (the film is awash with blood, but you don't hear any of the antiviolence critics denouncing this one!) and to have a sado-comic scene in which the police torture a young rebel by means of an electrically charged piano, which, so to speak, plays him, and from which, suddenly, an army of cockroaches pours out—a shaggy-roach story.

Why should we care about the dreams of supernumeraries? A dream becomes interesting in relation to the waking personality of the dreamer, but if he remains a passing blank, of what concern are his grotesque dreams to us? Yet even the principals' dreams remain in this film unrevealing, unfunny, unconvincing. It would seem (as Buñuel has more or less admitted) that some of those dream episodes were originally intended as strange but real events—as, for example, in *The Milky Way*—but that the film-maker lost his nerve and explained the thing away as dreams within dreams.

Typically, we'll see a character wake up after a grotesque dream, and another, equally grotesque, sequence begins. Then a second character is seen waking up, and he tells us that he dreamed both foregoing sequences, that even the first dream was dreamed by him, the second dreamer. Yet the protagonist of the second dream was really a third character, whose dream that should have been. If this doesn't make sense to you reading it, don't worry—it won't make sense viewing it, either.

The shaggy dogs spill over into the waking sequences. There is one in which an elderly peasant woman promises to tell a bishop why she hates the gentle Jesus, but is whisked off before she can do so. Again, the police commissioner receives a phone call from the minister of justice to release his prominent prisoners. Why? he asks. The minister explains, but the noise of a low-flying jet obliterates the explanation. Asked for a repeat, the minister wearily obliges, but another jet interferes. The frustrated commissioner passes the order on to his sergeant, who also requests an explanation. As the commissioner answers, the radiator pipes drown out his words—shaggy upon shaggy upon shaggy dog.

All the humor is pathetic. A bishop is summoned to give absolution to a dying old man. He turns out to be the gardener who, years ago, killed the bishop's parents who employed and tormented him. The bishop absolves the old man, then shoots him dead—another blood-spattered corpse. And people laugh at this! But they'll laugh at anything. We first glimpse the bishop innocently walking up to a front door to ring the bell; in the audience, hearty laughter. Why? Surely they have seen a soutane before, and the churchman is not walking on his hands or backward or hopping on one foot.

Then there is a visual refrain, a periodically repeated shot of the six main characters walking down a highway. This is no one's dream or vision and may be an auto-*hommage* to Buñuel's own *The Milky Way*, in which a highway was the connecting metaphor. Here, however, the three or four recurrences of the shot with incremental variations tell us no more than that our bourgeois sextet is trudging down the road of life with a different expression on each face. So what else is old? To resort to grandiose symbolism in order to say what plain narrative has already conveyed (and what, anyhow, is self-evident) is arrant pretentiousness.

Coitus or co-eatus interruptus and the shaggy-dog story are the two faces of the same debased coin. They are an impotent old man's cacklingly sadistic interference with his own fictional characters, and an exhausted mind's failed search for meaningful conclusions. Buñuel is merely rehashing his earlier and better films (themselves often enough marred by incoherence), without the fascinating love-hate or righteous indignation that informed them. We knew what was assailed in *Los Olvidados* or reduced to absurdity in *Simon of the Desert*. In *The Discreet Charm of the Bourgeoisie* we have not so much a shaggy as an old dog, unable to learn new tricks or even adequately recall old ones.

This latest Buñuel film is a haphazard concatenation of waking and dream sequences in which anything goes, and which would make just as much, or just as little, sense if they were put together

. . . an impotent old man's cackingly sadistic interference with his own fictional characters, and an exhausted mind's failed search for meaningful conclusions. (*The Discreet Charm of the Bourgeoisie*)

in any other disorder. Since there is no plot and the characters are just pawns—oily businessman, dissembling diplomat, spaced-out debutante, haughty matron, frivolous wife—able performers are reduced to striking permanent attitudes and hoping they will add up to performances. The talented Delphine Seyrig, for instance, opts for one unrelieved smirk from beginning to end.

Why, then, such slavish adulation, placing the film on every Best List from high to low? Buñuel is a Grand Old Man—antifascist, anticlerical, antibourgeois—well into his seventies and still swinging. Secondly, he is European and has been through all those prestigiously arcane cults like surrealism, dadaism, fetishism, sadomasochism, and can provide nothing so shallow but that it is somehow chockful of profundities. Thirdly, his films are in a foreign language and must contain subtleties submerged in the subtitles. The reviewers, like good Pavlovian dogs, salivate away at the ring of Buñuel's name.

Audiences, in turn, have the unanimous rapture of the critics and all those awards to rely on. Dogs multiply: shaggy begets shaggy, Pavlovian conditions others into Pavlovians. *Dr. Strangelove*, a satire that did have meaning, predicted the world's end by hydrogen bomb. This Buñuel bomb merely ushers in the end of common sense in movie appreciation.

TAMPERING
WITH REALITY   Charles Thomas Samuels

. . . .

By common consent, the most interesting films of the season (I write in the time warp peculiar to quarterlies) are Luis Buñuel's

From *The American Scholar*, Summer 1973. Reprinted by permission of Lawrence Graver for the estate of Charles Thomas Samuels.

The Discreet Charm of the Bourgeoisie, which won the National Society of Film Critics' top prize, and Ingmar Bergman's *Cries and Whispers,* favored by the New York Film Critics. In my judgment, the Buñuel is silly and the Bergman hollow (although brilliantly acted and photographed). Yet both films are interesting because they shed light on a central choice between fantasy and realism.

Owing to its photographic medium, the essence of cinema seems to be verisimilitude. The Lumière brothers, who startled late-nineteenth-century Parisians with moving pictures of trains, crowds and so on, are generally credited with having set the form's aesthetic identity. No sooner had they proven the camera's documentary genius, however, when another Frenchman, Georges Méliès, showed it to be an equally good tool for actualizing fantasy.

For the most part, Méliès's fantasy films were a trivial combination of vaudeville and circus; but when commercial interests began to dictate that realistic films contain narrative and that they arrange their stories according to contrived stage formulas, fantastications like those of Méliès became, arguably, no falser to life. Materializing imaginary worlds isn't any more artificial than representing human behavior through the conventions of melodrama. Nor is it necessarily more honorable. Most realistic films resemble literary best sellers, which adopt the style of realism in order to lend daydreams a comforting credibility. Fantasy films may seem to offer an alternative, sacrificing reality in the interest of truth, but most works in this mode try only to be exciting and spectacular. Between plausible daydreams and sensational fantasies, there is little difference in seriousness.

Faced with the fact that most films carry false messages or none at all, critics often shift their attention to the envelopes; commerce may cause a filmmaker to lie, but art can still express itself as invention. Audiences are also drawn toward a brilliant surface because, notoriously, most of them go to movies as an escape from life. Therefore, it is no accident that even among the handful of films that are serious, only the exotic prove widely popular. Hence directors like Fellini, Buñuel or Bergman (when he is mystical) enchant even those who don't understand their films, whereas a realist like Antonioni doesn't pull crowds until he flirts (in *Blow-Up*) with expressionism. Reality, in movies, at least, is what critics and the *hoi polloi* make common cause in shunning.

I do not want to say that movies shouldn't be diverting or that reality equals realism. Purely diverting films are pleasant, and realism (which is one style among many) is not the only way to represent truth. I do want to say that our desire to clothe a taste for thrills in some dignity shouldn't make us ascribe truthfulness to methods aimed primarily at excitement.

In special ways, Buñuel's and Bergman's films are exciting. *The Discreet Charm* has some good comic premises, titillating shocks, and beautiful women wearing lovely gowns; Bergman's film is visually ravishing, dramatically sensational, and its women are even better to look at. The Buñuel also lays claim to being a serious, although comically articulated, comment on the middle class, while the Bergman purports to treat human isolation. In this, each film is pretentious.

The Discreet Charm commences as a plausible lampoon. A smartly dressed couple, the wife's sister, and their ambassador friend arrive for dinner at the house of a third couple. As might well occur, they have come a night too soon; but being urbane as well as pleasure loving, they cover their embarrassment and assuage their disappointment by insisting that the hostess accompany them to an inn. Their refusal to wait until she changes into street clothes believably marks them as oversophisticated, as does the condescension with which they choose a meal (finding the inn unfashionable, inexpensive and empty of customers, they fear that the food will be contaminated). While the men are ordering, the women wander off to a nearby room, where they discover a funeral being held for the previous owner, who had died that afternoon. This surprise is amusing but barely credible; since it comments on the greed of merchants rather than on the privileged class (the new manager explains that this restaurant is always *à service*), it is irrelevant to the film's announced subject. Henceforth, credibility and relevance fade away.

Midway in the film, a lieutenant, who has been staring at the three women from a distant table at a café, comes over, asks if they had a happy childhood, and, without further ado, recounts his own. The following memory scene, since it includes ghosts, is acceptable only as fantasy. Later, the interrupted meals that give the film a narrative motif are ever more bizarrely managed. In one, another soldier gratuitously describes a dream. Subsequent scenes turn out to be dreams by a given character or by one character about another who is also dreaming. The whole film eventually disclaims realistic status through intercuts of the six characters walking aimlessly on a road—a device that presumably symbolizes the bourgeois aimlessness of which prior scenes are the symptoms.

Buñuel's gradual erosion of reality is itself aimless, however. The dreamlike arbitrariness cannot imply, as one might suppose, that middle-class reality is as senseless as a dream. For that point to be made, Buñuel would first have to convince us that he is presenting middle-class life accurately and only exposing its fundamental illogic. Instead, the film's absurdity is Buñuel's style, not an inference about the middle class; the gradual erosion of reality is only an excuse for the preposterousness of the film's details. A true absurdist like Ionesco distorts reality to uncover some underlying truth; Buñuel, on the other hand, denies reality so as to buffer us against the pain of taking anything he shows as a judgment. This, I think, explains why middle-class moviegoers find so charming a film that consists of unrelieved and irresponsible slander against them. Since it is all a fantasy, why worry?

Critics, on the other hand, have taken the film seriously. The male half of the film's three principal couples deals in cocaine; one of the husbands easily leaves his wife in the apartment of the ambassador after discovering that she had been hiding in the man's bedroom; neither fact is a likely representation of middle-class behavior, yet the film is called an incisive satire. Many of the details aren't even this plausible. For example, the ambassador, on discovering a terrorist pretending to sell stuffed animals outside his window, obtains a carbine and shoots one; and a café, established as existing in the real world and not in a dream, runs out of both coffee and tea. Neither surprise has the remotest relationship to satire, but both induce a laugh that greets the unexpected.

The Discreet Charm is little more than a succession of switcheroos, some of which are not only unexpected but contradictory. A scene in which the original host and hostess insist on making love despite their maid's announcement of luncheon guests suggests a vitality, impulsiveness and disdain for social forms that are exactly contrary to the traits elsewhere ascribed to the middle class. In another scene, when an army invades the couple's dinner party and begins smoking pot, one of the three female protagonists, on learning that pot is also favored by Americans in Vietnam, steps out of character to raise the cogent objection that as a result they bomb their own troops.

But, of course, this disorderly and opportunistic little film has no consistent characters, just as it has no consistent meaning. The repeatedly interrupted dinner party lends a specious air of unity, but this plot device does not support the implication that the middle class is successfully rapacious. Several elements in the film don't even seem to belong to that subject. For instance, Buñuel introduces the character of a bishop whose parents were killed by the family gardener. For no apparent reason, the bishop applies for such a post at the house of one of the couples and is later, coincidentally, asked to confess the dying murderer. This he does, only to turn around and shoot the man. Such a sequence we owe not to the film's announced subject but to Buñuel's obsessive anticlericalism. Similarly, the long subplot about the mythical dictatorship of Miranda is not an attack against the bourgeoisie but rather, with embarrassing circumspection, a sidelong gibe at Buñuel's native Spain. As if in recognition that he had stopped dramatizing his announced subject long before the film's conclusion, Buñuel resorts to flat-out assertions in the last scene, where, for example, one of the guests reports that the traffic through which they hurried to reach their meal forced them to run over about 150 cyclists.

Half the film is neither satire nor farce. The lieutenant's memory scene, in which his dead mother advises him to murder the father who'd killed his true sire, would be horrifying were Buñuel not as inept at picturing corpses as he is fond of devising irrelevant occasions for doing so. Similarly horrific—at least by intention—is a scene in which the French police torture a suspect by placing him in a wired piano where his writhings draw music

from the strings and—in a final Buñuelian touch—red cockroaches that fall on the keys as a substitute for blood.

These scenes, oddly neglected in the ecstatic notices for Buñuel's
"comedy," are disjunctive in meaning as well as effect. The
lieutenant's dream is slightly relevant since it ends with his
assertion that the crime was never punished and so supports the
presentation of a blithely criminal middle class. Even so, it goes
on too long, and when we hear the second soldier's dream, we
understand that both episodes contribute not to Buñuel's satire of
the bourgeoisie but to his preeningly outrageous disdain for
motherhood (the lieutenant's mother makes him a murderer and
the soldier's mother frustrates the longing that she had gratuitously inspired).

Buñuel's film doesn't deserve to be called surrealistic because its
dislocation of reality isn't dictated by theme but by narrative
opportunism. Nor is it absurdist, because the details are too silly
and incoherent to be taken as cogently interpretive. Rather *The
Discreet Charm* is yet another sign of Buñuel's commitment to
incongruity. For people in search of titillating diversion from
their daily lives, switcheroos may seem exciting; but such trifling
doesn't deserve to be taken as a reflection of anything significant,
unless—owing to its successful reception—it reflects a middle
class whose most salient fault may turn out to be a tolerance for
insult.

THE DISCREET CHARM OF THE BOURGEOISIE   Raymond Durgnat

. . . .

Four smart people call on a friendly couple for a dinner party and
find they've come on the wrong night. They repair to a restaurant

From *Film Comment* (May-June 1975). Reprinted by permission of the author. The
piece also appears in a shorter form in Durgnat's *Buñuel* (revised and enlarged
edition, University of California Press, 1978).

Buñuel's film doesn't deserve to be called surrealistic because its dislocation of reality isn't dictated by theme but by narrative opportunism. (*The Discreet Charm of the Bourgeoisie*)

and leave because the owner's corpse is laid out in the back of it. A tearoom has been strangely busy and has run out of tea, coffee, milk, and anything except water. One meal is disrupted by a social call by a Colonel and a roomful of soldiers; another by an irascible police-commissioner who arrests everyone; another by the arrival of gangsters who exterminate everyone. . . .

The spectator who prefers easy butts can easily dismiss these characters' commensalist nostalgias as simply some insect-dance, or a deluded and delusive ritual of solidarity, or an essentially egoistic need for reassurance of social acceptability. Yet dinner parties are a residual—and a potentially meaningful—form of potlatch.* And, even if it's hopeless, it's only human to attempt to

---

*Potlatch: a ceremonial feast among Indians living on the Pacific Coast of Washington, British Columbia, and Alaska, at the end of which the host gives valuable material goods to the guests who belong to other kin groups, or destroys property to show that he can afford to do so.

recapture a tribal fraternity by such psychological surrogates as the gang, the clique, the set. Part of the irony is that real needs are denied, and the quest is switched from solidarity to food—seven guests in search of a Host.

Some doubtless hurried critics have implied that Luis Buñuel's *The Discreet Charm of the Bourgeoisie* depicts a *continuous* stretch of time, but such a form would have been pointlessly contrived. The characters certainly eat between meals they miss; and Buñuel has selected only those meals whose bill of fare—or circumstances, or relationships with dream, love, or business— illustrates how a round of dinner parties can do as little to preserve their participants from the emptiness which society has sowed within their hearts as communing with nature could do to redeem the Victorian middle class from its materialism. Non-chalance where concern should be has long been a mainspring of Buñuel's method; certainly, here, passages of dialogue evoke Ionesco, the theater of the absurd, and a livelier, less stylized *Marienbad*.

Not that his culinary pilgrims are a band of Sancho Panzas looking for a Don Quixote, or Che Guevara, or Godot, or Lefty, or Haggerty, or even some Jesus-Sade to turn their wine to blood. Buñuel has conspicuously spared them some "typical" vices of their class. There's no structure of mutual betrayal, no conspicu-ous pecking order; their plague is not the Exterminating Angel but the Interrupting One. As a French critic observed of Resnais' *Muriel, "La vie moderne est faite de ruptures."* Distraction, rather than prohibition, is the conspicuous mode of modern repression. Conversely, their personal neuroses can interrupt normal social discourse, but can propose no alternative. Inconsequential whims and mental blanks replace even nostalgic yearning.

The film draws also on another source of mental dilatation. Frederic Vitoux: "November 1970. Luis Buñuel and Jean-Claude Carrière are collaborating for the fifth time, on a scenario which still has to find a title. They enter a restaurant where a table has been reserved for them. The restaurant is almost empty . . . and suddenly the Maître-d'hotel brings them a newspaper and announces solemnly, 'De Gaulle is dead.' Suddenly something clicks, and abruptly they find the title for which they have been seeking."

An alertness to subtle incongruities drives humor as it goads logic—which may be why humor and logic so often seem mutually exclusive options, and yet so often go well enough together to inspire satire. The affinities of Buñuel and Swift are worth a passing thought. Both are theologians *manqués,* both concerned with the thin line between madness and sanity. As Buñuel's *The Milky Way* is to *A Tale of a Tub, Discreet Charm* is to "Genteel and Ingeniose Conversation." Both are tragicomedies of mediocrity, and it's intriguing to imagine what might happen if the hitch-hikers of Buñuel's theological satire were to encounter the hosts and guests of its profane successor.

The *Discreet Charm* scenario identifies the local country as "Miranda," and specifies that military uniforms, auto number plates, etc., will be "indefinite," presumably so that no particular city (country) can be identified. Jacques Perret is probably right in assuming anti-precensorship precautions. In certain scenes, however (notably the seizure of the guerilla girl), a typically Parisian streetplaque is conspicuously visible, and reinforces every spectator's immediate assumption that Parisian-speaking, Parisian-styled actors imply Paris, France. And isn't Paris, France, still, in many ways, the cockpit of Europe, and thus Europe's spiritual capital?

The interplay of ambiguities and incongruities, of trivialities and dreams, permits the film its uniquely allusive style. The rumble of distant artillery is ominous; and the sudden appearance of an army in battle dress may suggest either civil war in our mythical country, or Algerian paras returned to France to roost, or maybe mercenaries going off abroad. But our army is only on maneuvers, and the process of anticlimax continues. The troops' weakness for marijuana recalls the legendary inefficiencies of the American army in Vietnam. Indeed, they also behave like the sensitive, humane army of TV recruiting commercials. And what is more appropriate—since the cultured bourgeoisie quite agrees with Surrealism about the poetic content of dreams—than that this amazing best of all possible armies should tarry to hear a sergeant tell his dreams? Thus the film ironizes over the paradoxes of a peacetime army (and conscription) continuing twenty-eight years after the "last" war. And it also gratifies our Marxist (*tendance* Groucho) anarchism with images of military chaos for which some sort of mythic correlative exists in *M*A*S*H*.

The hilarious idiocy of everyday chitchat is surely not over-played, but merely deprived of its ballast (or roughage) of sense. M. Thévenot recommends a restaurant to his friends. When they find it under new management, he's exasperated into lamenting the impossibility of eating well in restaurants. His companions find the reasonable prices and absence of overcrowding an om-inous combination. The color of the wine determines the choice of dish. The candles, which normally suggests an intimate, indeed aphrodisiac atmosphere, are disquietingly large—almost funereal. And in one of a series of logically impeccable, but subtly absurdist ironies, the *new* owner is newly *dead*, so newly that he's lying on a table in a back room. (There are meats and meat. . . .)

If this is a variant of the old folk joke about the hidden corpse (used by Tati in *Jour De Fête*), it's a new variant on it, for it depends on the incompatibility of bourgeois "business as usual" and bourgeois-peasant respect for death, both of which attract the derisive laughter of the Surrealist and the picaro. First of many deaths, this is the film's only natural one. The association of empty commensalism, of mankind as carnivore, of a well tem-pered cannibalism, hovers over this first supper as well as over the last: the Ambassador crouches on all fours, like an animal, under a table, while one almost autonomous hand—groping, like the beast with five fingers, for the leg of mutton above him—betrays him to his uninvited guests.

The film's structure is a matter much less of allegory than of such association-atmospheres, implications, expectations. We are made to expect that Florence (Bulle Ogier) will turn out to be the anarchist, the rebel, the agent of an at-least-briefly-saving dis-order (like Sylvia Pinal in *The Exterminating Angel*). One shot carefully emphasizes her sullen, desperate, lively face, and its potentialities are emphasized by her status as a semi-outsider, her willfulness (snatching a bouquet), her tipsiness (apparently chronic), her unsentimental indifference to the corpse's presence (like that of Buñuel's Young One). Our expectations are further aroused by Bulle Ogier's previous roles, by the frail, sad, mu-tinous insolence which has such meaning for Women's Lib; her name is one of those litanized in Monique Wittig's *Les Guerillères*.

But all these possibilities fritter away in her mixture of alcoholic befuddlement and vague illogic. Directly after the company has got the maid's age wrong by thirty years, Florence enquires the date of the Ambassador's birthday. The Zodiac character reading to which she then treats him hilariously whitewashes his "well-adjusted" mixture of paranoia and megalomania, except that it suddenly switches into what would be very good advice if she took it herself: "Your sensitivity harmonizes with your humanitarian conscience. But if you wish to rise above commonplace ideas, you must replace them by a personal morality." Failing which, she remains at least as forlorn as the Symbolist girl in the street in *Un Chien Andalou*, who was partially liberated (for, though she is fastidious, she is also unsqueamishly fascinated by human meat), but can go no further than a dead hand, and a death wish of which Florence's heavy drinking is a more respectable, gradual counterpart.

The Sénéchals (Jean-Pierre Cassel and Stéphane Audran) represent the bourgeoisie at its most youthful, flexible and engaging. But they take everything for granted, including a lighthearted skepticism, and remain rigidly within its limitations. They too begin by going through the motions of spiritual emancipation, and rush off into the shrubbery for a quick copulation before their guests arrive—much as a heroin addict might flee to the john for a fix, and maybe for much the same reason. Sexuality can be short-circuited into a tranquilizer quite as effective as, albeit more cumbersome than (to quote M. Thévenot) a dry martini.

The Thévenots (Paul Frankeur and Delphine Seyrig) are a few years older. Less capricious, more dignified, companionable rather than passionate, they are what the Sénéchals will become. They may seem the most colorless and stable of the group; in fact, they are the champions of the conversational *volte-face*, of inconspicuous disorder, of confusion of appetite. Just when they glimpse a reality that demands emotional authenticity, they retire into a tactful imperceptiveness that is similar to Sartre's idea of "bad faith." Madame Thévenot's affair with the Ambassador has nothing to do with passion, or even with modern permissiveness. It resembles elegant adultery in the style of *La Ronde*, although its elegance is undermined by something obstinately natural, realistic, and physical—a disfiguring skin rash which may or may not be psychosomatic.

Madame is very sensitive about it; with her hypocrisy goes shame. And M. Thévenot, rather than face a fact which would require (or allow) for some sort of decision (or resolution), and because he's too ashamed to confess that he doesn't know what a "sourcique" is, allows his suspicions to be quickly lulled, thus allowing his wife and her lover time for another high-speed coupling. We suspect that the Ambassador has invented the word *sourcique*, which suggests *sourire, sarcastique, sourcil* (raised eyebrow?): the mocking laughter which the bourgeois fears so much, particularly when confronted by the aristocracy. Indeed, Thévenot so fears the Ambassador that he dreams he *is* the Ambassador; to be precise, the Ambassador dreaming of a reception where everyone so insults him that he loses his diplomatic cool and outrages every canon of respectable violence—he shoots the Colonel almost without warning and almost in the back. But Thévenot is the man the Ambassador is cuckolding; and Thévenot ought, by the Mirandan code, to have challenged the Ambassador to a duel. In such ways, the film scrupulously observes Freudian theories of dream as wish fulfillment.

In status, in style, in age, in cunning and in self-assurance, the Ambassador (Fernando Rey) marks the apex of the little group. He is the least confused and the most violent. (In Buñuel, the two characteristics often go together.) His apparent mixture of paranoia and megalomania fits reality surprisingly well. His friends think he's mad when he levels his rifle at a street vendor's furry toy. But he was right: its seller *was* spying on him. His mental deviousness appears in largely triumphant forms, as in his cat-and-mouse game with the too-innocent, too-honorable and, to judge from her friend's car, too-bourgeois assassin (although she compares very favorably with another young apostle of violence). The Ambassador is not the victim of his own hypocrisy. Thus, after a complex game of gallantry, seduction, and superiority, he delivers the girl to a couple of heavies. Many critics have understood them to be the plainclothes police, although the implication that the French police may extradite her into the hands of their Mirandan colleagues, for Brazilian-style torture, may be mistaken. Perhaps they are simply Mirandan agents, operating with or without the tacit consent of the French authorities.

In his nightmare, the Ambassador suffers from a very animal passion: hunger. For, as the Marseilles gang guns his fellow-guests down, he permits his hand to stray upwards for a leg of lamb, as his prudence is overwhelmed by the combination of physical hunger, spirituality (overconfidence), and professional deformity (diplomatic immunity). The gangsters are described as our friends' rivals in the heroin business. If they prevail against the Ambassador it is partly because they, like him, are outside the law—although below it rather than above it—and because their ferocity is undiluted even by his dissimulation. The film's progression to this climax generates premonitions that some apocalypse is in the offing for this coterie, and for the style it represents; but it turns out that the return of the repressed has been indefinitely postponed—for lack of interest?—and the dreamer awakens to raid the fridge for a midnight snack.

The Ambassador's closest rival, in deviousness and in immunity, is of his generation also. The very phrase "worker-bishop" is an oxymoron, and possesses a plenitude of ironies. "Workers" classifies bishops (and priests) with the unproductive, the parasitical; while "bishop" obstinately asserts hierarchy while parading a climax of democratization. We may remember how effectively the hierarchy crushed the worker-priest movement about twenty years ago. Now this bishop (Julien Bertheau) applies for a job as a gardener, in a home exactly like his parents', thus remaining within his own class, which negates the purpose of the worker-priest movement. He acquires avuncular status at his employer's table, accepts a little glass of whiskey "exceptionally" in almost every scene, and secures the union rate—which his predecessor was sacked for demanding. In a film of plot rather than of ruptures, we might have seen him creep as relentlessly back to his dominant status as Tristana's uncle's priests.

The Bishop's earthly toil is little more than a rich amateur's hobby, for which, in the style of rich amateurs, he contrives to get paid. With the patness of a dream, he inquires for the gardener's job just as the Sénéchals have slipped off to commune with nature,

The very phrase "worker-bishop" is an oxymoron, and possesses a plenitude of ironies. "Worker" classifies bishops (and priests) with the unproductive, the parasitical; while "bishop" obstinately asserts hierarchy while parading a climax of democratization. (*The Discreet Charm of the Bourgeoisie*)

belly to belly. The comic possibilities are only too obvious, especially since he whimsically finds his way as far as the toolshed. A few steps more and he'd find his employers-to-be in a situation which, though it isn't illegitimate (since they're bound in holy matrimony), also isn't sinless (since they're enjoying it). The embarrassments of their encounter might generate an intriguing aftermath, which Buñuel sacrifices to a brilliantly devious throwaway: the new gardener respectfully picks a blade of grass off his employer's coat, gardening *that* and suspecting nothing.

Later he is the victim, or beneficiary, of a second piece of split-second timing. Just as he is expounding his ideas for improving the flowerbeds beside the drive (thus completing nature's transformation into a matter of social appearances), the horticultural has perforce to yield to the agricultural: conscience bids him rush off to a farm to hear a dying man's confession. The farmer turns out to have been the Bishop's parents' ex-gardener, whose "devotion" would seem to have influenced the Bishop's choice of lay vocation. Now, dying, he confesses that he hated his employers, who made him work too hard, and poisoned them. The Bishop, with uncanny objectivity, gives the farmer absolution—and only then, it seems, has the idea of picking up a handy shotgun and blasting the farmer's head off.

Perhaps the act resulted from a rage which, crystallizing more slowly than the impersonal reflexes of duty, only slowly penetrated the crust of mechanical forgiveness which is *his* professional deformity. Perhaps it's absurdist, resulting from the coincidence of an otherwise *insufficient* rage with the sight of a shotgun. But however one psychologizes this moment (and it would surely be unnatural to feel no curiosity about what's going on in the Bishop's mind at this point), Buñuel's external approach and the Bishop's impassivity make the murder look almost as matter-of-fact as any weeding process. Perhaps it implies the apogee of "otherworldliness"—a mixture of somnambulist's calm and madman's deliberation.

The insanity resides not in the revenge but in the lack of passionate expression, and the Bishop's calm complacency, even after the act of murder, isn't at all illogical. For he can be pretty sure of absolution in his turn, his being the most filial of *crimes passionels*. And he can also evince the fatalism of a peasant observing the code of the peasant feud—although, of course, he is a peasant only by virtue of his surroundings and, maybe, of the church's oft-proclaimed affinity with those who work the soil and follow its conservative code of *"famille, travail, patrie"*. At any rate, the farms where food is grown get him to the nitty-gritty quicker than the ornamental suburban gardens.[1]

---

[1] From *L'Age d'Or* we may remember the gamekeeper shooting his son in park land while the lovers vainly seek fulfillment in the shrubbery. Vegetation imagery is reiterated as a hanging flower-pot intensifies the hero's mental strain. He comes closest to happiness in the mud, and again, later, in the garden, with its broad pathways and its statues. The Sénéchals' manicured garden may resemble that one, but it comes nearer the desert than the mud, or than the jungle luxuriance of other Buñuel settings for passionate fulfillment: *Mexican Bus Ride* and *La Mort Dans ce Jardin*, where the "garden" of the title is a jungle. *L'Age d'Or* begins in mud and

The fact that the victim is a dying man anyway both mitigates the crime and aggravates it, renders the revenge both more unrelenting and more petty. These contradictions add their gruesomely comic tensions to the scene. The act of vengeance might be *redemptively* passionate, and one would certainly expect it of a magnificently "black," Buñuelian romantic hero like Heathcliff. (Buñuel's 1953 film, *Cumbres Borrascosas*, is an adaptation of *Wuthering Heights*.) But the Bishop remains conspicuously unchanged, unliberated by it. Perhaps he has briefly become the victim of confusion of codes (clerical vs. peasant); perhaps his revenge represents not a moral emancipation but the filial-Oedipal maintenance of a falsely idealized childhood home.[2] If he becomes briefly free from the tyranny of legalism ("Vengeance is mine," saith the State), he complacently returns to it. Still, "A little revenge is more human than no revenge"—so Nietzsche.

---

ends in snow. One might hazard the continuity; jungle-warm mud-garden-desert-stone-snow.

Where stone-and-shrubs gives way to park land, a gamekeeper kills his son. Where a manicured garden gives way to a farmyard, a gardener kills the gardener who killed his parents. To note this similarity isn't to suggest a rigid meaning for the garden-desert antimony. The setting is only one of many factors in the scene. For this reason, the degree of desert is not a direct index to the degree of spiritual sterility represented by the action. All the other aspects of the scene have their part to play. In the same way, the Bishop is more than just a variation on the theme of "Bishop." Not only does the very idea of a variable theme suggest internal counter-tendencies, but the variations may arise by borrowing from other themes. Thus the Bishop's residual ability to wreak a point-of-death revenge is a point in common with Jesus-Blangis, who is generally considered as a transformation of the rebellious hero in *L'Age d'Or*, and this Bishop's action is certainly more heroic than anything achieved by the bishop skeletons on the rocks of the island of the Golden Age. A structuralist analysis of an author's schematic can't remain content with single antimonies, but must cope with the existence of mosaics (many themes intertwining, yet constantly transforming themselves by lending aspects to one another). In a tightly constructed film like this, each scene represents an unstable equilibrium between several tensions, and the sequence of scenes will arise from constantly changing permutations of the same basic elements or "particles." Thought isn't just a "bisociation" of two themes, but a continuous reorganization of the multiple aspects of its themes.

[2] As so often, the apparent absurdities of Buñuel's films have real-life counterparts. For many years Lord Reith, the John Grierson of the BBC, carried in his pocket a wrench with which he intended to kill the hit-and-run driver who had killed his father. Had Lord Reith met that man, how much would his behavior have differed from the Bishop's? I take it, incidentally, that the Bishop's status guarantees his immunity from circumstantial evidence. Or that, to avoid a scandal, the police would classify the crime as "unsolved." Or, at least, that the Bishop thinks this.

To indicate the range of possible attitudes, let's imagine that a similar situation had befallen Buñuel's Archibaldo de la Cruz, *after* his liberation from the musical box and its repetition-compulsion. I can imagine that Archibaldo would pick up the gun, leave chance to decide whether it's loaded or empty, pull the trigger, and, smiling ironically at the "click," return it to its place. This acceptance of chance would imply a proper disrespect for all possible codes and taboos, and indicate a nihilism from whose vantage-point an acceptance of the entire personality and a new, more human, "Surrealist" morality become possible.

The Bishop's filial revenge climaxes a trio of episodes centering on the theme of dead parents. All originate from traditionally monosexual groups (the clergy, the army)—as if, in this debilitated world, the transcendence of the natural order is abandoned, by marital complacency, to conclaves of deprivation and reaction from which, alas, it can't break free. On the one hand, the Surrealist must seek liberation from the pious emotions conventionally associated with the (bourgeois) family and the (Christian) afterlife; the two converge in the idea of God the father, the sacrificed Son, and the Virgin Mother. But, on the other hand, all "primitive" people believe in ghosts, especially those of their ancestors; and the Surrealist may well wish to retain the freedom to "hallucinate" the afterlife of the dead, or some transcendence of separation in time. Similarly, however universal or local the Oedipus complex may be felt to be, the Surrealist will wish to defend both the existence and the legitimacy of incestuous emotions against the taboos under which they labor. Certainly the Oedipal triangle offers a handy schema for the complex weave of desire, taboo, and death. And the three dreams in *Discreet Charm* offer three solutions—or dissolutions—of its Gordian Knot.

I. The Bishop, who is desexualized, always speaks of his parents as a pair. His choice of job, and the outrageous speed with which he adopts a gardener's robes (or at least apron), suggest a childhood identification with an idealized servant.[3] The Bishop's murderous yet glib reaction to disillusionment suggests an only-too-effective

---

[3]A servant as father-figure is as easily understandable as, in England, Nanny and mother-figure. Another convenient analogy exists in the Ronald Neame film called, patly, *The Spanish Gardener.*

sublimation of his own rivalry with his father. Here, a murder by *poisoning* provokes a murder by *shooting*.

II. The Lieutenant's dream shows a far less complete, far more tortuous, pattern of repressions. As a child, he was instructed by his mother's ghost to poison her husband, who, in a duel, has just killed her lover (another lieutenant and the boy's real father). The situation contrasts two conceptions of the family: the husband's (bourgeois-feudal, based on appearances and honor) and the mother's (extralegal, based on love and biology). This *real* family avenges itself but cannot reconstitute itself. And the Lieutenant with the sad, romantic eyes is left, helplessly, dependent on three bourgeois women who don't know what to say to him because the current dissolution of codes makes comment almost impossible. His dream leads nowhere. Here, a killing by *shooting* provokes a murder by *poisoning*.

III. In his dream the Sergeant meets a lost love (who once repulsed him, but now seeks him), and two old friends. In his attachment to his equals and his peers, in a street which is like an indefinite space, the dream comes closest to that image of tentative camaraderie which crowns Buñuel's *Cela s'Appelle l'Aurore*. The atmosphere is that of limbo; at any moment we expect the dreamer to be told that his girl, his friends, and he himself are dead. Instead, he leaves her to search for his friends. His concern for them is preceded by a cutaway to a corpse topped by a crucifix—as if to signify that this emotion is "Christian" (that is, insufficiently animal), and that, if he were worthy of *l'amour fou*, he would have no thought to spare for them and wouldn't abandon the search for his beloved even for a moment. This "Christ-like" solidarity, going with the meekness of the Sergeant's style, is as distractive as the call from the Minister of the Interior in *L'Age d'Or*, and only superficially like the lucid and ferocious solidarity of the Doctor in *Cela s'Appelle l'Aurore*. When the Sergeant returns from a labyrinth of shops-like-a-church (the ecclesiastico-capitalist complex), he is alone, and he is calling, not for his girlfriend, but for his mother, as if a confused repression were underway.

At least, in this dream, any father-figure is present in the much less authoritarian guise of "mates." But, coming and going in this maze, they haven't the solidarity of "comrades," and they provoke him to a futile detour. In this dream, all hostility is softened, although the girl's calm confirmation of her earlier indifference may evoke the indifference of the young mother to her son in *Los Olvidados*. Is the Sergeant's absence of reproach exemplary? Or is it a hint of a certain weakness? The equal and opposite excess, an impotent fury with the beloved, leads only to an alternative impasse, the love-hate hallucination of *Wuthering Heights*.

Although the dream can thus be moralized, roughly in terms of the ethic of *Cela s'Appelle l'Aurore*, one can't dismiss the more troubling overtones in the evasion of fraternal abrasiveness, of potential rivalries for one woman. While this evasion is of a piece with the dreamer's rank, it also avoids a real crux, just as Surrealist moralizing tended to be romantic rather than realistic, and although it raised the issues it didn't adequately discuss the inevitable conflicts involving *l'amour fou*, revolutionary solidarity, and jealousy vs. fraternity. The Sergeant's rank suggests a lower-class origin. His dream comes nearest to being a non-hierarchical. Perhaps that's why, of the "parental" dreamers, the Sergeant is the least clearly distinguished from his surroundings, and from the mass of soldiers who are his false friends. Almost free, yet just as lost, he remains part of the machine, to the point of securing promotion within it.[4]

The trio of masculine-world dreamers about parental deaths becomes a quartet if we include father-figures and so admit the legend-cum-dream of the Bleeding Brigadier (a lay counterpart of the Bleeding Nun). The zealous excesses of this ferocious cop have regularly sabotaged the police's attempts to be well loved by the public, and his ghost now atones for his dysfunctional severity by releasing all the prisoners in the jail, once a year, on the 14th of June. The date may suggest the 14th of July, famous for dancing in the streets and as a fiesta of national reconciliation. (In a very

---

[4]Maneuvers leave no time for him to tell his second dream, that of "the train." Addicts of micro-symbols may surmise that the train is a social collective which can't quite go off the rails, or at least, not for long—although a streetcar enjoys a stealthy vagabondage in an earlier Buñuel comedy, and the village omnibus of *Mexican Bus Ride* wreaks its picaro-anarchic ravages with the company timetable. Ideally, perhaps, the Sergeant's train would have cut loose and sliced neatly through a bourgeois household, where a reception would be in progress, proving as splendidly omni-and auto-destructive as that in The Marx Brothers' *Go West*.

interesting review of the film, Irving Louis Horowitz does in fact substitute "July 14" for the script's "June 14".)

During the Brigadier's lifetime, his hatred was turned against the agent of another kind of street liberation, a demonstrating student. Our first associations—provided by his long hair, and by the freshness of our memory—will be with the events of Paris in May 1968 (to which Buñuel paid a graceful, but not optimistic, tribute in *The Milky Way*). But Buñuel's memory is long, and he acidly evades any sentimentality about students as a class being the vanguard of the proletariat, or the spearhead of spontaneous uprising, or the conscience of the country. This one behaves like a saintly martyr—idiotically—and the dialogue leaves the possibility that his crime is in fact terror-bombing *à la* OAS (a right-wing colonialist terrorism in which schoolboys and students were extensively involved).

Not that the police come out of things well. Although the police elaborately make a scapegoat of the ferocious Brigadier, the policemen under his command show no reluctance at all to obey his orders, and indeed it is they who maintain the theme of parenthood: they threaten the student's genitals, while tauntingly enquiring if he has a girlfriend, and discussing a colleague's wife's pregnancy.

They lay their victim on an electrified piano, like the dead donkeys of *Un Chien Andalou* (but in a prone position like the priests); his screams may recall the amplified Jesuit orchestra in *L'Age d'Or*. One may reasonably free-associate in several directions: backward in musical styles to the Bourgeois Concerto (music, being the most abstract and rarefied of the arts, is nothing but the beautified anguish of sublimation—repression); sideways to the electric-organ music of St. Simon's New York; and forward to the death-by-pleasure-machine in which Vadim's Barbarella (Jane Fonda) is ensheathed, like a Super-Vibrator.

But these *pianos à queue* have "electrified" tails, like scorpions. The ants-in-the-hand recur, as insects scurrying out of the keyboard, played by hands like Tristana's. The script specifies "bees"; electric shocks can feel rather like bee-stings, which is how another donkey dies, in Buñuel's *Las Hurdes (Land Without Bread)*. Most critics, myself included, interpreted the insects as beetles or cockroaches. And though this detail struck some of my colleagues as arbitrary, one would, realistically, expect such a torture-machine to be inhabited by insects which scurry out when disturbed, providing another mode of dream-realism. (That the electrified piano is not a very real idea wouldn't matter; the less real the idea is, the more it needs authentication by physical detail. Siegfried Kracauer's *Theory of Film* is useful here.)

Ginette Gervais, who is honest enough to write about this film with frank disappointment, rather than running for cover behind an indiscriminate approbation of everything Buñuel does, observe that, like most of the film's other "shock-images," this one doesn't work, and looks like an "academic citation." I'm not sure how it would strike the 99.9 percent of the *Discreet Charm* audience who haven't seen *Un Chien Andalou*, but I'm inclined to defend it as a matter of Buñuel's wryly observing that violence now has no *liberating* meaning in a world whose style of hypocrisy has changed, and aiming accordingly at disquiet rather than shock.

The theme of supernatural father-figures undergoes a further modulation, in the "theatrical" dream (apparently M. Sénéchal's). Awaiting their host the Colonel, our friends find a globe, and a hat of Napoleon's worn in battle, which Sénéchal impertinently claps first on his own head and then on the Bishop's. After these sacred relics come the props, the servants bringing chickens which, spilled, bounce on the carpet but are nonetheless served, with a relentless blandness at which the guests hardly dare protest. (We may be reminded of Jan Němec's *Report on the Party and the Guests*, which in some ways is this film's soul sister.) The horrors of a gourmet's Marienbad announce another: one wall rises like a curtain and they realize they are on a stage. By now we are all accustomed to parodies of role-playing in reality—and in reality's unreality—and Buñuel doesn't bother to develop such reflections any further.

It must have been tempting to show our friends exposed, not to *cinéma-vérité*, but to *théatre-vérité;* feeling required to entertain the public (*vox populi, vox dei*) by witty impromptu conversation and panicking at the prospect. Theoretically, this might be the moment in which an enforced exhibitionism reveals, to them or to us, their inner emptiness. And even though this world looks like the world of fashionable theatergoers (the world of people like themselves), the public could function as a kind of alter ego—a vast, unknown monster-mass onto which the hapless actors project their fears (which is, of course, the mechanism of stage fright). But the effect is too easy, and wouldn't prove any inner emptiness—for who wouldn't be startled at being in such a situation? Buñuel prefers absurdity to facile moralizing.

The guests are expected to know their text by heart; and the reference to Don Juan's dining with the Commander's statue brings ghosts, sex, and guilt back into the picture (as well as relating the play to *L'Age d'Or*, whose heroine must suck a statue's toe while her beloved converses with his conscience). The Bishop, being used to obediently reciting things, obediently repeats what the prompter whispers. But as the others hurry off, Sénéchal awakes, just in time to go off for dinner with the Colonel.

Indeed, this dream anticipates the dinner, in strict accordance with the common or textbook rules for anxiety dreams about events scheduled for the following day.

Far from arriving too early, as the dream predicted, they are affably reproached for being too late, but having quit the realms of eternity, it is only to be caught in an experiment with time—for, exactly as predicted by the dream, Napoleon's hat is in evidence, except that this time it's on Florence's head, on whom it sits almost as incongruously as it had on M. Sénéchal's. The Bishop's head fits it well enough, however, and Madame Thévenot observes that it's a "bicorne," which may remind us of a cuckold's horn. (In this respect the unconscious mind of her husband, whose dream this will turn out to be, is more alert than his conscious mind is to her adulterous liaison.)

But, as throughout this pair of dreams the hat goes from head to head, so do the thoughts. This second dream's emphasis (as well as our identification) promptly deserts Sénéchal to follow the Colonel, and as briefly deserts him to finally come to rest with the Mirandan Ambassador, who, suddenly and surprisingly, feels obliged to defend his brave new world against all comers. The Colonel rudely repeats rumors that the Mirandan government tortures students (which the French police will be doing in the next dream). The Ambassador succeeds in defending himself diplomatically enough, and observes that rebels are part of Miranda's folklore—a neat tilt of Che Guevara's functions in student hagiography, which prepares the introduction of the ambivalent, or romantic, or confused student in the dream of the Bleeding Brigadier. In both cases mention of students is followed by references to insects. ("We swat malcontents like flies," says the Ambassador.)

But this diplomatic calvary has scarcely begun. The Bishop gets with his church's evolution by observing that, in Miranda, the rich get richer while the poor get poorer. (If Miranda is beginning to sound like *Las Hurdes*, it's also true that large tracts of South America *are* like *Las Hurdes*.) The Ambassador makes a quick getaway only to come to face with the Colonel's brother-officer whom the script calls "The Commandant," as if to recall the Commander in the play-within-the-other-dream. He accuses Miranda of police corruption, which does sound plausible, since it's an increasingly evident problem in many countries. By now fuming, the Ambassador again encounters the Colonel, who observes that Miranda has the world record for the number of homicides, an accusation which the Ambassador, losing a short, sharp struggle within himself, renders all the more plausible by drawing a revolver and shooting the Colonel three times, a murder which, occurring after second thoughts and a slow burn, pairs with the Bishop's double-take.

It may look like an explosion of rage, a scandalous self-liberation, like the slap in the salon in *L'Age d'Or*. But it's really an atavistic resurgence of an obsolescent code—not, in this case, that of peasant vendettas, but of aristocratic dueling (recalling Don Lope in *Tristana*, or the lieutenant's mother's husband in this film). This skid-around dream eventually locates itself in the head of M. Thévenot, who perhaps because he's the most "anonymous" of our little group, is also the most confused as to which member of it he is. At any rate, the pair of nightmares are complementary: one is a social fiction where almost everyone is struck dumb, the other a social function where almost everyone speaks the truth.

The attribution of dreamer and dream grows wilder as we're plunged into the dream of the police commissioner (Claude Piéplu), who doesn't appear in reality until after he wakes up from it. Contrasting with the Ambassador's paranoia, his is cast in the petit-bourgeois mold. From the furious way in which he both rails against and tramples on the civil rights of his social superiors, he seems animated by either an idealistic moral rage, or a petty bourgeois resentment of the idle rich, or the fantastic notion that rich and poor are equal before the law, or all three. His dream of the bleeding brigadier is another anticipatory anxiety dream, and it comes as true as Napoleon's hat: when he awakes from it, the Minister of the Interior insists he free the Mirandan Ambassor and his friends immediately. The Minister's explanations are drowned by the noise of typing, or airplanes, which exasperates the Commissioner; but they're hardly likely to be true anyway, since the Commissioner's suspicions that our friends are engaged in heroin trafficking are perfectly correct. It's only his style that's paranoid, although his moral rage suggests that he is also paranoid in fact, even though he doesn't suspect his superiors (the Ministers) enough.

Heroin, that apparently esoteric and exotic drug, marks the rendezvous of three themes: food (insofar as it is ingested by the body), complacency (for heroin provokes illusions of detachment, immunity, invulnerability), and politics. In a sense, *Discreet Charm* is a parody-retort to two American accusations of France's moral-political fibre, *Topaz* and *The French Connection*—the first directly inspired by France's refusal to toe to C.I.A.'s Cold War line, the second making France a scapegoat and overlooking the Indochina U.S.A. supply-route. Just to clarify the point, the Minister of the Interior is played by Michel Piccoli, the Communists' mastermind in *Topaz;* and in an earlier speech, some of which was also drowned by passing airplanes, the Ambassador observed that forty kilos of heroin were found on his U.S. counterpart. Elsewhere, a joke about "Quasi-Cola" paraphrases both the familiar French gibe "coca-colonization" and the French winegrowers' contention that one brand of American Cola contained inordinate amounts of an addictive drug.

The train of thought is revived when, just after the Colonel's guests have been offered not wine but (ugh) Cola, the Prompter whispers, "You put us to sleep with a narcotic drug." Not that Buñuel's politics are one-sided, since the Bishop reminds us that, in the First World War, French soldiers were usually issued with wine before being sent over the top, although he puts it in a hilariously garbled form: each soldier was required to drink three liters of wine a day. The reference to deserters which got *Paths of Glory* banned in France is brought to the point of sacrilege with "It's even said that it happened at Verdun." The troops' impenitently smoking marijuana on maneuvers is justified by the American precedent in Vietnam. Madame Thévenot, an amoralist of the old school, hazards that this was probably why the Americans bombed their own troops once a week. But the Colonel, defending not so much marijuana as professional honor among soldiers, feels that if they did that they must have had their reasons—which the Bishop provides, weighing in with rumors about gendarmes shooting deserters by the hundred.

All in all, the film's overtones about the morale of the West are enough to make a drill sergeant weep, while reminding the spectators that the modern military machine is as big a threat to its own soldiers' limbs as any enemy in front. In criticizing France and stressing the need for drugs in war, the Bishop may seem to be adopting a properly Christian line, tending to pacifism and unpatriotic impartiality. But his use of the word *fuyard,* with all its implications of cowardice, reveal him as chauvinistic hawk rather than Christian dove. Doubtless he would have despised German deserters just as much; God, as usual, is on both sides, just to be sure of winning.

Such sequences of rapid, subtle, dizzying dissonances and incongruities—in effect, twists—give the film that hilarious onirism which is also close to the uncertainties and ambivalences of real *or* feigned attitudes in informal, off-the-cuff, oral culture. The themes of food and drugs modulate into that of poisonings, and the film's subtitles might be "You are what you eat" and "You dream what you aren't."

The threats of violence intimated by the military and then the police are consummated with the appearance of the gangsters. Their leader's dyed hair evokes a certain type of muscular homosexual, or maybe the gangsters of bad French films. The abstraction of these "scorpions" suggests that they stand in for a universal tendency in human nature generally, as well as for something particular to the Ambassador (in whose dream they appear). Maybe they're his "Mr. Hyde": the repressed roots of his violence, and of the narcissism suggested in his dandy style. Their ultra-vulgarity makes them the Ambassador's antithesis, his *nightmare* alter ego; and it's just because they're vulgar and brutal that they succeed where the intelligent, dedicated guerrillas failed.

The gangsters have no more idealism than the Ambassador, and don't get caught playing things his way. They're the climax of a series of gate crashers, all from the lower orders. It began with the would-be gardener (who isn't really from the lower orders at all) and includes the chauffeur and the maid. The chauffeur unsuspectingly wishes his patrons good health, not realizing that he's being used as a demonstration of how not to savor a dry martini; this may be why the guests are punished, in their turn, by being exhibited on a theater stage. The maid, assumed to be about twenty years old, turns out to be fifty-two, which may suggest just how time flies with respect to someone who's become part of the furniture and is just as functional. Its sudden temporal jolt, carefully underlined by exact instructions as to cooking time, preludes the climactic disruption of order, and combines the themes of time and heat. A concern with the latter was intimated in Piccoli's concern with central heating in *Belle de Jour* (as if he were a cold-blooded animal); here, the hot-cold game lends a tactile dimension to the sensuousness of taste.

If *Discreet Charm* briefly lends itself to a structural analysis of sensations, it's perhaps by way of a parody of *Teorema;* the Buñuel film constitutes the reverse angle to Pasolini's highly theoretical erotico-political Q.E.D. Buñuel has even amused himself, and us, by concocting a bizarre configuration in which the Ambassador explains overpopulation to Florence by holding a globe up near the fire. Later, far from the fire, he puts his hand on Madame Thévenot's back, during a discussion of the exact glacial temperature at which a dry martini should be savored. This almost constitutes a diagram of the solar system, with the earth near the fire and the outer orbits frozen; Florence's interest in the zodiac adds to the imagery. One can't put it past the man who gave us the anti-Last Supper photographed through a beggar woman's vagina.

While the film is structured on the eccentric orbits which these earthly bodies follow through the outer space of bourgeois politeness, it also includes cutaways to the six principal characters strolling along a country road. Modified by Buñuel from an early version in which they become progressively more exhausted with each shot (and so paraphrase the burial-in-the-sand of *Un Chien Andalou*), these interludes now look more like a "time out," a country walk in which the very blankness of their minds brings the characters as close as they'll ever come to freedom, nature, and unself-consciousness. Not for them the pilgrimage of *The Milky Way*, or the guerrillas' last stand in *L'Age d'Or*.

The ironic distance of the "citation" from *Un Chien Andalou* recurs insofar as Florence is the chief custodian of the imagery of Buñuel's first two films. She keeps worrying about some otherwise inexplicable cyclists, and expresses her revulsion at the ugly hands of a cellist. She's half tipsy throughout—which may recall Buñuel's humorous confessions of dipsomania. Many authors incarnate themselves as women in their work; and both *Un Chien Andalou* and *Viridiana* deal quite freely with transvestisms of various kinds. It's possible to see (though one obviously wouldn't want to impose this view) Florence as a figure of something in Buñuel's *anima* which isn't quite able to break free from a world which nonetheless it can't endure. Perhaps she is Buñuel's auto-caricature—a portrait of the artist had he never exposed himself to Surrealism.

Florence is often placed in a special relationship with the Ambassador. Since Fernando Rey is one of Buñuel's stock company, auteur theory and post-Freudian common sense would converge to suggest that he represents another auto-caricature: an aspect of Buñuel's internalized father-figure, an identification, a rascally sympathy, from which Buñuel derives an inspiration that is at once continuous, critical, and detached.

Obviously, aspects of Buñuel in the film are only fragments of the total pattern of the film; and that, in turn, is only a part of the Buñuel who makes the film. The cellist's hand which horrifies

Florence (provoking nausea and evasion, but not revolt) antic-ipates the torture-pianos. But perhaps its closest recall is the Ambassador's hand, slyly creeping up for the meat, and betraying him to the gangsters whose brutal directness is all the guerrilla girl lacked. The deftness of figures is also prominent in testing the heroin, and in the Colonel's preparation of marijuana. So we're probably right to be reminded of similar gestures in earlier films and of their Freudian associations with masturbation—including pure thought, or all futile activities. Either way, they're a psychic surrogate for touching reality—or for clenching into a fist.

Such theme-images are far from being merely personal fetishes. Everything suggests that Buñuel, in one way or another, has an exceptionally easy access to (and knows the importance of) hyp-nogogic mental strata which most of us are too busy, materialistic, or incautious to investigate. Far from taking them to an analyst for "cure," he is particularly attentive to their closeness with "ra-tional" conversation, conscious thought, and perception of social reality. Where we systematically choose the socially relevant remark and forget the others, Buñuel's films also follow up the alternatives which (understandably) we don't speak of, but (sui-cidally) forget—thus progressively obliterating a full reality that might help us replace the living death of hypocrisy by a patient, tolerant, ferocious lucidity. The radical opponent of a system, even the Marxist or Surrealist in a "free" society (though films are hardly free), lives under constant mental strain. Especially if he is an intellectual or a filmmaker, he must often—not just in order to live, but in order to say anything—force his mind to appear to function along lines he abhors, and maintain a tactful façade while keeping an alternative value-system clear in his mind. One can't speak of alienation, in the usual sense, since the strain comes precisely from maintaining two contradictory value-systems and personal styles, in his mind and his behavior. This may be why a sense of silent resistance, of mental labyrinths, of precarious communication, is so strong in so many films by Resnais, Marker, Franju, and other veteran left-of-center directors.

At any rate it may explain how Irving Louis Horowitz can determine that in *Discreet Charm* Buñuel at last relents. Horowitz feels that Buñuel shows his erstwhile enemy, the Bishop, a friendly respect for hankering after the simple life: "The exiled genius has at last made his peace with Spain under Franco." Perhaps the Bishop *has* left his Palace for the middle-class garden, like Opus Dei. But surely this film is more of a cry of despair at the survival, for nearly forty years, of the "anachronistic" Franco regime, and of the Fascism which it represents. For despite the Parisian references, Buñuel's nationality, the *Viridiana* affair, and the Ambassador's style, all ensure a diffuse but general atmosphere whereby Miranda is more than Spain or Mexico or some banana republic.

Perhaps the touchstone of the common market bourgeoisie is the survival, at its head or heart, of an elegant Fascism that isn't quite so obsolete as we may easily assume. For seven years, the Greek Colonels repeated Franco's success, and while they ruled there were lively fears of their effectively supporting a Fascist coup in Italy. The Algerian Colonels nearly brought off a coup in France. The film's anachronisms are also a useful warning that reactionary tendencies, far from being spent, may enjoy a rebirth at any moment, and that the exclusion of reality from the dinnertables of the bourgeoisie is a sign of weakness or blindness in what purports to be a liberal, stable, apolitical center.

Horowitz is quite right to sense a personal, Buñuelian anachronism about aspects of the film. No doubt its Ambassador's style is anachronistic when compared with that of, say, the executives of multinational corporations such as I.T.T. Nonetheless the persistence of the older style, in Latin America as in Spain, is indicated by Glauber Rocha's film, *Land in a Trance.* The general line of *Discreet Charm* wouldn't be incompatible with a story in which international connections involving heroin were replaced by international connections involving oil. If the Ambassador (the film's one anachronistic character) is also its most lucid character, its most duplicitous, its most ferocious, and a foreigner, it's because he's the closest to the "gangster-generals" who, at the right moment, might decide to dispense with diplomacy. Diplomat and gangster are Jekyll-and-Hyde, yin and yang, A.C. and D.C. of a world whose liberalization is, as usual, indefinitely postponed.

BUÑUEL'S
BOURGEOISIE

Irving Louis Horowitz

. . . .

The Discreet Charm of the Bourgeoisie might be called a continental version of *Dinner at Eight*, 40 years later. The difference is that the nouveaux riches are no longer nouveaux, but have learned to live within their means and have lost their moral sense in the process. Both films are organized by the dining room. *Dinner at Eight* is concerned with everything that happens before the eating begins, a last fling before the Great Depression impinges its ugly truths on the lives of a still confident middle class. In *The Discreet Charm of the Bourgeoisie*, worries of economic depression have long since yielded to concerns about political revolution, although such concerns are expressed only in nightmares and fantasies. *The Discreet Charm* is, from beginning to end, a dining room farce; every "action" scene takes place around eating. In this way, Luis Buñuel leads us to see the difference between affluence and opulence, wealth and waste.

Buñuel has employed the device of the collective eating scene before. In both *The Exterminating Angel* and *Viridiana*, dining is employed surrealistically, to show the depravity of people by comparing them to the beasts from which Darwin elevated them. In these films, Buñuel's eating scenes tended to be of Hogarthian proportions—ribald as well as revolting. But in *The Discreet Charm*, depravity is given a specific class character: manners intersect with eating to produce a shadow of civility while disguising the absence of its substance. Here the joys of the feast are punctuated by a comedy of errors: missed cues, coming to eat at an associate's house on the wrong day, going to a restaurant and finding a funeral, and experiencing sexual desire at a socially embarrassing moment. But in the end, Hogarth is displaced by Mao. The feast is disrupted by the slaughter of the meat eaters.

From *Society*, Vol. 10, No. 5 (July–August, 1973). Copyright © 1973 by Transaction, Inc. Reprinted by permission of Transaction, Inc.

From Garcia Lorca's *Blood Wedding* to Carlos Fuentes' *Aura,* modern Spanish and Latin American literature has echoed the theme of death as the expiation of private and social guilt. The search for sensual pleasure, while inevitable, is countered by the resolution that only death can bring. The old gardener who had poisoned the bishop's parents is given absolution and the final rites of the Church by the bishop—after which he murders him, despite the fact that the gardener is about to die a natural death. This is necessary, not because the bishop is depraved or seeks revenge, but rather because a violent death is just. No matter what consolations the last rites of the Church may provide in the next world, the biblical laws of this world must be met. And so, every death, real or illusory, factual or fantasized, must be violent to the degree that people in the natural world have sinned.

It is no wonder that Buñuel has an ambiguous relationship to Christianity here, as in every other one of his films. The hypocrisy of the Church, the wickedness of its excesses, the vanities of its ecclesiastical leaders, are again apparent; but here, Buñuel has made peace with his own deep religiosity, his own beliefs in a just and good Providence. The bishop, for all his vanity, is strangely human; he desires a pastoral life and takes joy in wearing the clothing of a gardener and using the sickle of the toiler. "You have heard of the worker-priest movement," he says in seeking the gardener's job from the incredulous bourgeois family. "Well, I represent the worker-bishop movement." The bishop turned gardener still seeks the reward of his ecclesiastical position—deference from others—but he is happier with the inner rewards of returning to the land toiled by his parents. Buñuel does not reconcile his attitudes toward Christianity in this movie because such a pretentious and preposterous aim is not intended. Instead, the agony of the two faces of the Church: opulence and poverty, devotion and defiance, is revealed with a greater sense of compassion and less tendentiousness than in Buñuel's previous films. If Spain under Franco has not yet made its peace with Buñuel, the exiled genius has at least made his peace with Spain under God.

The French critic André Breton has noted in Durkheim-like fashion, that "what is most remarkable about the fantastic is that the fantastic does not exist. Everything is real." Buñuel, true to his earlier work in *Un Chien Andalou* and *L'Age d'Or*, has a few surrealistic pigeons up his sleeve in *The Discreet Charm*. A coffee shop claims to be out of coffee and tea (but does have water). A restaurant conducts a funeral for a deceased owner (but food is being served). At parties, generals pass marijuana to colonels (while ambassadorial drug dealers pontificate over the evils of pot and how it leads to higher evils). A married couple leaves guests waiting downstairs because of a passionate need to fornicate (in their own garden). Couples come to supper on the wrong evening (matching army maneuvers in the French countryside taking place on the wrong day).

What is special about surrealism in the seventies is its subtlety. No longer are temporal and causal time reversals done primarily for shock value. Rather, they illustrate the pretentiousness of bourgeois discretion; the impossibility of reconciling every trifling incongruity into a polite middle-class framework, and the need to try. Here too art and criticism intersect with more telling effect than in previous films. A foremost member of the Spanish "generation of 27" has evolved into a "revolutionist of 72."

Buñuel has produced a masterpiece in film making, the crowning achievement in a career of continuous film innovation. But as in so many of his other films, the tension between artistic entertainment and social energy remains intact. This is exemplified in the dream sequences in which neo-Freudian Oedipal complexes compete with neo-Marxian social messages for attention: the young military officer poisons his father on instructions from his mother (who has been dead six years) after she tells him that his real father (shown in spattered blood) was killed by the imposter father; the prison chief inspector dreams of a police officer who, doing penitence for having been cruel and heartless to young prisoners, returns each July fourteenth (again, spattered with blood) to open the jails in expiation of his crimes. In a final dream, the Ambassador of Miranda (played brilliantly by Fernando Rey) highlights the theme of revenge and death, as bloody carcasses are strewn about in demonstration of the violent end to meaningless lives.

This ambiguity can be understood, if not entirely resolved, by appreciation that this is a Spanish film made in the French language. Its passions and emotions are derived from the soil of

Spain, not the more delicately laced French tradition of *cinéma vérité* as exemplified by Jean Renoir's *Rules of the Game* (with which *The Discreet Charm* invites comparison). Lorca-like themes of repressed love, maternal domination, justice as expressed through violent death, are all symbolized by the constancy of bloodletting (even one of the dream victims of death through poisoning is seen bloodied about the mouth). This evokes the angular violence of Spanish interpersonal history, which more than anywhere else in Europe, was carried over into its political structure. Buñuel's skill is in relieving the tension by having the storytellers react normally to their dreams. Waking up in a cold sweat and downing food becomes a test of being alive. The general relief felt when finding oneself alive and out of the dream world is expressed by a return to bestiality rather than an elevation in humanity.

The dream sequences are of two types: those recited ritualistically by the teller before an audience, in which the teller receives relief and absolution in a thoroughly psychoanalytic manner; and dreams actually experienced and portrayed, not as exhibitionistic releases from tension, but as expressions of that tension. In these latter dreams, social values are most directly expressed as the thoroughgoing frustrations of the police lieutenant with the contradictions of a job that ostensibly ensures law and order, but does so through such lawless devices as torture and castration of political prisoners. The quintessential dream of the ambassador, which in effect is the nightmare of the bourgeoisie itself, is to be brought face to face with reality by being brought to the edge of death by guerrillas and revolutionists who do not understand the limits of bourgeois civility.

The final dream sequence is organically linked to the final eating sequence to form a Gotterdammerung of meaning in death. Political reality and social consciousness impinge on the bourgeois representatives only as a result of fear of violence, that form of seemingly spontaneous violence that can take place at any time and under any circumstances because it is outside the law, outside the norms of polite society. Were it not for such lawlessness, nothing could awaken the bourgeoisie from its torpor. Buñuel is quite clear on this point: the barrel of the gun, not reason, is the source of consciousness—for victim and victimizer alike. But even here, Buñuel adds a distinctive touch: a brilliant dialogue between the ambassador and a guerrilla girl *cum* assassin who is caught by the ambassador. Their conversation is punctuated by the ambassador's effete wave of a handkerchief, signaling that his guards should remove the guerrilla girl and do away with her. So even at the most intimate level, the bourgeoisie is incapable of doing its own killing without the aid of hired assassins. Buñuel's distinction between those who kill for principle and those who buy protection to defend privilege is quite strong. Again, this is a thoroughly Spanish aspect of the film scenario.

The organization of the film into eight eating-dining segments is a brilliant device for moving the viewer from scene to scene with continuity. It also expresses the simple truth that so much of all life, not only bourgeois life, is organized by pedestrian activity. But the film does much more than that: it shows how the bourgeoisie takes questions of eating and drinking (how to prepare a martini, in what sort of glass, and at what speed to drink it) as the essence of life itself. Good housekeeping relates not just to their life-style, but permeates the substance of their existence. Table conversation is taken up with matters of food, and when it drifts from this omnipotent subject it either leads to astrological banalities of a most hilarious nature or to discussions of certain minor embarrassments that occur in Miranda (hunger, torture, harboring Nazi war criminals) which call forth even more incredible banalities ("One should not exaggerate the number of Nazis in Miranda, they are to be found everywhere. . . . I have spoken to the Nazi you mention; the word butcher is far too strong; he is a quite civilized sort.") In effect, politics itself is bad manners. Reality at the dinner table is in poor taste. And that, after all, is what the discreet charm of the bourgeoisie is all about.

The film takes place in a political vacuum; we are in the midst of the private lives of a diplomat and his entourage. The one thing the diplomat seems incapable of rendering is a political judgment or a sober thought on worldly affairs. Even in describing his own country, he can only sound like he is conducting a travelogue. His nation becomes some sort of grotesque admixture of Argentina, Uruguay and Chile, called Miranda—simply a delightful place for his business associate (the business is heroin traffic) to visit. The word "bourgeoisie" is thus linked to business and commerce as well as manners and mores—the huge, illegal trafficking in heroin, under the cloak of diplomatic immunity, underwrites the entrepreneurial spirit of three families of friends, lovers, pushers and dipsomaniacs. The wonderful thing is that Buñuel is able to make all of these strange goings-on happen in a value-neutral, morally irrelevant context.

The shocking coming to true consciousness for the bourgeoisie is the scene towards the end of the film where the diplomat dreams

The word "bourgeoisie" is thus linked to business and commerce as well as manners and mores - the huge, illegal trafficking in heroin, under the cloak of diplomatic immunity, underwrites the entrepreneurial spirit of three families of friends, lovers, pushers and dipsomaniacs. (*The Discreet Charm of the Bourgeoisie*)

of his dinner being invaded by guerrillas who, in revenge for a quite real hygienic murder of a would-be female assassin, wipe out the dinner guests in a bloodbath—while the diplomat hero hides under the table from where he attempts to sneak his unfinished dinner. He awakens from the nightmare as the guerrillas take aim at him. In a scene reminiscent of *The Loved One*, the ambassador is caught in the act of raiding the refrigerator just after the dreamed blood bath.

The "message," sometimes obscured by the levity of the dinner proceedings, is nonetheless permitted to surface in key dialogues between the young female guerrilla and the old diplomat. For only when he is confronted by the force of weapons, or better, by the threat of annihilation, does reality intrude upon the discreet charms of the bourgeoisie. There is no responsiveness to the sufferings of the poor, no sensitivity to the needs of this quasi-mythic Latin American country he presumably serves. The purpose of guerrillas in the film, and no doubt for Buñuel in reality, is to bring some sort of reality to bear on the culinary proceedings. Without the guerrillas, the life of the diplomatic corps would be simply a round of parties and dining engagements. It is precisely this goal that the guerrillas frustrate in reality and in the dream sequences. The bourgeoisie lack a consciousness, but retain a capacity to react to the destructive aims of their adversaries. They do not think through causative sequences, but try to rid themselves of nuisances which would disturb the delicately woven patterns of self-deception that substitutes manners for morals and elevates style to substance.

One serious problem with *The Discreet Charm* is whether the portrayal is typical or stereotypical—a true representation of the bourgeois cum diplomat or a false representation based on a radical chic of a deracinated European consciousness. This is not an unimportant distinction, since so much hinges upon the accuracy of the portrayal. And it is at this point that the plot of this plotless film dissolves. Is the diplomatic corps, above the third attaché level at least, composed simply of swindlers, gourmets and transparent fools? I suspect not. Indeed, the time has long since passed when diplomacy was organically linked to the manners of the European bourgeoisie. Diplomacy has become mechanized, coldly efficient, part of the scientific determination of national interests in a war-gaming universe. Ironically, the diplomatic corps, like its bureaucratic counterparts elsewhere, remains strangely indifferent to real politics, very much linked to a hygienic view of national realities and moral imperatives.

Buñuel's genius as expressed in *The Discreet Charm* is something of a period piece, more a reflection of a time of his youth rather than the present universe of nuclear fear and trembling. Latin America is simply no longer a place of reactionary banana republics harboring fugitives and fascists from justice; nor are its embassies passive recipients of the glories of French cuisine. It is not that Buñuel is unaware of such changes, but that he seems unsure how to give such change expression. The coldly mechanical and methodical bureaucratic reality of the bourgeoisie (certainly the diplomatic variety) is only partially captured by Buñuel. In this respect, the film should be judged for its metaphorical aims rather than on empirical terms. Luis Buñuel himself would probably rest content with that.

A Buñuel Filmography

. . . .

Un Chien Andalou (1928) (France)
> Produced, written, and directed by Buñuel and Salvador Dali. Photographed by Albert Dubergen. Decor by Schilzneck. Edited by Buñuel. Music by Beethoven and Wagner, plus a tango. With Pierre Batcheff (Cyclist), Simone Mareuil (Girl), Jaime Miravilles, Salvador Dali (Priest), Luis Buñuel (Man with Razor). 24 minutes.

L'Age d'Or (1930) (France)
> Produced by the Vicomte de Noailles. Written by Buñuel and Salvador Dali. Decor by Schilzneck. Edited by Buñuel. Music by Georges van Parys, Beethoven, Wagner, Mendelssohn and Debussy. With Gaston Modot (Man), Lya Lys (Woman), Max Ernst (Leader of the Bandits), Pierre Prevert (Péman, a Bandit), José Artigas, Jacques Brunius, Caridad de Lamberdesque. 60 minutes.

Las Hurdes (Land Without Bread) (1932) (Spain)
> Produced by Ramon Acin. Commentary by Pierre Unik. Photographed by Eli Lotar. Assistants: Pierre Unik and Sanchez Ventura. Music: Brahms. Edited by Buñuel. 27 minutes.

Films made in Spain on which Buñuel was executive producer:
Don Quintin El Amargao (1935)

La Hija de Juan Simon (1935)

Quien Me Quiere Mi? (1936)

Centinela! Alerta! (1936)

Contributions to: *España Leal en Armes* (1937)

Supervision of: *Espagne 39* (France)

Gran Casino (1947) (Mexico)
> Produced by Anahuac (Oscar Dancigers). Screenplay from a novel by Michel Weber. Adapted by Mauricio Magdaleno. Dialogue by Javier Mateos. Decor by Javier Torres Torija. Music by Manuel Esperon. Edited by Glora Schoemann. Photographed by Jack Draper. With Libertad Lamarque (Mercedes Irigoyen), Jorge Negrete (Gerardo Ramirez), Mercedes Barba, Agustin Insunza, Julio Villareal, Charles Rooner. 85 minutes.

El Gran Calavera (1949) (Mexico)
> Produced by Ultramar Films (Oscar Dancigers). Script by Raquel Rojas and Luis Alcoriza from a comedy by Adolfo Torrado. Decor by Luis Moya and

Darío Cabanas. Photographed by Ezequiel Carrasco. Music by Manuel Esperon. With Fernando Soler (Don Ramiro), Charito Granados, Rubén Rojo, Andres Soler, Maruja Grifell, Gustavo Rojas, Luis Alcoriza. 90 minutes.

Los Olvidados (1950) (Mexico)

Produced by Ultramar Films (Oscar Dancigers). Script by Buñuel and Luis Alcoriza. Photographed by Gabriel Figueroa. Decor by Edward Fitzgerald. Edited by Carlos Savage. Music by Rodolfo Halffter from themes by Gustavo Pittaluga. With Alfonso Mejía (Pedro), Roberto Cobo (Jaibo), Estela Inda (Pedro's mother), Miguel Inclán (the blind man), Hector Lopez Portillo, Salvador Quiros, Victor Manuel Mendoza, Alma Delia Fuentes (Meche). 88 minutes.

Susana (1951) (Mexico)

Produced by Internacional Cinematográfica (Oscar Dancigers). Script by Jaime Salvador from a novel by Manuel Reachi. Photographed by José Ortiz Ramos. Decor by Gunter Gerzso. Music by Raul Lavista. With Rosita Quintana (Susana), Fernando Soler (Guadalupe, the Father), Victor Manuel Mendoza (Jesús, the Ranchero), Matilde Paláu (Doña Carmen, the Mother). 82 minutes.

La Hija del Engaño (1951) (Mexico)

Produced by Ultramar Films (Oscar Dancigers). Script by Raquel Rojas and Luis Alcoriza from a story by Carlos Arniches. Photographed by José Ortiz Ramos. Decor by Edward Fitzgerald. Music by Manuel Esperon. With Fernando Soler (Don Quintín), Alicia Caro, Rubén Rojo, Nacho Contra, Fernando Soto, Lily Aclemar. 80 minutes.

Una Mujer Sin Amor (1951) (Mexico)

Produced by Internacional Cinematográfica (Oscar Dancigers). Script by Jaime Salvador, from *Pierre et Jean* by Guy de Maupassant. Photographed by Raúl Martínez Solares. Music by Raúl Lavista. With Rosario Granados, Julio Villareal, Tito Junco, Joaquín Cordero.

Subida Al Cielo (1951) (Mexico)

An Isla Production, written and produced by Manuel Altolaguirre. Photographed by Alex Phillips. Decor by Edward Fitzgerald and José Rodríguez Granada. Music by Gustavo Pittaluga. With Lilia Prado (Raquel), Carmelita González (Oliviero's wife), Esteban Márquez (Oliviero), Manuel Dondé (Don Eladio, the Deputy), Roberto Cobo (Juan), Luis Acevez Castaneda (Silvestre, the Chauffeur). 85 minutes.

El Bruto (1952) (Mexico)

Produced by Internacional Cinematográfica (Oscar Dancigers). Script by Buñuel and Luis Alcoriza. Photographed by Augustín Jimenez. Decor by Gunther Gerzso. Edited by Jorge Bustos. Music by Raúl Lavista. With Pedro Armendariz (Pedro, el bruto), Katy Jurado (Paloma), Rosita Arenas (Meche), Andrés Soler (Cabrera). 83 minutes.

El (This Strange Passion) (1952) (Mexico)
Produced by Nacional Film (Oscar Dancigers). Script by Buñuel and Luis Alcoriza, from a novel by Mercedes Pinto. Photography by Gabriel Figueroa. Decor by Edward Fitzgerald. Edited by Carlos Savage. Music by Luis Hernández Bretón. With Arturo de Córdova (Francisco), Delia Garcés (Gloria), Luis Beristein (Raúl), Aurora Walker (Doña Esperanza), and Martinez Baena (Padre Velasco). 100 minutes.

La Ilusion Viaja en Tranvia (1953) (Mexico)
Produced by Clasa Films Mundiales (Armando Ozive Alba). Script by Mauricio de la Serna and José Revueltas. Photography by Raúl Martínez Solares. Decor by Edward Fitzgerald. Music by Luis Hernández Bretón. With Lilia Prado (Lupe), Carlos Navarro (Caireles), Domingo Soler, Fernando Soto (Tarrajas), Agustín Isunza (Pinillos), Miguel Manzano, Javier de la Parra, Guillermo Bravo Sosa, Felipe Montojo. 90 minutes.

Cumbres Borrascosas (Abismos de Pasión) (1953) (Mexico)
Produced by Tepeyac (Oscar Dancigers). Script by Buñuel from *Wuthering Heights* by Emily Bronte. Photography by Agustín Jiménez. Decor by Edward Fitzgerald. Music by Raúl Lavista and Wagner. With Irasema Dilian (Katy), Jorge Mistral (Alejandro), Lilia Prado, Ernesto Alonso, Luis Aceves Castaneda, Francisco Requiera. 90 minutes.

Robinson Crusoe (1954) (Mexico)
Produced by Ultramar Films (Oscar Dancigers and Henry F. Ehrlich). Script by Buñuel and Philip Roll, from the novel by Daniel Defoe. Photography by Alex Phillipa. Decor by Edward Fitzgerald. Edited by Carlos Savage and Alberto Valenzuela. Music by Anthony Collins. With Dan O' Herlihy (Robinson Crusoe), Jaime Fernandez (Friday), Felipe da Alba (Captain Oberzo), Chel Lopez (Bosun), José Chavez, Emilio Garibay (Mutineers). 89 minutes.

El Rio y La Muerte (1954) (Mexico)
Produced by Clasa Films Mundiales (Armando Ozive Alba). Script by Buñuel and Luis Alcoriza from the novel by Miguel Alvarez Acosta. Photography by Raúl Martínez Solares. Decor by Edward Fitzgerald and Gunter Gerzso. Edited by Jorge Bustos. Music by Raul Lavista. With Columba Dominquez (Mercedes), Miguel Torruco (Felipe Anguiano), Joaquín Cordero (Gerardo Anguiano), Jaime Fernández (Romulo Menchaca), Victor Alcocer (Polo). 90 minutes.

Ensayo de un Crimen (The Criminal Life of Archibaldo de la Cruz)
(1955) (Mexico)
Produced by Alianza Cinematográfica (Alfonso Patino Gomez). Script by Buñuel and Eduardo Ugarte, from a story by Rodolfo Usigli. Photographed by Agustín Jiménez. Edited by Pablo Gomez. Music by Jesús Bracho and José Perez. With Ernesto Alonso (Archibaldo), Miroslava Stern (Lavinia), Rita Macedo (Patricia), Ariadna Walter (Carlota), Rodolfo Landa, Andres Balma, Carlos Riquelme, J. Maria Linares Rivas, Leonor Llansas. 91 minutes.

Cela S'Appelle L'Aurore (1955) (France-Italy)
>   Produced by Les Films Marceau (Paris) and Laetitia Film (Rome). Script by
>   Buñuel and Jean Ferry from the novel by Emmanuel Robles. Dialogue by Jean
>   Ferry. Assistant directors: Marcel Camus and Jacques Deray. Photographed by
>   Robert Le Febvre. Decor by Max Douy. Edited by Marguerite Renoir. Music by
>   Joseph Kosma. With Georges Marchal (Dr. Valerio), Lucia Bosè (Clara), Giani
>   Esposito (Sandro), Julien Bertheau (the Commissioner), Nelly Borgeaud
>   (Angela), Jean-Jacques Delbo (Gorzone), Robert Le Fort (Pietro), Brigitte
>   Elloy (Magda), Henri Nassiet (Angela's father), Gaston Modot (a Corsican
>   peasant), Pascal Mazotti (Azzopardi), Simone Paris (Mme. Gorzon). 102
>   minutes.

La Mort en Ce Jardin (1956) (France-Mexico)
>   Produced by Dismage (Paris) and Teperac (Oscar Dancigers). Script by Buñuel,
>   Luis Alcoriza, Raymond Queneau, and Gabriel Arout. Photographed by Jorge
>   Stahl. Decor by Edward Fitzgerald. Edited by Marguerite Renoir. Music by
>   Paul Misraki. With Simone Signoret (Gin), Georges Marchal (Chark), Michel
>   Piccoli (Father Lizzardi), Michèle Girardon (Maria), Charles Vanel (Castin),
>   Tito Junco (Chenko), Luis Aceves Castaneda (Alberto), Jorge Martínez de
>   Hoyos (Captain Ferrero), Alicia del Lago, Raúl Ramirez (Alvaro). 97 minutes.

Nazarin (1958) (Mexico)
>   Produced by Manuel Barbachano Ponce. Script by Buñuel and Julio Ale-
>   jandro, from the novel by Benito Pérez Galdós. Dialogue supervision: Emilio
>   Carballido. Photographed by Gabriel Figueroa. Decor by Edward Fitzgerald.
>   Edited by Carlos Savage. Production advisor: Carlos Velo. With Francisco
>   Rabal (Nazarin), Marga Lopez (Beatrice), Rita Macedo (Andara), Jesús
>   Fernandez (Ujo, the dwarf), Ignacio Lopez-Tarso (the "good thief"), Ofelia
>   Guilmain (Chanfa), Noe Murayama (El Pinto), Luis Aceves Castaneda (the
>   "bad thief"). 94 minutes.

La Fièvre Monte à El Pao (1959) (France-Mexico)
>   Produced by C.I.C.C., Cité Films, Indus Films, Terra Films, Cormoran Films
>   (Paris), and Cinematográfica Filmex (Mexico). Script by Buñuel, Luis
>   Alcoriza, Louis Sapin and Charles Dorat, based on the novel by Henri
>   Castillou. Dialogue by Louis Sapin. Photographed by Gabriel Figueroa.
>   Music by Paul Misraki. Edited by James Guenet and Rafael Lopez Caballos.
>   With Gérard Philippe (Ramon Vasquez), Maria Féliz (Ines Vargas), Jean
>   Servais (Alejandro Gual), Miquel Angel Ferrez (Governor Vargas), Raoul
>   Dantes (García), Domingo Soler, Victor Junco, Roberto Canedo. 97 minutes.

The Young One (1960) (Mexico)
>   Produced by Producciones Olmeca (George P. Werker). Script by Buñuel and
>   H. B. Addis (Hugo Butler) from the novel *Travellin' Man* by Peter Matthiesen.
>   Photographed by Gabriel Figueroa. Music by Jesús Zarzosa. Edited by Carlos
>   Savage. Decor by Jesús Bracho. With Zachary Scott (Miller), Key Meersman
>   (Evvie), Bernie Hamilton (Travers), Graham Denton (Jackson), Claudio
>   Brook (the Minister). 95 minutes.

Viridiana (1961) (Spain-Mexico)

Produced by Gustavo Alatriste (Mexico) and Uninci Films 59 (Madrid). Executive Producer: R. Muñoz Suay. Script by Buñuel and Julio Alejandro. Photographed by José A. Agayo. Decor by Francisco Canet. Edited by Pedro del Rey. Music by Handel. With Silvia Pinal (Viridiana), Fernando Rey (Don Jaime), Francisco Rabal (Jorge), Margarita Lozano (Ramona), Victoria Zinny (Lucia), Teresa Rabal (Rita), José Calvo, Joaquin Roa, Luis Heredia, José Manuel Martin, Lola Gaos, Juan Gardia Tiendra, Maruju Isbert, Joaquin Mayol, Palmira Guerra, Sergio Mendizabal, Milagros Tomas, Alicia Jorge Barriga (the beggars). 90 minutes.

El Ángel Exterminador (The Exterminating Angel) (1962) (Mexico)

Produced by Uninci and Films 59 (Gustavo Alatriste) Script and dialogue by Buñuel from a story by Buñuel and Luis Alcoriza, suggested by an unpublished play by José Bergamin. Photographed by Gabriel Figueroa. Edited by Carlos Savage. Decor by Jesús Bracho. With Silvia Pinal ("the Valkyrie"), Enrique Rambal (Nobile), Jacqueline Andere (Señora Roc), José Baviera (Leandro), Augusto Benedico (the doctor), Luis Beristein (Christian), Antonio Bravo (Russell), Claudio Brook (Majordomo), Cesar del Campo (the colonel), Rosa Elena Durgel (Silvia), Lucy Gallardo (Lucia), Enrique Garcia Alvarez (Señor Roc), Ofelia Guilmain (Juana Avila), Nadia Haro Oliva (Ana Maynar), Tito Junco (Raul), Xavier Loya (Francisco Avila), Xavier Masse (Eduardo), Angel Merino (waiter), Ofelia Montesco (Beatriz), Patricia Moran (Rita), Patricia de Morelos (Blanca), Bertha Moss (Leonora). 95 minutes.

Le Journal D'Une Femme De Chambre (Diary Of A Chambermaid) (1964) (France-Italy)

Produced by Speva-Filmalliance-Filmsonor-Dear (Henri Baum). Script by Buñuel and Jean-Claude Carrière from the novel by Octave Mirbeau. Photographed by Roger Fellous. Edited by Louisette Hautecoeur. Decor by Georges Wakhevitch. No music. With Jeanne Moreau (Célestine), Michel Piccoli (M. Monteil), Georges Géret (Joseph), Françoise Lugagne (Mme. Monteil), Daniel Ivernel (Captain Mauger), Jean Ozenne (M. Rabour), Gilberte Géniat (Rose), Bernard Musson (the sacristan), Jean-Claude Carrière (the curé), Muni (Marianne), Claude Jaeger (the judge), Dominque Sauvage (Claire), Madeleine Damien, Geymond Vital, Jean Franval, Marcel Rouze, Jeanne Perez, Andrée Tainsy, Françoise Bertin, Pierre Collet, Aline Bertrand, Joelle Bernard, Michelle Daquin, Marcel Le Floch, Marc Eyraud, Gabriel Gobin. 95 minutes.

Simon del Desierto (Simon of the Desert) (1965) (Mexico)

Produced by Gustavo Alatriste. Script by Buñuel. Photographed by Gabriel Figueroa. Music by Raúl Lavista. With Claudio Brook (Simon), Silvia Pinal (Temptations), Hortensia Santovena (Mother). 42 minutes.

Belle de Jour (1966) (France)

Produced by Henri Baum for Paris Film Production (Robert and Raymond Hakim). Script by Buñuel and Jean-Claude Carrière from the novel by Joseph Kessel. Photographed by Sacha Vierny. Decor by Robert Clavel. With

Catherine Deneuve (Séverine), Jean Sorel (Pierre), Michel Piccoli (Husson), Geneviève Page (Anaïs), Francisco Rabal (Hyppolite), Pierre Clementi (Marcel), Georges Marchal (the duke), Françoise Fabian (Charlotte), Maria Latour (Mathilde), Francis Blanche (M. Adolphe), Francois Maistre (the teacher), Fernard Fresson (pock-marked man), Macha Meril (Renée), Muni (Pallas), Doninque Dandrieux (Catherine), Brigitte Parmentier (Séverine as a child). 100 minutes.

La Voie Lactée (The Milky Way) (1969) (France-Italy)
Produced by Greenwich Film Productions (Paris) and Medusa (Rome) (Serge Silberman). Assistant directors, Pierre Lary and Patrick Saglio. Script by Buñuel and Jean-Claude Carrière. Photographed by Christian Matras. Art direction by Pierre Guffroy. Sound by Jacques Gallois. Edited by Louisette Hautecoeur. Music by Luis Buñuel. With Laurent Terzieff (Jean), Paul Frankeur (Pierre), Delphine Seyrig (The Prostitute), Edith Scob (The Virgin), Bernard Verley (Jesus), Georges Marchal (the Jesuit), Jean Piat (The Jansenist), Jean-Claude Carrière (Priscillian), Julien Guiomar (Spanish Priest), Marcel Peres (The Posadero), Michel Piccoli (the Marquis), Alain Cuny (Man with the Cape), Pierre Clementi (The Devil), Michel Etcheverry (The Inquisitor), Julien Bertheau (M. Richard), Francois Maistre (French priest), Claudio Brook (Bishop), Claude Cerval (Brigadier), Denis Manuel (Rodolphe), Daniel Pilon (François), Ellen Bahl (Mme. Garnier), Augusta Carrière (Sister Françoise), Agnès Capri (Teacher), Muni (Mother Superior), Jean-Daniel Ehrmann (Condemned Man), Pierre Lary (Young Monk), Bernard Musson (Innkeeper), Michel Dacquin (M. Garnier), Gabriel Gobin (Father), Pierre Maguélon (Civil Guard Corporal), Marius Laurey (Second Blind Man), Jean Clarieux (Apostle Peter), Christian Van Cau (Apostle Andrew), Claudine Berg (Mother), Christine Simon (Thérèse). 98 minutes.

Tristana (1970) (Spain-Italy-France)
Produced by Robert Dorfmann, Epoca Film-Talia Film (Madrid), Selenia Cinematografica (Rome) and Les Films Corona (Paris). Scenario by Luis Buñuel in collaboration with Julio Alejandro, based on the novel by Benito Pérez Galdós. Director of photography: José F. Aguayo. Assistants to the director: Jose Puyel, Pierre Lary. Art director: Enrique Alarcon. Production manager: Juan Estelrich. Edited by Pedro del Rey. Sound engineers: José Nogueira, Dino Fronzetti. No music. With Catherine Deneuve (Tristana), Fernando Rey (Don Lope), Franco Nero (Horacio), Lola Gaos (Saturna), Jesus Fernandez (Saturno), Antonio Casas (Don Cosme), Sergio Mendizabal (headmaster), José Calvo (bellringer), Vicente Soler (Don Ambrosio), Fernando Cabrian (Dr. Miquis), Juan José Menendez (Don Candido), Candida Losada (citizen), Maria Paz Pondal (girl), Antonio Ferrandis, José Maria Caffarel, Joaquim Pamplona. 98 minutes.

Le Charme Discret de La Bourgeoisie (The Discreet Charm of the Bourgeoisie (1972) (France)
Produced by Greenwich Productions (Ully Pickard). Assistant director: Pierre

Lary. Script by Luis Buñuel and Jean-Claude Carrière. Photographed by Edmond Richard. Art direction by Pierre Guffroy. Sound by Guy Villette. Edited by Hélène Plemiannikov. With Fernando Rey (Ambassador), Delphine Seyrig (Simone Thévenot), Stéphane Audran (Alice Sénéchal), Jean-Pierre Cassel (Sénéchal), Paul Frankeur (Thévenot), Claude Piéplu (colonel), Bulle Ogier (Florence), Julien Bertheau (bishop), Michel Piccoli (minister), Muni (peasant), Milena Vikotucic. 105 minutes.

Le Fantôme de la Liberté (The Phantom of Liberty) (1974) (France)
Produced by Greenwich Productions (Serge Silberman). Script by Luis Buñuel with the collaboration of Jean-Claude Carrière. Director of photography: Edmond Richard. Edited by Hélène Plemiannikov. With Adrianna Asti (prefect's sister), Julien Bertheau (first prefect), Jean-Claude Brialy (Mr. Foucauld), Adolfo Celi (Dr. Legendre), Paul Frankeur (innkeeper), Michel Lonsdale (hatter), Pierre Maguélon (Policeman Gerard), Helen Perdriere (aunt), Michel Piccoli (second prefect), Claude Piéplu (commissioner), Jean Rochefort (lost girl's father), Bernard Verley (captain), Milena Vikotucic (nurse), Monica Vitti (Mrs. Foucauld). 104 minutes.

Cet Obscur Objet du Désir (That Obscure Object of Desire) (1977) (France)
Produced by Serge Silberman. Script by Luis Buñuel with Jean-Claude Carrière, suggested by the novel *La Femme et le Pantin*, by Pierre Louys. Director of photography, Edmond Richard. Edited by Hélène Plemiannikov. With Fernando Rey (Mathieu), Carole Bouquet (Conchita), Angela Molina (Conchita), Julien Bertheau (judge), André Weber (valet), Milena Vikotucic (traveler). 100 minutes.

Index

* *

Note: For films other than those by Buñuel, directors' names appear in parentheses following the film titles.